Pax

~~Gilbert Henninger~~
St. meinrad Seminary
St. meinrad, Indiana
6-12-31

~~Harley, B.~~

~~Gilbert Henninger~~
~~Gilbert Henninger~~

SIMON BRUTÉ DE RÉMUR

SIMON BRUTÉ DE RÉMUR, FIRST BISHOP OF VINCENNES

SIMON BRUTÉ DE RÉMUR

FIRST BISHOP OF VINCENNES

By
Sister Mary Salesia Godecker, O. S. B., Ph. D.
Convent Immaculate Conception
Ferdinand, Indiana

With a Preface by
His Excellency,
The Right Reverend Joseph Chartrand, D. D.
Bishop of Indianapolis

Published by
ST. MEINRAD HISTORICAL ESSAYS
ST. MEINRAD, INDIANA
1931

NIHIL OBSTAT:

CYRILLUS GAUL, O. S. B.
Censor Deputatus

IMPRIMATUR:

✠ JOSEPHUS CHARTRAND, D. D.
Episcopus Indianapolitanus

In Festo Sti. Joseph
Die 19 Martii, 1931

2360

PRINTED BY
THE ABBEY PRESS
ST. MEINRAD, INDIANA

TO THE SUCCESSORS IN THE APOSTOLIC WORK
OF THE
RIGHT REVEREND SIMON BRUTÉ
FIRST BISHOP OF THE DIOCESE OF VINCENNES, NOW INDIANAPOLIS,
IN PROFOUND RESPECT
THE AUTHOR DEDICATES THIS VOLUME

FOREWORD

Every deliberate act of intelligent man is sponsored by a primary motive. This fact is obvious in the simple recording of the deeds of Vincennes' first bishop. But far, yes, extremely remote lies this motive from one that prompts and permeates a glorious deed of fame. Bishop Bruté, one of the most humble, simple, and learned of the Great Master's chosen shepherds, who in life resented everything that savored of pride and worldly splendor, would look with disdain from his heights of peace eternal on the smallest degree of pomp or ostentation associated with his biography. Hence to harmonize the purpose of this labor of love with the silent, yet fruitful, career of our saintly prelate, the writer is influenced by one humble motive, namely, to ransom from oblivion the story of a supereminent life that those who read it may as an Augustine of old be led to comprehend, and inspired to follow the example of one who drew eternal profit from the use of all transitory things and thereby accomplished marvelous good in planting the Faith in the hearts of past generations.

Bishop Bruté possessed in an eminent degree the same courage, zeal, simplicity, and heroic sacrifice that abounded in the hearts of those faithful apostles who crossed the bar long ages before him; those who worshipped in moss-covered catacombs; those who bled and died in the arena of ancient Rome; those who met and suffered the same fate as the martyrs of today. And as the old Coliseum still stands to tell the story of numerous heroic saints of bygone days so, too, the numerous churches, religious, and educational institutions within the original Diocese of Vincennes bear testimony to the fruitful labors of the zealous Founder; labors that will always remain monumental and a proof of what a true apostle's strength can accomplish.

May the Holy Spirit grant to every reader of these pages the light to profit by the example that humble Bishop Bruté gave to the world. Clergymen, religious, laymen, youths, and children all may find within this modest volume many timely lessons that if heeded will lead them nearer to God. While we honor and revere this saintly apostle who has laid the foundations on which we build, let it be a permanent honor that we accord him—one that perpetually arises from an imitation of his worthy deeds and a transmission of like deeds down through the ages of our glorious historic faith for the benefit of the future masses.

S. M. S.

Written in the Coliseum,
at Rome, October 8, 1929.

*   *   *   *   *

The writer wishes to acknowledge with unfeigned appreciation her indebtedness to His Excellency, the Right Reverend Joseph Chartrand, D. D., Bishop of Indianapolis, the Right Reverend Monsignor James H. Ryan, S. T. D., Ph. D., Rector of the Catholic University of America, Washington, D. C., the Reverend James R. Shea, Brownsburg, Indiana, the Reverend J. P. Armstrong, M. A., Dublin, Ireland, the Reverend Leon A. McNeill, M. A., Superintendent of Schools, Wichita, Kansas, and Reverend Leo Lindeman, New Albany, Indiana; to Reverend Mother M. Seraphine and Community, and to all who in any way assisted in the work.

Owing to the fact that a portion of this work was submitted to the Catholic Sisters' College of the Catholic University of America in partial fulfillment of the requirements for the degree of Doctor of Philosophy, it is with considerable pleasure as well as from a sense of justice that the writer expresses her sincere thanks to the Right Reverend Patrick J. McCormick, Ph. D., Dean of the Catholic Sisters' College, and to all her professors, especially the Reverend George Johnson, Ph. D., and Doctor Patrick J. Lennox. She takes occasion to express her deep obligation to the Reverend P. W. Browne, Ph. D., S. T. D., under whose guidance the dissertation was prepared and the complete study was outlined, and to the Reverend Francis P. Lyons, C. S. P., D. D., for his inestimable assistance in reading numerous French documents.

To the Reverend Cyril Gaul, O. S. B., Vice Rector of St. Meinrad Seminary, Professor of Ecclesiastical History, and Editor of St. Meinrad Historical Essays, St. Meinrad, Indiana, the Reverend Doctor Francis P. Lyons, C. S. P., St. Mary's Church, Chicago, Illinois, and former Rector of St. Paul's College, Washington, D. C., the Reverend Doctor Gilbert J. Garraghan, S. J., Research Professor of History, St. Louis University, St. Louis, Missouri, and Editor of Mid-America, Chicago, Illinois, the Very Reverend Doctor Charles L. Souvay, C. M., Rector of Kenrick Seminary, Webster Groves, Missouri, and the Reverend Doctor Patrick W. Browne, Professor at the Catholic University of America, Washington, D. C., who by their careful and painstaking reading of the manuscript, and their valuable suggestions and constructive criticism rendered the work less imperfect than it would otherwise have been, the author wishes to express in a very special manner her profound gratitude.

ILLUSTRATIONS

CONTENTS

PREFACE

Effective organization, quick results, grand achievements are characteristics of our age.

It is well to appreciate fully temporal advantages and opportunties and make the most of them, but in so doing, we must not lose sight of other truths and facts equally, and even more, important. Heedless of the admonitions of religion and the warnings of history, our vision will not be clear and sober, and we may easily become the victims of our own prosperity, inviting decadence, mental and moral.

While not wishing unreservedly for a return of the alleged good old times, we should not be altogether unmindful and indifferent as to what our forefathers endured and wrought in laying the foundation of our great religious and civil institutions.

We cannot hope or expect to preserve and perfect these monuments of divinely guided human endeavor, unless we understand the motives, the sacrifices, the ideals they embody.

In every department there have been leaders; seers, to whom the future unfolded its secrets; pioneers, undaunted by formidable obstacles; determined men and women, with singleness of purpose and indomitable energy, who inspired others and led them into the march of progress. Forgetful of self, wholly absorbed in the cause to which they gave their lives, they passed on, some into oblivion, and others into the memory and honor of men.

Among the earliest builders of the nation none served with greater zeal and devotion and magnificent results than the pioneer European missionaries who came to this country with the sole purpose of extending the stakes and multiplying the tents of the Christian conquest.

Memorable names, not a few, are recorded in the annals of the Church in this country, names, which, after many years, have lost nothing of their lustre.

Some of these great Churchmen were noted for keen intellect, consummate oratory, intrepid defence of revealed truth, administrative ability or other exceptional gifts. Many others who performed all the duties of their exalted calling faithfully, fearlessly, have passed to their eternal reward, and were soon forgotten on earth.

There is one figure in the early Hierarchy of the Church in America, learned, fervent, gentle, unassuming, whose sanctity was generally, and frequently acknowledged by his contemporaries, and the people whom he served.

Bishop Simon William Gabriel Bruté, first bishop of Vincennes, for nearly a century has been accorded a singular veneration, which can be explained in no other manner than that his personality was of the highest and holiest type. His numerous letters and his memoirs reveal a mind unusually alert and a heart ablaze with the love of God and man.

It is most gratifying, therefore, that Sister Mary Salesia of the Order of St. Benedict has chosen to make a scholarly study of the life of Bishop Bruté. By reading this interesting and instructive biography, may we become better acquainted with the early history of the Church in this country, and with the life and labors of one who should be regarded as one of her chief glories—the first Bishop of Vincennes.

✠ Joseph Chartrand, D. D.
Bishop of Indianapolis.

Indianapolis, March 19, 1931.

BRUTÉ BIOGRAPHICAL SOURCES

No manuscript material has been the prey of vandalism more lamentably than the personal papers of the Right Reverend Simon Bruté, First Bishop of Vincennes. The earliest extant information relative to the Bruté Collection is a letter signed J. R. Bayley, Secretary of the Archbishop of New York. A transcript of this letter reads thus:

New York, July 9, 1852.

Dear Sir:

The Most Reverend Archbishop being hindered by his many occupations from answering your letter of the 24th of May, has requested me to write to you in his name.

The papers of the late Bishop Bruté were far from being complete when they came into the Archbishop's hands; they had evidently been examined by some one, who had taken from them many important papers, especially those of an historical nature. When they first arrived here, I examined them myself, in the hope of finding, important information upon certain matters, to which I had turned my attention—and discovering nothing worth preserving, tho' during his whole life he had employed more or less time in making researches connected with the history of the Catholic Religion in this part of the world. As, however, I did not examine them particularly in reference to the Indian Missions, there may be some documents connected with them, that I may have overlooked—and I will take an early opportunity of looking them over so that if I discover anything likely to interest you, I will let you know. The Rev. Mr. Shea of the Society of Jesus, has been for some time engaged upon a History of the Jesuit Mission amongst the Indians—and from his peculiar fitness for the task, as well as the valuable documents in his possession, I have no doubt that it will prove a valuable addition to the early history of our country. The Most Reverend Archbishop requests me to convey to you his kind regards.

I remain, with sincere Respect,

Very truly yours,

J. R. Bayley, Secr. Archb. of N. Y.[1]

Jas. H. Causten, Jr., Esq.
Washington, D. C.

The contents of this letter are contradicted, at least in part, by another letter dated two years later and addressed to Right Reverend J. R. Bayley, by Reverend E. Audran. Herein the pastor of St. Francis Xavier's Cathedral, Vincennes, Indiana, states that the entire Bruté Collection was shipped to the Most Reverend John Hughes, Archbishop of New York.

Vincennes, Nov. 23, 1854.

Right Reverend dear Sir:

About five years ago, upon the receipt of a letter of yours and of Archbishop Hughes, and at the request of Bishop de la Hailandière, I sent you the manuscripts and papers of our venerable first Prelate, Doctor Bruté. A good deal of anxiety has always been felt here for those papers—and I may confess to you that I was at the time very much censured for sending them so far away with no other authorization but the promise once made by Bishop de la Hailandière who having resigned at that time could not be entitled to dispose of them. A long time has elapsed since already, and I understand that the papers are in your hands altogether. I would feel much relieved to hear from you that they are safe, all of them; and that they may without much greater delay be restored to the Archives of our Diocese.

I took them from a particular spot in which they had been placed by Bishop de la Hailandière, and packed them all in a box without examining first whether there were not other papers not belonging to Bishop Bruté that should not have been sent. It thus happened that a manuscript Indian Dictionary was among them, which probably can be of no service to you. As it is a precious relic you would confer a particular favor by sending it back now as

[1] *Researches*, (ACHS), IX (1892), p. 132.

well as all other papers of which you would have no more use.
With much respect,

> Your obedient and humble servant in Xto.,
> > E. Audran,
> > > Rector of St. Francis Xavier's Cathedral,
> > > Vincennes.[2]

Despite the above request of Reverend E. Audran, the
Bruté Collection was not returned to the diocese of Vincennes. On the contrary, it was scattered out among several writers of that day. Archbishop Hughes denied John
Gilmary Shea access to it, but His Grace gave a trunk full
of these valuable papers to Henri de Courcy, a Frenchman,
who at the time was engaged in mercantile affairs in New
York. Likewise, J. R. Hassard came into possession of an
appreciable amount of this material.

This Bruté Collection served Henri de Courcy to great
advantage in the production of his articles relative to the
history of the Catholic Church in America. But Henri de
Courcy did not write for the American people. His articles
were written in French, and were contributions to a French
paper published in his native country. These articles were
never collected in book form in French, but the John Gilmary Shea translation of them was issued in book form in
America in 1856, and for many years served as the most
comprehensive account of the history of the Church in this
country. The credit for the valuable information given us
in the de Courcy-Shea edition belongs in the main to Right
Reverend Simon Bruté, who preserved in his manuscripts
the records of the early noteworthy events. The volume, in
all justice, should have been entitled, Bruté-de Courcy-Shea.

Shortly after this, Henri de Courcy, owing to ill health,
was forced to return to France. He took with him many of
the valuable Bruté documents. Immediately he set to work
to prepare the de LaMennais-Bruté Correspondence for
publication, but death overtook him before the manuscript

---

[2] Original in CA of A. Notre Dame, Ind.

went to press. His project was carried through by M. Eugène de la Gournerie, and the letters were published at Nantes, in 1862.

In 1865 Right Reverend J. R. Bayley, Bishop of Newark, compiled the *Memoirs of Right Reverend Simon Bruté*. The greater part of this volume is made up of the original notes and records of Bishop Bruté. This fact makes the volume all the more valuable. However, at the time the author compiled this work he did not have access to the entire Bruté Collection, owing to the fact that many of these papers were in France. This valuable work, however, was in great demand and a revision of the volume appeared in 1876.

In 1869 Dom Paul Jausions, O. S. B., a monk of Solesmes, came to America for the purpose of writing the Life of Right Reverend S. Bruté. Dom Jausions spent scarcely one year in research, but in that time he collected the remnant papers that remained in New York, several letters preserved by the Quebec Historical Society, and a few documents still extant in Indiana. In late summer, 1870, Dom Jausions fell ill with fever and died at Vincennes, September 7. The entire diocese, as well as his Community abroad, lamented the great loss and the cessation of the work. However, at the time, there was no one else who cared to accept the responsibility for the research, and the task remained untouched for a period of twenty years.

In 1870 Lady Herbert, at London, produced a *Life of Right Reverend Simon Bruté*. This author had in her possession no original documents or letters, and the work was based wholly on gleanings from the few articles that had been written previously.

Abbé Charles, now M. le Chanoine Bruté de Rémur, gave us *Vie de Monsiegneur Bruté de Rémur*, in 1887. The extent of original material at his disposal in addition to the voluminous family correspondence was the Archives at St. Sulpice, and at Ploërmel, together with the England-Bruté, Cheverus-Bruté, and Grassi-Bruté Correspondence. He also used the de LaMennais-Bruté Correspondence, published at Nantes, in 1862.

In the meantime the Dom Jausions Collection, though scanty in quantity, was packed and shipped to St. Meinrad Abbey, St. Meinrad, Indiana, where it perished in the destructive conflagration of 1887. A portion of this material, namely, the letters procured from the Quebec Historical Society, was preserved in a translation and was published in the *Ave Maria*.[3]

In 1890 Reverend Edmund J. P. Schmitt, a priest in the diocese of Indianapolis, became interested in the life of Bishop Bruté, and began the research anew. His parish duties did not permit him to visit Archives at a great distance, but he did visit all within the State of Indiana as well as Chicago and St. Louis, where he copied all extant material. Father Schmitt also advertised for available material, in several German and English publications. Likewise, he succeeded in getting in touch with the more remote places through correspondence, and in this manner he procured, both here and abroad, many valuable letters and much information relative to the first Bishop of Vincennes. In addition to the unpublished material he procured by purchase and by gift several volumes from France, and the two volumes of the *Bruté-Seton Correspondence* from the Sisters of Charity at Emmitsburg, Maryland.

The following letters addressed to Reverend Edmund J. P. Schmitt, disclose several interesting facts, such as: the loss of material at Louisville, Kentucky; the destruction of an early Indiana paper, at Vincennes; the New York story regarding the Bruté Collection; the John Gilmary Shea information concerning the fate of the Bruté papers; the interest of Right Reverend C. Maes, Bishop of Covington, Kentucky; the information of Reverend R. Seton, Miss Mary Meline, and Reverend E. P. Allen, President of Mount St. Mary's, Emmitsburg, Maryland.

[3] *Ave Maria*, V (1869), No. 34, 35, 37. Notre Dame, Ind.

Louisville, Feast of St. Joseph, 1891.

Reverend E. J. P. Schmitt,

Dear Father:

I fear me much that the letter you refer to in your favor of the 6th inst., has been lost, and others with it upon which I set great store. I am now an old man, and I live with my oldest child and daughter, with her large family of children, among whom I am grieved to say, there are some who have little care of their grandfather effects. Within two years, I am certain, I held in my hands the old stringless portfolio in which I had gathered these previous letters. Now I can find it nowhere. From the day I received your letter, I have sought for it diligently, but without result. I shall continue to do so, and should it turn up you will hear from me at once. The letter you speak of was written in French, of which I have little knowledge. The paragraph quoted from it was translated by my friend, Reverend P. J. Jenkins, now pastor of St. Lawrence Church, Daviess County, Kentucky (Knottsville). I suppose he must have read the entire letter, and he may remember its contents.

I have memory of having seen your venerable Bishop but on a single occasion. He was then visiting Bishop Flaget at Bardstown, and I and many others of the congregation of the then Cathedral of St. Joseph's had the happiness of receiving Holy Communion at his hands. Every since, his face and bearing, the one so saintly and the other so impressive have been present to me. Kentucky and Indiana were truly blest in their first Bishops, and it pleases me to know that you are engaged in the effort to perpetuate the holy name of this saintly Doctor Bruté.

The Metropolitan Catholic Almanac of 1843 contains a short sketch of the life of Bishop Bruté, taken, if I mistake not, from an address by Doctor McCaffrey on the occasion of his death. However, you have no doubt seen this.

I am obliged, even at the risk of being unintelligible, to address you in pencil. A pen is utterly abhorrent to my lame and tremulous fingers.

Begging your kindly remembrance of me, I am, Reverend dear Sir,

Yours respectfully,

Benj. J. Webb.[4]

Archbishop's House, 452 Madison Ave.,
New York, March 11, 1891.

Reverend dear Sir:

Some few years ago the grandnephew of Bishop Bruté, a Benedictine Monk of Solesmes, by name of Dom Paul Jausions (as far as I can remember), came to this country for the purpose of collecting material for the French life of his venerated granduncle. This Reverend Gentleman got possession of all the manuscripts that had been left in New York by Bishop Bruté, as well as several others which Archbishop Bayley had brought with him to Newark, and which at that time were in my keeping as his successor. All the papers of the Bishop that had been left in New York and Newark were handed over to Dom P. Jausions, and must now be in the keeping of his heirs in France.

My impression is that the French life of Bishop Bruté has already been published, so that you would be likely to find in it all that you require.

I am, Reverend dear Sir,

Very faithfully yours,

M. A. Corrigan, ABP.[5]

Elizabeth, N. J., Jan. 1, 1892.

Reverend dear Father:

I forward volumes two and three and before the end of the month will send volume four. It has been a hard struggle to complete it and see it through the press as my health is wretched, constant pain, sleeplessness, and increasing weakness make literary labor very difficult.

Bishop Hughes had a great esteem for the Reverend Mr. Bruté and apparently very little for Mr. Dubois, in his Emmitsburg days.

[4] Transcript in Edmund J. P. Schmitt's Historical Notes. CA of A., Vol. 2, pp. 18–21.

[5] Transcript in Edmund J. P. Schmitt's Historical Notes. CA of A., Vol. 2.

He had an idea of writing a life of Bishop Bruté, and the papers were sent to him. As he was not a man of research or study he did nothing. I asked his permission to examine them, but he refused—although he sent the trunk or trunks to H. de Courcy. Bishop Bayley used his *Recollections of the French Revolution* and took the papers to Seton Hall College. Some were given away, some lost, and many perished in a fire. It was only a remnant that went to Dom Jausions. I learned later that this clergyman died of a contagious disease, and that after his death the papers in his room, including what he had selected from Bishop Bruté's papers were burned.

The Abbé Charles Bruté de Rémur in 1887 published *Vie de Mgr. Bruté de Rémur.* He seems to have had no documents and says he bases his work on an abridgment of Bishop Bayley's book by Lady Herbert. He never had Bishop Bayley's book. He used the books on the Sisters of Providence, Barberey's life of Mother Seton, and letters of the de LaMennais brothers (the good and bad) which H. de Courcy printed in the French periodical.

He speaks of the Archives of St. Sulpice but apparently did not glean much and letters in the possession of a Community of Brothers founded by de LaMennais.

Now what material have we? He was a great letter writer, and writer of notes, often hasty and incorrect. Prof. Edwards of Notre Dame must have many letters of his. I have a few, and others are scattered. His life at Mount St. Mary's seems most vague and yet there was his great work accomplished. Miss Mary Meline of Cincinnati went to Mt. St. Mary's and did some work on a history of that institution. She may help you.

For his period as Bishop there is a series of contributions signed "Vincennes" in the volumes of the *United States Catholic Miscellany* which are evidently and clearly his and have never been used by any writing about him.

In his hasty way he misled Judge Law in regard to the first settlement of Vincennes, confounded by a tanning venture at the mouth of the Ohio with Vincennes. I was very sorry to see this historical error dressed up in most fantastic guise in the Indianapolis Catholic paper, with intrinsic absurdities, making an expedition from Detroit accompanied by a Jesuit priest, when there were none at Detroit and Cadillac hated them too heartily to have one there.

When I am free from my volume, and can rest, I will see what I have that may help you. But I feel that my days, especially my working days are numbered.

Pray for me.

Yours sincerely,

John Gilmary Shea.[6]

Covington, Ky., Jan. 11, 1892.

Reverend E. J. P. Schmitt,
Weltes P. O., Indiana.

Reverend dear Sir:

I am delighted that you put your leisure time to such good account: the *Life of Bp. Bruté* by the late Archbishop Bayley is more of introduction to his missionary and Episcopal life than a real Biography. A new Life will be a welcome addition to Catholic History.

The Reverend Nerinckx's letter of 1806, referred to, is in the Archives of Baltimore. You might get it by writing to His Eminence, but I think I took out of it all that concerns Bishop Bruté and Vincennes.

The letter of 1807 has never been found.

I am so busy now that I must request you to write again, say in the beginning of February. I have among my papers an unfinished sketch of the *Life of Reverend Rivet* written many years ago, also several of his manuscript letters. The latter are in French, should you understand that language, I will send you my unfinished sketch and the letters, to use freely. If not, I will then try to finish the sketch and give it to you as my mite to the good work.

Sincerely yours in Christ,

Camillus P. Maes, Bp. of Covington.[7]

[6] *Ibid.*, pp. 3–6.
[7] *Ibid.*, pp. 23–4.

Saint Joseph's Rectory,
Jersey City Heights, N. J., Jan. 11, 1892.

Reverend dear Sir:

Your letter of inquiry just received. I regret that I can be of no
use to you whatever. Letters of Bruté used in my *Mother Seton*
were all returned to Emmitsburg. I doubt if anything exists fuller
as regards the prelate's early and home life than what must have
passed through Bishop Bailey's hands in preparing his most interesting *Memoir;* unless you have access to the papers of that
monk—a nephew I believe of Bruté's—who was travelling in this
country—in your Western parts—some 18 years ago preparing (as
I understand) a life of the Bishop of Vincennes.

Respectfully yours in Dno.

Robt. Seton.[8]

1406 Hopkins Place,
Washington, D. C., January 17, 1892.

Reverend E. J. P. Schmitt,

Dear Sir:

Your note of the 6th inst. was forwarded to me from Cincinnati.
I shall be glad to give you any assistance I can by the use of my
manuscript *History of the Old Mountain.* But it is there, at the
college,—unfinished. If you write to Reverend E. P. Allen, the
President, and tell him that you have my permission to use it—he
will send it to you I suppose—There is a great deal of data at the
college, besides that which I have winnowed also in the Archives
of the Baltimore Cathedral. The Cardinal kindly placed all of this
at my disposal when I should need it. (When my History will be
finished I cannot tell) and you will find also much data with the
Sulpicians at Baltimore. Archbishop Elder's oldest living brother
Mr. Basil T. Elder of 3842 Windsor Place, St. Louis, Mo., remembers his college days very vividly and has anecdotes of Bruté.
He is very lame however in his hands from gout and it would be
easier for him to talk than write. I have some very interesting
letters from him at home (in Cincinnati) and will be back there

[8] *Ibid.,* p. 27.

some time in February, when I will copy them for you if you desire it.

Very truly yours,
Mary M. Meline.[9]

Mount St. Mary's College,
Near Emmitsburg, Feb. 7, 1892.

Reverend E. J. P. Schmitt,
Dear Reverend Sir:

Excuse my delay in answering your letter. The examinations
have kept me so busy that I could not reply sooner. I am glad
you propose to write the *Life and Times of Rt. Rev. S. G. Bruté*,
for I am sure the work can be made a most interesting one. I
suppose you have seen the French Life of the saintly bishop, recently published by his nephew.

We have a great many letters and notes of Bishop Bruté, but
while I am anxious to aid you in your work in any way in my
power, I would not wish to send these documents out of the college.
Some years ago some valuable documents, including Bishop Bruté's
correspondence with the unhappy de LaMennais, were lost in this
way. In regard to Miss Meline's manuscript as long as it remains
in its present shape, we would not care to have it go out of the
college, though we would be quite willing to have you examine it
here. I send you by this mail, a copy of the *Jubilee at Mt. St.
Mary's College*. Please return it after you are through with it.
The book is out of print and it is hard to get a copy of the work
now. We would be glad to see you at the Mount any time you
find it convenient to pay us a visit. Wishing you success in your
work, I remain, Dear Sir,

Very truly yours,
Edw. P. Allen, President.[10]

Archbishop Corrigan's statement, regarding the Dom
Jausions Collection having been sent to France, is refuted
by the following letter written by the Right Reverend Germain Cozien, Abbot of Solesmes.

[9] *Ibid.*, pp. 28–30.
[10] *Ibid.*, pp. 49–51.

Quarr Abbey, Ryde,

Isle of Wight, 9 févr. 1926.

Ma Révérende Mère,

Veuillez m'excuser d'avoir tardé à repondre à votre lettre du 12 Janvier. La raison en est que je suis venu en visite dans une de nos maisons.

J'ai pu cependant avant de quitter Solesmes m'occuper de l'affaire que vous me recommandiez. J'aurais été heureux de vous être utile, mais j'ai en le regret de constater que nous n'avons pas les documents que vous cherchez.

Tous les papiers que Dom Jausions avait mis à part, toutes les copies de pièces, toutes ses notes furent considérés comme la proprieté de l'Evêche de Vincennes, et rien ne parvint à Solesmes.

M. Charles Bruté de Rémur dans l'ouvrage qu'il a consacré au Jausions; et dans ce volume quelques pages seulement se rapportent à l'episcopat de Mgr. Bruté.

J'espère trouver encore en librairie les deux volumes que vous desirez et, dans ce cas, je vous les ferai adresser.

Je bénis votre travail, et en me recommandant moi-même à votre prière, je vous offre, Ma Révérende Mére, l'hommage de mon religieux respect in Christo Jesu.

Fr. Germain Cozien,

Abbé de St. Remi de Solesme.[11]

Reverend Edmund J. P. Schmitt spent ten years collecting material for the biography of Bishop Bruté. At the close of that period ill health forced him to go south. The good priest died at St. Rose Sanatorium, San Antonio, Texas, May 5, 1901, and the *Life of Bishop Bruté* was destined to remain undisturbed for another twenty-five years.

The Reverend Edmund J. P. Schmitt Collection became the property of Right Reverend Joseph Chartrand, D. D., present Bishop of Indianapolis. Bishop Chartrand deposited this material in Notre Dame University Archives until such a time as he should wish to recall it. Several priests were urged to take up the task, but the labor was too mas-

[11] Convent of the Immaculate Conception Archives. Ferdinand, Ind.

sive to be undertaken by any priest engaged in parish work.
The results were that the material continued to be left to
the destructive hand of time.

According to the foregoing letter of Miss M. Meline, the
Archives of St. Mary's, Baltimore, should possess valuable
material. The Reverend Father Boyer, S. S., however,
states that their Archives possess nothing relative to Bishop
Bruté, except one valueless letter. The following letter discloses the fact that the Chancery Office Archives at Charleston, South Carolina, have, likewise, suffered the loss of Bishop Bruté's correspondence with Bishop England.

Chancery Office,
Charleston, S. C., May 19, 1928.

Dear Sister Salesia:

    Bishop Walsh handed me your letter of April 18 regarding letters
of Bishop England.

    Father Wolfe and I searched the archives but could not locate
the letters you are looking for. You are possibly aware that Doctor
Guilday, in preparing his work, *The Life and Times of Bishop
England*, worked at the material in our archives, and it might be
possible that he has information regarding the letters, if they are
extant.

    Regretting that I have to disappoint you, and with best wishes
for success in your work, I remain,

Sincerely,
John Steigner, Chancellor.[12]

From the foregoing it is evident that the hand of time has
dealt ruthlessly with much of the material that after the
lapse of a century would have aided a biographer in portraying the life and labors of Indiana's pioneer bishop.
Nevertheless, it will be apparent to the reader of the following pages that a great amount of original material is
still extant in the numerous archives listed in the biblio-
graphy.

[12] Convent of the Immaculate Conception Archives, Ferdinand, Ind.

Among the European Archives that of Canon Bruté de
Rémur is of prime importance. This Collection contains
about 500 pages of family correspondence, written in
French, dating from Simon Bruté's college days to the close
of the venerable prelate's episcopal career. While many of
these letters are of a personal nature and intensely spiritual
in character, they contain much that is of value to the historian. In addition to this the Collection contains ap-
proximately 130 transcripts which include the correspondence of Grassi, England, Du Bourg, and Cheverus with
Bruté; also the correspondence between Madame Bruté de
Rémur, the mother of Father Bruté, and Monsieur James
Emery, Superior of St. Sulpice, and their letters to Father
Bruté. The most valuable portion of this material is Father Bruté's correspondence embracing his episcopal career.
Every phase of progress made in the new diocese and its
needs were imparted in lengthy and frequent letters to the
zealous bishop's brother, Doctor Augustine Bruté de Rémur,
at Rennes.

The Monastery Archives of the Brothers of Christian Instruction, Ploërmel, France, contain nine lengthy letters,
thirty-one pages of fools cap, written in French by Father
Bruté to the worthy Founder of this institution, Abbé Jean
de LaMennais, and his brother Abbé Félicité. These letters
were written between the dates 1810 and 1824. They are
most valuable from the viewpoint of delineating Father
Bruté's admirable missionary spirit and his zeal for the
spread of God's kingdom in the United States.

The Archives of St. Sulpice, Paris, possess eighteen
lengthy letters about eighty pages of fools cap written in
French by Father Bruté. Of this number three letters were
addressed to Father Garnier, one to Father Emery, one to
Father Dubois, and the remainder were written to Father
Duclaux. The earliest one dates back to June 21, 1811, and
the last one bears the date of September 30, 1824. Newman
says the only adequate story of a man's life is his letters.
This is true in regard to Father Bruté. These letters, in

addition to portraying his spirit of sacrifice and his intense
desire to see Catholicism flourish in America, tell in a most
charitable manner the story of Mount St. Mary's hardships
and struggle for existence. Moreover, these letters reveal
the part that Father Bruté took in saving this institution
for the future Church.

The Musaeum Bollandianum, Brussels, possesses two important volumes, Folios 552 and 868, of letters written by
Most Reverend John Carroll and the early missionaries in
the United States to their relatives and clergymen in Belgium. A goodly number of these letters are written in
French but the greater number are written in Flemish. The
letters of Carroll, Nerinckx, Malevé, Henry, Urbain—the
Trappist, and the appeal of Du Bourg to the French people
for assistance give a vivid insight into the condition of the
early Church in America. Father Nerinckx's letters in
Flemish are the most valuable for our purpose. They contain a very thorough account of the progress of the Church
in the Bardstown diocese at the period when Indiana was
subject to Bishop Flaget's jurisdiction. The two folios contain hundreds of pages of priceless material but the most
valuable of these letters date from 1806 to 1815 and were
very helpful in preparing the chapter on Catholicism in
Indiana Prior to 1834.

The Archdiocesan Archives of Quebec also contain rich
stores of material that aided in the preparation of the chapter mentioned above. The correspondence of the inhabitants
of Vincennes, in 1769, with the Bishop of Quebec; the correspondence between Father Gibault and the Bishop of
Quebec from 1769 to 1788; and the correspondence between Bishop Carroll and the Bishop of Quebec from 1788
to 1794, rendered untold service in depicting the condition
of religion throughout our territory in the pioneer days. In
addition to this material there is one lengthy letter written
by Bishop Bruté to Bishop Signay, in 1839. This letter
gives the reader an insight into Bishop Bruté's scholarly
ability for research.

The Sulpician Archives at Montreal while rich in historic lore possess only two letters written by Father Bruté. These two letters were addressed to Bishop Cheverus, the first bishop of Boston.

Following the brief survey of the most important of the European and Canadian Archives we now turn our attention to the priceless archives in our own country. Among the archives here in the States that of Baltimore Cathedral occupies the first place. This fruitful Collection yielded the following assistance to our story: twenty-four letters written by Father John Francis Rivet—letters that gave appreciable aid in delineating the condition of religion in and around Vincennes from October 26, 1795 to November 6, 1803; several letters written by Bishop Flaget of Bardstown; one letter written by each of the following, Fathers Kundek, Lalumière, Champion, and Madame Bruté; and ninety-six letters, or more than three hundred pages, written in French by Father Bruté. These letters with the exception of four or five were addressed to the Archbishops of Baltimore in succession as they filled the office, Carroll, Neale, Maréchal, Whitfield, and Eccleston and bear the dates from 1810 to June 22, 1839, four days prior to the saintly prelate's death. Besides producing an authentic story of Father Bruté's labors at Baltimore, and Emmitsburg, these letters give us a true picture of the four and one-half years of his episcopal life in which he served so faithfully and so nobly the poverty-stricken Diocese of Vincennes.

The Catholic Archives of America, Notre Dame—the invaluable storehouse of research—yielded a rich harvest of information. This collection embraces the following writings of Bishop Bruté: ten French letters addressed to Bishop Blanc; eight written to Father Timon; twenty penned to Father François; thirty letters, mostly French, written to Judge Gaston of South Carolina, besides several to Bishops Flaget, Purcell, and Rezé, Fathers Vabret, Chance, Gartland, Ferneding, Shawe, Wathen, Babade, Zocchi, and Pise. In addition to this there are the following let-

ters addressed to Bishop Bruté: thirteen letters from the
Sacred Congregation, Rome; nineteen letters from the pen
of Bishop Du Bourg; eleven written by Bishop Cheverus;
and twelve letters addressed by Bishop England. This last
collection has been depleted since 1883 when it numbered
twenty-three letters. However, the missing numbers were
happily found in transcripts in the valuable Canon Bruté de
Rémur Collection. Notre Dame is also in possession of a
goodly share of the Bruté-Seton Correspondence. Over and
above these collections numerous other letters—correspondence of the early bishops—were winnowed for information.
The Edmund J. P. Schmitt Collection is also deposited at
Notre Dame.

The Central Bureau of the Central Verein, St. Louis,
graciously granted our research the assistance of the *Berichte der Leopoldinen-Stiftung im Kaiserthume Oester-
reiche*, Vienna. This series contains eight lengthy and
highly descriptive letters written by Bishop Bruté in which
he gave, from time to time, a detailed account of the missionary activities within his new diocese. The letters of
Bishop de la Hailandière and Father Kundek also gave additional information.

The Georgetown University Archives possess the Bruté
writings that were in John Gilmary Shea's possession together with several letters written by Bruté to the President
of the University. The most noteworthy of these papers
is a brief *Journal* recording the principal events of his life.

The Government Indian Archives, Washington, D. C.,
have in their files the following sixteen letters concerning
Indian affairs in Indiana:

Father Deseille, Missionary to A. C. Pepper, Indian
    agent at Logansport. 2
Lewis H. Sands, assistant agent to A. C. Pepper. 2
S. T. Badin to Lewis Cass, Secretary of War. 1
S. Bruté to H. C. Harris, Washington, D. C. 2
A. C. Pepper to H. C. Harris. 2
John Law to H. C. Harris. 1

While these letters are few in number they reveal much relative to the story of the Indians in Indiana from June, 1834, to June, 1838.

The Souvay Collection, Kenrick Seminary, Webster Groves, Mo., possesses valuable transcripts of Du Bourg's correspondence with Bruté; the lengthy letter of Bruté asking Bishop Chabrat's advice regarding his nomination to Vincennes; and a volume of correspondence between Bruté and the Mountain.

Mount St. Joseph-on-the-Ohio Archives possess several original letters and a goodly store of original papers of Bishop Bruté. The greater portion of them are of a deeply spiritual character. The store of Bruté notes at Mount St. Mary's, Emmitsburg, has been sadly scattered. Nothing remains but a few valueless letters written by parents of students. Mount St. Vincent-on-Hudson Archives are in possession of a Journal of Mother Seton. In this Journal is a lengthy account of her life written by Father Bruté immediately after her death. The most noteworthy original material in St. Francis Xavier Cathedral Archives, Vincennes, are the registers containing the deaths, marriages, baptisms, and minutes of the trustee meetings, and a lengthy letter of John Hughes to Father Bruté. St. Joseph's Convent Archives, Emmitsburg, still possess, over and above the two volumes of *Bruté-Seton Correspondence*, a goodly store of unpublished notes together with several letters. The greater portion of these writings are meditations, prayers, and spiritual exhortations.

The St. Louis Chancery Archives rank next to Baltimore in possessing authentic original information on Bishop Bruté. This gold mine of documents tells practically the entire story of our pioneer bishop's apostolic life. The

Bruté letters preserved in the St. Louis Chancery Archives number one hundred and thirty-five or 470 pages of fools cap written in French. If all other material had perished a very thorough history of Bishop Bruté's administration could be woven from his numerous letters to Bishop Rosati, who was the ideal of the Bishop of Vincennes.

The St. Louis University Archives possess but a few letters of Bishop Bruté. These were addressed to Father Elet, S. J., President of the University on the occasion of Father Benjamin Petit's illness and death. St. Mary's Church Archives, Chicago, possess the early baptism and marriage registers dating back to the period when Chicago belonged to the Diocese of Vincennes. Bishop Bruté's signature bears testimony to his ministrations at Chicago late in the summer of 1838.

In addition to this short account of the more important Archives there are other places that have furnished small quantities of original matter. Nevertheless, these brief pages will give our readers at least an idea of the number of Archives in Europe, Canada, and the United States, that have been examined in person, and of the amount of unpublished materials, not to speak of the published sources, that have been gathered and incorporated in the present biography of Bishop Bruté.

BIBLIOGRAPHY

MANUSCRIPT SOURCES

European Archives:

Archdiocesan Archives, Rennes, France.
Brothers of Christian Instruction Archives, Ploërmel, France.
Archives of St. Sulpice, Paris.
Bruté de Rémur Archives, Rennes, France.
Musaeum Bollandianum, Brussels, Belgium.
Propaganda Archives, Rome.

Canadian Archives:

Archdiocesan Archives, Quebec.
Government Archives, Quebec.
Government Archives, Ottawa.
Sulpician Archives, Montreal.

United States Archives:

Baltimore Cathedral Archives, Baltimore, Md.
Catholic Archives of America, Notre Dame, Ind.
Central Bureau of Central Verein, St. Louis, Mo.
Convent of the Immaculate Conception Archives, Ferdinand, Ind.
Georgetown University Archives, Washington, D. C.
Files of the Indian Office, Dept. of the Interior, Washington, D. C.
Kenrick Seminary Archives (Souvay Collection), St. Louis, Mo.
Mount St. Joseph-on-Ohio Archives, Ohio.
Mount St. Mary's Archives, Emmitsburg, Md.
Mount St. Vincent-on-Hudson Archives, New York.
St. Francis Xavier Cathedral Archives, Vincennes, Ind.
St. Joseph Convent Archives, Emmitsburg, Md.
St. Louis Chancery Archives, St. Louis, Mo.
St. Louis University Archives, St. Louis, Mo.
St. Mary's Church Archives, Chicago, Ill.
St. Meinrad Abbey Archives, St. Meinrad, Ind.

PUBLISHED SOURCES

Annalen der Gesellschaft der Verbreitung des Glaubens, Einsiedeln, 1832–1837.
Annales de L'Association de la Propagation de la Foi, Lyons, 1828–1841.

Berichte der Leopoldinen-Stiftung im Kaiserthume Oesterreichs. Vienna. 1836–1850.

Bishop Kenrick's Diary and Visitation Records, 1830–1851. Lancaster, Pa. 1916.

Bruté-Seton Correspondence. Emmitsburg. 2 vols. 1884, 1886.

Concilia Provincialia, Baltimori habita ab Anno 1829 usque ad Annum 1849. Baltimore. 1851.

David-Bruté Letters, Ave Maria. Notre Dame. Vol. 5. 1869.

Lettres Inédites de J. M. & F. de LaMennais. Nantes. 1862.

McCaffrey, Discourse on Bishop Bruté. August 19, 1839. Emmitsburg. 1839.

The Metropolitan Catholic Almanac and Laity's Directory, 1834–1843.

The National Pastorals of the American Hierarchy, 1792–1919. Washington, D. C. 1923.

GENERAL WORKS

Alerding, H., *A History of the Catholic Church in the Diocese of Vincennes.* Indianapolis. 1883.

    The Diocese of Fort Wayne. Fort Wayne. 1907.

Aubrey de Vere, *Heroines of Charity.* New York. 1896.

Azais, L'Abbé, *Monseigneur Maurice d'Aussac de St. Palais.* Nimes. 1880.

Barberey, Madame de, *Elizabeth Seton.* Paris. 1880.

Bayley, J. R., *Memoirs of Rt. Rev. S. W. G. Bruté.* New York. 1865, 1876.

Belloc, Hilaire, *The French Revolution.* New York. 1911.

Bennett, W. H., *Catholic Footsteps in Old New York.* New York. 1909.

Bilger, Charles, *History of St. Mary's Parish, Madison, Indiana.* Madison, Ind. 1915.

Birkbeck, M., *Notes of a Journey in America from the Coast of Virginia to the Territory of Illinois.* Philadelphia. 1817.

Blanchard, C. C., *History of the Catholic Church in Indiana.* 2 vols. Logansport, Ind. 1898.

Boggers, A. C., *The Settlement of Illinois, 1778–1830.* Chicago. 1908.

Bruté, Abbé Charles, *Vie de Monseigneur Bruté de Rémur.* Rennes. 1887.

Bruté, S., *The Sons of St. Dominick.* Baltimore. 1812.

Carr, M. W., *A History of Catholicity and Catholic Institutions in Evansville, Indiana.* Indianapolis. 1888.

    Catholicity in Terre Haute and Vigo County, Indiana. Indianapolis. 1888.

    Catholicity in Tipton City and County, Indiana. Indianapolis. 1890.

    History of Catholicity in New Albany and Jeffersonville. Indianapolis. 1890.

History of Catholicity in Richmond and Wayne County. Indianapolis. 1889.

Carron, Guy, *Les Confesseurs de la Foi dans l'Eglise Gallicane a la fin des XVIII Siècle*. Paris. 1820.

Cassidy, F. P., *Catholic College Foundations and Development in the United States (1677–1850)*. Washington. 1924.

Cauthorn, H. S., *History of St. Francis Xavier Cathedral, Vincennes, Indiana*. Vincennes. 1892.

Clarke, R. A., *Lives of the Deceased Bishops of the United States*, 3 vols. New York. 1872–1888.

Code, J., *The Life of Elizabeth Seton*. New York. 1927.

Corbinière, C. de La, *An Apostolic Woman*. New York. 1882. St. Louis. 1917.

  L'Indiana. Paris. 1886.

Currier, C. W., *Carmel in America*. Baltimore. 1890.

  History of Religious Orders. New York. 1894.

Dauphin, L'Abbé Joseph, *Histoire des Seminaires de Rennes et de Dol et L'oeuvre du R. P. Blanchard*. Paris. 1910.

De Courcy—Shea, *The History of the Catholic Church in the United States*. New York. 1856.

De Smet, P. J., *Western Missions and Missionaries*. New York. 1858.

Deuther, C. G., *The Life and Times of Rt. Rev. J. Timon*. Buffalo. 1870.

Dilhet-Browne, *Beginnings of the Catholic Church in the United States*. Washington, D. C. 1922.

Dillon, J. B., *A History of Indiana*. Indianapolis. 1859.

Dunn, J. P., *Indiana and Indianans*. 5 vols. Chicago. 1919.

Erskine, M., *Mother Philippine Duchesne*. New York. 1926.

Esarey, L., *A History of Indiana*. 3 vols. New York. 1922.

Farley, John Cardinal, *The Life of Cardinal McCloskey*. New York. 1918.

Finotti, J. M., *Bibliographia Catholica Americana*. New York. 1872.

Fitzmorris, S. M. A., *Four Decades of Catholicity in Texas*. Washington, D. C. 1926.

Fox, S. C., *The Life of Rt. Rev. B. J. David*. New York. 1925.

Fullerton, Lady G., *Life of Venerable Madeline Barat*. Roehampton. 1880.

Gallouédec, L., *La Bretagne*. Paris. 1916 (5th ed.)

Garraghan, G. J., *Catholic Church in Chicago, 1673–1871*. Chicago. 1921.

Gautherat, G., *Histoire Politique des Massacres*. Paris. 1927.

Goodrich and Tuttle, *A History of Indiana*. Indianapolis. 1875.

Gosselin, Abbé A., *Le Venerable François de Montmorency Laval*. Quebec. 1906.

Greene, G. E., *A History of Old Vincennes and Knox County*. Chicago. 1911.

Grente, Joseph, *Les Martyres de Septembre 1792 a Paris*. Paris. 1926.

Guilday, "John Gilmary Shea," *Historical Records and Studies*, XVII (1926). New York.
    The Life and Times of John Carroll. New York. 1922.
    The Life and Times of John England. 2 vols. New York. 1927.
    The National Pastorals of the American Hierarchy, 1792–1919. Washington. 1923.

Hassard, J. R. G., *The Life of Most Rev. John Hughes*. New York. 1866.

Heineman, J. L., *The Early Days of St. Gabriel's*. Connersville, Ind. 1925.

Henny, J. M., *Ein Blick ins Thal des Ohio*. Muenchen. 1836.

Herbermann, Charles, *The Sulpicians in the United States*. New York. 1916.

Herbert, Lady, *The Life of S. W. G. Bruté*. London. 1870.

Howard, T. E., *History of the University of Notre Dame*. Chicago. 1895.

Howe, W. M., *The History of Louisiana from the Earliest Period*. New Orleans. 1882.

Howlett, W. J., *The Life of Rev. Charles Nerinckx*. Techny. 1915.

Jausions, Dom P., *Vie de L'Abbé Carron*. 2 vols. Paris. 1866.

Jeannin, A., *Histoire de L'Eglise de Saint Sulpice*. Paris. 1901.

Kehoe, L., *Complete Works of Most Rev. John Hughes*. New York. 1865.

Kenton, E., *The Jesuit Relations*. New York. 1925.

Kirlin, J., *Catholicity in Philadelphia*. Philadelphia. 1909.

Lambing., A. A., *The Catholic Church in the Diocese of Pittsburg*. New York. 1880.

Lamott, J. H., *History of the Archdiocese of Cincinnati*. New York. 1921.

Lathrop, G. & R., *The Story of Courage*, New York. 1894.

Law, J. J., *The Colonial History of Vincennes*. Vincennes. 1859.

Levesque, E., *Les Bienheureux Martyrs du Seminaire Saint-Sulpice*. Paris. 1928.

Lindley, H., *Indiana as seen by Early Travelers*. Indianapolis. 1916.

Macleod, X. D., *History of Devotion to the Blessed Virgin in North America*. Boston. 1879.

Maes, C. P., *Life of Rev. Charles Nerinckx*. Cincinnati. 1880.

McCann, S. M. A., *The History of Mother Seton's Daughters*. 2 vols. New York. 1917.
    Archbishop Purcell and the Archdiocese of Cincinnati. Washington. 1918.

McCarthy, S. M. B., *Napoleon Bonaparte and the Restoration of the Catholic Religion in France*. Nazareth, Mich. 1925.

McGill, A. B., *The Sisters of Charity of Nazareth, Kentucky*. New York. 1917.

McGirr, J. E., *Life of Rt. Rev. William Quarter*. New York. 1850.

McGovern, J. J., *History of the Catholic Church in Chicago*. Chicago, Illinois. 1891.

Meline, M.—McSweeney, E. F. X., *The Story of the Mountain*. 2 vols. Emmitsburg. 1911.

Minogue, A., *Loretto—Annals of the Century*. New York. 1912.

Munro, W. B., *Crusaders of New France* (Chronicles of America Series). New Haven. 1921.

O'Connell, J. J., *Catholicity in the Carolinas and Georgia*. New York. 1879.

O'Daniel, V. F., *An American Apostle*. Washington. 1923.
    Life of Bishop Fenwick, O. P. Washington. 1920.
    The Father of the Church in Tennessee. New York. 1926.

O'Donnell, J. H., *The Catholic Hierarchy in the United States, 1790–1922*. Washington, D. C. 1922.

O'Gorman, T., *A History of the Roman Catholic Church in the United States*. New York. 1895.

Parkman, F., *La Salle and the Discovery of the Great West*. Boston. 1898.

Reuss, F. X., *Biographical Cyclopedia of the Catholic Hierarchy of the United States, 1789–1898*. Milwaukee. 1898.

Reynolds, I. A., *The Works of Rt. Rev. John England*. 5 vols. Baltimore. 1849.

Rothensteiner, J., *History of the Archdiocese of St. Louis*. 2 vols. St. Louis. 1928.

Roy, Pierre-Georges, *Le Sieur de Vincennes, Fondateur de L'Indiana*. Quebec. 1919.

Ryan, J. P., *Travel Literature as Source Material for American Catholic History*. Chicago. 1928.

Salzbacher, J., *Meine Reise nach Nord-Amerika im Iahre 1842*. Vienna. 1845.

Schlarman, J. H., *From Quebec to New Orleans*. Belleville. 1929.

Schmitt, E. J. P., *Geschichte der deutschen St. Marien Gemeinde von New Albany*. Cincinnati. 1890.

Seton, R., *Memoirs, Letters, and Journal of Elizabeth Seton*. 2 vols. New York. 1870.

Shea, J. G., *History and General Description of New France*. New York. 1870.
    History of the Catholic Church in the United States. 4 vols. New York. 1886.

The Hierarchy of the Catholic Church in the United States. New York. 1886.

Spalding, M. F., *Sketches of the Early Catholic Missions of Kentucky.* Louisville. 1844.

The Life of Rt. Rev. B. J. Flaget. Louisville. 1852.

Tourscher, F. E., *The Hogan Schism.* Philadelphia. 1930.

Thwaites, R. G., *France in America* (The American Nation Series). New York. 1905.

Wallace, J., *The History of Illinois and Louisiana.* Cincinnati. 1893.

Webb, B. J., *The Centenary of Catholicity in Kentucky.* Louisville, 1884.

Wharton, C. H., *A Concise View of the Principal Points of Controversy between the Protestant and Roman Churches.* New York. 1817.

White, C. I., *Life of Mrs. Eliza Seton.* New York. 1878.

Wilson, G. R., *History of Dubois County.* Jasper, Ind. 1910.

Winsor, J., *The English and French in America.* 1689–1763. New York. 1887.

ANONYMOUS:

Catholic Encyclopedia.

Eighteenth Annual Report of the Bureau of American Ethnology. Washington. 1889.

Life and Life-Work of Mother Theodore Guérin. New York. 1904.

Life of Very Rev. Felix de Andreis. Baltimore. 1861. St. Louis. 1900.

Memorial Volume of the Centenary of St. Mary's Seminary of St. Sulpice. Baltimore. 1891.

Oeuvres Posthumes de Féli de LaMennais. 2 vols. Paris. 1858.

St. Paul's Church, New Alsace, Indiana, Souvenir of Diamond Jubilee. 1908.

Souvenir of the Silver Jubilee of Archbishop Feehan. Chicago. 1891.

The Indiana Gazetteer or Topographical Dictionary, Indianapolis. 1833. (2nd. ed.)

PERIODICAL LITERATURE

Historical Reviews and Magazines.

Alma Mater. St. Meinrad. Vol. 4. 1895.

America. New York. Vol. 37. 1927.

American Catholic Quarterly Review. Philadelphia. 48 vols. 1876–1923.

American Ecclesiastical Review. Philadelphia. Vol. 35. 1906.

Ave Maria. Notre Dame. 1865–1930.

Brownson's Quarterly Review. Boston. Vols. 1–4. 1847–1850.

Historical Records and Studies. New York. 19 vols. 1899–1929.
        Monographs. 12 vols. 1902–1930.

Indiana Magazine of History. Bloomington. 26 vols. 1904–1930.

Literarischer Handweiser. Muenster. No. 36, 1865; No. 530, 1891.

Michigan Historical Magazine. Lansing. Vol. 2.

Mississippi Valley Historical Review. Cedar Rapids. Vol. 4.

Notre Dame Scholastic. Notre Dame. Vol. 21.

Pastoral Blatt. St. Louis. 59 vols. 1866–1925.

Proceedings of the Mississippi Valley Historical Association. Cedar
        Rapids. Vol. 10. 1920.

Publications of the Indiana Historical Society. Indianapolis. 9 vols.
        1897–1930.

Records of the American Catholic Historical Society. Philadelphia.
        41 vols. 1884–1930.

St. Meinrad Historical Essays. St. Meinrad. Vol. 1. 1929–1930.

The American Catholic Historical Researches. Philadelphia. 29
        vols. 1884–1912.

The Catholic Historical Review. Washington. 15 vols. 1915–1930.

The Catholic Historical Society of Indiana. Bulletin No. 1 & 2. 1927.

The Catholic World. New York. 131 vols. 1865–1930.

The Metropolitan. Baltimore. Vol. 1. 1830.

The Religious Cabinet. Baltimore. Vol. 1. 1842.

The St. Louis Catholic Historical Review. St. Louis. 5 vols. 1918–
        1923.

The United States Catholic Historical Magazine. New York. 5 vols.
        1887–1892.

The United States Catholic Magazine. Baltimore. Vol. 5. 1846.

Newspapers

Catholic Record. Indianapolis. Vols. 7–10. 1889–1893.

The Boston Pilot. Boston. 1836.

The Catholic Advocate. Bardstown—Louisville. 1836–1840.

The Catholic Herald. Philadelphia. 1833–1841.

The Catholic Mirror. Baltimore. 1849.

The Catholic Telegraph. Cincinnati. Vols. 1–15. 1831–1846.

The Indiana Catholic and Record. Indianapolis. Vols. 1–21. 1910–
        1930.

The New Record. Indianapolis. Vols. 1–3. 1883–1885.

The New York Catholic Register. New York. 1839.

The New York Weekly Register and Catholic Diary. New York. 5 vols. 1832–1836.

The Shepherd of the Valley. St. Louis. 1832–1836.

The United States Catholic Miscellany. Charleston. Vols. 1–19. 1822–1841.

The Vincennes Gazette. Vincennes. Vol. 4. 1835.

The Western Sun and General Advertizer. Vincennes. 1825–1840.

Wahrheitsfreund. Cincinnati. Vols. 1–3. 1839–1842.

INTRODUCTORY

The ancient province of Brittany comprises the north-western peninsula of France and is situated directly south of the British Isles. Owing to its geographical features, it is generally termed Upper or West, and Lower or East Brittany. It bore the name Armorica, meaning the *Land of the sea*, until the Celts from Britain took up their abode in the land.

The surface of Brittany consists of a plateau in the north, dominated by Monts d'Arée; while the Montagnes Noires are a continuation of the southern plateau. The water-ways are of little value. The Vilaine which flows through Rennes is the only river basin of any importance. The coast-line is very irregular and the mouths of the rivers form deep estuaries, all of which makes approach to the province very difficult. Nature herself condemned Brittany to remain in isolation.

Prior to the coming of the Romans, we have no definite knowledge of the history of Brittany. The primitive population left no records, no traces save megalithic monuments. The Romans destroyed the fleet of Veneti in the year 56, B. C. The Armoricans joined in the insurrection of the Gauls against Caesar in the year 52, B. C., but they were subdued by him during the following year. Under the Roman Empire Brittany formed part of the Third Lyonnesse. However, it became a kingdom in 383 and remained independent until 509.

The first migration of Celtic inhabitants to Armorica occurred about the year 450, and was occasioned by the invasion of the Angles and the Saxons. Then in the two centuries following they migrated in great numbers until practically the entire peninsula was populated. They were converted to Christianity, built monasteries, cleared the land, and became prosperous. Under the Merovingians, Brittany ranked as a countship. Nomenoë established in 845 the

Kingdom of Brittany, which was destined to be short-lived. In 874 this kingdom was parcelled out among a number of counts, of which the Count of Rennes was the most important. Goeffrey I, Count of Rennes, took the title of Duke of Brittany in 902. However, the final union of France and Brittany was not consummated until 1532, when Francis I, married Claudia of France, daughter of Anne of Brittany and Louis XII.

The Bretons by nature are very conservative, and local customs have been rigidly observed down through the centuries. Nevertheless, the flair for marvelous legends exists nowhere as in Brittany. Recent research indicates that there exists within its boundaries an extensive folk-literature. In addition they possess a keen appreciation and love of the beautiful, a characteristic that is universally manifested throughout the province. They are an industrious, economic, and thrifty folk. Their homes are quaint, but abound in natural and artistic beauty. Their dress is rich and odd, but modest and pleasing in character. In manner they are courteous and obliging to the extent of burdening and inconveniencing themselves to render services to others. The Bretons, staunch in their religious beliefs, have admirably preserved the Faith under the most excruciating pangs of persecution during the French revolutions.[1]

Rennes, the ancient capital of the province of Brittany, is situated in Upper or West Brittany at the confluence of the rivers Ill and Vilaine. From its position at the conjunction of two streams it was called Condate. Later it received the name Rennes from the inhabitants of the province whom Julius Caesar called Rhedones. At present it is the principal city of the department of Ill-et-Vilaine.

In the year 1720, the Rhedones suffered the overwhelming loss of more than one-half the city by fire. This failed, however, to discourage the inhabitants for immediately they set about rebuilding it on a more modern plan. The only remnants of antiquity existed in the vicinity of the Cathedral.

[1] L. Gallouédec, *La Bretagne*, Paris, 1916.

Rennes is the seat of an archbishopric. The palace occupies part of the site of the abbey dedicated to St. Melaine. Authentic historical mention of the See of Rennes dates to the year 453. Records reveal that her bishops participated in the early councils which convened at Angers, Tours, and Orleans.

Religion flourished and this ancient city became the possessor of many beautiful churches. Various religious communities found peaceful quarters within those walls and numerous monasteries were erected. During the Reign of Terror, the government confiscated all those sanctuaries and either sold, destroyed, or used them for profane purposes. Nevertheless, persecutors failed in their attempt and the Faith again waxed strong.

Another feature of interest and beauty is the old Parliament House, which is considered the finest building in the city. It was designed by Jacque Debrosse in the seventeenth century. The ceiling of the Parliamentary chamber was painted by Jean Jouvent, a genius from Rouen. His art was beheld with such enthusiastic admiration that Louis XIV awarded him a pension of 1,200 livres at the completion of the work in 1696.[2]

[2] Bruté notes, Original in CA of A. Notre Dame, Indiana; E. Rivière, *Guide Illustré de Rennes*. Rennes, 1925; L. Gallouédec, *op. cit.*

CHAPTER I

THE CHILDHOOD OF SIMON BRUTÉ DE RÉMUR
1779–1791

The ancient capital of loyal Brittany deserves to be enshrined in the heart of every Catholic, not only within the confines of historic Indiana, but throughout the United States. Chiefly the states of the East and the Middle West owe her a debt of deep gratitude. It was there, at Rennes, that Simon William Gabriel Bruté de Rémur,* who was destined one day to become the Father of the Church in Indiana, was born. His brief autobiography reads: "Born at Rennes, Little Brittany, on the twentieth of March, 1779, of a rich family but half ruined since the French Revolution."[1] Simon was baptized in the church of St. Germain, on the day of his birth, and special designs seemed to be upon him from his infancy.[2]

According to a general custom, which was common in those days, the new-born son was sent into the country to a foster nurse. He remained with this nurse for about fifteen months, and she sometimes lent him to another poor woman who used to hold him on one of her arms to excite compassion while she begged. Simon may have deplored later

---

* Pronounced Brōō'tay.

[1] Original in Georgetown University Archives, Fol. 92, 6. Washington, D. C.; Abbé C. Bruté de Rémur, *Vie de Monseigneur Bruté de Rémur*, p. 1. Rennes, 1887; J. R. Bayley, *Memoirs of the Rt. Rev. S. W. G. Bruté de Rémur*, p. 9. New York, 1865.

[2] *Bruté—Seton Correspondence*, p. 515. Emmitsburg, 1886.

Extract de Registre concernant l'Etat civil de Citoyens de la cidevant Paroisse de St. Germain de Rennes pour l'anne 1779.

"Simon Guillaume Gabriel, fils de Simon Guillaume Gabriel Bruté de Rémur, et de Renée Jeanne Le Saulnier de Vauxelle, né et baptisé le meme jour vingt mars mil Septcent soixants dix neuf. Parrain, François Pierre René Vatar de Jouanner; Marraine, Victoire Françoise Bruté de Rémur. Le Valler, Curé.

Souissigné a Rennes le Quatore Thermidor, an sept de la Republique Francaise, une et indivisible. Durbreil."

THE PALACE OF JUSTICE, BIRTHPLACE OF SIMON BRUTÉ DE RÉMUR

THE CHURCH OF ST. GERMAIN, WHERE SIMON BRUTÉ DE RÉMUR
RECEIVED BAPTISM AND HIS FIRST HOLY COMMUNION

in life the great deprivation of a mother's affection which he
suffered in his infancy; nevertheless, he considered himself
favored by Providence and experienced a sense of gratification in knowing that even in his helpless babyhood he had
been an occasion of aid to God's needy.[3]

This young Breton's ancestors were of genuine French
extraction. His father, born at Paris in 1729, belonged to
an ancient and wealthy family. He was married twice. His
first wife was Mary Jeanne Le Chat by whom he had seven
children. After her death he married Madame Vatar at
Rennes. She was a native of St. Brieux and the widow of
Francis Vatar, printer to the King and Parliament at
Rennes. Of this union were born two worthy sons, Simon
and Augustine. The father had an uncle and two brothers in
Holy Orders. They were distinguished for both their virtue and their learning. Abbé Jean, the older of the brothers,
was a doctor of the Sorbonne and pastor of Saint Benedict's
Church in Paris. He was also the author of several valuable
literary works. The younger, Abbé Bruté de Loirelle, was
royal censor of Belles-Lettres at Paris, and was the author
of several works in prose and in verse. Moreover he made
valuable translations from the writings of German and English authors. The mother, too, had relatives who were
dedicated to the service of God. The Reverend Peter Robert,
an uncle, was Prior of Etables of the Order of Premonstra-
tensians and died in Guingcamp Hospital, a prisoner for the
Faith during the Reign of Terror in 1795. Her sister, a
member of the Daughters of St. Vincent de Paul, spent
forty-four years in religion.[4] Owing to the numerous religious vocations among their relatives, it would not have
been astonishing had both Simon and Augustine devoted
their lives to the same cause.

The family resided in the Palace of the Parliament where
the mother's ancestors for several generations had occupied

[3] J. R. Bayley, *op. cit.*, p. 11.

[4] Abbé C. Bruté de Rémur, *op. cit.*, pp. 1–2; J. R. Bayley, *op. cit.*,
pp. 211–212.

apartments in one of the wings. The father was Director
of the Finances of his native province with the promise of
succession to the more remunerative office of Farmer-
General of the revenues at Paris. This promised a brilliant
career for their son, as far as wealth could contribute to it.
His mother often addressed him in the words, "You were
born to live in opulence." This prophecy was not fulfilled
for within a few years, time wrought manifold changes in
the parental home. Military officers and nobles gathered no
longer within its portals. The sumptuous banquets ceased,
and where wealth once abounded now came financial difficulties.

The father's sudden death, February 27, 1786, resulting
from a major operation, came as a serious blow to the
family. It all occurred within the course of a few days and
allowed him no time to balance his accounts. He had never
questioned the honesty of anyone, and as a result the state
of his affairs proved that many had taken advantage of his
goodness. Madame Bruté de Rémur was amazed to discover that in addition to her husband's confused estate, he
was surety for others to the amount of one million francs.
Friends and lawyers advised her to renounce the succession
but honesty bade her act otherwise. Therefore, she sac-
rificed her personal possessions to pay the debts of her
husband and opened a printing office to support her family.[5]

In 1785 the mother realized that the days of infancy for
her son had passed and that other teachers must assist her
in Simon's education. Accordingly, he was sent to the best
schools in his native city. The first school he attended was
kept by Mademoiselle Rosé in the *Rue aux Toulons,* where
he learned to read and write. At the time of his father's
death in 1786 he was attending Madame Badier's boarding
school. After the death of the father, the mother cheerfully assumed the duties of both parents towards her children. The spirit of the nation was continually growing
more godless. Startling tragedies were soon to follow. It

[5] Bruté Journal, Georgetown University Archives. Fol. 92, 6.
Washington, D. C.; Shea, III (1890), p. 640.

was in prescience of these coming evils that Madame Bruté de Rémur fostered more prudently the religious and intellectual character of her son.

By nature this young Breton was gentle, affectionate, and cheerful. He possessed a strong sense of humor, and this, together with a lively imagination and tenacious memory, won for him the affection of fellow-students and teachers. Simon proved to be an apt scholar. After completing the preliminary requirements he attended the College of Rennes from 1788 to 1791 and was particularly fortunate in having as teachers priests who were eminent for piety and learning. However, the college student has left us in his notes little information concerning this period. It may be penned in a single line: "Educated at the College of Rennes with all the collegiate honors."[6]

Again Simon was singularly favored in having the celebrated Father Carron as his first guide and confessor. This eminent priest admitted Simon to his First Communion in 1791. The child's preparations for this sacred act were made with the utmost sincerity. The series of instructions, the solemn surroundings, the retreat, the general confession, and Holy Communion, impressed him so deeply that their memory was never effaced. From his notes, on this memorable event, we learn the state of sanctity his soul possessed at this time. He stated that although he had attended the public schools for five years he was a stranger to all improper notions. He went to confession regularly, but up to that time, he had little to confess. His chief matter of reproach, at the time of making his general confession for First Communion, was having taken an apple from the stand of an old woman who sold fruit. Simon was ever grateful to God for the state of innocence and piety in which he received his Eucharistic Lord for the first time. In 1791 all public exercises of religion ceased in France, the College of Rennes was forced to close, and Simon Bruté pursued his studies under private tutors.

[6] *Ibid.*

CHAPTER II

A TARSICIUS OF THE REVOLUTION
1791–1796

The résumé of personal experiences during the agonizing Revolution that swept over his native land during the period of boyhood is a prominent feature in the biography of Simon Bruté de Rémur. It gives an insight into the spirit of the day and casts light on Simon's private life. Likewise, it reveals the influence that environment exercised on the formation of his character and the indelible impression that it stamped upon his life.

The Reign of Terror came not as an unheralded avalanche upon the French nation. On the contrary, it bore rather the complexion of a raging tempest growing in fury and increasing in violence as it swept along. It had been roused by rationalists, who claimed to have found nothing except slavery around the throne and superstition at God's altar. Hence they considered it their sacred duty to share in the task of annihilating the monarchy and the Catholic faith. In the beginning the rationalists were not wholly averse to all religious worship. They practised no religion themselves; yet they maintained it was indispensable for the people. The incompatibility of the Catholic system with the principles of government which they proposed to substitute for the existing monarchy was obvious to all. Therefore, the leaders resolved to give the people a religion evolved from their own false theories.

The French world, prior to this, had been living in a spirit of dangerous unrest, for a period of two hundred years. The infallibility of the Sovereign Pontiff and his superiority to a general council of bishops was the vital question that caused the agitation. Gallican claims in opposition to this doctrine were wholly contrary to the teachings that had prevailed in the Church for the previous 1600 years. Ill

humor between the French and the Papal courts was provoked in 1663 by a quarrel between the servants of the
French ambassador at Rome and the Corsian guard. Following this in 1680 the deputies of the clergy, at the request
of Louis XIV, wrote a flattering letter in favor of the king's
claims and against the Pope. Many ecclesiastics had been
provided with benefices by the government and many bishops, unworthy of the name, occupied high and influential
places. It is well known that royal patronage together with
intrigue ruined the French Church.

From the opening of the States-General on May 5, 1789,
to the promulgation of the "Civil Constitution of the
Clergy" on August 24, 1790, the nation rapidly sank into
an abyss of impiety and corruption and nothing remained
undone to extirpate Catholicism in France. Violent measures were taken to force the clergy to subscribe by oath to
the civil constitution. Catholics were ill-treated, bishops
were cast into prison, and finally the death sentence was
passed on the clergy who refused to take the oath. These
various degrees of persecution followed each other in rapid
succession until the height of the Revolution prevailed
throughout the nation.

The close of the year 1792 beheld France deluged in horrors. Ecclesiastics, together with those who harbored them,
fell victims to the guillotine within twenty-four hours after
their capture. Frequently the officers and soldiers rushed
into private dwellings for the purpose of ransacking and
searching for victims. The members of suspected homes
were forced to be very watchful lest they betray some innocent priest or themselves, for as soon as the last sympathy was manifested for anything religious, they were immediately distrusted and in some cases even denounced to
the tribunal without further evidence. Thus disappeared
the exterior charm and comfort of home-life, and terror
reigned in their place; nevertheless, within the hearts of
the faithful the love of God waxed more vigorously.

Historians have, in numerous volumes, preserved to us
the record of the deeds of this period; yet the greater num-

ber have been content to treat solely of the crimes and horrors of the time.   The iniquities of the oppressors have been
unveiled, while the virtues of the sufferers, for the most part,
have been hidden.   Our heroic Breton in his *Recollections
of the French Revolution* changed this picture. His sketches
vividly portray not only the trials and persecutions suffered,
but also the charity, patience, and heroism manifested by
those who in the midst of those wretched days remained
faithful to God and His Church.   Likewise, his simple narrative brings out in strong relief his own deep faith and
intrepid courage.   It was during this trying ordeal, when
the glory and the shame of France seemed to meet in a
death-struggle, that Simon Bruté de   Rémur   witnessed
events which were to influence his future ever after.[1]

Simon was then fourteen years old and, being a tactful
observer, was often sent by the family to attend the tribunal
that was in session in the Parliament House.   He witnessed
the trials of many priests and related their fate to his mother and other members of the household.   However, he never
had the courage to witness the execution of any of the
victims.   Because of the excessive terror which prevailed
throughout the nation and the fear of committing themselves by manifesting their feelings amid the savage mob
that generally gathered for the occasion, the elders dared
not attend these trials.

During these days of persecution Simon remained for the
greater part of the time with his mother at Rennes, and the
rest he spent at the home of Madame Jausions, his half-
sister, who resided at La Chapelle Bouexie.   His memoranda
show that even in those troubled days he was exact in the
employment of his time.   He rose early and applied himself
diligently to his studies.   From various citations of his own
we learn that his education was continued without interruption during 1791 and 1792 under priests who were in hid-

[1] J. R. Bayley, *Memoirs of the Rt. Rev. S. W. G. Bruté de Rémur*,
pp. 93–217;   H. Belloc, *The French Revolution*, p. 254.   New York.
1911.

ing. On the reverse side of a letter Simon wrote: "This letter is from M. Despres, who before the Revolution was curé at Reguiny, in the diocese of Vannes, then in prison at Vannes. He had been a long time in concealment at Rennes, in the house of M. Troublet, and I studied my Philosophy under him."[2] In a list headed "Places where I studied" Simon records four years under M. Muriel. He also studied under M. Delaitre, a young and fervent priest who was in concealment at the Bruté home. Relative to this clergyman Simon states that they became very intimate, studied together, and then stole out into the country and roamed about.

In the midst of these dark days Simon was devoted to a number of priests, and he proved his sincerity by favouring them secretly. These clergymen frequently wrote to him soliciting information concerning their friends and other members of the clergy. To obtain this information Simon was often forced to enter the prison. He visited the guards; entered into conversation with them until he became acquainted, and then awaited opportunities to visit the prisoners. Frequently he was prevailed upon to carry concealed letters from friends and loved ones to the imprisoned. Nevertheless, his courage did not end with these small acts. Within the prison walls his name was extolled for greater deeds of consolation. To Simon was granted the office of Tarsicius of old, for on numerous visits to the prison he carried, concealed on his bosom, the Blessed Sacrament. On such occasions he was accompanied by a priest who came disguised as a baker, carrying a basket of bread. The guards, anxious to be relieved of the responsibility of providing food for their charges, freely permitted the friends of prisoners to supply the necessary bread. Unknown to the guards, the clergy and the laity availed themselves of this opportunity to renew their spiritual strength by the reception of the Sacraments of Penance and Holy Eucharist. Lest our readers be mistaken regarding the distance between Simon's

[2] *Ibid.*, p. 23; *Records* (ACHS), XIII (1902), p. 325–333.

home and the prison, we may state that one of these places of incarceration was within the Palace of Justice, adjoining the Bruté apartments. Simon was not destined to be among the incarcerated or to die a martyr's death; nevertheless, he aided many prisoners to procure strength to remain faithful to the end.

The Revolution continued to generate new and more grievous troubles and of those one especially caused the interruption of Simon's studies during 1793–4. He recorded this in a note which evinces Madame Bruté's extraordinary ability to deal tactfully with the public in those clamorous days. During the height of the Revolution his mother made him work in the printing office[3] to save him from being enrolled in a regiment formed of boys, fourteen, fifteen, and sixteen years of age, named "The Hope of the country." This mob of young scoundrels asked and obtained permission from the Revolutionary Tribunal to preside at the condemnation and execution of some of the victims. Madame Bruté was strongly pressed to allow her son to join them, but she was released from the alarming situation on the plea that her woeful reverses necessitated her son's service in the printing office.

Madame Bruté's plea was not deceptive because the Revolution had practically ruined her sources of revenue. After the death of her second husband she obtained the reversion of Francis Vatar's title of printer to the King and Parliament. This occupation afforded her only support for the family. The books edited at her office were chiefly those on Jurisprudence of the Province, the Customs, and Collections of Ordinances. Her stock of books was valued at 130,000 francs, when the Constituent Assembly abolished all local laws and customs. Consequently, this destroyed the entire present value of her store, and it was necessary to rush new publications to press in order to preserve her business from complete destruction.

[3] Bruté Journal, Georgetown University Archives, fol. 92, 6. Washington, D. C.

From the close of 1792 until 1795 the Catholic religion in France seemed to have become extinct. All exterior worship was supplanted by the *festivals of reason*, and the *decadi* superseded the Sundays. Churches, convents, and religious houses were confiscated and converted to profane uses. Likewise, a great number were destroyed for the wealth of their material, while some few were changed into *temples of reason*. Countless pictures of these profane celebrations have been penned, but Simon Bruté, in contradistinction to the secular view on this subject, portrays "a little bit of heaven" granted to privileged homes that God deigned to cheer with His Sacred Presence, and with concealed priests.

Although the family lived in the Parliament House, the secret altar was not wanting. The chapel of the Palace was immediately over the Bruté apartments, but Simon relates that even in time of peace, this chapel, generally, was a solitude. Mass was celebrated in it only once a year, at the opening of the Courts of Law. It was rarely used on other occasions; however, one of his earliest recollections was his assistance at Mass there, at the age of four years, when his elder sister was married to M. Mazois. Within an interior room immediately beneath the sanctuary of that chapel, and the same room in which Simon was born, Madame Bruté erected their secret altar. Two priests officiated there daily. These clergymen were concealed in the Bruté quarters with all that awful and anxious privacy which their own safety and that of the household demanded. One of them, Father de Rosaire, a Dominican, was the confessor of Simon's mother. He was a venerable friar of seventy-eight years, with snow-white hair, calm features, and the simplicity of a child. The other, Father Pacificus, a Capuchin, was slightly younger. In that secret sanctuary they both slept and lived, and there also they offered up the Holy Sacrifice. Each morning when they had finished their private devotions, Simon's mother having seen that all things were prepared, called the family together and led them to that sacred room. One or two were left to keep watch each day, and to give notice in case of any alarm. For almost two years Mass was thus celebrated beneath the chapel of the Parliament House, which was then utterly profaned and made a den of thieves being a part of the Bureau of the Revolutionary Committee. This was not the height of its desecration. Later one of the three Tribunals, which supplied the guillotine with victims, took possession of it and for a while profaned the sacred name of Justice within those walls where the divine Sacrifice had been so often celebrated.

The Bruté home escaped unharmed although not without suspicion and danger during those two years. Despite the depletion of the nation, life was daily growing more difficult. The domiciliary visits were made with greater rigor and frequency. The officials became more shrewd and deceitful. Nevertheless, Madame Bruté, a woman of extraordinary prudence and equal virtue was not to be entrapped. She, therefore, decided to abandon the rare privilege which had been their precious consolation and thereby to establish the household in greater safety. The two venerable clergymen, who were concealed in the home, were transferred to smaller and more secure quarters which they dared not leave lest they fall captives to their persecutors. Simon, too, was forced to abandon the sacred charge that had been confided to him. Much to his sorrow he was no longer permitted to carry Holy Communion to the imprisoned.

From this time forth the Bruté household suffered the deprivation of Holy Mass, as did countless other homes. Although forbidden under the penalty of death to give Sunday any recognition, they sanctified the day to the best of their ability by performing devotions in secret. The mother of the household assumed the responsibility for conducting the services. Simon relates that his mother summoned them on Sunday before breakfast, usually to the parlor, and there kneeling before a large ivory crucifix, which she brought from her small oratory, they recited the prayers of Mass. They stood at the gospel and stopped in silence at the time

marked for the Consecration. He says that the King of men
and angels was indeed present, invisibly, but alas! not
present in the divine Sacrament of Love for both priest and
altar were absent. Not unfrequently were they disturbed
during these devotions by the noise and tumult attendant
upon the capture of a priest or of persons, politically ob-
noxious who were being brought for trial and execution.

The gloomy days of the Revolution ushered in countless
tragical scenes, many of which Simon witnessed. Numerous
others were imparted to him by persons who were present
at the time of their occurence. Frequently there were three
Tribunals in session on the same day at Rennes. The priests
were generally tried at the Criminal Court. The so-called
political conspirators were brought before the Revolutionary Tribunal; while those persons captured in arms or at a
place of some encounter were judged by the Military Commission. These three tribunals observed no strict limits
of jurisdiction and each one considered itself authorized to
decide the fate of all accused persons, regardless of the nature of their imaginary guilt. Simon sympathized especially with the clergy, therefore, he seldom attended other than
the Criminal Court. Courageously he entered the court
room and ventured so near that not unfrequently during
the trial did he lean upon the back of the bench where the
accused were seated.

Simon's *Recollections of the French Revolution* contains
detailed descriptions of numerous, cruel, mock trials. In
proof of the wretched barbarism and injustice practised in
those days we here insert accounts of several of those trials.
That of Father Raoul-Bodin, Curé of La Chapelle, St. Au-
bert, and the three La Gracière sisters who harbored this
priest, impressed the young Breton so indelibly that after
twenty-seven years had elapsed he was able to reproduce the
event in a pen-sketch. Simon was particularly captivated
by the noble, religious countenance of the priest, as well as
his calm, impressive manner of speech. M. Raoul, together
with two other priests, had been denounced by a workman

who saw them in the La Gracière home when he was mending the roof. The two younger clergymen escaped before the soldiers arrived.

Another scene, that left upon him a lasting memory, occurred one morning at five-thirty o'clock. Simon was engaged in study. Suddenly he was disturbed by the chanting of the *Libera me Domine* at a distance. The singer, evidently, was being hurried along the way, for very shortly he approached near to the Bruté home. All services of that nature had been proscribed for more than two years; hence the singular incident astonished Simon and he rushed to the window. There he beheld two men in peasant attire, bound together, and hurried along by a mob of soldiers. Immediately he perceived the one to be a priest and it was he who was singing his own *Libera*. The peasant wore a calm and fearless, yet, serious countenance and was engaged in prayer. Simon's devotion to priests would not permit him to remain in doors. He left the house and followed them to the end of their street and then reluctantly retraced his steps, for he dared not venture within sight of the fusillade. Before entering the house he knew from the report of the guns that both the priest and the peasant were in eternity.

Towards the close of the Revolution a new sorrow afflicted Simon in the loss of Father Sorette. This young priest had been his professor of humanities at the College of Rennes during the first year of the Revolution. Owing to a particular interest in his youthful student, Father Sorette had often dined at Simon's home and a mutual endearment made their lives almost inseparable.

When the Revolution accomplished the destruction of the college, Father Sorette retired to the scene of his first clerical labors, a country parish at Le Chatellier, about eighteen miles distant from Rennes. From the beginning he had the affection of his own people, as well as the esteem and veneration of those in the adjoining parishes. During the most tragical days he exercised, with undaunted zeal, the duties of his holy ministry. He escaped during the whole reign

FATHER BRUTÉ'S PEN SKETCH OF A REVOLUTIONARY SCENE
THE TRIAL OF FATHER RAOUL-BODIN AND THE LA GRACIERE SISTERS

of Robespierre and until the death laws were repealed and again replaced by the milder orders of banishment, for the younger clergy, and perpetual imprisonment, for those advanced in years.

The most zealous Jacobins were infuriated at this relaxation of the law and deliberately violated it at every opportunity. Consequently, upon the capture of a priest, if not restrained by a magistrate, they immediately put their victim to death on the spot, rather than to deliver him up to authorities.

The continued crimes of these assassins caused Father Sorette's life to be constantly in danger; nevertheless, he spent himself zealously in the discharge of his duties. One day while returning from a labor of love he was captured by a party of Contre-Chouans in disguise. The good priest surrendered as soon as they fired upon him and bade them lead him into the city. The blood-thirsty mob knew that if this injunction were obeyed their victim would suffer only banishment; thereupon, they acquainted him with their resolve, which was immediate death. Father Sorette entreated them to grant him a few minutes to prepare. He knelt down on the grass and within a few moments his murderers shot him.

Simon also witnessed the trial of Father Francis J. Sacquet, Rector of St. Martin at Rennes. Dignity, self-possession, and mildness were stamped upon this priest's countenance. He answered the questions slowly, briefly, and in a calm, gentle tone. His trial seemed to differ vastly from that of other clergymen and all who were present, both judges and spectators, were greatly impressed by this singular scene. In referring to this trial at a later period many of those in attendance said: "it seemed as if it was our Lord during His passion," and others remarked: "he was like a lamb before so many ravening wolves."

The youth watched the executioner strip and prepare the holy confessor for the scaffold. In cutting his hair and the collar from his shirt the executioner wounded the priest in the neck and the blood was flowing down his breast as he passed along the corridor of the Palace of Justice. The guillotine was only two hundred steps away but the heart of Simon was too tender to behold such horrors and he fled home to relate the tragedy to his mother.

At the Military Tribunal he witnessed but two trials. The first was that of a Brother of the Christian Schools of La Salle. This Mr. Martien was innocently accused and sentenced to death on false evidence that he was implicated in a conspiracy. The second was the trial of two brothers, laymen, who were condemned to death as enemies of the Republic. This scene also touched him deeply as one was a father leaving a wife and children at the mercy of a heartless mob.

One of the most striking revolutionary tragedies that Simon witnessed was the trial of Father Maréchal and the Countesses de Renac. The home of these virtuous ladies was denounced to the authorities as certainly harboring some of the victims. Valeray, an active, villainous agent of the Revolutionary Committee, was appointed to make the search. He had been informed that the concealed priest was Mr. Maréchal, who had been his school-mate and intimate friend. Valeray came with his gang and after spending hours in the search found nothing. Fearing that his cause would be defeated he took the ladies aside and said to them hypocritically: "You see how diligently my men search, it is positive that Mr. Maréchal will be discovered. I want to save him, my dear school-mate, but the only chance is for you to tell me the place where he is concealed that I may keep my men away from that particular spot." One of the ladies deceived by his wily entreaties pointed out to him the place of concealment. As soon as this was done Valeray called to his men to come and pull down the boards that concealed their victim. Upon perceiving Father Maréchal he addressed him sarcastically and ordered the priest and the countesses to follow him to the tribunal.

No sooner had the news of their arrest been received, than Simon made his way to the court and took his place very near to the victims. The priest, as usual, was interrogated first. Then the ladies were called upon to answer in their turn. The whole matter was carried on in a hurried manner and the sentence of death passed upon all three. One of the ladies fainted when she heard the word, *death*, and lay senseless upon the floor. The three victims were hurried from the tribunal to the guillotine. Father Maréchal had to suffer death last. The one who fainted at the tribunal, again fainted on the scaffold and was guillotined in that condition.[4]

The horrid days of delirium ran their agonizing course, waned, and disappeared. The rationalists' cause was foiled, religion was not extirpated, and heaven preserved the work of Christ's mission for souls. Among those spared for greater accomplishments was the youthful Breton, Simon Bruté de Rémur. He survived, pure and untainted, the wretchedness of those years; however, we cannot question the fact that they stamped an impression upon the youthful genius and influenced his life's career. From his intense application to study, obedience to a prudent mother, and a continual association with concealed clergymen, he possessed a store of wisdom beyond his years. Young as he was, he experienced how sad and desolate life can be; nevertheless, he tells us that this desolation seemed to bind his heart more strongly to the cause of Faith. The sentence of death that he heard pronounced frequently, when attending the trials of numerous victims, caused the word, *Eternity*, to dwell with him as a life companion, and he ever cherished the remembrance of the holy martyrs of that period, keeping always before him their noble example of heroism and fidelity to God.[5]

[4] J. R. Bayley, *op. cit.*, pp. 93–158; *The Catholic World*, XVII (1873), pp. 711–17.

[5] M. Meline,—E. McSweeny, *The Story of the Mountain*, I, p. 356; Ave Maria, XXVI (1927), p. 404. Notre Dame, Indiana.

CHAPTER III

ACADEMIC YEARS
1796–1810

The storm of violent persecution gradually abated; the nation then slowly assumed a more normal complexion and, accordingly, Simon Bruté entered upon a career better suited to his tastes and intellectual habits. He had acquired, in early years, habits of study, of close, patient, mental application which, fortunately, the Revolution had failed to disturb. In the public schools and the College of Rennes he had been distinguished, although modesty prevented his ever speaking in his own praise. He was versed in the most cultural passages of the French writers and of the Latin poets. He had read the Greek classics to great advantage and with pleasure. Nevertheless, his education had been seriously interrupted since 1793; and, owing to the wretchedness of the country, it was utterly impossible for Simon to decide definitely upon his future career. At one time he contemplated entering the French Polytechnic School in preparation for which he devoted two years to an extensive course in mathematical science. After more thoughtful study he became convinced that his vocation must be guided by the sole desire of obeying the Divine Will and of rendering commendable service to mankind. In view of this he looked forward to the study of medicine. If he had any inclination at the time to enter the ecclesiastical state, the conditions of France rendered such aspirations hopeless. Having decided as to his future career, he made no delay in entering upon a timely preparation.

On February 10, 1796, Simon began the study of medicine under Doctor Duval, an eminent surgeon in the city of Rennes. Here for three years he applied himself diligently, acquiring knowledge through practical experience, study, and informal instruction. His fondness for the profession, his talent and industry, gave indications of eminent success. Yet if success was to be realized in an appreciable measure Simon must enter a Medical College. This would necessitate his leaving Rennes and a virtuous mother who had daily guarded him from his infancy. Madame Bruté was resigned to this course of events and hastened to prepare the necessaries for his departure. As she bade her son adieu she placed in his hands a pamphlet written in her own hand, containing lengthy and prudent counsels by which he should govern his life.

Simon's mother was a woman of ability and thoroughness, discharging her duties always in an efficient manner. She availed herself of every opportunity to foster a like character in her children. In her educational methods she stressed the complete development, or the physical, intellectual, and moral training of man. Simon was admonished to pursue but few courses upon his arrival at the Medical College, however to master those few thoroughly. His mother maintained that many courses could not be followed satisfactorily at one time and that such procedure engendered confusion. Practical counsel concerning the proper care of health was her next advice to Simon. She requested him to accept a few invitations, especially in the beginning, and to spend a reasonable amount of time in amusements. However, he was warned to avoid theatres. Following this he was reminded never on any ocasion to neglect God; moreover, to permit nothing to disturb his soul, but to keep it always in great tranquility; to do his best each day, never worry about the coming day, and above all to choose a good director. She credited him with a knowledge of his religion, bade him to keep and preserve it, also to read good books, such as the scriptures and the works of St. Francis de Sales. Simon was admonished to do all for God, whether it be study, prayer, or amusement. She closed with the words: "Be your own master. Write to me weekly. Practice charity. Reflect upon all you have to do."[1] After the

[1] Original in the Canon Bruté de Rémur Collection. Rennes, France.

perusal of those admonitions one would scarcely attempt to question Simon's repeated statement: "I owe everything to my mother."

In 1799 at the age of twenty years, Simon entered the Medical School at Paris where he pursued courses conducted by the first masters of the age, such as Pinel, Esquirol, Fourcroy, and Bichat. Many of these distinguished professors were avowed infidels and tried to instill their false principles into the minds of students. The boldest atheism and materialism were studiously professed and it was assumed as an established truth that death is annihilation. They taught that man, like the beast of the field, has no God and no accountability; therefore, he should entertain neither hope nor fear of any life beyond the grave. This insidious propaganda succeeded in a measure, and thus Simon was surrounded not only by infidel professors but also by libertine fellow-students. However, he was daily mindful of the admonitions addressed to him by his mother. He openly practised his religion and organized a group of Breton students to oppose the false teaching to which they were obliged to listen. This group selected such subjects for their theses as enabled them to sponsor and defend their belief in Christianity. At this time Napoleon, First Consul, was laboring to restore Catholicism as the only means of reorganizing society in the sundered nation. When he heard of the expedients pursued by the students, he commanded those professors to confine their lectures to medicine alone and not to make religion the subject of their fallacious reasonings.

Simon found the study of medicine attractive and fascinating. He became deeply absorbed in his chosen field; still he did not permit it to produce a narrowing effect upon his other studies. On the contrary, the science of medicine stimulated and gave his additional studies a definite aim. He excelled in mathematics, drawing, philosophy, and derived much pleasure from a course pursued in music. Thus he was living in the midst of the world, in immediate contact with eleven hundred other medical students, as well as numerous students pursuing other professional courses, qualifying himself for a secular profession, and encompassed by more than the ordinary dangers of youth. There was everything to seduce him to abandon God and to neglect his soul. Within the school itself there was the ardent and vigorous pursuit of science with hundreds of competitors contending for the prize. Beyond the school he was confronted with the dissipation of one of the most effeminate cities in the world. In addition to this there was also the frantic excitement caused by the numerous victories of Napoleon which almost maddened the youthful minds of France. Although surrounded by the spirit of alluring vice and profligacy, Simon retained his innocence and neither became entangled in the meshes of infidel sophistry nor was he lured from the profession and practice of his faith. His life corresponded to the advice of his mother: "Be your own master."

Despite Simon's dauntless character that neither flattery nor persuasion could influence, he had hosts of staunch friends both among fellow-students and professors. Various incidents occurred that illustrate his fidelity to his colleagues and on every occasion his actions portrayed an earnest, fearless character. We have a proof of this in the case of a fellow-student, named Collins, who fell under suspicion by the Imperial Government and was arrested, tried, and cast into prison. This young physician had been called to attend a conspirator, injured in the explosion of the *Infernal Machine,* on December 24, 1800. The purpose of this conspiracy, which ended in failure, was the assassination of Bonaparte. As Collins was a Breton, naturally Simon Bruté de Rémur was very active in his behalf. The faculty likewise encouraged the medical students in their attempt to have Collins freed, for every one at the school considered him a victim of a secret of honor and medical duty. On April 16, 1801, Collins was acquitted of any implication in the plot, but he was condemned to another three months imprisonment and a fine of three hundred francs for having failed to make an immediate declaration to the police. At the expiration of this term he received a new sentence of another six months. Simon visited him several times during his imprisonment at Ste. Pelagie. On January 28, 1802, Collins was dismissed from Ste. Pelagie with an order to go to Nantes, and from thence to be exiled to the Ile de France. Simon Bruté went security for him. The Prefect at Nantes, as a personal favor to Bruté, making an excuse of the English blockade, permitted Collins to remain there. He was still in that city when his thoughtful friend in the Seminary of St. Sulpice made another unsuccessful attempt to petition the Emperor in Collins' favor.

Xavier Bichat, the famous physician and one of Simon's professors, died at the home of Madame Dessant at four o'clock on the morning of July 21, 1801. Simon related that this wretched woman used every means to prevent Dr. Bichat from seeing a priest. However, his former confessor, Abbé Pinlibert, succeeded in reaching his bedside on the night before his death and administered absolution *in extremis*. Simon wrote a favorable account of Dr. Bichat and solicited prayer for his soul.

In the course of the following year Simon lost his aged aunt, his mother's sister, who resided at Paris. She had been a Sister of Charity for forty-four years. He was called to her bedside early on the morning of September 4, 1802, and she expired within a few moments after his arrival. Her nephews, Lisineau, Mazois, Simon Bruté de Rémur, and his friend Parrier attended the obsequies at St. Roch's Church, and accompanied the remains to the cemetery of Montmartre.[2]

A written examination, open to all candidates for the prize, was conducted at the Medical College during the four days of September 27 to 30, 1802. Doctors Sabbatier, Lassus, Deyeux, Leclerc, and Boyer were the examiners. The result of this first test showed that of the 1100 students in attendance there were only 120 competent to enter the con-

[2] J. R. Bayley, *Memoirs of the Rt. Rev. S. W. G. Bruté de Rémur*, pp. 183–212.

test. Simon was among the chosen number. He was summoned to appear for an oral examination conducted by Doctors Desgenettes, Petit, and Randal, on October 14, 1802. Evidently, he passed it successfully for he was again summoned to a continuation of the examination conducted by Doctors Pinel, Richard, and Sabbatier, on October 24, 1802. Two days later, on October 26, 1802, Simon Bruté de Rémur was unanimously accorded the first prize, known as the Corvisart Prize,[3] by the impartial decision of his professors. They proudly congratulated and encouraged their distinguished pupil, and his friends predicted a brilliant and successful career in the profession which he had chosen. Simon immediately sent the prize to Dr. Duval, at Rennes, in recognition of the kindness of his first teacher and master in the profession. That the young physician lawfully rejoiced in his own success, we learn from a line in his journal where he relates having dined with his friends, Buisson, Tizeau, Maisoneuve, Frain, Parrier, and Villeneuve.

Six days later, he was on his way back to Rennes, where he was cordially welcomed by his mother and friends. The three years of separation had been painful to the maternal heart of Madame Bruté, but she rejoiced now at the hope that her son would soon finish at the Medical College and be established in his profession near her. This, however, was not the intention of the young physician, but he preferred to be silent for the present. After a sojourn of two months he returned to Paris, on December 29, 1802, to complete the academic year.

When Simon Bruté entered the Medical School at Paris in 1799, he chose for his director the virtuous priest, M. Bourdier-Delpuits, who had belonged to the Society of Jesus before the suppression. Simon also became a member of the confraternity established by this priest, who accomplished untold good by preserving numbers of young men from the evil principles of the day. M. Julien Duplessis,

[3] Abbé C. Bruté de Rémur, *Vie de Monseigneur Bruté de Rémur*, p. 81.

another youth from Rennes, and student at the Polytechnic
School in Paris, also belonged to the confraternity. Duplessis was seized with a fever about two and one-half weeks
before Easter in 1803. M. Teysseyre, a friend of both Bretons, wrote the following to his mother, concerning the last
illness of Duplessis:

> We watched alternately at his bedside. Early in his illness we
> called Father Delpuits, who administered to him all the consolations
> of our holy religion. M. Bruté de Rémur, who obtained the first
> prize at the Medical College, an angelic young man, watched at the
> bedside of the dying youth on Easter night. At one-thirty o'clock
> he called us to witness the last moments of our good Duplessis.[4]

Relative to this event Simon recorded the following:

> *On Easter night 1803*, Julien Duplessis of Rennes, died in my arms
> at midnight, after 17 days' illness—19 years of age. Student in the
> Polytechnic School; studious, intelligent, amiable, loved by his
> fellow-students, a pious and faithful child of M. Delpuits.[5]

According to Teysseyre's letter, M. Bruté de Rémur had
received the Corvisart Prize before the death of M. Duplessis. Simon stated that this young man died on Easter night
1803. Hence it is an established fact that Simon Bruté de
Rémur received the prize in 1802 and not at the time of
graduation, as some maintain. From the date of his appointment to the First Dispensary it is evident that he received his doctorate early in 1803.

This signal triumph in a class of eleven hundred students
brought Dr. Bruté prominently before the public and made
Napoleon eager to obtain his service. Therefore, he was
officially appointed Physician to the First Dispensary in
Paris, on Saturday, April 21, 1803. Simultaneous with his
appointment was that of his intimate friend, Dr. Parrier,
who was named Surgeon to the *Maison de Force*. Two days

[4] *Ibid.*, p. 77.
[5] J. R. Bayley, *op. cit.*, p. 213.

previously Simon had met his bishop, Jean Baptiste-Marie de Maillé, at Passy. In the course of the interview Simon made his intentions known to His Lordship, who not only approved of them, but encouraged their fulfillment. Therefore, Doctor Bruté did not accept the honor tendered him by the Imperial Government. In the fruition of his youthful triumph his thoughts were turned from the cure of the human body to the cure of the immortal soul, to a vocation which was more worthy of his endowments than medicine. Many years later in a note to Mother Seton, relative to this event, he said: "After I had studied pretty far (some especially), all the human sciences, and perceived enough of their bearing, I—Oh, perpetual thanks!—surrendered my whole soul to the invisible and eternal things, as says St. Paul" (2 Cor. 4:18).[6]

On July 14, 1803, Doctor Bruté returned to Rennes. It is not to be assumed that he relinquished the profession, to which he had devoted years of laborious study, through any feeling of disgust. On the contrary it was no small sacrifice for him to abandon it. He always honored it as one of the most noble to which talented philanthropists could devote their lives. After he became a priest and even when elevated to the episcopate, he acknowledged his attachment to the medical profession to which he still felt himself strongly linked by honorable study and pleasing associations. The young physician was prompted only by the purest motives when he turned his thoughts to a higher calling. The numerous body of fellow-students, in the Medical College convinced him that physicians for the human body would never be wanting; while physicians for the souls of men would be more difficult to supply, owing to the fact that seminaries and religious houses had been closed for ten years.

Madame Bruté enjoyed the company of her son for four months. During this time her friends, who had rejoiced in his singular success, used every influence to dissuade the

[6] *Bruté—Seton Correspondence*, p. 40. 1886.

young physician from abandoning the profession. If we view it from their standpoint, which, indeed, was a purely human one, such actions were a veritable mystery. His mother's hopes, too, had been frustrated by his unexpected decision; yet she was, above all, a Christian mother and, therefore, did not hesitate to sacrifice the plans she had formed for the future. Relative to his departure from Rennes, on this occasion, he has left us only one line in his Journal: *"Nov. 13, 1803.* Started for Paris, with my brother, Augustine; mother approved of my choice." Doctor Bruté was on his way to the Seminary, an aspirant to the priesthood. Augustine, his brother was entering the Medical College to continue the traditions of honor and of science that his brother had left to the faculty of Paris.[7]

Thus far the life of Doctor Bruté had wielded admirable influence and had proved an inspiration to virtue. He had been an example to youthful students at the College of Rennes. During the Reign of Terror he resembled a Tarsicius and a Tertullian in his courageous assistance to the persecuted and at the Medical School at Paris, by his purity and stainless honor, he played well the parts of both an Aloysius and a Bayard. From the moment he entered the seminary, that quarry whence come those living stones that reenforce the glorious edifice of the Church, Simon became a Bede.[8] He records his first work at the seminary in the following words: *"November 24, 1803.* My first lessons at the seminary under M. Montague, Professor of Moral Theology at the Seminary of St. Sulpice, Rue Notre Dame des Champs, No. 1456."

However, before Simon had entered regularly at the seminary, Madame Bruté grew ill at ease concerning him. Early in August 1804, she wrote to M. James Edward Emery, superior of St. Sulpice, to this effect. She needlessly feared that Simon was becoming too serious and formal; moreover, if he continued at the seminary it would be impossible

---

[7] Abbé C. Bruté de Rémur, *op. cit.,* pp. 82–3.

[8] M. Meline,—E. McSweeney, *The Story of the Mountain,* II, p. 361.

for him to take care of his brother. Permitting maternal solicitude to control her on this occasion, she desired Simon to leave the seminary and follow the medical profession. In a prompt but courteous reply M. Emery assured her that Simon did not lack in gayety, but, on the contrary, he was quite vivacious. While M. Emery agreed with Madame Bruté that Simon would have made an excellent physician, still he maintained that her son would be more serviceable to the Church. Moreover, she was assured of Simon's continued care of Augustine.[9]

Seemingly, this letter did not calm her fears for she continued to question Simon's vocation. To her second letter M. Emery responded: "You have a great son—a true blessing for a mother. His vocation for the priesthood is truly evident, although you are opposed to such a vocation."[10] Apparently, her mind was now at ease for in all future letters to M. Emery she never again questioned her son's choice. She was not really opposed to it at any time but merely wished to be positive that Simon had a true vocation. He was entered regularly into the Seminary of St. Sulpice on October 10, 1804. Shortly after this Simon suffered the loss of Jean Baptiste-Marie de Maillé, his much beloved Bishop of Rennes, who died at Paris on November 25, 1804.[11] Simon was at the bedside of His Lordship, received his last sigh and closed his eyes.

This zealous seminarian had courted honors neither at home nor at the Medical College. Far less did such worthless ambitions disturb him in the seminary where he was leading a life of seclusion and wholly absorbed in laying a worthy foundation for his ecclesiastical career. Apparently, honors seemed to seek him regardless of his age or place of abode. On December 10, 1804, he was appointed to serve daily at Cardinal Fesch's Mass at the Tuileries in the pres-

[9] M. Emery to Madame Bruté, 8–20, 1804. Canon Bruté de Rémur Collection.

[10] M. Emery to Madame Bruté. *Ibid.*

[11] Abbé J. Dauphin, *L'Oeuvre du R. P. Blanchard 1797–1830*, p. 297. Rennes, 1910.

ence of Bonaparte. This was agreeable only because he hoped it would afford him an opportunity which up to that date had seemed impossible. Simon had not forgotten the fate of his fellow-student, Collins. He was convinced of his innocence, and repeatedly, although in vain, had sought to have his sentence revised. As a last effort he prepared a memorial to the Emperor in favor of Collins. This petition was signed by himself and Frain, another fellow-student from Brittany. But as yet he had had no opportunity to present it. He now seized one which he thought was offered him while serving Mass in the Imperial Chapel. As Mass was ended he hastened from the sanctuary with a hope of meeting the Emperor as the latter hurriedly retired by a private passage. Failing in the attempt he threw the memorial before Bonaparte, but owing to the Emperor's rapid gait, he was not noticed. This, however, was fortunate for him because he was in danger of losing his life instantly at the hands of the gendarmes in attendance. Simon's imprudent boldness was censured by his superiors, but his fidelity to his friend was admired by all.

Following this appointment as acolyte came a second privilege which left in the heart of the fervent seminarian a lasting and happy memory. On December 18, 1804, Simon Bruté de Rémur was granted a private audience with the Holy Father, Pius VII, who had come to Paris for the coronation of Bonaparte and was being held captive by this impious Emperor. Simon had been entrusted with commissions to the Holy Father, yet his manner of procedure displays to us the character of his preparation for the priestly career. Kneeling at the feet of this holy pontiff, Simon begged Pius VII to bless him that he might become a good priest. After hearkening to the Holy Father's words of wisdom and consolation, Simon presented to His Holiness copies of M. Champion's books together with a letter in regard to the reestablishment of the Society of Jesus. He related in his Journal that Pius VII raised his eyes and hands to heaven and exclaimed *Faxit Deus* "God has done it." Simon listed that interview among the most precious remembrances in his life.[12]

Doctor Bruté had sought with unremitting toil for secular knowledge when preparing himself for a secular profession, but now with increased ardour, enthusiasm, and self-sacrificing labor did he pursue that knowledge which was necessary in preparation for the ecclesiastical state. In the science of Scholastic Theology he became a gifted scholar. He also searched the works of the Fathers of the Church, the primitive sources of ecclesiastical history, and the acts and canons of Church Councils. The Sacred Scriptures were read daily and ample time was assigned to the study of Hebrew. Incessant application was devoted to the principles of the various sects and his voluminous memoranda testify how carefully he recorded everything that could be utilized to defend or illustrate truth and to expose or confute error. The great defenders and ornaments of religion that appeared in every age were familiar to him. Hence there were few subjects on which he was not able to converse. This, too, was a result of never having belonged to the category of surface scholars. Simon always read with pen in hand and the note-books written during his seminary days illustrate and develop each subject so profoundly that his readers would be more inclined to class him with the faculty than with the student-body. He also began at this time to accumulate precious volumes that formed the nucleus of the large and valuable Bruté library.

To credit Simon Bruté with having devoted all his time to formal study and prayer would be exaggerated and untrue. He was not living an isolated, quiescent life in ethereal heights. On the contrary, he was human and faced the same problems that confront all seminarians. Not unlike legions of others, he, too, enjoyed the company of his own and possessed numerous friends whom he loved sincerely. Among those for whom he preserved a life-long intimacy were the brothers, Jean and Félicité de LaMennais. Simon was

[12] J. R. Bayley, op. cit., p. 214.

acquainted with Félicité for some years only indirectly
through Jean but, on account of his profound attachment to
Jean he developed an equal interest in Félicité.

Jean de LaMennais and Simon Bruté were kindred souls.
They possessed similar admirable qualities of soul and
mind. An affection tender and reciprocal bound them very
closely. Both were natives of Brittany. Their families had
preserved the same traditions of faith and honor. Moreover, both were trained in the same school of virtue and
passed through the same degrees of sorrow. The Reign of
Terror with its sadness and horror made these two youths
mature far beyond their years. Around the home of de
LaMennais lingered the same sweet memories as perfumed
the Bruté de Rémur household for both had given asylum
to persecuted priests. Early in life the two friends had
differed on the matter of vocation. Jean, on the day of his
First Communion, at the age of nine years, decided his future and promised God he would become a priest. Simon,
however, had in view divers vocations, yet always with the
primary intention of serving God. When Jean was pursuing his studies in the seminary, Simon was distinguishing
himself through science in the Medical School and by virtue
in the confraternity of Father Bourdier-Delpuits.

The correspondence between these two souls portrays
the nature of their relations more strikingly than any description would be able to effect. Theirs was an ideal friendship, the union of two hearts by a common affection, two
souls by the same faith and piety, and two minds by similar
aspirations. They were privileged souls from whom God
later demanded the sacrifice of their natural affection for
the purpose of drawing them closer to Himself and spirit-
ualizing their love. Unfortunately only too few of Simon's
letters have been preserved and some of those only in part.
Moreover, the greater number are of a personal nature, and
hence less interesting than they otherwise would be. The
earliest one, of which a mere fragment remains, was written during his seminary career and dated May 24, 1806. To

quote the closing lines will suffice to demonstrate the characteristics of Simon's affection for Jean.

> Adieu dear sir and friend. Never while I live shall I forget the proofs of affection which I received from you here during a sojourn much too brief for the health of us both. Oh! for the love of our dear Lord and His Church take the best care of your health. Please be docile to all that prudent friends ask of you in that regard. Do not hasten to say the *laetatus sum*, but rather in view of the evils which surround us, sincerely accept the prolongation of your exile and make use of the efficacious means. I pray you not to accuse me on this account of not loving you, for it is from the depth of my heart that I have vowed for life the attachment with which I am your devoted servant and friend.[13]

On numerous occasions Jean de LaMennais also acquainted Simon Bruté of his continued affection for him, assured him it is always in Jesus Christ that he loves him. Men of the present day may be inclined to consider such friendships effeminate. Many, too, may fail to comprehend the utility of such effusions of affection, and even pass an unfavorable judgment upon them. However, all prejudice would disappear if they could but fathom the nature of the love that united the hearts of these two friends. The following letter beautifully illustrates this bond of union.

> Saint Malo, February 2, 1808.
> I can scarcely express to you, my dear friend, my gratitude for your kind remembrance and for all the agreeable things you have written to me; I repeat, I am deeply grateful and assure you it has been a long time since I have felt such an intense joy! Ah! as a favor I ask of you, my dear Bruté, to strengthen the bonds which unite us. I desire absolutely to place my soul within yours, for I know that yours is already entirely in that of Jesus Christ. I desire more and more that we love one another with His own love, that we help one another to serve Him well, that His divine Spirit take possession of us, and that our hearts be filled with His ardent charity.

[13] Abbé C. Bruté de Rémur, *op. cit.*, pp. 109–110.

And at what moment were it more necessary, my dear friend, in which we should be more firmly united, in which we should stand closer together as it were than at this time? Is not our Holy Mother Church attacked from all sides? And if Her enemies have combined their talents, their means, their hatred, their audacity, why should we not combine our efforts to oppose theirs and encourage one another to fight and win. Yes, in spite of the distance which separates us, we can edify one another, encourage one another, help one another; and since our prayers are our best arms, let us unite and united ask our Lord to send France a true apostle, who shall renew the face of the earth....

Farewell, my dear Bruté; do not fail to write me, and especially to inform me of the time of your ordination. I pray you to give me a place in your *memento*, and to place on your paten the best of your friends. Farewell, once more, let us live, I repeat, let us live in the bowels of divine charity. We must have great courage to serve God as nobly and as valiantly as possible, for why should we think that He would have wished to make a single heart of two, unless this heart were extraordinarily strong, brave, courageous, constant, and loving in its Creator and Saviour, by Whom and to Whom I am,

Always yours,

J. M. de LaMennais, Curé, St. Malo.[14]

In the meantime Madame Bruté continued her correspondence with Saint Sulpice. On every occasion M. Emery in his reply compliments the virtue of Simon. He also lauded his talent affirming that the young seminarian, owing to his extraordinary gifts, would be capable of pursuing higher studies.[15] At every opportunity the superior of St. Sulpice congratulated the mother for having such a wonderful son. In 1807 M. Emery informed Madame Bruté that he had counselled Simon to defer his ordination to the priesthood because it was the opinion of St. Sulpice that he could

---

[14] *Lettres Inédites de J. M. & F. de LaMennais*, pp. 17–21. Nantes, 1862.

[15] M. Emery to Madame Bruté, 10–7, 1805. Canon Bruté de Rémur Collection.

serve the Church better elsewhere than in Rennes. His second reason for such advice was that they desired to detain Simon longer at St. Sulpice because of his piety and the great edification which he gave the seminarists and the faculty.[16] Although Simon was pursuing his studies under the Sulpicians, yet, during his seminary days he was not a member of their Society. M. Emery's action was satisfactory to Madame Bruté for she, too, entertained the same opinion that her son would aid the Church more profitably elsewhere than in his native city. While the superior of St. Sulpice commended the piety of the young seminarian, he was no less aware of his charity and compassion especially for his poor fellow-students. On one occasion Simon made a collection to assist a certain Mr. J—to continue his studies. The result of his efforts were gratifying and Simon happily recorded in his Journal for 1807:

> M. Pied de Nogent gave me 100 francs. Lord Shaftsbury, who was at that time at Paris with the Duchess of Devonshire, sent me 240 francs, through his friend, Mr. Nicholas McCarthy, to assist this poor seminarist. He had seen the seminarians at St. Sulpice, in the parish Church, and in giving this money to Mr. McCarthy he said that he wished those angels to pray for him. He has an excellent heart said Mr. McCarthy to me, very near the true Faith.[17]

From the time that Doctor Bruté entered the seminary, M. Emery prophesied that great deeds would be wrought by him. On several occasions he told the young aspirant there was a sufficient number of preachers but few who were capable of pursuing higher studies. Regardless of this advice, it is evident from the notes recorded during Simon's early retreats that he felt an inward call to become a foreign missionary. He had already arrived at a great spirit of detachment from home and family, and prepared himself to make every necessary sacrifice the moment he felt it to be

---

[16] M. Emery to Madame Bruté, 8–26, 1807. *Ibid.*

[17] J. R. Bayley, *op. cit.*, p. 215.

the Will of God that he should leave France. In September 1806, he made a retreat at the *Carmes*—formerly the church of a Carmelite Monastery—to decide his special vocation in God's ministry. His mind was permanently engaged with the question as is verified by the fact that his papers contained numerous statements regarding different foreign missions and even the mode of travel best suited to reach them. In 1807 his attention was turned towards India and he resolved to go thither, in so far as it depended upon himself to decide the future. The thought that his medical knowledge would serve him to good advantage on the Eastern Missions afforded him no small degree of pleasure. Recalling his fondness for books and study, one is not surprised to find in his "list of sacrifices to be made, if called to the foreign missions," that of not being able to take his library with him.

As time advanced Simon Bruté passed through the intermediate stages preparatory to the priesthood. On December 22, 1804, he received tonsure from Right Reverend de Belmont, Bishop of St. Flour, who was delegated to act for Cardinal Jean Baptiste du Bellay, the Archbishop of Paris. Minor Orders were conferred on him a year later, December 21, 1805, by Right Reverend de la Roche, Bishop of Versailles. Five months later, Bishop du Voisin, Bishop of Nantes, ordained him sub-deacon, May 31, 1806. The Right Reverend Etienne Celestin Enoch, Bishop of Rennes, was the officiating prelate when Simon Bruté was ordained deacon. At this date M. Emery still served in the capacity of superior of St. Sulpice. Fathers Boyer, Duclaux, Garnier, and Frayssinous were Simon's professors. Father Duclaux, of whom he often spoke with the greatest veneration *mon saint et tout bon père*, was his spiritual director. The learned deacon was ordained priest on Saturday preceding Trinity Sunday, June 10, 1808. The solemn ceremony took place in the parish church of St. Sulpice and was performed by the Right Reverend André, the retired Bishop of Quimper. The newly ordained priest read his first Mass at

ALTAR OF THE BLESSED VIRGIN, ST. SULPICE, WHERE FATHER BRUTÉ
CELEBRATED HIS FIRST HOLY MASS

the altar of the Blessed Virgin in the Seminary of St. Sulpice on Trinity Sunday, June 11, 1808.[18]   Immediately after these sacred events Father Simon Bruté joined the Society of St. Sulpice.

When Simon Bruté abandoned worldly pursuits and entered the seminary, his name did not pass into oblivion in the world around him. Those who appreciated the worth of his noble character followed his progress with interest, and more than one bishop awaited the day of his ordination to the priesthood. He was held in such esteem that immediately after ordination Napoleon again sought to confer honors upon him and accordingly appointed him with M. Feuteur to the Imperial Chapel.[19] He declined this distinction because his humility did not seek honors. The Bishop of Nantes eagerly sought to obtain the services of Father Bruté for his diocese, but his request was refused. The Bishop of Rennes recognized the worth of this young priest and wished to utilize his talents within his native city. Therefore, in obedience to his bishop, he repaired to Rennes to enter upon the charge assigned him as professor of theology in the diocesan seminary. At the same time the bishop offered him a canonry in his Cathedral, but he did not accept this dignity.

The professorship of Father Bruté at the seminary was characterized by the same traits that had marked his student-career. During the two years of invaluable services in this institution he was a worthy model for imitation, especially in fidelity to duty, spiritual exercises, and recollection. The students confided to his charge loved and respected their eminent master and his teaching. Even the less devout seminarians were impelled to laud his virtue and to reveal his austerities which at times were perceived despite the precaution he took to keep such practices concealed. They related of him that he frequently took the dis-

[18] R. Seton, *Memoirs, Letters and Journal of Elizabeth Seton*, II, p. 216. New York, 1870.
[19] Bruté Journal, Georgetown UA, Fol. 92, 6. Washington, D. C.

cipline when he thought every one in the house to be asleep. Likewise, he was often found late at night prostrate before the Blessed Sacrament engaged in fervent prayer.[20]

It was during his sojourn at the Seminary of Rennes that an intimate friendship was formed with M. Rene-Jean Sebastian Breteau de la Guéretterie. This priest, descended from a family in Maine, was born at Vitré, educated at the Seminary of Angers, and ordained in 1782. Repairing immediately to St. Germain at Rennes, where he had been appointed curate he became distinguished for his zeal and firmness. During the Revolution he continued to minister to the faithful in Rennes and in the surrounding country. In 1798 he was assigned to the pastorate of St. Martin at Vitré, and in 1807 he was named Director of the *Grand Seminaire de Rennes*. A year later Father Bruté was made professor in the same institution. Father de la Guéretterie was in very delicate health, suffering from a tumor in his side for which all remedies proved useless. The newly appointed professor possessing a thorough knowledge of medical science recommended the application of various ointments and the use of different drugs, but all was in vain. The afflicted priest suffered excruciatingly. One morning as Father Bruté was repairing to the sacristy to vest for Mass he met Father de la Guéretterie who was in great agony from pain. He knew the sufferer was beyond human aid, and sympathetically whispered to him, "I am going to pray to God for you." The Holy Sacrifice was scarcely ended when Father de la Guéretterie found himself relieved of all pain. He removed the bandages and to his utter surprise found that the tumor with all its evil effects had disappeared. The entire institution was amazed at the sudden cure and called Father Bruté who also shared in the general astonishment. "When human aid is exhausted," said he, "shall we not have recourse to Divine Providence?" From that day the two friends became more intimate and often united in their prayers and good works.[21]

[20] Abbé C. Bruté de Rémur, *op. cit.*, pp. 97–106.
[21] *Ibid.*, pp. 104–106.

Regardless of the numerous tasks that encroached upon the limited time of Father Bruté, his relations with the de LaMennais brothers daily became more intimate. According to their correspondence he continued to aid them in all their difficulties regarding research, seminary affairs, reading of manuscripts, and giving advice on their published material. He was also called upon to arrange with the Superiors for a retreat that the de LaMennais brothers wished to make at the Seminary of Rennes. Prior to this he had never met Féli, although they corresponded from time to time, and from the following letter, we learn how anxiously the poor, unhappy Féli longed to meet his generous friend.

February 17, 1809.

My excellent friend, with what impatience do I await that moment when I shall be able to express verbally my deepest gratitude for that friendship so good, so sweet, so amiable that you deign to show me, who have merited it so little. You resemble our Good Master Who went about seeking out the poor and the sinners to encourage them, to raise them up, to console them. And who ever had more need than I of those helps and consolations? It is a great consolation for my heart to hold even a little place in yours. Keep it for me, I beg of you, all unworthy as I am, and particularly, dear friend, pray for me, ask our Lord for the graces I need so much; ask Him to deign to cure my weakness, my coldness, my dryness, my languor in His service. Alas! dear Bruté, your poor friend is nothing but pure misery. When I reflect on my past life, on that life of sin, that all the most rigorous austerities, the most severe penance and the longest, will not be sufficient to expiate, and after that, when I consider my present state, this tepidity, this indolence, this weight of judgment which tires me and bears me down, this self-love which only half sacrifices itself and which springs up again even under the knife, I enter into frightful misgivings which have only too real a foundation, and I ask myself if it is possible that such an unfortunate should penetrate within the sanctuary, and if rather I ought not to prostrate myself at the foot of the altar as that sinner of the Old Testament, less of a sinner than myself? However, one thing re-assures me a little. I am obeying counsels which I must respect, and that is my one reason to hope from the mercy of God the help that is necessary, and on which I shall count the more if you will deign to ask it from God for me. My brother and Father Hay are also writing to you today; you know how much they love you, that is to say you know how well they know you. May the Lord, my friend, unite us forever in His holy love and in that of his Holy Mother,

All yours in Christ,

Féli de LaMennais.[22]

Intimate relations through frequent correspondence was preserved between the superior of St. Sulpice and the young professor at Rennes. From a letter written by Father Emery we learn that the absence of Father Bruté from St. Sulpice was a great loss to his superior. Nevertheless, the latter continued to depend upon him for important research and consulted him on many questions concerning ecclesiastical history. In turn the learned professor acquainted his superior at Paris with all plans and progress of his work at Rennes. The experienced Father Emery failed not to give prudent counsel in reply. While his letters were always courteous and affectionate,[23] yet on many occasions he warned the young priest against acquiring an unquiet and restless spirit; exhorted him not to become over zealous, for such a spirit would prevent the good that he otherwise would be capable of effecting. Moreover, he should not write too frequently to his bishop for it would make him appear too solicitous. If we may infer from two letters written in October 1809 and still extant, this latter advice seems to have been a timely counsel. At this date the French government was again curtailing the rights of clergymen by forbidding missions. Father Bruté wrote in haste to his bishop, stating that seculars had ruined education; that parishes were on a continual decline and that the

[22] *Lettres Inédites de J. M. & F. de LaMennais*, pp. 28–29.
[23] Cf. 21 Letters of M. Emery to M. Bruté, 1808–1810. Originals in Canon Bruté de Rémur Collection.

bishop should be cognizant of this state of affairs. Gleaning from the contents of this letter we discover that he and his colleagues at the seminary accused the bishop of lacking in zeal. The bishop, however, was aware of prevailing conditions and responded thus: "I have done all within my power to protect the Church and to resist the unreasonable demands of the government. Why should they at the seminary find fault with their Bishop?"[24]

The maternal solicitude of Madame Bruté never waned and, consequently, she kept a continual correspondence with the superior of Saint Sulpice. At one time she feared her son was not appreciated by his superiors. Again she regretted the fact that he had not been retained in Paris. Father Emery frankly contradicted the first statement. As to the latter he agreed with her, but answered that even though he was superior of the Society he had no power to resist the wishes of Bishop Enoch who wished to keep her son at Rennes.[25]

Father Bruté was ordained almost a year before he had any opportunity for parochial work. His first experience was ministering to the Catholics of Brütz whither he was sent during the Easter vacation of 1809. He spent three weeks there assisting the pastor, Father Massiot. From the correspondence of de LaMennais, we learn that the young curate preached during Holy Week. In his sermons he dwelt especially on divine love and happily found his audience responsive to his zealous counsels.

During this same year Félicité de LaMennais began his studies for the priesthood and was permitted to receive tonsure. His brother wrote to their friend at the seminary to arrange with the bishop concerning this event. As usual Father Bruté attended to the matter immediately and responded:

[24] S. Bruté to Etienne Celestin Enoch, 10–15, 1809. Etienne Celestin Enoch to S. Brute. Originals in Canon Bruté de Rémur Collection.
[25] M. Emery to Madame Bruté de Rémur, 8–28, 1809. *Ibid.*

I received your letter at ten o'clock. At eleven o'clock I called at the Bishop's House, and now at noon time I respond to you from the home of my mother where I have repaired to take my dinner. The bishop bids me to express to you his delight at this good news and assures you that it is with great satisfaction that he will come to the seminary, in our little Bethlehem, to give the tonsure to your excellent brother. I unite myself with you in advance for this day and bid you both to have pity on me before the Lord.[26]

Visits of these two clergymen were alternated frequently and Father Jean de LaMennais passed a portion of the vacation of 1809 at St. Sulpice with Father Bruté, who had arranged the trip. There he made precious acquaintances, among whom were M. Emery, superior, and M. Duclaux, one of the directors of the seminary. It was on the return from this trip that he wrote to Father Bruté:

My friend, my tender friend, I can never repay you for all the kindness and attention which you showed me during this visit. We love each other too dearly to be permitted to write one line or say one word that savors of complimentary. In my position with regard to you, I must lock all in my heart and taste in secret, how sweet it is to have a friend like you.[27]

Evidently, it was well for Father Jean de LaMennais that he knew not the secrets of the near future when he penned the foregoing lines.

[26] Abbé C. Bruté de Rémur, *op. cit.*, p. 124.
[27] *Ibid.*, pp. 118–119.

CHAPTER IV

DEPARTURE FOR THE MISSIONS

Augustine Bruté de Rémur, who entered the Medical School at Paris, in 1803, completed his studies, passed successful examinations, and was graduated as a Doctor of Medicine in 1809. He returned to Rennes during the same year and established himself in the profession. The venerable mother rejoiced at the thought of having her two sons settled in their respective vocations. Additional consolation came to her in the announcement of Augustine's approaching nuptials. The news of this event was welcomed by the family, chiefly because of the rare gifts both natural and spiritual that adorned the young physician's chosen fiancé, Mademoiselle Camille Bourgeois. On the eve of their nuptial day Father Bruté addressed a note to his mother asking her to remind Augustine and Camille that a portion of the banquet should be given to the poor. It was with the greatest cheerfulness that the devoted servant of God officiated on this occasion, blessed the marriage, and interrupted his occupations to spend these festal days in the midst of the family. However, he was forced to shorten his days at the festivity because duty awaited him with other problems.

While he discharged the obligations incumbent upon him in the diocese of Rennes, he never abandoned the resolution to follow his special call to the foreign missions. Thus far the time for him to enter upon this work had not arrived. The care of his aged mother had been a hindrance to following this call earlier. Now that Augustine was in a position to supply all her needs, the young priest resolved to decide immediately upon his future career. Accordingly, he betook himself to the Seminary of St. Sulpice where he spent several weeks.

During his sojourn at Paris he happily met another member of the Society, a colleague that he had always loved and esteemed highly, and one who had already spent a number of years on the American missions. It was at this time that Father B. J. Flaget was appointed first bishop to the newly created see of Bardstown in Kentucky. He refused the office and returned to Saint Sulpice to beg his superior, Father Emery, to assist him in being released from such a weighty responsibility. Although he failed in the primary purpose of his voyage, great good accrued from his journey.

Thus far Father Bruté had been aided by no other guidance than his own mind; therefore, he entertained views of only an Eastern field of labor. But this was not the design of Providence in his regard. After several interviews with Father Flaget, a supernatural light manifested to the young priest that his field of missionary labor lay not in the East but in the West. Upon his return to Rennes he made known his decision which surprised but few. He had resolved to depart with Father Flaget for the American missions. Conformable as was his will to the divine call he had other obstacles to encounter. Bishop Enoch of Rennes, who held him in singular esteem, loathed to part from him, but God disposed the good bishop's heart favorably and he granted the young missionary leave to go. Madame Bruté could not be reconciled to such a blow, and to preclude the family ties from being severed forever she appealed to the Superior of St. Sulpice in a very pathetic letter. Father Emery who held her undivided confidence responded thus:

I can well conceive how painful to you must be the part which your son has chosen. It is indeed a separation from a dear son who merits to be loved. Moreover, it is a long separation, although he has every reason to assure you that he can return. Imagine that he is going on a long voyage, and that he will return with increased piety, well moulded, and with enriched knowledge that will render him more useful to the Church in France and in America. You know how much I love and esteem him. I shall not cease to watch over him and I shall avail myself of all opportunities to receive news concerning him and to impart this information to you. It will be possible to hear from him every month, especially if peace, which cannot be long delayed, be concluded. If he had gone to the Oriental Missions you would have no longer any hopes of seeing him again. Be assured, Madame, you shall participate in all his good works, and by the consent you have no doubt given to his departure, you will partake in a great measure of the merits of his mission. Believe me that through this your own predestination will be better assured.[1]

Upon reading Father Emery's timely advice, Madame Bruté realized how appalling it would be to resist the designs of God in a soul and her sacrifice was consummated. Father Bruté, relieved by the change in his mother's attitude, hastened at once to prepare for his departure. To acquaint Father Jean and Félicité de LaMennais with his immediate intentions he sent them the following note:

Read low and alone.—It is at this moment that I have need of my friends before the Lord. I confide to you and to Féli my designs under secrecy. I depart for the American Missions. My spiritual directors have been unanimous in their opinion. The bishop consented with a readiness that confirmed me in the hope that it is a call from Providence. Mother did not resist. Her sacrifice is complete. I have my exeat. I shall sail from Bordeaux with two new bishops. I hope to leave Rennes next Friday.[2]

To this information Félicité responded with a letter deeply spiritual, dated May 25, 1810, and addressed to Bordeaux, the port whence the missionaries were to take passage. In the course of his letter he drew Father Bruté's attention to the increase of atheism in Europe, and to the fact that from this very period of darkness comes forth apostles of love who go to establish the Faith in other parts of the world. He assures their friend of their companionship with him, in spirit, on the sea and of their constant union with

[1] Abbé C. Bruté de Rémur, *Vie de Monseigneur Bruté de Rémur*, pp. 138–142.

[2] *Ibid.*, pp. 142–3.

him in the incomparable loving Heart of the Divine Master. Félicité closed with a pledge of sincere loyalty to their friend, when he said:

> Can you doubt it, dear friend? Your mother is also our mother, and we regard it as one of our duties to sweeten the cruel pain which your departure has given her heart. Not that we rely on the efficacy of our words; but when God wants to relieve a soul suffering for Him, He sometimes allows His consolation to flow through the most obscure channels.[3]

The assurance of his two friends' affection for his mother was a great consolation for the heart of the departing missionary, albeit he knew she would never want for anything as long as the Lord spared his brother, Augustine. This was the first request to his brother after he obtained the bishop's permission to leave France. Again, while on his farewell visit to his sister, Madame Mazois, he wrote to Augustine charging him to care for their good mother.[4]

While Father Bruté longed for the day of departure for the foreign missions, this desire was not a sublimated disgust for his own native country. On the contrary, he always remained deeply attached to his dear France. Even his last letter from Bordeaux written June 9, 1810, eve of his embarkation for America, shows no abatement of interest in his fatherland. These lines addressed to the de LaMennais brothers bespeak the same enthusiasm, the same desire for the progress of the persecuted Church, as well as the advancement of his two friends in ecclesiastical knowledge. The greater part of this letter is an overflow of such interest.

Bordeaux, June 9, 1810.

My dear friends,

> I impart to you with intense joy a very happy discovery that I have made here and of which I now regret not to be able to profit. I desire earnestly to place you in a position to draw more ad-

---

[3] *Lettres Inédites de J. M. & F. de LaMennais*, p. 75.

[4] S. Bruté to A Bruté, 5-9, 1810. Canon Bruté de Rémur Collection. Rennes, France.

vantageously from it than myself. I have found a young priest as
professor of theology in the Seminary. He is very young, nevertheless, he has enjoyed a distinguished reputation for some time.
If you could meet him only a few times as I have had the consolation to do you would readily agree that he merits this reputation.
He is well versed in good literature and in the sciences. He devotes
himself with zeal and an excellent spirit to ecclesiastical studies,
principally to those of ecclesiastical history and of disicpline,
embraced under the same point of view as that of yours; that is
to say, with an intense desire to search to the origin of sources, to
disentangle badly presented questions, to establish correct
boundaries; in a word, he will be your colleague. I behold in him
sympathetic sentiments and others as well, that I wish through this
letter to send him, with all other means that my feeble part would
play in it, to St. Malo, to you, to become associated with your
prudent plan of studies. He lacks books only, but the seminary
has an adequate library, profane as well as religious. Commence
a correspondence relative to study and impart the consoling news to
me. His ardor still flourishes in his present position through the
honor he has just received in being appointed professor of ecclesiastical history in the faculty of Bordeaux. I do not cease to hope
that you will also be appointed, willing or unwilling, to that of
Rennes. It is to you that these chairs extend invitations, and
how much good is to be done there! I bid him to open the
correspondence with you and to propose his first views of his course
and the manner of procedure. I leave to him blank paper for
this . . . .

My dear friends, here I am on the eve of my departure and never
has my heart been more filled with my friends. But thanks be to
God, without that regret which would be unworthy of our friendship. On the contrary, however, with a true emotion of joy, since
this friendship formed solely for the Lord could never on either
side be more happy. Ah! I beseech you to continually pray to
the Lord that He may grant a great increase to those first blessings
so consoling, that He has already bestowed upon these distant
Churches, to which He seems to draw nearer to console old Europe.
For after all, she cannot hope or desire more delightful consolation
than to see the glory and Kingdom of the Sovereign Master, of so

good a Master, spread itself in such promising and encouraging ways as to assure them of a fortified bulwark against all the vain efforts of the infernal one.

Pray for me, save me while at sea. I shall remain with you and in spirit I shall not leave you for a moment; no, no, never— it is necessary for the parting ones to remain and for the remaining ones to depart.

Farewell, to God, to God alone, to Jesus, to Mary, I am

Yours in time and eternity,

S. Bruté.[5]

Father Bruté was a member of the Society of Saint Sulpice; and hence no stranger to his co-members at St. Mary's Seminary in Baltimore. Nevertheless, before his departure he procured authentic letters introducing him to the Archbishop in the United States. On May 30, 1810, Reverend M. Champion, at Rennes, recommended him to His Grace, the Most Reverend John Carroll of Baltimore, Maryland, in the following brief but touching message.

Rennes, May 30, 1810.

Your Grace,

Please accept the *Nouvelles Lectures de Pieté* and other volumes which kind Providence has given me the opportunity of offering Your Grace, by the hands of Monsieur l'Abbé Bruté, who has already had the honor of presenting the same work to His Holiness, Pius VII, in Paris.

This gentleman, to whom I am doubly indebted for this kind deed so greatly appreciated by me, is a treasure which heaven confides to you. Let us respect its decrees, and not speak of our regret at our loss which will be a rich gain to your country.

I am with the most profound respect,

the very humble and obedient servant of

Your Grace,

Champion—Pontalier,—Priest and former member of a Society whose spirit you know and possess.[6]

[5] S. Bruté to J. M. & F. de LaMennais, 6–9, 1810, Archives—Ploërmel, France.

[6] BCA, Case 2–B[12], p. 3.

On the same day Madame Bruté addressed a letter similar in character, to the venerable Father of the Church in America. She acquainted him with the virtuous character of her son, pleading that His Grace show him the care and affection of a father and, when he should no longer be needed in America, return him to France that he might be her solace in her aged years.[7]

Father Bruté sailed for America on June 10, 1810, on the *George Dyer*, Captain P. Collard. Among the American passengers was a Dr. Johnson, bearer of dispatches from General Armstrong, who was at that time United States minister to France. Bruté also lists among his fellow passengers, a poet; an Ursuline nun; five Trappists— Père Mauvais and four brothers; Father Cary of the Society of Jesus; Father B. J. Flaget, S. S.; Mr. Gras, a deacon who afterwards joined the Jesuits at Georgetown; M. Chabrat, a deacon and later Bishop of Bardstown, Kentucky; Mr. Anthony Deydier, who was to become the pioneer priest of Evansville, Indiana, in Bishop Bruté's diocese; and Messrs. Derigaud and Romeuf.[8]

[7] Madame Bruté to John Carroll, 5–30, 1810. BCA, Case 2–B[12], p. 1.
[8] C. de la Corbinière, *L'Indiana*, p. 416. Paris, 1886; J. R. Bayley, *op. cit.*, p. 40; H. S. Cauthorn, *St. Francis Xavier Cathedral*, p. 38. Indianapolis, 1892; *The Catholic Record*, April 16, 1891. Indianapolis.

CHAPTER V

IN THE NEW FIELD OF LABOR
1810–1815

The ship on which the missionary band took passage from Bordeaux to Baltimore came safely to port on August 10, 1810, after a voyage of two months. The passage had been tedious and distressing because of the rigors of the Continental blockade and the reprisals of the French against the English. Consequently, the vessel on which they sailed was twice overhauled, detained by English frigates, and was even in danger of being carried into an English port. However, on both occasions it was released out of consideration for Right Reverend B. J. Flaget, bishop-elect of the newly created See of Bardstown.

Upon his arrival Father Bruté was welcomed both by Archbishop Carroll, the Father of the Church in America, and by his colleagues at St. Mary's College and Seminary. Nevertheless, his missionary career lay before him an unwritten page, and peculiar circumstances, both civil and religious, were to be met with in the land of his adoption.

The territory included within the limits of the United States, at that period, extended from the Atlantic Ocean to the Rocky Mountain watershed on the west, and southward to the Spanish possessions of East Florida. Territorially the new nation was a unit. Expansion had followed natural lines, variety of soil, and climate. The extent of coastline and the vast area at her command made the region occupied by the United States not only worthy of the home of a great nation, but over and above that characteristic, preeminently suited for the home of a deep and active Catholicism, as this French missionary beheld it. The population, too, had been growing apace and at that period the inhabitants numbered 7,200,000, however, the distribution of population was very different from that with which we of the present day are familiar. In 1810 there were in the United States only eleven cities whose census registered eight thousand or over and the urban population comprised less than five per cent of the inhabitants. Less than one-third of the total area of the country was settled and opportunities were rare for the inhabitants of the backwoods. Nevertheless, a new period of industrial development was just beginning. The passage of the Embargo Act, the Non-Intercourse Act, the Napoleonic decrees, and the British Orders in Council practically ended for a time the importation of European manufactures and forced the Union to rely upon its own resources. Consequently, the development from previous small beginnings of manufactures became astounding. The annual value of these American manufactured products was estimated in 1810 at nearly $199,000,000 and they were used almost exclusively for home consumption.

The infant nation had advanced admirably, but still there remained much to be desired. The Catholic Church was only beginning to thrive. Just one score of years had elapsed since the first bishop of the See of Baltimore had been appointed and in 1810 there was only one bishop for the whole United States, the Most Reverend John Carroll. Two years previous Baltimore had been elevated to an archiepiscopal see with four suffragan sees, yet thus far no bishops occupied them and all administration and responsibility still rested upon the Father of the American Church. One of the four bishops-elect, Bishop Luke Concanen, appointed to the see of New York, had received consecration on April 24, 1808; but, owing to the distracted times in Europe, he died at Naples, June 19, 1810,[1] without ever reaching America. To that date the remaining three bishops-elect had not received consecration. In a brief note Father Bruté relates that he was present at their consecrations in Baltimore late in 1810, the year of his arrival in the episcopal city. Right Reverend John Egan, bishop-elect of

[1] Shea, II, p. 626. New York, 1888; V. R. Hughes, *Richard Luke Concanen*, p. 295, Freiburg, Switzerland, 1926.

Philadelphia, was elevated to the episcopacy on October 28, in St. Peter's Church. Right Reverend John Cheverus, nominated to the See of Boston, was consecrated in the same church on November 1, and the ceremony for Right Reverend B. J. Flaget, first bishop-elect of Bardstown, was conducted in St. Patrick's Church three days later. All three were consecrated by Archbishop Carroll.

The sole motive of Father Bruté in leaving France and coming to America was to devote his life to the missionary cause. He was staunch in his purpose for his spiritual directors assure us that he had been inclined towards this vocation since his youth.[2] Nevertheless, he was a member of a religious Society, and as such he was subject to a Superior. Therefore, the capacity in which he would serve was to be determined by his Superior and the Archbishop. He was retained as professor of Philosophy in St. Mary's Seminary at Baltimore. Here the young priest was to consecrate his time, talent, and energy to the great work for which his Society had been founded. Here he began his missionary career in America under the auspices of St. Sulpice and in accordance with the spirit of a true son of the Society. While he belonged to the Sulpicians by profession, they soon perceived that he belonged to all by charity; and this spirit of charity, imbibed at the bosom of his mother, was to him a lamp warming and lighting not only his own life, but also the lives of his colleagues and students. Thus, it was a singular advantage to the growing Church in America that Father Bruté was not the type of missionary who might impress an Indian tribe. In learning, scholarship, and culture, he was vastly superior to the average American priest in his day; and while he neither courted nor wished for such occasions, he was well equipped to mingle in society.[3]

[2] Cf. Letter of M. Emery to Madame Bruté, May 1810. Canon Bruté de Rémur Collection. Rennes, France.

[3] Cf. C. G. Herbermann, *The Sulpicians in the United States*, pp. 1–15. New York, 1916.

As a professor this model clergyman ranked second to none. His knowledge was profound and his skill in the class-room admirable; therefore, his daily program was always well filled. From a letter to his superior, Father Emery, at Paris, we find his schedule for 1811 to embrace the following duties. In the morning he taught a class of Philosophy in Latin, numbering fourteen students of whom three were seminarians, and a Latin class containing twelve pupils. The time period for each class was one and one-half hours. In addition to this he spent some time in study for he related that his first occupation in the afternoon was to take a lesson in both the English and the Spanish language, after which he gave a one-half hour English class to a student who knew less than himself. Following this he daily taught a Catechism class in French. Moreover, he took his turn at preaching every five or six weeks, and performed his share of the parochial duties which consisted in hearing the confessions of the children.[4] He never thought of exalting or aggrandizing himself. On the contrary, his one continuous effort was to hide his virtues and his talents; nevertheless, his worth was soon recognized and he was sought out on frequent occasions to decide momentous questions and to assume additional responsibilities in the absence of any of his confrères. Hence when transactions of major importance in behalf of St. Mary's College demanded the president, Reverend W. Du Bourg, to sail for the Isle of Martinique late in 1810, it was to Father Bruté that he confided the First Communion and the Confirmation classes, saying: "Upon my return I shall find all this accomplished and I shall be indebted to you for having fulfilled my tasks."[5] Likewise, after the departure of Father David from St. Mary's Seminary to the Kentucky country, Father Bruté had to assume the parochial work of the absent priest, namely, to hear the confessions in English of about forty girls.

[4] Cf. P. S. to Letter of S. Bruté to M. Emery, 6–21, 1811. Archives of St. Sulpice. Paris, France.

[5] W. Du Bourg to S. Bruté, 12–5, 1810. CA of A. Notre Dame, Indiana.

This last task, he admitted, was very embarrassing owing
to his meagre knowledge of the English language, but he
added, "those who frequent the Sacraments are confined to a
certain number of good souls."[6]

This zealous priest was always cheerful, happy, and contented in his position. From the very beginning his correspondence with St. Sulpice, at Paris, proved the solidity
of his vocation for the foreign missions. He was intensely
interested in the welfare of the Society's American foundations, as well as in the universal development and spread of
Catholicism in the young nation. Yet he was a genuine
Frenchman who never forgot his fatherland. Apparently
a portion of his heart remained in France, for the following
letter to Father Emery reveals both his sincere zeal for the
missions and his tender affection for his friends and country.

Baltimore, 21 June, 1811.

Very Reverend Father,

Father Zocchi has just visited us and left us your letters, but he
stayed only fifteen minutes at the seminary and then repaired to
Georgetown to visit the Archbishop. I earnestly desire to see him
on his return, in order, personally, to hear more details of you and
of my mother whom he saw at Rennes enroute to his port of
embarkation.

I have not received the letter which you were kind enough to
write me as stated in your letter to Father Nagot. This is another sacrifice. I am often tempted to count them when I think of
my dear and venerable friends from whom I am so far away that
probably I can no longer look forward but to the eternal reunion.
This sacrifice from time to time saddens me unto tears, nevertheless, this sadness wanes during my occupations which consume
whole days and which will soon have consumed the entire first year.
It is impossible to pass whole days without thinking of you and of
poor France. From the day of my arrival you were mirrored in
my memory and the vision never leaves me but brings before me at

[6] Cf. P. S. to Letter of S. Bruté to M. Emery, 6–21, 1811. Archives
of St. Sulpice. Paris.

times a list of names of which yours, M. Duclaux and two or three others have not escaped me a single time. This is a mere tribute of love and gratitude that is left me to offer you. As for letters, their fate is so uncertain that one dares not undertake to write them. Of twenty-nine written to my Mother I know of only two that were received. I am ashamed to tell you this number but I think I owe that to this poor Mother and it is only by writing a great number of letters that in the end one arrives.

We are all enjoying good health except Father Nagot who is completely incapacitated from a serious fall which he had in Passion Week. We found him unconscious and bathed in blood at the foot of the stairs. We feared we would lose him, but he recovered and on St. Joseph's Day he recommenced saying Mass and he continued every day with the exception of two or three times. This last month he seemed more or less himself and was able to go for a walk with us. But he remained incapable of applying himself mentally—being extremely fatigued after writing a few lines. Since last week the intense heat has overcome him and he probably will not be able to write. It is a type of nervous prostration which makes him incapable of the least mental work; however, he again said Mass today. He comes to the refectory, to the recreations with a peaceful countenance, resigned, even joyous, and is our entire consolation. We have great need of this after your last letters because in view of our situation and our extreme needs at the little seminary at Emmitsburg. It is overwhelming to see that it will not be possible for you to send those we ask for with the exception of Father Maréchal. God's Will be done and we shall do our best—how heartrending all this is! We do not doubt the good will of our Father and his profound interest in the American foundations; but it is a frightful time for us—all hope has vanished. One must keep silence and say nothing, only I did not think that I had planned too far in advance by having my eye on certain priests in France—such as Father Tharin.

Our Kentucky missionaries have arrived at Louisville after a pleasant voyage down the Ohio river. From the letters of Bishop Flaget and Father David you would think you were reading Chateaubriand, but for them these events are delicious realities—a permanent chapel erected in their boat—Mass every day and four on

Sunday and everyone receiving Holy Communion on the waters in the midst of forests. Across the prairies from time to time the first vestiges of culture, the first houses, sometimes small villages, sometimes cities half built—the site of active industry could be seen. Their hearts were all filled with hope in this ark of salvation where were kept regular exercises as in the seminary, from the hour of rising to the hour of repose, from the Feast of the Ascension when they embarked from Pittsburg to the day of their debarkation at Louisville on June 4. This was the life and preparation of our modern apostles, my dearest Father. You in your turn do lift your hands in prayer for them—you and Father Duclaux and all our Fathers and good friends.

Father Du Bourg was announced as being in harbor yesterday. We believed it, awaiting him all day, but we must still have patience. Father Pasquit continues to hold his position. He is an admirable man—admirable beyond all description. Father Joubert is another precious addition, being procurator of the college, he teaches several classes in addition to administrating with talent, profit, and remarkable economy. Moreover, he is sacristan and pious to the point of needing reproach for the length of time he takes to say Mass and to make his thanksgiving. I enjoy telling you all this. There is another colleague whom we must love as well as respect and whom I dare praise. This is the worthy Father Dubois, who, unaided, maintains with indefatigable activities the entire establishment of Emmitsburg. Such men are so necessary to us in the abandonment in which you are forced to leave us; yet they are rare.

My Father, I finish without almost having begun. I cast myself at your feet or if you will permit me in your heart to rest there and in this solitude of 1300 leagues away I beg you to speak of me to all your children in your continual prayer—speak of me to Our Lord, to Our Holy Mother, to our holy Founders, so that I may have the pleasure of lessening each day the enormous weight of miseries that burden my heart. Not that I am sad or afflicted here, I do not wish our Father to think that—on the contrary, I am happy and consoled in my position and my only difficulty is to turn so many obstacles to good, but I do not worry. I await all love and mercy from Our Sweet Saviour.

My dear Father take care of yourself and send me news often. Likewise, have the greatest possible pity on our extreme necessities. Remember me to all, I beg of you.

Your submissive child,[7]
S. Bruté.

In the month of July during the summer vacation of 1811, Father Bruté visited the Mountain near Emmitsburg, where his colleague Father Dubois had opened a college.   He also visited St. Joseph's Valley two miles distant, where the first Community of the American Sisters of Charity had located.   It was on this occasion that Mother Seton first met this zealous French priest, who later proved a devoted friend.   "I first met Mother in 1811.   She read with me the *Following of Christ* to form my English pronunciation— marked out especially Chapter Twenty-one, Third Book."[8] During this same visit at Mount St. Mary's, he also made the acquaintance of Madame Melmoth.[9]   No one, not even the energetic priest himself, foresaw that this historic spot was to offer him asylum during the greater portion of his life in America.   Father Bruté was a nature lover, and he loved the Mountain and the Valley at first sight.   However, he was too zealous to tarry long.   His vacations were always brief.   He was no spendthrift of golden moments, but economized time to such an extent that in passing from one place to another he always read, or recited the Divine Office. Thus on this occasion, after a few days of relaxation he departed to attend to the spiritual needs of a French Community of Trappists, exiles from France, who had settled temporarily at Pigeon Hill.   This task having been satisfactorily accomplished he returned to Baltimore.

Upon the opening of the academic year Father Bruté resumed his class in Philosophy at St. Mary's Seminary. Scarcely more than a year had elapsed since his arrival in

[7] Original in Archives of St. Sulpice. Paris.

[8] *Bruté—Seton Correspondence*, p. 52. 1886.

[9] S. Bruté to Madame Melmoth, 8–1, 1812. Archives of St. Joseph's Convent. Emmitsburg, Md.

America, yet his mind was occupied with problems more
profound than the assigned duties in the class-room. The
missionary spirit possessed him completely and despite his
meagre knowledge of the English language he had already
taken an inventory of Catholicism and its pressing needs
throughout America. He beheld eighty students, housed at
the Mountain under the sole charge of one master, Father
Dubois. It was impossible for Baltimore to give assistance
to this new foundation. Hence our enthusiastic Missionary
wrote to M. Duclaux, at Paris: "If you have anyone to
spare please do send them." Viewing the Kentucky missions, he witnessed Bishop Flaget and Father David accomplishing marvelous work in the new diocese. According
to their letters many conversions had already been effected;
yet, religion was restrained because the bishop lacked the
necessary quota of zealous and devout priests. Father
Bruté learned that Philadelphia was peopled with French
Catholics but for the want of a shepherd to guide them
these people retained scarcely more than the name of
Catholics. Through correspondence with Bishop Cheverus,
he discovered there were only three priests at Boston,
where everything was to be accomplished. In order to care
for his flock it was necessary for the bishop to make journeys of three hundred and more miles. Seemingly without
a conception of distance as he was his thoughts were suddenly fixed upon remote China. He beheld religion dying
there from the same cause—a lack of priests, and in his
superabundant zeal for the salvation of all mankind he
wrote his superiors to send him to China. Upon a second
thought he realized "Our America, too, is suffering," and
writing again to his superiors, at Paris, he advocated sending men from France, maintaining that Europe would profit
by their sacrifices and for every ten priests sent away they
would gain double. He reminded St. Sulpice that the seminaries had more students than the country ever could employ. He begged his superiors in France to interest pious
souls in the welfare of America and to send their American

foundations as many books as could be spared, together with *good living books.*[10]

Silently this humble priest was rising in the estimation of his confrères and he commanded the esteem of all with whom he came in contact. His colleagues, as well as the Archbishop, had previously experienced with what promptness and efficiency he discharged his tasks, consequently, over and above his class-room responsibilities Archbishop Carroll frequently entrusted to him some important correspondence. Thus Bishop Flaget of Bardstown, on June 10, 1812, wrote that he had received from Reverend Mr. Bruté a letter written in the name of Archbishop Carroll, stating that it was "in contemplation to convene" a Provincial Council in the following November and requesting his attendance.[11] And Reverend W. Du Bourg at Conewago, wrote to Reverend M. Tessier, at Baltimore, saying: "Reverend Mr. Bruté begs me to remain for the Council."[12]

The duties of Father Bruté increased daily. His own correspondence was becoming wide-spread even in America. An exchange of lengthy and frequent letters was carried on with the Bishops of Boston and Bardstown; and, likewise, with Fathers David, Dubois, Matignon, Du Bourg, and others. But he never permitted himself to become so engrossed that relations with home and friends suffered. On the contrary he wrote frequently to his aged mother, to his brother Augustine and family, to his superiors and confrères at St. Sulpice, and to Father Jean and Félicité de LaMennais. At this period transportation was both slow and unreliable. Often it required ten or twelve months[13] for these letters to reach their destination and it is to be regretted that many of them were destroyed at sea; yet this scholarly priest succeeded astonishingly in keeping in touch

[10] S. Bruté to M. Duclaux, 11–11, 1811. Archives of St. Sulpice. Paris.

[11] M. J. Spalding, *Life of Rt. Rev. B. J. Flaget,* p. 106. Louisville, 1852.

[12] W. Du Bourg to M. Tessier, 8–28, 1812. Canon Bruté de Rémur Collection.

[13] S. Bruté to J. M. de LaMennais, 6–15, 1812. *Ibid.*

with every movement in France, as well as in communicating information concerning the progress of the Church in America.

Seemingly the unswerving zeal for the spread of Catholicism in the United States made Father Bruté appear importunate at times. Although on such occasions he may have voiced the opinion of his confrères, his actions assume the complexion of unauthorized responsibility. Such an opinion is gained in reading a letter of July 12, 1812, to the Archbishop of Baltimore. He told the Archbishop how much it pained him to perceive the little interest that His Grace apparently manifested in the various institutions at Baltimore and the Mountain. He charged him with being a stranger to the seminarians when these clerics should be regarded as the hope of religion in this country. He compared the attitude of the Bishop of Rennes and the Archbishop of Baltimore and stated that the latter seldom accepted an invitation to the seminary whereas the Bishop of Rennes frequently visited both the *petit* and the *grand* seminary. He also attended the examinations in all the subjects and his words of encouragement to the diligent and of reproach to the indolent were effective. Then in the name of his superiors and confrères he invited the Archbishop to attend the exercises in their seminary, assuring His Grace that the sole interest of his colleagues was to form a priesthood worthy of spreading God's kingdom within this new nation.

Even though Father Bruté did appear importunate at times, he deserves to be lauded for his sound philosophy of ecclesiastical life: "Your Grace," said he, "English, French, Irish, Sulpicians, or Jesuits, all this amounts to nothing here. The American clergy ought to be of one heart, one soul, and one zeal for the glory of God and the good of the Church in this country. All differences, and especially all national or individual differences, ought to be lost in the midst of the weighty cares that press upon us."[14] He wisely maintained that they were all Catholics and that racial dis-

---

[14] BCA, Case: 13–p. 12. (Apparently wrongly catalogued.)

tinctions should be merged in the nation which had adopted
them regardless of the country of their birth.

In the summer of 1812 Archbishop Carroll sent Father
Bruté to St. Joseph's mission on the eastern coast of Maryland to assist Father Monelly for two months. There he
made courageous attempts to preach in English. Within a
month he had visited six different missions and at each one
he said Mass, administered the consolations of religion, and
delivered a sermon. He acknowledged in a letter to Bishop
Flaget that it was bad preaching, indeed, filled with blund-
ering pronounciations and grammatical errors. But far
from being dejected he strove more eagerly, as he himself
said, "to force this dreadful English into my backward head,
or I must renounce forever to know it." His intense ardor
to save souls was profoundly manifested in this brief mission tour. If one would examine his activities on the eastern coast where he labored to gather the Master's sheep
into one fold, one would scarcely believe that his time could
have embraced more. Nevertheless, we find him spending
the evenings in advising others through correspondence.
One of his earliest letters of this type, still extant, bears
date of August 1, 1812, and is addressed to Madame Melmoth in New York.[15]

Entering upon the second month of this mission career,
Father Bruté received a letter bearing the first intimation
of his transfer to Mount St. Mary's near Emmitsburg. It
came from his confrère at Conewago, Father Du Bourg,
who said:

> As for you, my friend, I have written to Reverend Mr. Tessier that
> you should be sent to the Mountain. I have given my reasons in
> detail, none of which I have imparted to Father Dubois. You per-
> ceive very well that I love you, because nothing could please you
> more. I would advise you to return as soon as possible and I am
> convinced that without much opposition the council will adopt the
> measure.[16]

[15] Cf. Original in Archives of St. Joseph's Convent. Emmitsburg.
[16] Cf. Original in CA of A.

Shortly after this Father Bruté received official notice of his transfer. He returned to Baltimore late in September and departed on the twenty-eighth of the same month to enter upon his new field of labor at Mount St. Mary's. This institution is located about fifty-two miles distant from Baltimore, on the side of the Catoctin spur of the Blue Ridge Mountains in the state of Maryland. Its elevation, seven hundred feet above the sea, is sufficient to afford a wholesome atmosphere, as well as a clear view of the surrounding picturesque landscapes.

At the time of Father Bruté's coming to the Mountain, the college and its surroundings were primitive. The buildings consisted of two parallel log houses a short distance apart, and a small structure at the entrance of the garden. The one known later as the "White House" lodged the president, vice-president, and students. It also contained the study room, class-rooms, and dormitory. The refectory, store-rooms, and cellar were arranged on the basement floor. The other building contained the kitchen, clothes-room, and infirmary; the small building at the garden entrance was occupied by three lay teachers. The buildings were equipped with coarse furniture and nothing savored of comfort, for frequently the dire essentials were lacking. Everything from basement to roof wore the aspect of poverty. The war between the United States and England had increased the prices of merchandise, which circumstance subjected the institution to even more rigid economy. Therefore, the daily meals were exceptionally frugal. Breakfast consisted of dry bread and coffee. The same courses, with the addition of a small quantity of butter were served at supper. The college grounds, too, were very primitive. The stumps of the original forest trees were still standing in the yard, while the wood-pile was within a few feet of the refectory door. The water supply for the institution was kept in two long troughs in the yard near the door.

The year 1812 brought marked changes at the Mountain. Father Dubois in his eagerness to supply the Church with an educated clergy admitted almost every youth who gave promise of a vocation. He trusted all men and judged them by his own honesty; but in acting thus he was often too good to accomplish good. He was a profound scholar, but unfortunately did not possess great executive ability. The property had been purchased on credit and in a short time the institution was overwhelmed by financial difficulties. The origin of this state of affairs, however, cannot be attributed wholly to Father Dubois' incapacity, but also to his confrères, who figured prominently in the purchase. In this hour of need Father Bruté became the confidential adviser of Father Dubois and supplied some of the qualities in which the president was deficient. He was appointed treasurer of the establishment and began immediately to keep an account of the income and expenditures and by his method extricated the institution from pecuniary embarrassments. After taking an inventory of the financial condition of the college in 1812, he exclaimed: "O Providence! that a cart so overladened did not stop in the mire—yet it came out, with a loss indeed. It needs hammering and screwing and mending."[17]

Prior to this date Mount St. Mary's had been only a *petit seminaire* and the students who wished to continue their studies for the priesthood after completing the humanities were transferred to the Sulpician seminary at Baltimore. This arrangement ceased with Father Bruté's coming to the Mountain, and those students who desired to pursue studies in divinity were instructed by him. Accordingly, an ordination, the first at Mt. St. Mary's, occurred on October 8, 1812. Archbishop Carroll conferred tonsure on John Delaney, Wm. Byrne, Francis Grandchamps, George and Alexis Elder, George Boarman, and M. Clauzel.[18]

[17] M. Meline,—E. McSweeny, *The Story of the Mountain*, I, p. 52.
[18] Some years later Father Bruté recorded the following: "John Delany—dead. Wm. Byrne, priest keeps school for Bishop Flaget. Francis Grandchamps, returned to the islands, secular—. George Elder, priest, president of Bardstown College. Alexis Elder, priest now, Sulpician, George Boarman, returned to the world, and M. Clauzel, I believe,—dead." (Cf. *Bruté—Seton Correspondence*, p. 314. 1886.

Archbishop Carroll, owing to a sudden indisposition, was detained at Emmitsburg on this occasion and his absence from Baltimore was a source of regret to Father Du Bourg, who had been appointed administrator of the diocese of New Orleans and had completed arrangements to sail for this port on October 15, 1812. The Archbishop had promised to provide him with three letters of recommendation; one to Father Olivier, one to Governor C. C. Claiborne, and the other to the Superior of St. Ursula's Convent; but not having received these letters Father Du Bourg dispatched to Father Bruté on October 13, by special carrier, a letter requesting him to give the affair his immediate attention. He enclosed the essential points that these letters should contain because he supposed, as was the case, that his confrére was fulfilling the office of secretary to His Grace during the latter's stay at Mt. St. Mary's.[19]

Academic conditions at the Mountain differed vastly from those at the seminaries of Rennes and Baltimore, respectively, where Father Bruté had served prior to this transfer; however, he possessed the happy faculty of always knowing how to make school-life agreeable as well as profitable to his student. At this particular institution work was combined with study. The boys enjoyed cutting trees, planting others, removing stumps, clearing off stones, and in general beautifying the premises. They especially rejoiced to work with Father Bruté because he was a man of utter unselfishness and simplicity. He also supervised cleaning the undergrowth from some of the many points on the mountain-side from which the beautiful landscapes could be enjoyed. On pleasant days he would often lead his students to one of these quiet hermitages for study. From a letter to his uncle at Rennes, we learn that he spent all recreations in trying to improve the college grounds. He also carried stones to a suitable spot on the mountain-side and erected a grotto to our Blessed Mother. A path was then cut and cleared between the grotto and the church. Crosses were

[19] Original in CA of A.

erected on the trees at equal distances to afford his students and confrères an opportunity of making the Way of the Cross between the two shrines of devotion. Another incident relative to the Church on the mountain manifests his unselfishness and also his charity, measured by the standard established by Christ, namely, "Whatsoever you have done to the least of My brethren you have done unto Me." The ascent to the church was very steep and tiresome, particularly on winter mornings when the ground was covered with ice and snow. One zero morning the faculty and students were surprised to find the steepest portion of this path terraced with wood. It had been done in the darkness of night or early in the morning. The workman was soon discovered to be Father Bruté, and the idea suggested was immediately grasped by the students who set about at once and terraced the remainder of the pathway.[20] Despite his skill in landscape gardening, this occupation was not practised to excess or to the detriment of the essentials in academic life. On the contrary, he made many of the articles used in the class-room. While studying medicine at Paris, he had pursued courses in drawing and singing. Great accuracy was acquired in the former and it served the devoted priest to good purpose while teaching at the poverty-stricken Mountain. All the maps that the institution possessed in those early days were his own production. A globe neatly carved from a block of wood was another practical addition to their equipment.

If Father Bruté was solicitous for all at the Mountain he was no less generous in granting favors to others who appealed to him, regardless of the weather or the hour of the day or night. One winter evening William Seton was sitting in the good Father's room when the mail was brought in. Among the papers and letters was a message from His Grace, at Baltimore, asking information regarding a quotation from one of the Fathers of the Church. The scholarly professor glanced up along the lines of his library shelves,

[20] M. Meline,—E. McSweeny, *op. cit.*, I, pp. 1–55.

rose, took down a book, tucked it under his arm, picked up his hat and bidding Master Seton, "good-night," with his customary admonition, "be a good boy," left the college. On the following morning when Archbishop Carroll entered his breakfast room he was greeted by the vice-president of Mt. St. Mary's and the desired book. Apparently it was impossible for Father Bruté to respond in the affirmative to all requests, because there were times when he deemed it more prudent to refuse, even though the petition was addressed to him by an intimate friend. Thus on September 1, 1813, Father Du Bourg wrote him a lengthy account of the deplorable conditions in the Louisiana diocese and begged him to exchange the Mountain for the south. On this occasion the prayers of Du Bourg remained unanswered and his confrère remained with Father Dubois in the capacity of professor.[21]

Previous to Father Bruté's transfer to the Mountain, Father Dubois had gone daily to celebrate Mass for the Sisters of Charity. Now his colleague came from the Mount on Monday, Tuesday, Wednesday, and Thursday of each week to celebrate Mass in St. Joseph's Chapel.[22] On Sundays the two priests alternated regularly in saying the early Mass for the Sisters and they observed the same order in regard to the High Mass which was sung alternately at the Mountain and at the Village. Father Bruté was neither confessor nor spiritual director to the sisterhood at this period; yet he gave the community the full benefit of his spiritual and intellectual accomplishments. He and Mother Seton were kindred souls, possessing minds of the same delicate mould, and from their first meeting they sympathized heartily. Immediately he beheld and admired in her the eternal womanly and she recognized him to be a priest according to God's own heart. Throughout her remaining years we find in Mother Seton that continued ever-present supremely effective power of the eternal womanly

---

[21] W. Du Bourg to S. Bruté, CA of A.
[22] *Bruté—Seton Correspondence*, p. 88. 1884.

identifying her with the apostolic work of Father Bruté. Her beautiful soul was able to follow him in his lofty flights and she delighted to commune with him on eternal truths, and to derive thence peace amid the trials that are the portion of every pioneer Community.

Regardless of the pressing duties at the college, together with serving the Sisters at St. Joseph's and answering numerous and distant sick-calls, Father Bruté continued to live a life of mortification and self-denial. He slept but part of the night; as soon as he awakened, he arose regardless of the hour, and spent the remainder of the night prostrate in adoration before the Most Blessed Sacrament, and in writing lectures and sermons. He was ever ready to deprive himself of even that meagre rest if he knew his services would mitigate the pain or sorrow of another. At the close of a spiritual exhortation written to Mother Seton, he added: "I have passed the night with one of the sick children. I feel weak, but it is a languor so sweet, of thoughts, of desires, of regrets, of love, of union, views of that beautiful Heaven of St. Vincent, confusion, desolation of doing nothing for it."[23] Shortly after this we find him keeping the night vigil at the bedside of a dying pupil. Theophilus Kaufman of Philadelphia, a boy of twelve years, had been fatally wounded in the breast by falling upon an open knife while at play. He had not yet made his First Communion but on all occasions he had displayed extraordinary faith and piety. The fatherly priest remained up all night with the child, prayed with him, assisted him in making his general confession, and at one o'clock in the morning on Tuesday of Holy Week, administered the Holy Viaticum which was the dying child's First and Last Communion. Then kneeling at the bedside in profound adoration of his Eucharistic Lord, he united with the suffering child in making a gladsome thanksgiving. So eager was he to catch every whisper of love coming forth from this innocent heart that he leaned his head directly over the wounded breast of

[23] *Bruté—Seton Correspondence*, p. 62. 1886.

the expiring boy until the latter breathed forth his pure
soul into the hands of his Creator. That all the students
looked upon Father Bruté as a tender father and implicitly
confided their personal cares to him is manifested in this
same incident. Upon receiving Holy Viaticum, Theophilus,
after a few moments of silence, asked the priest at his side:
"What shall I say?" This question was easily answered
in all simplicity by one who spent long vigils in ecstatic
adoration and whose heart was saturated with love for the
Master.[24]

Four years had elapsed since Father Bruté's coming to
America, but the sacred friendships that bound him to the
opposite shore—France, were not to be weakened by absence. Jean and Félicité de LaMennais never ceased pleading with him to return to his fatherland. Every available
means was used to convince him that he could accomplish
greater good, and, more effectively, in France than in
America.[25] At the same time Father David was trying to
influence Father Bruté to join him in the West. Catholicism
was constantly spreading and becoming more firmly established and Father Bruté welcomed every message, that came
from Bishop Flaget or Father David, imparting news of
their mission-field. He was particularly fond of these two
pioneers of the Church on the western frontier and was
interested in all they did. It was not difficult for him to
realize the position of Bishop Flaget and to perceive how
closely he was pressed for priests to care for the straying
flocks. Although this devoted missionary had been destined
by Providence to found a new diocese in the Northwest Territory, his hour to join the pioneer apostles on the frontier
had not yet arrived. Many years of hardship and laborious
toil were to fill the interim before he was to become Simon
of Vincennes. Nevertheless, the correspondence from the
two shores seemed to vie with each other in the attempt to
procure the services of this apostolic missionary. Both

[24] M. Meline,—E. McSweeny, *op. cit.*, I, pp. 51–3.
[25] *Lettres Inédites de J. M. & F. de LaMennais*, pp. 84–88.

knew his zeal and his worth and it was the future of the Church in these two vastly remote sections that prompted both French and American clergy to seek Father Bruté.[26]

The scourge of a second war for Independence had made its cruel lashes felt throughout the nation for more than two years before the battle scenes approached the Mountain. . Late in the summer of 1814 a British fleet under Admiral Cochrane and an army of four thousand men under Major General Ross appeared on the Chesapeake. General Ross landed at Benedict on the Patuxent, forty miles from Washington, and marched unopposed on the city. A battle ensued at Bladensburg, five miles from Washington, in which the Americans retreated. On the eve of the same day, August 24, 1814, the British entered Washington, burned the capitol and the White House. A fortnight later they attempted a raid on Baltimore, which was frustrated by the alertness of the Maryland militia and the defense of Fort McHenry. Maryland had collected fourteen thousand men, and Emmitsburg had furnished its quota in the defense of Baltimore. On this occasion, Father Bruté addressed the volunteers in sentiments of true patriotism, urging them to do their duty as brave sons of the nation. He himself became so anxious that he walked to Baltimore to render ministerial services if needed.

On November 16, 1814, Father Bruté wrote to his superior, M. Duclaux, at Paris, asking permission to go abroad. He wished to see his mother and to bring back his library, but his primary reason was that he felt the voyage would produce good results for the Church in America. Apparently up to that date it had never been definitely decided whether Father Bruté was to remain in America or whether he was to be recalled at some future date. Consequently, he asked his superior to decide where he was to live—either one shore or the other. The decision was immaterial to him; however, if he was ever to be

[26] Cf. *Ave Maria*, "Letters of Father David to Father Bruté," V (1869)), p. 547 ff., 561 ff., 595 ff.; *Records* (ACHS), XXIX (1918), pp. 50, 53, 154.

permitted to see his mother he requested to be allowed to come immediately.

At that date the college at Baltimore was on the decline. It registered only thirty-four boarders and six of those were unable to pay. Father Bruté remarked that the Baltimore institution had a saint, but no superior. At the Mountain everything was progressing. They had one deacon, four clerics, and Mr. Hickey had just been ordained on the seventh of that month. Father Bruté was confessor at the seminary and at the Mountain church. Père Duhamel, a priest of the Society of the Holy Ghost, lived near the Mountain institution and aided Father Dubois in the parochial work at the village church.[27] The interest of Mount St. Mary's, of St. Joseph's Valley, and of the Village were almost identical in those days. The vice-president loved all three and many anxious moments had been spent in planning how to serve them more efficiently. Despite all this a sudden change saddened the happy scenes; Father Bruté was recalled.

[27] S. Bruté to M. Duclaux, 11–16, 1814. Archives of St. Sulpice. Paris.

CHAPTER VI

PRESIDENT OF ST. MARY'S COLLEGE, BALTIMORE
1815–1818

St. Mary's Seminary, Baltimore, the parent foundation of the Sulpician Fathers in the United States, was the first of its kind in the young Republic and, accordingly, it demanded time and feeders for growth. Catholicism in America was too young at that epoch to produce numerous spontaneous vocations. It was expedient, then to find students or candidates for the priesthood, and this could be accomplished only by founding a twin establishment that would provide for the training of boys from childhood in the correct principles of the true Faith. Consequently, St. Mary's College was an institution that sprang from necessity. It was first conceived in the mind of Father Du Bourg. The work was wholly foreign to the purpose for which the Society had been founded; yet the Sulpician Fathers had emigrated to foreign shores, and the nation which offered them asylum differed vastly from their native country.

The college thrived under the direction of the capable president, Father Du Bourg, until 1812, when he accepted the more responsible office of administrator of New Orleans. Upon this vacancy a secular priest, Father Pasquit, succeeded to the office, and as he was thoroughly acquainted with the needs of the place the college continued to advance until the opening of the academic year, in 1814, when a surprising decrease in attendance was witnessed. Father Pasquit resigned late in that same year and with M. Cotineau of Nantes departed for the mission on the Island of Bourbon.[1] The next choice fell to Father Bruté, whose Journal

---

[1] S. Bruté to A. Bruté, 6–23, 1821. Canon Bruté Collection. Rennes. France.

bears the following entry: "In 1814 I was appointed president of St. Mary's College of Baltimore and for it early in 1815 I went to France."[2]

In the meantime Father Bruté received an agreeable reply from Father Duclaux, at Paris, and, consequently, before entering upon the office of presidency, he was to go abroad. This voyage, however, could not be undertaken immediately. Although the treaty of peace between Great Britain and the United States was signed at Ghent December 24, 1814, it was necessary to give the nations time to right themselves; hence the newly appointed president of the college displayed prudence in delaying his voyage.

Mother Seton was at this time deeply concerned about her older son who had reached the age when it was necessary to choose some vocation in life. The unsettled conditions of the time made it difficult for her to determine the course which would prove most to his advantage. A naval profession was not her choice, and the distracted state of commerce made it almost impossible to place him in a desirable mercantile establishment. Father Bruté aided her to solve the difficulty by informing her of his pending voyage to Europe. Immediately she resolved to send her son abroad under the protection of her counsellor and place him with her friends, Messrs. Filicchi at Leghorn.[3]

Father Bruté and William Seton sailed from New York on April 6, 1815, on the *Tontine* bound for the French port, Bordeaux. The seas were free, and at the time of their departure the scholarly priest intended to visit Italy before returning to the States. These plans did not come to fruition. Peace in France had been short-lived, although the report thereof had failed to reach America before they sailed. Napoleon had escaped from the Isle of Elba on March 1, 1815, hence, when they arrived at Bordeaux, the royalist city, on May 22, they found themselves in the midst

[2] Bruté Journal, Georgetown UA. fol. 92, 6. Washington, D. C.
[3] C. I. White, *Life of Mrs. E. A. Seton*, pp. 314–355. New York, 1878; R. Seton, *Memoirs, Letters, and Journal of Elizabeth Seton*, II, pp. 180–186.

of a terror-stricken people.   The rival factions were wrang-
ling violently and inevitable disaster threatened every section.   Southern France was under undisciplined troops, and
the whole nation was thrown into consternation.   There
were additional dangers lurking between Marseilles and
Leghorn;   the coasts were infested with Algerian pirates.
Murat, whom Napoleon had made King of Naples, marched
on Rome, and the Pope was again an exile.   He fled to
Genoa, where he arrived early in April, whither he was followed by thirteen Cardinals.   All this forced Father Bruté
to change his course.   Instead of accompanying William Seton farther he was obliged to hasten the youth's departure
on the following day.   He dispatched the lad by way of
Marseilles in care of Mr. Prud'homme, provided with a
passport and letters from the American consul at Bordeaux
to the one at Leghorn.[4]   On the following day he wrote to
the Messrs. Filicchi, from Bordeaux, to recommend William
Seton and to express his regret at not being able to continue the journey to Leghorn.

From Bordeaux Father Bruté betook himself to Rennes
and was forced to find security in hiding.   Even before
escaping from Bordeaux he had been afraid that he would
be arrested as a priest.[5]   Bonaparte's return made life disagreeable for this zealous priest who was anxious to achieve
the purpose of his voyage and to return at an early date.
This sudden disorder compelled him to live in constant
alarm from the date of his arrival May 22, until July 17,
when the white flag was again raised.   During this visit
with his mother, he occupied the room directly beneath the
Chapel in the home of his childhood, the Old Parliament
Building.[6]   This room was regarded as sacred quarters, owing to the fact that it had been the hiding place of two confessors during the Reign of Terror.   The memories of those

[4] J. B. Code, *Elizabeth Seton by Mdme. De Barberry, (translated)*
p. 377.   New York, 1927;   R. Fleming, *The Catholic Veto and the*
Irish Bishops, p. 44.   Dublin, 1911.

[5] R. Seton, *op. cit.,* II, pp. 188–194.

[6] J. R. Bayley, *Memoirs of the Rt. Rev. S. W. G. Bruté de Rémur,*
pp. 180–181.

dark days occupied his mind again, and he thanked God
Who sent the two priests to bless his youth and his family in
such days of gloom. He visited the churches of his native
city and said Mass in several of the ruins of the Revolution.

During this alarming period it was impossible for Father
Bruté to meet his friends who lived beyond the city of
Rennes. Consequently, he and Jean de LaMennais were
forced to be resigned to the course of events and patiently
to await happier circumstances and more peaceful times.
However, a continual correspondence bound their hearts
the closer and de LaMennais, the Vicar of Saint-Brieuc, insisted that the American missionary should not leave the
country before they spent some days together.

This visit occurred between June 26 and July 17. It would
be difficult to determine which of the two priests experienced the greater joy at this reunion. The precious
hours they spent in each others company were profitable
to both. They encouraged each other to greater good and
greater accomplishments for the spread of religion. The
visit, however, was despoiled of some of its pleasure by the
absence of Abbé Guy Carron and Féli de LaMennais. The
Richerists and Blanchardists had become so enraged over
the late volume, *La Tradition sur l'Institution des Evêques,*
written by Félicité, that he was obliged to expatriate himself. Consequently, he fled to London and sought refuge
with Abbé Guy Carron, the mutual friend of the Brutés'
and the de LaMennais'. The Vicar kept his promise and
accompanied Father Bruté back to Rennes where Madame
Bruté welcomed both as her cherished sons, after which de
LaMennais spent a short time with his aged father and then
retraced the route alone to Saint-Brieuc. Upon his return
he became greatly depressed, ill at ease, sad, and as one in
a dream. The soul of the Vicar was knit to that of the missionary and he felt that in Father Bruté's going he had lost
the half of himself.[7]

[7] *Lettres Inédites de J. M. & F. de LaMennais,* pp. 94–97 & 103–105.

Peace was restored July 17, 1815, and Father Bruté went forth immediately to accomplish the purpose of his voyage, which was to interest the young clergy in embracing the American missions.[8]   However, before leaving Rennes he wrote William Seton at Leghorn, charging him to obtain news through the Messrs. Filicchi regarding Father Zocchi's books and the personal effects of Bishop Concanen and then to write him at St. Sulpice.[9]   He then visited the seminaries in northern and central France and everywhere he strove to arouse in the hearts of the young clerics a true fervor and zeal for souls.   Some writers maintain that the purpose of his going to France in 1815 was to bring back his library to America.   Without doubt he desired to do this also, but it was neither his primary motive nor the one which he actually accomplished.[10]   At this date Father Bruté had not yet reached Paris; hence he knew not what orders awaited him there for his immediate or deferred embarkation.   If his sojourn was to be prolonged he would visit the southern seminaries for the purpose of awakening their interests in America.[11] On the first Monday in August, he went to Lyons and thence to Paris where he conferred with his Superior at St. Sulpice.   He had hoped for an immediate or an early embarkation, but again he was disappointed.

Father Du Bourg was in Rome at this time.   Both he and his confrère had crossed the Atlantic for practically identical purposes, but the condition of France was all but encouraging to Father Bruté.   He wrote to his colleague from Paris, saying he would return to America without having accomplished much, although he hoped to take several missionaries back with him.   Du Bourg was not slow to fathom the spirit of the writer and responded at once to console his "Little Brother" in the ill luck that had befal-

---

[8] *Ibid.*, pp. 100–103.

[9] R. Seton, *op. cit.*, II, pp. 194–196.

[10] S. Bruté to J. M. & F. de LaMennais, 11–12, 1815.   Archives-Ploërmel, France.

[11] *Idem.* 7–30, 1815.

len him on his visit to France and tried to convince him
that the patience and devotedness with which he accepted
the trials would be the means of drawing great blessings
upon his worthy enterprise. He also imparted news of Father Bruté's nephew whom he had met at the French Em-
bassy and who had impressed him as an interesting character. Likewise, the administrator of the Louisiana diocese
had called on William Seton and the Messrs. Filicchi and
had learned from Cardinal Litta that the nomination to
Philadelphia was still pending. Information about Mr.
H.... was expected from Dublin. Du Bourg opposed the
consideration of Mr. H....'s name and did all in his power
to have the nomination given to Father Ambrose Maréchal.
He made investigations relative to Father Zocchi's books.
He then informed Bruté that it was almost useless to in-
quire concerning the effects of Bishop Concanen since, according to the bishop's last will, these were to be delivered
to his successor.[12]

In a letter to his brother Augustine of September 2, 1815,
Father Bruté acknowledged the receipt of, and expressed his
gratitude for, Mother Bourgeois' gift to America. He also
announced his early departure.[13] Nevertheless, just the contrary was awaiting him. Jean de LaMennais took advantage of his friend's delay in sailing and wrote him twice
more at Bordeaux. The last letter was mailed from La
Chênaie where he was on retreat, after having completed a
visitation of the diocese. He gave an account of the conditions as he found them, and Father Bruté was gratified
to learn that the good being effected by the dismissal of
Fouche, Talleyrand, and others of similar character partially counterbalanced the evil of religious indifference that had
sprung forth since the return of Bonaparte.[14]

Father Bruté's sojourn in France extended ten weeks
longer than he had planned; yet it terminated safely, and

[12] W. Du Bourg to S. Bruté, CA of A. Notre Dame, Indiana.
[13] Canon Bruté Collection.
[14] *Lettres Inédites de J. M. & F. de LaMennais*, pp. 119–121.

he sailed from Bordeaux on the *Blooming Rose* on October 17, 1815. His friends, on numerous occasions, attempted to dissuade him from leaving France. Apart from his staunch courage in not yielding to their entreaties, he succeeded in persuading three clerics to accompany him on his return to the mission country. While he considered this number small, he was grateful and felt extreme pleasure in being able to make even that small preparation towards the future of Catholicism in the young nation.

More than six months had passed since Father Bruté had left America, and another six weeks would be consumed by his return voyage. During that time many unforeseen events had passed into his life and claimed his attention, yet not to the exclusion of his friends at the Mountain and in St. Joseph's Valley. His request to Father Dubois in parting was for the president of the Mountain to keep a journal, but foreseeing difficulties in the way of its execution, he suggested to Father Dubois to entrust the little journal to Mother Seton. Fragments of the journal have been preserved. They show the simple home-life at the Mountain and in the Valley in early times. Mother's journal contained news about everyone, from the president to the colored servants. She detested flattery, yet in all sincerity she recorded the words of Archbishop Carroll, who said: "How unfortunate Mr. Bruté's going! Will he ever return? I hope so, indeed, and that very soon." Following this entry she added a gentle admonition: "Dear, dear, Archbishop, how tenderly he loves you! take care; you are so well and too much loved by all. I fear for you, would rather you should be in China than too much a *darling* here. It is only because they do not know you, my son,—yet those who know you so well, do they care less."[15]

Apparently Father Duhamel, who assisted Father Dubois in parochial work, had less sympathy than the Archbishop had with Father Bruté's going abroad. At all events his conversation would warrant such conclusion. In speaking

[15] *Bruté—Seton Correspondence*, pp. 280–307. 1884.

of him to Mother Seton he said, "Poor crazy Bruté, if his
neck ain't broke, the Lord help him! But you are very
happy ma'am to have such a gentleman take care of your
son." And on another occasion he remarked to Mother Seton
that "poor Hickey" (Father Hickey) had received a great
compliment this morning when an Irishman told him the
three priests at the Mountain all put together were not
worth one Bruté. Father Duhamel, personally, was very
fond of Father Bruté, yet he thought the congregation acted
foolishly when they said, "Now Bruté's gone, all is gone;"
and some of the parishioners told him they would not go to
confession until Bruté came back. Again he said to Mother
Seton: "Did you see his letter Ma'am *to everybody to save
souls?* Poor crazy Bruté! he says he will be on the high
seas; he would be much better here attending his congregation. He could 'tend ten congregations at least. He can
do what would kill ten men if you only give him bread and
two or three horses to ride to death, one after the other.
Poor gentleman! if he was only steady!"[16] The good old
priest had his fixed opinion and no amount of explanation
could change his view on the subject.

The *Blooming Rose* had weathered the high waves safely
for four weeks and was then sufficiently near its destination
for those on board to consider it a happy passage. Seemingly Father Bruté had spent much of his time in reviewing
to himself the results of his voyage. As for himself, he said,
the voyage was practically ended, and still there remained
sufficient time and distance to suffer shipwreck. He was
somewhat dejected and lonely. It seemed to him that he had
profited scantily by the voyage, yet it had been made in
such disagreeable circumstances. The impressions he received upon his arrival were so deep and sorrowful that
it seemed almost impossible to free himself from this experience of the upheaval. Then, too, his disappointment
had been threefold. At his departure he had envisaged his
native land happy and beginning new life. Instead of this a

[16] *Bruté—Seton Correspondence*, pp. 283–288. 1884.

very sorry contrast was realized when he arrived at Bordeaux. Likewise two of his intimate friends were absent in England. Thirdly on the return voyage high winds deprived the zealous priest of the consolation of celebrating Mass.

Father Bruté then turned his reflections from gloomy France to poor America. He viewed the immensity of the mission field but his courage almost abandoned him when he beheld the small force engaged in this vast harvest. Writing to the Vicar of Saint-Brieuc, he said, there was so much to be commenced, continued, and accomplished, if the spread of Catholicism in the New World was to be a success. He asked the Vicar to speak to his mother at Rennes about his books. They were sorely needed, but for the lack of means to defray their transportation he had been able to bring but very few with him. He feared that it would savor of egoism if he himself approached his mother with these troubles at a time of temporal suffering. He also requested de LaMennais to send several copies of his and his brother's latest work for the seminary, since the greatest poverty suffered in that institution was the insufficiency of literature on theology.

This voyage was called a "happy passage" by the energetic missionary, but from the hardships and deprivations to which he was subjected we of the present day evidently would place it in another category. He had to sleep on a bed equal in hardness to that of a Trappist and twenty times worse in other respects, and spend whole days in a cabin infested with insects, amid noise and smoke. The *Blooming Rose* landed at New York on the evening of November 20, 1815. As Father Bruté came ashore he received distressing news. The Most Reverend John Carroll, who had regretted his going and had offered prayers for his speedy return, now lay dangerously ill. This message was no small grief for the devoted priest. He loved the Archbishop as his venerable benefactor, and it was with an anxious heart that he, with his three companions, hastened to depart on the following day for Baltimore by way of Philadelphia.[17]

Three days later he bade a second farewell to the Mountain and repaired to Baltimore where he entered upon his new office as president of St. Mary's College. The two presidents who had preceded him were both men of extraordinary executive ability. His immediate predecessor possessed, moreover, a merited reputation as a scientist. Despite the fact that St. Mary's College had passed from the guidance of these noble characters, there was no cause for apprehension under the new president. Father Bruté was a scientist and a scholarly theologian, who was gifted with ample executive ability. He was also a gentleman of tact and ability wherever duty placed him. He would have been successful in any walk of life.

Most Reverend John Carroll died on the feast of St. Francis Xavier, December 3, 1815, and Father Bruté was present at the moment of the soul's departure. In a letter written on December 31, 1815, he described to Jean de LaMennais the holy death of the Father of the Church in America. At this hour Bruté looked upon the infant churches as a widowed mother would regard her dependent children. He beheld the development of Catholicism in the States from Carroll's appointment to his death and while great things had been accomplished, yet the churches were only in their infancy. Beholding their numerous needs and their crushing trials, he wept over the orphaned dioceses, but with these tears he mingled deep regrets for the misfortunes of his own unfortunate Fatherland, saying to the Vicar, de LaMennais, "Oh! if the excess of its misfortunes would bring some day one of you to weep with me here." Father Bruté described the obsequies of the Archbishop as having been singularly impressive. The population of Baltimore rendered homage, and deposition of the remains was made in the Sulpician Chapel until after the Cathedral should be

[17] S. Bruté to J. M. de LaMennais 11–12, 1815. Archives–Ploërmel, France.

finished.   He maintained that a like scene had not been witnessed in the United States since the burial of George Washington.[18]

According to Father Bruté's correspondence, St. Mary's
College was more progressive in 1815–1816 than it had been
during the preceding year.   The register numbered more
than forty boarders with a noticeable increase in day scholars.   Over and above discharging the duties connected with
the presidency, he taught Natural Philosophy.   Both the
management of the college and the subjects that he taught
received close attention, while the equal interest taken in
each student proved the president to be a man of interior
spirit.   The office was agreeable to him only in so far as he
beheld it to be the Will of God.   Humanly speaking he did
not relish it, for he wrote the Vicar of Saint-Brieuc to the
effect that he was far more in his element when instructing
the seminarians.   And to Mr. Garnier,   director   of   the
Seminary of St. Sulpice, he wrote:

> I am recalled from Emmitsburg and made president of the college
> at Baltimore.   Everyone considers it a fatal move, but Maréchal
> demands it.   We presented our protestations, but were unable to
> change matters.   However, things must follow their natural course
> since I have been taken away.   I accepted the presidency through
> urgency because Mr. Maréchal refused it.   You may hear of these
> facts without appreciating them, but nevertheless, it is true that M.
> Dubois is overburdened at the Mountain.[19]

However, we are not to deduce from his attitude towards
college work that Father Bruté withdrew from such subjects as did not directly treat of God or religion.   On the
contrary, he had the highest regard for all natural sciences
because they aided him in comprehending more fully the
Creator of all nature.   Apart from this he did experience a
particular vocation for training priests who would go forth

[18] S. Bruté to J. M. de LaMennais, 12–31, 1815.   *Ibid.*
[19] S. Bruté to M. Garnier, 12–17, 1815.   Archives of St. Sulpice.
Paris.

to further the work of the Divine Master in America. One can readily perceive that his was the heart of a missionary. In his correspondence he spoke little of the college or of the office that he held there, while on numerous occasions his letters were filled with ecclesiastical news. At this particular time Jean de LaMennais was informed of the erection of the new diocese of Louisiana, the designation of the episcopal city, and the appointment of the bishop-elect. Father Bruté desiring him to know its exact location drew the Vicar's attention to the map. Then his thoughts rushed on infinitely faster than his pen, and he said: "Ah! look at the entire globe! Soon we shall leave those missions to our successors, but alas! What beginnings shall we leave them?" He realized that it was the period when the most beautiful acts of religion were to be performed and that those acts depended upon the present generation of clergy for their execution.[20]

The president of St. Mary's College soon realized that his life was not to be hidden away in the company of books and executive duties. While the progress of the institution pointed to his practical management of affairs, yet he felt himself out of place in the position and continued in it only in obedience.[21] Aside from this he was deluged by correspondence, and momentous problems beyond the college walls beckoned for his attention. Moreover, he willingly concerned himself with many church affairs that he considered important. It was at this time that he requested Archbishop Neale not to dispense with Doctor Gallagher's expected oration on the late Father of the Church in America. He looked forward to printing the oration and thereby to preserve it to posterity as a ground-work for a future biography.[22] Likewise, at this same period he was deeply concerned about the Mountain and thought it an opportune time

[20] S. Bruté to J. M. de LaMennais, 12–31, 1815. Archives-Ploërmel, France.

[21] S. Bruté to M. Duclaux, 1–22, 1816. Archives of St. Sulpice. Paris.

[22] BCA, Case 12–A⁵.

to give Father Dubois practical counsel regarding some changes. Up to that date all domestic charge of Mount St. Mary's had been supervised by the Sisters of Charity. Concerning this arrangement, Father Bruté wrote:

I feel it is impossible to take care of Emmitsburg without the Sisters, yet perhaps it would be better to sever associations with the nuns as far as domestic charge of the college is concerned. Deliberate and do as you think best, my Brother. I love the Sisters as you do; my heart and heaven is for them, yet we must not be ruled by intrinsic gifts—this system was never used in France. Sectarian views must also be taken into account. However, encourage these genuine, pious, American, nuns.[23]

Shortly after this we find Father Bruté condemning some erroneous writings. During a brief visit to Philadelphia, he met Mr. Carey who presented him with a volume of Shobert's translation of Chauteaubriand's writings. This work was annotated with lengthy false interpretations by a certain Mr. Kett. The scholarly priest lauded the work of Shobert and pronounced it exact and elegant, but confuted the notes of Mr. Kett, pointing out numerous passages that were ridiculously erroneous. He requested Mr. Carey to suppress the notes in the next edition and to issue censures against these notes in the Philadelphia Magazines.[24]

Another test of Father Bruté's wide sympathies was his letter dated March 20, 1816 to C. H. Wharton, the first American apostate priest. Two years previous the zealous priest had written to the unhappy Wharton, but the recipient burned this letter and left no record of its content. Father Bruté reminded Wharton of the fleetingness of life, and the necessity of returning to God from Whom he had departed. Moreover, he upbraided Wharton for his venomous writings against Holy Mother Church and against Fenelon. After several gentle warnings he made a bold and last appeal with the hope of effecting the conversion. Seem-

---

[23] S. Bruté to J. Dubois, 1–25, 1816. Archives of St. Sulpice. Paris.
[24] Records (ACHS), XII (1901), pp. 98–101.

ingly Bruté failed. Wharton became indignant, published
the letter, and declared in reply on April 20, 1816, that the
spirit of Father Bruté's letter illustrated the "intolerance
and persecution which the Church always professed and
frequently realized when possessing civil power." Wharton signed the reply "Presbyter of the Apostolical Protestant Episcopal Church in the United States of America."[25]

Apart from these varied ecclesiastical and collegiate duties Father Bruté always found time to cheer, direct, and
console his friends. A continual correspondence was kept
up with Father Dubois, Mother Seton, and her children,
especially Rebecca, the *Little Sufferer.* On numerous occasions it would be difficult to determine which of the two,
Father Bruté or Mother Seton, held the position of counsellor to the other. While the latter assured her zealous director of the great good effected in her soul by his return to
America, she also addressed to him an abundance of advice
and good counsel. However, let us not be mistaken regarding the nature of their correspondence. It was at all times
the communing of two interior souls on spiritual subjects, in
which the news of transient earthly things received neither
consideration nor mention. It was the sole intention of both
to assist each other on the ascending path of virtue—a desire that is expressed on numerous pages of their writings.
Father Bruté considered it a duty to write to little Rebecca
Seton, and he always addressed her in terms of fraternal
endearment. He delighted to lavish upon her the same
tenderness that he would have bestowed on his own sister.
Rebecca reciprocated this affection to the utmost of her
ability by praying for her spiritual brother and by writing
him little notes as frequently as her suffering condition
would allow. In response to one of her letters he wrote:
"I thank you for your dear little note. I have pasted it
on the last page of my Bible." One may readily perceive
the joy these lines imparted to the dear child's heart. The

[25] C. H. Wharton, *A Concise View of the Principal Points of Controversy between the Protestant and Roman Churches*, pp. iv.–v. New
York, 1817.

learned priest knew the magic of simplicity and the art of making himself "all to all." At another time he wrote her: "I took you in my heart at Holy Communion and offered you to our Lord as completely as I could." Again he penned the holy names of Jesus, Mary, and Joseph, saying that he knew she would enjoy them more than roses or lilies. Rebecca profited richly by all these consoling messages and she proved a model of patience to all who saw her. During her intense suffering she begged her mother to keep Father Bruté's picture opposite her eyes at the foot of the bed.[26]

Owing to the scanty material relative to St. Mary's College, it is impossible to glean much information on its proceedings during the period of Father Bruté's presidency. Judging from his correspondence with St. Sulpice and from the commencement exercises we are justified in stating that it was successful under his administration. At that early period there were few attractions and amusements to allure the students beyond the campus borders; moreover, the college was located in the suburbs of Baltimore, and, owing to the long class hours which extended to six o'clock in the evening, pupils from the city were boarders. The students rose at five-thirty o'clock, recited morning prayers in common, and attended Mass in a body at six o'clock. At the close of divine services they repaired to the study hall where they devoted an hour and a half to study. This was succeeded by a brief intermission, followed by breakfast at quarter past eight o'clock. The mid-day repast was served at half past one o'clock and was preceded by thirty-minutes recreation. In those days the classes assembled at the beginning of September and continued until after the middle of July, leaving to the summer vacation an interim of only six weeks.

In the simple days of that period the commencement programs differed vastly from those now in vogue, especially where they have been reduced to the conferring of degrees

[26] R. Seton, op. cit., II, pp. 216–232; *Bruté—Seton Correspondence*, pp. 244–245. 1884.

and honors. The commencement exercises in 1816 opened
on July 16 and continued throughout two days. The morning of the first day was devoted to an exhibition of experi-
ments in Natural Philosophy. A demonstration of fire-
works produced from inflammable gases proved a brilliant
success which gave evidence of the skill of both the master
and students. One small balloon of hydrogen gas was
launched and soon disappeared, taking its course to the
north while another of larger size took fire. The afternoon
was passed in entertaining the assembled visitors by delivering orations on the following academic subjects: "The
Advantage of Natural Philosophy," "The Fine Arts," "Eloquence," "Chivalry," and "Astronomy." On the following
afternoon two dialogues were spoken: "Moderation in our
Pursuits," "Inconvenience of a Spirit of Mockery." The degree of bachelor of arts was conferred upon five candidates,
while an equal number received the M. A. degrees. Upon
this same occasion the premiums were distributed by a
member of one of the most prominent families of Baltimore,
namely, Colonel Howard, the hero of the battle of Cowpens
in the Revolutionary War.[27]

At the close of these exercises which terminated the scholastic year for 1816 Father Bruté walked to Emmitsburg to
visit the Mountain and the Valley. However, vacations
meant no relaxation for a man of Bruté's caliber. He neither wished nor accepted time for idling, because in his
estimation there were too many problems more essential
than vacations. Consequently such visits were short. According to a letter written by Mother Seton to her son at
Leghorn, Father Bruté visited at St. Joseph's Convent in
the Valley on July 22, and from the statement of Reverend
Felix de Andreis, we learn that the president of the college
was the only clergyman at home at St. Mary's on July 26,
1816.

[27] C. G. Herbermann, *The Sulpicians in the United States*, pp. 109–
123.

Father Bruté's dominant interest rested not in the presidency of the college or in any other worldly concern, but in the one act sacred to him above all others—namely, the laying of the foundation, broad and deep, for Catholicism in America. Therefore this day, July 26, was to him a record day. Unknown to the Sulpician Fathers at Baltimore, a band of thirteen missionaries of the Congregation of the Missions, with Father Felix de Andreis as their Superior, arrived at Baltimore and were searching for St. Mary's College, to which they had been directed by Bishop Du Bourg who had procured this foundation for his Louisiana diocese. These strangers were favorably impressed by the magnificent view of the harbor and the location of the city, nevertheless, they were tired and hungry after the voyage, and the abode they sought was situated outside the city at the very opposite end from the place where they had landed. After a tiresome tramp, they reached St. Mary's and were received by Father Bruté, whom Father Felix de Andreis described as "the most holy, learned, humble, and affable man" that he ever knew. The maternal-hearted Bruté welcomed the missionaries with the utmost cordiality. The other Fathers had gone to the country for a brief vacation, leaving the president alone at the college; nevertheless, Father Bruté cared for all their wants. He hastened to procure lodgings and to provide his guests with every comfort. Their baggage received immediate attention, as well as the payment of duties thereon. He was very considerate of these men; not only during their stay at Baltimore, but ever afterwards he ceased not to lavish fraternal kindness upon them. Owing to his thoughfulness, a generous collection was made in Baltimore for them, while he himself supplied from his own meagre income all that was needed for their individual comfort.[28] This overflowing charity of his heart caused him to be misunderstood by his confrères and his zeal brought humiliations and accusations of which he was not

[28] *Sketches of the Life of Felix de Andreis*, pp. 80–90. Pub. by Kelly, Hedian & Piet. Baltimore, 1861.

deserving.   Father Bruté considered all those early missionaries to be saints.   He cared for them because it was
necessary and served them the best he could without permitting those services to encroach upon his other duties.   However, his actions were wrongly interpreted, and he was un-
deservingly punished.   He was accused to his Superior in
France of having disturbed the order of the house by housing guests in quarters that were intended for students and
of spending his valuable time entertaining them, thereby
neglecting his assigned duties.   These accusations, however, were not formulated with sufficient cleverness to prevent them from bearing the stamp of falsehood.   It was
July when Father Felix de Andreis and companions arrived at Baltimore.   They remained but six weeks.   At this
time the students were away on vacation; hence their
quarters were vacant.[29]

Father Bruté always shared with others not only the
material things of life but also the events that gave him
pleasure.   Thus he hastened to impart the news of the arrival of Father de Andreis and companions to Bishops
Cheverus, Flaget, Father Dubois, Mother Seton, and Doctor
Augustine Bruté of Rennes,[30] each of whom thanked him
for the thoughtful message.   The Bishop of Boston said: "A
thousand thanks for your amiable and interesting letter.
The arrival of the holy missionaries for Louisiana is an
event of very great importance.   I think that it is there and
in Kentucky that we can have well founded hopes."[31]   In a
note addressed to Mother Seton on September 10, 1816, he
announced the missionaries' departure from Baltimore for
the Louisiana country, saying that Fathers Vespre, Cooper,
Xaupi, and he, just returned from the gate at ten minutes
past three o'clock p. m., after seeing their guests safely depart in a stage for Pittsburg.   He expected and predicted

---

[29] S. Bruté to M. Duclaux, 4–28, 1817.   Archives of St. Sulpice.
Paris.

[30] S. Bruté to A. Bruté, 8–28, 1816.   Canon Bruté de Rémur Collection.

[31] J. Cheverus to S. Bruté, 10–9, 1816.   CA of A.

FATHER BRUTÉ'S PEN SKETCH OF FATHER NAGOT, S. S.

that promising results would rise from this new foundation, owing to the fact that their superior was singularly virtuous.[32] The names of those who accompanied Father de Andreis may be considered interesting, not from the viewpoint of their immediate value but from the rôle they played in the Church and from further associations with Father Bruté. Therefore, according to rank, they were Father F. de Andreis, superior, Reverends Rosati and Acquaroni, both priests of the Congregation of the Mission, Reverends Carretti and Ferrari, secular clergymen from the city of Port Maurice on the Genoa river, the former being Canon of the collegiate church; Messrs. F. X. Dahmen, Jos. Tichitoli, Leo Deys, and Casto Gonzales, seminarians, Brother Martin Blanka, C. M., and three young laymen, Francis Moranviller, Medard di Latre, and John Flegifont, who had some intention of entering the Congregation as lay brothers.[33]

Another individual who shared in Father Bruté's zeal during the vacation of 1816 was Mrs. Post, a sister to Mother Seton. On August 6 he addressed to this lady, an Episcopalian, a lengthy letter with the hope of effecting her conversion to the Catholic Church. This discourse was too apologetical for an ordinary mind to comprehend and as a result the attempt was a failure. He who from infancy had been reared in the faith knew not from personal experience the trammels of ignorance and indifference and therefore failed in the method applied to overcome them. He did not realize how impossible it was for a Protestant to comprehend the Catholic interpretation of truths, how necessary it is to lead such souls step by step and to dissipate the darkness little by little.[34]

A favor of October 15, 1816, proved Father Bruté's continued interest in behalf of the Louisiana missionaries and

[32] *Bruté—Seton Correspondence*, pp. 102–105. 1886.

[33] *Life of the Very Reverend Felix de Andreis*, p. 91. Pub. by B. Herder. St. Louis, 1900; S. Bruté to F. de Andreis, 10–15, 1816. St. LCA. St. Louis, Mo.

[34] S. Bruté to Mrs. Post, 8–6, 1816. Archives of St. Joseph's Convent. Emmitsburg.

announced to Father de Andreis that he was forwarding to him one hundred and seventy dollars. This amount had been donated by three friends of Bruté, namely, Mr. Carroll, who contributed one hundred dollars; Father Grassi, S. J., who added a collection amounting to thirty dollars; and Mr. Tuite on the eastern coast who gave the remaining sum of forty dollars. Bishop Flaget of Bardstown exercised a like charitable spirit towards those needy missionaries. He housed them for six months and was happy to assist them in this manner, although Kentucky was far poorer than Baltimore. In a letter Bishop Flaget informed Father Bruté that he, too, was collecting in Upper Louisiana for Father de Andreis and companions.[35]

If Father Bruté was solicitous about the welfare of others and availed himself of every opportunity to assuage their wants, he in turn was not neglected by his devoted Jean de LaMennais. During that same year he shipped a goodly number of desired books to his friend in America. Likewise, he imparted the agreeable news of Félicité's ordination to the priesthood, an event that Bruté had long desired to see.[36] Books had such an attraction for the scholarly priest that his eye caught every announcement of new publications as well as the discoveries of antique manuscripts. At this same time he wrote Wm. Seton at Leghorn requesting him to influence the Messrs. Filicchi to procure and send to him a copy of the newly discovered manuscripts of classics. These antique volumes contained works of Fronto and Symmachus besides numerous unpublished letters of Sallust, Ennius, Plautus, Cato, Pliny, Antoninus Pius, Marcus Aurelius, Verus, and the historian, Appian. Father Bruté maintained that it would be an honor for St. Mary's College to be the first in America to possess these literary treasures.[37]

[35] S. Bruté to M. Duclaux, 4–28, 1817. Archives of St. Sulpice. Paris; S. Bruté to F. de Andreis, St. LCA.
[36] *Lettres Inédites de J. M. & F. de LaMennais*, pp. 125–130.
[37] S. Bruté to W. Seton, 10–7, 1816. Original in CA of A.

Father Dubois again cast academic cares aside for a few moments and wrote to Father Bruté on November 4, 1816. This message, however, differed from previous ones and was framed in a tone of sadness. It related the circumstances of Rebecca Seton's beautiful death, praised especially her heroic courage and lively faith, but left the details to be supplied by the good Mother herself. The Father Superior of the Sisterhood was careful to add the most important feature when he requested that each of his confrères at St. Mary's, Baltimore, offer the Holy Sacrifice for the departed soul. Father Bruté had expected this message for several months, and in the meantime, he had utilized every opportunity to prepare his spiritual sister for her departure; yet the news touched him keenly for the moment and his affectionate heart was moved to tears. Despite this, he hastened to console the good Mother and to urge her to the practice of greater calm, love, abandonment, and even to thanksgiving for the wonderful graces granted by Providence to her little daughter.[38]

Father Bruté had intended to enter upon a literary career in 1814, but the year following he visited France and gave his plans, together with his voluminous notes to Jean de La-Mennais, saying that he had abandoned the idea. This met with a sharp rebuke from the Vicar who accused him of being a genius at commencing things but not worth while in continuing or seeing his projects completed. In 1817 Father Félicité suggested that their friend now enter the literary field and write the history of the Catholic Church in America. He realized the practical need of this story of Catholicism in the New World and knew that the nations would welcome such a work because of its unique character. Father Bruté was impressed by this suggestion, yet it was impossible to devote himself to the task at that particular period.[39] His time was occupied with too many academic duties, too many bishops and confrères to keep in touch

[38] *Bruté—Seton Correspondence*, pp. 112–116.   1886.
[39] *Lettres Inédites de J. M. & F. de LaMennais*, pp. 130–133.

with, too many friends to counsel, and too many erring souls
to admonish, to allow him to take up writing beyond correspondence.   Several important messages were dispatched
to Father Dubois and to Mother Seton, announcing the arrival of Bishop Cheverus who would administer Confirmation at the Sisterhood and confer tonsure at the Mountain.
He requested them to be solicitous regarding the bishop's
health because he was suffering from a cold.[40]   Then to
Bishop Flaget and Father David, the college president hastened to send an account of the death of Father Thayer who
died like a saint at Limerick, Ireland.   This clergyman
formerly had belonged to the Boston diocese, and, owing to
the reasons of his departure for Europe, Father Bruté well
knew that his confrères at Bardstown would welcome a detailed account of the closing days of this clergyman's
career.[41]   Shortly after this Father Bruté furnished Tessier, Superior of St. Mary's, Baltimore, with an account of
the college for the past years.   Then to his superior in
France, he sent an account of his labors, which testified
that the college was progressing satisfactorily.   The attendance was ever on the increase, better discipline existed
everywhere and many favorable reports had been written
about the institution by dignitaries in the various dioceses.[42]
A continuous exchange of letters was carried on with Bishop Cheverus, who acquainted Bruté with many interesting
Church affairs.[43]   Then to Matthew Carey he sent a letter
of practical admonitions, encouraging this author and pub-
lisher to return to his Christian duty and to refrain from
his present conduct by which he was bringing detriment to
the Church.[44]   On the eve of St. Martin, Father Bruté addressed to M. Garnier at St. Sulpice another letter, re-
sembling a chronicle, which announced the safe arrival of

[40] *Bruté—Seton Correspondence*, pp. 116–122. 1886.
[41] S. Bruté to B. J. Flaget, 12–6, 1816. Original in CA of A.
[42] S. Brute to M. Garnier, 2–3, 1817; S. Brute to M. Duclaux, 4–28,
1817; Originals in Archives of St. Sulpice. Paris.
[43] J. Cheverus to S. Bruté, March 24, June 24, Aug. 21, 1817. Canon
Bruté Collection.
[44] *Records* (ACHS), XII (1901), p. 101.

M. Damphoux and companions who joined their confréres at St. Mary's Seminary. Likewise on the same day, November 10, the Bulls arrived for Father Maréchal who was forced to accept and who immediately became Archbishop of Baltimore. Another item of interest was the departure of Bishop Du Bourg on St. Charles day, by way of Pittsburg to Bardstown and thence to New Orleans, where he had recently lost, by death, three of his missionaries.[45] Gleaning from Father Bruté's correspondence with the de LaMennais brothers[46] and with Bishop Du Bourg, we discover that the latter arrived with his companions early in September and stopped with the Sulpicians at Baltimore until November 10, when they departed for St. Louis via Pittsburg and Bardstown. On November 13, the bishop wrote Bruté and described the perilous journey from Baltimore to Pittsburg, advising that no one attempt this journey by stage before the completion of the turnpike—an improvement that would require three or four years more. Bishop Du Bourg had experienced many hardships enroute to his bishopric. The stage coach "capsized" three times, their baggage was scattered along the way, and they were forced to travel a great part of the distance on foot.[47] However, in a letter to de LaMennais, Bruté described Bishop Du Bourg as travelling "in high spirits to his vast mission and more vast harvest."

The true missionary spirit of Bruté is fully displayed in a letter written to de LaMennais at the close of the year 1817. It reveals his heart riveted to that one sacred act, the founding of the Church in America. He centered his plans on no particular edifice or single diocese because his heart was all embracing and nothing less than the whole nation could satisfy this evangelizer; nevertheless, he realized that this work must be accomplished little by little. Constantly he planned and looked forth to the future, seldom, if ever,

[45] S. Bruté to M. Garnier, 11–10, 1817. Archives of St. Sulpice. Paris.

[46] S. Bruté to J. M. & F. de LaMennais, 9–24, 1817. Archives—Ploërmel, France.

[47] W. Du Bourg to S. Bruté, Original in CA of A.

living or thinking in terms of the present. The numerous population of coming generations ever stood before him, and his one sacred aim was to make their eternity secure by firmly establishing Catholicism in the hearts of the sparse population in order that the Kingdom of Christ might flourish in the generations to follow. Evidently Father Bruté was a full century in advance of his day. It is no exaggeration to say that no other clergyman in America at that period—no matter what his ideals or his influence—can in truth and justice be ranked above the prudent, thoughtful, and spiritual Bruté. Many of his confrères were heard more frequently and appeared in broader circles; but their issues and their interests fade and wane, when placed beside the "Silent Power"—the simple, unassuming Father Bruté.[48]

A further proof of his unswerving zeal to establish Catholicism throughout America is revealed in one of his compositions called the "Beads for the Missions." This rosary consisted of six decades introduced by three acts. The intentions for the decades were well chosen and distributed; hence the chaplet embraced petitions for all the needs of the infant churches. In order to preserve, unchanged, the beauty of his thoughts we insert here the original form of the

BEADS FOR THE MISSIONS

1. Invocation to the Holy Spirit and call for His unspeakable cries in our hearts.

2. Profession of faith as the groundwork.

3. The three Hail Marys to obtain the participation in the three main virtues of Faith, Hope, and Love as they were so exalted in the heart of Mary and that the spirit of them might spread over the land.

[48] Cf. S. Bruté to J. M. & F. de LaMennais, 9-24, 1817. Archives—Ploërmel, France.

1st. Decade

in behalf of the bishops as the representatives of our Lord and His Church and the head fountain of all the good graces to flow over our particular Church here in America.

2nd. Decade

the seminaries as the source of all the clerical graces and apostolic spirit to form the men of God and the Church in the various employs of the spiritual kingdom as pastors, doctors, etc.

3rd. Decade

all the priests over the land that Our Lord may grant them the grace to sanctify themselves first, so as to sanctify others—and support them through all difficulties, dangers, and tribulations of soul and body.

4th. Decade

all the nunneries and religious associations so eminently useful by their services, prayer the most fervent for the clergy, instruction of the ignorant, fairest example of the most beautiful things of Christian perfection, the angels of the militant church.

5th. Decade

all the faithful in their various conditions, particularly the heads of families on whom depend the rising generations of the elect— and also the young people who are that very blessed hope.

6th. Decade

the poor sinners to be rescued and the poor heretics to be enlightened so dear to Mary the great Refuge of all sinners and enemy of the heresies against the Kingdom of Her Son.

De Profundis

for the departed of this country that at last admitted from Purgatory to Heaven they may raise their best cry for the militant church.

Sub tuum praesidium
all earnestly recommended to Mary.[49]

[49] Original in Archives of St. Joseph's Convent. Emmitsburg.

The burden of the college continued to weigh more heavily upon its president, yet he did not shirk the most insignificant duty. In the bitter cold month of January of 1818 we behold him enroute to Annapolis for the purpose of procuring a favor for the college. Authorities had decided to pass a road through the college premises within two hundred feet of the door, but, owing to Father Bruté's wisdom and skill, the early plans relative to the turnpike were not carried out. While material favors were the sole purpose of the two trips to Annapolis, he failed not to avail himself of the opportunity to seek and to find the sheep strayed from the fold. During the five days spent in that city he gave thirty Holy Communions and administered the sacrament of Baptism three times.

Father Bruté's health was never robust, but under this continuous strain he was gradually declining and felt that a change must soon be made. While he was considering the best measures to adopt, another event occurred at the Mountain that hastened the change to realization. The Reverend Chas. Duhamel, who had assisted Father Dubois in parochial work at the village, died on February 6, 1818. The sympathy of St. Mary's president for Father Dubois who held a like responsibility at the Mountain, severed the last link that bound Father Bruté to Baltimore.[50]

[50] *Bruté—Seton Correspondence*, pp. 145–146. 1886; C. G. Herbermann, *op. cit.*, pp. 267–276; M. Meline,—E. McSweeny, *op cit.*, I, p. 74.

CHAPTER VII

AT THE MOUNTAIN AGAIN
1818–1824

Mount St. Mary's had suffered financially as well as from an inadequate faculty since the date of its establishment and its president was careworn. A gracious and tactful compeer had been granted him during the years 1812 to 1815 but early in the latter year this colleague was recalled to fill an important office in the parent foundation at Baltimore. As president and professor Father Bruté gave loyal service to St. Mary's College, Baltimore, from December 1815 until the month of February 1818, when Father Dubois suffered the loss of his assistant.[1] All the parochial duties then devolved upon the already over-burdened president; yet despite this weight of care he was soon to realize his ardent desire. He and Father Bruté had always been very devoted to one another and at last he succeeded in influencing his confrère to resign the presidency at Baltimore and return to take up permanent residence at Mount St. Mary's. Both the Mountain and the Valley were delighted over this change and Bruté, himself, believed that in deciding thus he was doing the Will of God. He felt that there was a good to be accomplished by him at the Mountain. However, his confrères at Baltimore who were not of the same opinion objected to his resignation,[2] although unsuccessfully.

The original purpose of Mt. St. Mary's was to prepare young men for the study of theology and the students who gave evidence of a true vocation were transferred to St. Mary's Seminary at Baltimore as soon as their preparatory studies were completed. From year to year Father Dubois supplied a considerable number of clerical candidates, most

---

[1] M. Meline,—E. McSweeny, *The Story of the Mountain*, I, p. 74.

[2] C. I. White, *Life of Mrs. E. A. Seton*, pp. 480–1; Bruté Journal, Original in Canon Bruté de Rémur Collection. Rennes, France.

of whom later entered the priesthood. In all probability the greater number of them would never have been admitted to this worthy vocation but for the Mountain institution. Nevertheless, the prospects of this establishment were at times so disheartening that even the energetic Father Dubois would probably have forsaken the great cause and returned to the ordinary labors of the mission had it not been for the consolation and support derived from the friendship and cooperation of him who was justly styled the "Angel Guardian" of the Mountain.[3]

Soon after this change was effected at the Mountain classes in philosophy and theology were opened. This made the college a school of divinity in addition to that of philosophy and the humanities, thus giving its present form and its present purpose. The new department was placed under the immediate direction of Father Bruté, who fully understood the responsibility that rested upon him. He was an intensely spiritual character who kept his thoughts and conversation in heaven and, therefore, was capable of teaching all the sacerdotal virtues by exemplifying them in his own life. When he resumed connections with Mount St. Mary's in 1818 the Baltimore foundation was seriously considering measures for the suppression of the Mountain. Contrary to the designs of Fathers Dubois and Bruté, their confrères had planned to reduce the institution to the grade of an ordinary school.[4]

During these trying days that engendered new difficulties and trials for the clergy at Mount St. Mary's Father Bruté again seemed to be the soul and inspiration of the institution. Because of his staunch, firm character it was useless for any one to try to prevail upon him once he had decided as to the better action. When the commissioners arrived from the Baltimore house for the purpose of suppressing the struggling institution Father Bruté, in opposition to his

[3] *United States Catholic Historical Magazine,* "Mt. St. Mary's," V (1846), p. 36.

[4] M. Meline,—E. McSweeny, *op cit.,* I, p. 76.

confrères at Baltimore, maintained that the Moutain Seminary should be continued. This struggle between the two foundations for the accomplishment of their opposing designs became more determined and seems to have left its traces on the close of the scholastic year. That no record of a commencement or a list of the graduates for 1818 is extant, seems to indicate that the closing exercises were dispensed with in that particular year. An old record containing the grades and interesting notes on the final examinations discloses to us that, despite the unsettled conditions, there were distinguished students in attendance until the close of the school.

On July 18, 1818, Father Dubois sent his colleague to entreat the Sulpicians at Baltimore not to suppress the Mountain. After a candid discussion in which each party felt justified in not acceding to the requests of the other, Father Bruté was given no hope of being allowed to continue the Moutain Seminary. He was sorely distressed at the verdict of his confrères and, before leaving Baltimore, appealed to Archbishop Maréchal in a very suppliant letter. He besought the Archbishop to use his paternal influence to protect the Mountain institution from destruction, maintaining that a suppression would, in various ways, be detrimental to the diocese. A goodly number of the students at Mt. St. Mary's came from homes that possessed little wealth and if the Mountain were forced to close it would be impossible for such parents to send their children elsewhere. Father Bruté's keen foresight caused him to visiualize the future and to comprehend all the detrimental consequences of such an imprudent action. He beheld as coming forth from the seminary many worthy priests well qualified to further the work of the Divine Master. To crush this institution in the bud would mean to rob the Church of faithful ministers and to deprive souls of fervent leaders. The zealous priest was likewise solicitous for the young Community in St. Joseph's Valley, and he told the Archbishop that suppression of the Mountain would bring both spiritual and temporal suffering to the Sisterhood. Having finished the letter to His Grace,

he again set out for the Mountain. His heart was ill at ease
owing to the fact that his confrères at Baltimore failed to
comprehend the value of the Mountain Seminary to the future diocese and to the future Church. He regretted that
their present views differed in regard to the institution. A
sigh was frequently sent heavenward accompanied by the
touching ejaculation: "O spare me, spare my friends, O
Lord,—O my Lord, if we did wrong," yet he was at peace
with all and he was fully convinced that all within his power
had been done to preserve the institution for the needs of
the growing Church.[5]

Archbishop Maréchal at once proceeded to consider the
cause and at his earliest convenience held an interview with
Father Tessier, Superior of St. Mary's Baltimore. In a letter, dated June 27, His Grace informed Father Dubois that
the seminary was to continue; however, sufficient security
should be given to relieve the Baltimore establishment of
Mount St. Mary's debts. Further negotiations to settle the
affair were to be taken up with St. Sulpice in Paris by the
Archbishop. On the same day Father Babade at Baltimore
wrote his confrères at the Mountain. The contents of these
letters were wholly contradictory to that of the Archbishop.
The contrast was so vast that Father Dubois impossed on
his colleague the task of answering for both of them. The
latter in his usual, gentle, yet frank manner, responded as
kindly as circumstances could allow. He again besought
his confrères to change their present attitude towards the
situation because this open war between the two institutions
was giving scandal to the laity. Father Bruté realized that
great good was being accomplished at both places and
pleaded for the preservation of a tender union between
them. In his estimation moments were too precious to be
frittered away—much less, squandered in useless disputes.
However, the closing lines of his letter testify that it was
far from this charitable heart ever to judge the intentions
of others. "The intentions doubtlessly are very good—they

---

[5] *Bruté—Seton Correspondence*, pp. 149–150. 1886.

will go with each one of us to our Eternity, but how much evil is done, and will be done in this world, with good intentions."[6] At this moment of trial many hearts were in sympathy with the Mountain, and many friends wrote consolingly to those struggling beneath the burden. From the far southland diocese Father Bruté received a message saying: "I have heard strange accounts about our dear foster-child, the Mountain. This must be particularly distressing to you and our friend Father Dubois. I partake in all your feelings on this occasion and I hope that our Divine Lord will direct everything for His greater glory."[7]

These petty contentions, although disagreeable, happily failed to engender strife and, without many noticeable changes, everything progressed as formerly. Towards the close of the month of June[8] Father Bruté succeeded to the charge of pastor at the village church, an office which he held alternately at Emmitsburg and at the Mountain.[9] Two months later, in August, he accepted the chaplaincy of the Community in St. Joseph's Valley.[10] Second to the inspiring mission of educating and moulding the young clergy was that of spiritual director and confessor to Mother Seton and her religious daughters. She had always esteemed him as a zealous director and even during his sojourn at Baltimore she had kept a constant correspondence with him on spiritual subjects. Immediately upon this assignment he addressed Mother Seton in the following lines:

My dear Mother:

In this new beginning it seems as we altogether want to renew our best confidence in Our Lord Himself, for how can I hope to be His blessed instrument but through His adorable Will and most tender mercies to souls so entirely offered to Him in the ways of His most perfect service on earth. Indeed, let it be all confidence,

[6] S. Bruté to M. Babade, BCA, Case 13–P[8].

[7] W. Du Bourg to S. Bruté, 7–4, 1818, Original in CA of A. Notre Dame, Ind.

[8] Bruté—Seton Correspondence, p. 309. 1886.

[9] Bruté Journal, Georgetown University Archives. Fol. 92, 6.

[10] Bruté—Seton Correspondence, p. 82. 1884.

all pure faith and love, and we may be sure that His grace will be confirmed in every heart, even by the most unworthy and unfit instrument. *Humility, Simplicity, Charity.* How well these blessed names of the three virtues marked out by St. Vincent will carry us through. Indeed it is my most sacred duty to try to assist your dear family, and yourself, Mother. My heart and my eyes, I might say, at this very moment fill at the thought, as it will appear to me when my Lord, and your Sovereign Creator, and most tender Saviour, will, at my death ask me what I did *feel*, and still more what I did fulfill of such a charge. Holy confidence in *Him*, is all on both sides, poor man nothing. Ah, so well do I feel it for me,— but, I am glad to feel so, and wish to feel more so, that truly Our Lord be all in all!"[11]

As a director Father Bruté was ever constant in his endeavors to lead to higher perfection the souls entrusted to his care. His unswerving fidelity to the charge was supported by humility, gentleness, and vigilance. On all occasions his chief principle was to advance souls as gently as possible and the devoted priest prayed God daily to uphold him and not permit him ever to become a "diminution of grace" to those souls entrusted to his guidance. He desired the religious to perform all duties in the spirit of preparation for *Eternity;* yet he wished that this necessary preparation be peaceful, loving, patient, and silent. He likewise maintained that no particular preparation was ever necessary for religious who assisted daily at the Holy Sacrifice and frequented the sacraments. One of the qualities of Father Bruté's direction was his apostolic fervor. At the close of his frequent notes to Mother Seton he invariably recommended the Church in America to the prayers of the Community. On one occasion he closed with the words: "Pray, pray, pray continually for the Church, especially for America, and for this diocese—*Our prayers and our work for ages to come, and soon for our account."*

Thousands of souls have been inspired and consoled by the words of a native of Normandy, whose birth, life, death,

[11] *Ibid.,* pp. 149–150. 1886.

and canonization have occurred since Bishop Bruté answered the last call. But, we may ask, wherein did her principles differ from those of Father Simon Bruté de Rémur? When Saint Thérèse of the Child Jesus said, "I will spend my heaven in doing good upon earth," her words were but an echo of the sentiments voiced eighty years previous by the devout Father Bruté in the foregoing note to Mother Seton. "Pray, pray—*Our prayers and our work for ages to come* ..."[12]

Since the Archbishop's letter had stated that all things were to be continued unchanged, the Mountain institution resumed classes on the usual date early in September. Permission to teach theology for a definite time had been given by His Grace. Mr. J. Anduze was the first student allowed to pursue the course during two years It was obligatory to take the third and last year at Baltimore. Archbishop Maréchal visited Mt. St. Mary's during the second week in December, 1818 and conferred tonsure on five seminarians.[13] During this scholastic year, 1818—1819, the school increased in student body, character, and efficiency. The register contained the names of many brilliant students who later became shining lights in the Church. Among them we find the name of John McCaffrey, whom Providence preserved to the establishment sixty-two years. We find Father Bruté busily engaged at the close of this particular academic year in writing to Archbishop Maréchal to recommend J. Anduze for a continuation of the study of theology.[14]

The vacation offered the vice president more time for visiting and observing his congregation. A note headed "A Day of the Missions at Emmitsburg" gives us an insight into how these days were spent. On the feast of St. Ignatius, Father Bruté left the Mountain at a quarter to five o'clock in the morning and returned home at five-thirty

[12] *Bruté—Seton Correspondence*, pp. 162–165. 1886.
[13] S. Bruté to G. Carron, 12–19, 1818. Canon Bruté de Rémur Collection.
[14] BCA, Case 13–P[10]. 6–23, 1819.

o'clock in the evening. Within this time he travelled thirty miles and conversed with sixty-two persons on matters relative to their religious duties. Some were reminded of their Easter duty; several were spoken to for circulating evil reports; while still others were warned not to attend a camp-meeting that was scheduled for the following week.[15]

Notwithstanding the great and visible good that he was accomplishing in the capacity of pastor, professor, and chaplain, he was frequently assailed by a spirit of restlessness. At one time he was wholly absorbed with plans for the future of the Mountain and Valley, at another he was planning to go far away to the mission-field of China. At times this affliction tended to make him pensive, morose, and even distrustful of friends. From Mother Seton's correspondence it is evident that these feelings were manifested once in his notes to her. In this hour of trial God directed Mother Seton to advise him, and the note that she wrote to him on this occasion is admirable for its prudent and frank content. No description could portray a more vivid picture of both characters.

> Your restless thoughts strike me to the soul. You make the lesson of *the grace of the moment* so very plain to me I owe you perhaps my very salvation by the faults and sins it has saved me from, yet physician you will not heal yourself. You surely would not leave your brother (Father Dubois) *now*, and if our God does indeed graciously destine you for China, will He not, seeing the overflowing of your boiling heart for it, open an evident door....
>
> All is a true mystery to me in your disposition. Much greater mystery than any of Faith. A man of your particular graces, not given drop by drop, as to other souls, but poured over your head in a daily torrent. Yet I seldom see you but in such wild enthusiasms of your own particular impressions of the moment, that you can see nothing, hear nothing but that one object; or else quite *reserved, hurt, and anxious* because you have not been consulted in things *which spoke for themselves*, or others, which we would not

[15] M. Meline,—E. McSweeny, op. cit., I. p. 84; J. R. Bayley, *Memoirs of the Rt. Rev. S. W. G. Bruté de Rémur*, p. 50.

dare to take your advice about, without knowing the Superior's will—or others again, which like the poor German smiths go over in blind ignorance, and I never even guess I have not done well until some one points it out.

You speak as if your Mother's confidence is deficient, but it is surely not at this time I am to open your eyes on my situation in this Community.

As to private concerns, I have none, unless it be my trials occasionally at the conduct of different sisters, and that you have forbid me speaking of, and since you think it proper, and I am acquitted before God, I am too happy it is so.

For the *rest*, as to confidence, devoted love, and happy heart, our dear Saviour is witness that no soul could be more blessed than mine with regard to you,—too much for the few days of my life.

If you could *feel* as I do, the *union* of Betsy, Joanna, and Margaret with me in the management *since you are here*, you would bless God, as I do, *in peace*, instead of your restless desires.[16]

In the month of September 1830, a new affliction befell the Community in St. Joseph's Valley. Mother Seton was suffering from a severe affection of the lungs which threatened to rob her of life. On the feast of "Our Lady of Mercy" her spiritual daughters believed her to be dying and two sisters rushed to the village church to call Father Bruté. He arrived shortly and, finding the patient's condition serious, he administered to her the consolations of religion. Mother Seton was extremely weak yet the good priest perceived that she was not so near the passage to Eternity as her daughters thought her to be. Consequently, he returned to his parochial duties at the village.[17]

Father Bruté's life continued to be one of restless activity filled with parochial and academic duties to which was added a wide-spread correspondence. Bishop Cheverus appealed to him for favors.[18] Bishop Du Bourg entrusted to his "Little Brother" important affairs in behalf of his

[16] *Bruté—Seton Correspondence*, pp. 261–4. 1884.
[17] *Ibid.*, pp. 3–20.
[18] Original in CA of A. 1–5, 1820. (not catalogued.)

diocese,[19] while laymen, living at a distance, wrote the devoted priest to visit sick members of their family.[20] Over and above responding to these entreaties, there were many other problems that required him to write frequently. His unrivaled missionary spirit prompted him to write to St. Sulpice, beseeching Father Duclaux to send men and books to assist the Mountain.[21] To Abbé Carron he introduced, by letter M. Chabrat who was returning to France for a brief sojourn.[22] Then turning his attention to the one sacred aim of his life, he wrote His Grace concerning the genial spirit that existed among the bishops in 1810. These founders of the pioneer dioceses were of one heart and one soul and Father Bruté urged that this spirit should be fostered and continued.[23]

Another duty that received Father Bruté's punctilious care at this time, was that of watching the ebbing life of Mother Seton. She grew weaker day by day and to the great sorrow of her spiritual daughters and friends it became evident that her days were few. She, too, felt convinced of her approaching death and under the watchful eye of her director she continued her preparation for it. On the morning of January 3, he heard her last confession. Mother Seton died on the following morning, January 4, 1821.[24]

Scarcely had the mortal remains of Mother Seton been consigned to the earth when Father Bruté bade the Sisters at St. Joseph's collect and deposit in a safe place the writings of their venerable foundress. Here again, as on numerous other occasions, the prudent director visualized the future when he addressed the Community in the following words: "Preserve all carefully and gather up the fragments lest any be lost, for some day how precious they will be!"[25] He had

[19] Originals in CA of A. 10–4, 1819. 7–22, 1820.
[20] R. Brooke to S. Bruté, 1–14, 1820. Original in CA of A.
[21] Original in Archives of St. Sulpice, 4–8, 1820. Paris.
[22] Original in Canon Bruté de Rémur Collection, 1820.
[23] BCA, Case 13–Q[12]. 12–7, 1820.
[24] *Bruté—Seton Correspondence*, p. 29. 1884.
[25] *J. B. Code, Elizabeth Seton by Mdme. de Barberry*, p. 510.

My dear William,

A LETTER OF FATHER BRUTÉ TO WILLIAM SETON, JUNE 29, 1821

known the good Mother for ten years. During the greater part of this time he was her spiritual counsellor, and since August 1818 he had been her confessor. No other individual could have hoped to possess a keener insight into her soul than he had acquired. Hence it was but natural that he should be the first to realize the worth of her deeds. Immediately after her death he recorded in Mother Seton's Journal a brief account of her singular and admirable life.[26]

The continual excitement, together with the burden of many cares, began to leave their traces, and from all appearances it was only too evident that Father Bruté's health was on the decline. Archbishop Maréchal warned Father Dubois to take care of the vice president. To this gentle command Dubois responded on January 9, 1821, "You tell me to take care of him,—he is not a man to allow himself to be taken care of—He is restless, and lets no one else rest."[27] These words affected Father Bruté but slightly and still less did he heed them. Not one duty less did he discharge. The retreat for the First Communion class, suspended by the death of Mother Seton, was again resumed on January 10, and the same devoted services were tendered the Sisterhood as before the visit of the "Angel of Death." The loss of a friend on earth meant to the fervent priest the gain of another in heaven, and such events did not cause him to become melancholy. On the contrary, they rather pressed him on to more loyal service.

At this date all financial relations between the Baltimore establishment and the Mountain had been severed and the latter existed independent of Baltimore. The clergy in charge still remained members of the Society of St. Sulpice and their yearly compensation was apportioned by the Baltimore superiors. This, however, was one phase of life that never disturbed the vice president. The misers' coffers were never installed by him for he detested the slightest manifestation of greed, and the more so when he perceived

[26] Mother Seton's Journal, Original in Convent Archives. Mt. St. Vincent-on-Hudson, N. Y.

[27] M. Meline,—E. McSweeny, op. cit., I, p. 154.

it among the clergy. On one occasion it happened that his stipend had not been sent to him for two years. When it did arrive the sum amounted to only one hundred dollars. Forthwith he dispatched a letter containing the half of it to His Grace at Baltimore. The generous priest maintained that the needs of the Archbishop were more pressing than his own, and that His Grace would accomplish the surest good with the money.[28]

The location of Emmitsburg was not inviting so that the newcomers were scarce, and older emigrants were migrating to more promising sections. This retarded the growth of the parish. Father Bruté failed to comprehend the real cause for the diminishing numbers of the congregation and felt that his mission was a failure. His interest in parochial labors was wholehearted, yet he himself realized that he was more interested in seminaries and seminarians. This knowledge caused him to attribute the seeming failure in the former to his own inability for missionary work. Owing to the spirit of discouragement that arose from these undesirable conditions, he earnestly besought the Archbishop to withdraw him from the pastorship.[29] This request, however, was not acceded to since a month later we behold him seeking a delinquent member of the parish.[30]

The course of events and the manner in which the Emmitsburg and surrounding congregations were being administered did not coincide with Father Bruté's views. Consequently, he appealed once more to the Archbishop to recall him from the parish at Emmitsburg. Although he was pastor, he was subject to Father Dubois. These two clergymen were always devoted to each other, still they were different characters and disagreed on many points. Father Dubois was strong-headed, obstinate, and somewhat self-sufficient. Father Bruté was a mystic, pious, zealous, and maternally gentle, but indubitably he, too, was firmly fixed

[28] BCA, Case 13–Q[16]. 4 .... 1821.
[29] BCA, Case 13–Q[17]. 5–13, 1821.
[30] S. Bruté to J. Smith, 6–20, 1821; 9–9, 1821. Originals in CA of A.

in his ways. He notified the Archbishop to the effect that the Emmitsburg parish should have a pastor who was independent of Dubois at the Mountain. Likewise, Craigstown, Waynesboro, and Millerstown, each should be given an individual pastor.[31] Father Bruté maintained that nothing had been definitely arranged at Emmitsburg, and under such conditions it was impossible to render satisfaction. Father Dubois reserved to himself all the temporal administration, called the assemblies, even in the absence of his vicar and presided over them. Moreover, Father Dubois continually regulated without him whatever seemed useful. The trustees appealed to Father Dubois and generally referred their observations, petitions, and complaints, directly to him instead of consulting the pastor. The difficulty was that Father Dubois had too many cares to attend properly to temporalities, and Father Bruté had not sufficient authority to administer them. Hence Father Bruté concluded that it would be an advantage both to the Mountain and to Emmitsburg to have a local pastor at the latter station.[32] He also complained to the Archbishop that not only were the temporalities suffering at Emmitsburg, but in some cases the rubrics also were being disregarded. Owing to the poverty of the congregation they were forced to make many concessions that otherwise would never be tolerated. Despite this, Father Bruté firmly opposed the use of a paper box in which to keep the Sacred Hosts in the tabernacle while the ciborium was being purified. To impress upon His Grace the fact of this abuse he drew on the front page of his letter an exact likeness of the carton.[33]

The See of Baltimore had been erected thirty-one years, but up to this date no one of those who had occupied it had visited Rome. Several momentous problems demanding readjustment forced Archbishop Maréchal to sail for Rome in the month of October, 1821. The preparation for this voyage and the drawing up of a memorial, which embodied

[31] BCA, Case 13–R[21]. 8–2, 1821.
[32] *Bruté—Seton Correspondence*, pp. 318–319. 1886.
[33] BCA, Case 13–Q[19]. 6–13, 1821.

all the problems that were to be laid before the sovereign
Pontiff, had occupied His Grace for months. This forced
the minor details of the diocese to await a seasonable time
for hearing. Hence Father Bruté's request to be released
from the pastorship at Emmitsburg failed to be granted.

During the interim of the Archbishop's absence in
Europe, Father Bruté's attention was attracted by exciting
news that began to pour into America from the far-distant
land of Australia. When the Original Colonies of America
rose in rebellion and declared themselves free and independent of England, the latter was forced to find another
home for exile subjects whom they considered dangerous
to the public. Consequently, a penal colony was established
in January, 1788, at Botany Bay, Australia. At that period
practically little was known concerning this sparsely inhabited continent. It was as yet an unexplored primeval
wilderness referred to under the name of New Holland.
Among the victims transported to these shores there were
many Irish Catholics. Here in exile they were reviled and
persecuted for their faith by the cruel governors. Not until the year 1803 were the exiled priests permitted to say
Mass for their fellow-Catholics. In general, the conditions
there were shocking. The Catholics were not only deprived
of priests and the consolations of religion, but they were
also forced by the authorities to attend Protestant services.
To counteract this abuse several priests volunteered to minister to these suffering people. One of these volunteers was
Father Flynn, a Cistercian monk. After ministering for a
short time he was arrested on the street, and without being
allowed to return to the temporary chapel he was deported
to England. The Davis family, in whose home the chapel
had been arranged, piously guarded the Blessed Sacrament
for a period of two years until the next priest arrived in the
colony.[34]

Upon reading the startling account of the persecuted
Catholics, Father Bruté also decided to volunteer for New

[34] America, "The Next Eucharistic Congress," XXXVII (1927),
pp. 563–564.

Holland, but considering the influence of his confrères greater than his own he felt convinced that the request would sooner be granted if it were presented through another clergyman. Accordingly, he wrote to Rome through a renowned Jesuit, who responded, to the satisfaction of Father Bruté, that he was accepted for missionary work in New Holland. Notwithstanding this permission he never reached the Australian shores. Archbishop Maréchal, as we have recently observed, was in Rome at the time that these negotiations were in progress. Owing to the persistency of His Grace in withholding his consent, the missionary's desires were never realized.[35] However, this incident is another testimony to a foregoing statement, that, although he belonged to the Sulpicians by profession, he belonged to all by charity. Likewise, it is a proof that nationality was not a dominant figure in this clergyman's life. The Australian exiles belonged for the most part to the staunch Irish race, while he himself was a loyal son of Brittany. First and above all Father Bruté was a priest, a Catholic. As such he stood for Christ and the religion of Christ and he looked upon all duties through this two-fold light. Again he was a loyal member of St. Sulpice, and regardless of all life's vicissitudes he preserved the spirit of this Society unto the moment of his death. Nevertheless, he was again misunderstood and falsely accused to his superiors in France of desiring to sever associations with the Society when he offered himself for New Holland. On the contrary, his affection for St. Sulpice continued unmitigated.[36] Despite this he never looked with disdain upon the members of other Societies. In this he again belonged to all by charity for he associated with members of every Society that labored with him in this missionary country.

Bishop Du Bourg who had labored in the Louisiana country for the past ten years was at this time seriously considering the division of the vast diocese committed to

[35] Bruté Journal, Georgetown UA. Fol. 92, 6.
[36] S. Bruté to M. Duclaux, 10–10, 1822. Archives of St. Sulpice. Paris.

his charge.   It is evident from the following letter addressed to Bishop Plessis of Quebec, that Bishop Du Bourg wished to have Father Bruté as a co-laborer in the episcopacy.

New Orleans, 19 March, 1822.

I have cast my eyes on two men, one French, the other Italian; the one a Sulpician, who has been in Baltimore for twelve years, and is a man of universal knowledge, of eminent sanctity, whose zeal was in the past considered excessive, but which age and experience have toned down to the proper degree; for the rest, possessing in a high degree the power of making himself beloved, because his heart is the tenderest and humblest that I know of, blessed, finally, with strength proportioned to the immense labors that he would have to undertake.   He is Mr. Simon Bruté, of Rennes, about forty-two or forty-four years of age.   The other is a disciple and child of St. Vincent de Paul, superior of my seminary and my vicar general, only thirty-two years of age, but with the wisdom and maturity and poise of a man of fifty.   He is Mr. Joseph Rosati, a Neapolitan.   It would be difficult for me to say which of the two deserves the preference; both are known, respected, and beloved by all my priests.   However, the last named being the only man whom I can for a long while hence put at the head of my seminary, the only one also who can form his increasing Congregation in my diocese, which by God's grace is here making great progress, I should not hesitate to decide on Mr. Bruté.   The difficulty in regard to either one of them will be to get him to accept the burden, and I am certain beforehand that nothing short of a formal order of His Holiness would be able to gain this important victory over their modesty.   I forgot to add in Mr. Bruté's favor that Mr. Rosati, although ten years younger than he, is far from enjoying as robust health as his senior, for he is already subject to infirmities that prevent him from riding for any great length of time on horseback; and, finally, that he is threatened with a permanent lameness of an arm that he was so unfortunate as to break last September whilst returning on horseback from visiting a sick person.   L. Wm., Bishop of New Orleans.[37]

[37] *Records* (ACHS), XIX (1908), p. 198.

Providence designed otherwise, hence Bishop Du Bourg's wishes did not come to fruition. The diocese was not divided until four years later.

The years brought little change in the exterior life of the Superior of Mt. St. Mary's Seminary. His duties, modified by slight variations, were a mere repetition of those of preceding years. In 1822 the Mountain registered one hundred students. Seventy-eight were in college and the remainder were hopeful seminarians to whom Father Bruté taught Theology, Philosophy, and Geography. On the holidays he held a class in Sacred History.[38] The scholarly professor related that he taught daily four classes, held an ecclesiastical conference on Thursday and a Holy Scripture conference on Saturday. Besides this he ministered to the parish that lay two and one-half miles distant from the Mountain. Saturday afternoons and Sundays were wholly devoted to this mission work. Father Dubois served at the Mountain church and Father Hickey attended St. Joseph's in the Valley, thereby releasing Bruté from one of three-fold charges, namely, the chaplaincy of the Sisterhood.[39] In the following year the Mountain witnessed the ordination of two seminarians to the priesthood. The theologians then numbered fourteen, and there were five in Philosophy, all of whom would become good priests according to the judgment of their zealous master.[40] In the course of this same year Father Bruté was released from the pastorship of Emmitsburg, and the Mountain Seminary was now his sole charge.

Early in 1823 the death of Bonaparte was announced. A French paper stated that "a priest, the Abbé Vignoly from Corsica, sat by the corpse—a crucifix was placed upon his breast—the rites were performed at the burial." Further than this nothing definite was made known regarding his last moments. Father Bruté had been in Paris at the time

[38] S. Bruté to F. de LaMennais, 1822. Canon Bruté de Rémur Collection.

[39] S. Bruté to J. Rosati, 4–15, 1822. St. LCA. St. Louis, Mo.

[40] S. Bruté to A. Bruté, 9–26, 1823. Canon Bruté Collection.

of the Emperor's coronation, and having known this con-
queror personally, he was much concerned as to how the
exile died.   In a letter to Judge Gaston, relative to the conquered ruler, he wrote:

> I underline a word which speaks volumes of eloquence, or poetry—
> of religion and philosophy. Proud Bonaparte his *Crucified Lord* on
> his breast, his poor heart cold, the blood stopped, his eyes closed,
> mouth silent, death and judgment present and silent for us—the
> judgment of absolute truth and justice and not to be changed, no,
> not if heaven and earth were moved—finally that *Eternity* which
> alone answers though some would choose to call for *nothing*.

In addition he testified to the fact that Bonaparte had not
received the sacraments at the time of his coronation, although some persons had expected it.   However, it was
sometimes observed that the Emperor, at heart, possessed
the Catholic Faith and was unable to shake it off.[41]

Archbishop Maréchal returned from Rome late in 1822.
On Trinity Sunday, 1823, Bruté sent His Grace a letter
headed *secretum tibi in Christo*.   Once more he enclosed to
the Archbishop one-half of his salary of one hundred
dollars.   This donation was intended to defray the expenses
of His Grace in visiting the Virginia country.   The donor
was well aware of the condition of Catholicism in that
State, and he knew how necessarily zealous missionaries
were needed, yet owing to his faulty English he hesitated
to offer himself for Richmond.[42]   Nevertheless, unknown to
himself, he was, according to the following, recommended
again for episcopal charge of a new diocese.

> On June 21, 1823, Propaganda wrote to Maréchal, stating that
> it was the opinion of the Sacred Congregation that a separate
> diocese should be erected at once for Florida and Alabama. Two
> priests had been recommended to the Holy See for the episcopal
> charge of the new diocese, viz., Enoch Fenwick, S. J., and Simon

[41] S. Bruté to W. Gaston. 2–5, 1823. CA of A.
[42] BCA, Case 13–S³³. 1823.

Bruté. The first was President of Georgetown College, the other was a teacher in the Sulpician Seminary at Emmitsburg. Maréchal was asked to advise the Holy See on the merits of these two men.[43]

As to the nomination Maréchal responded to Propaganda testifying to Father Bruté's learning and piety but added that "he was so light-headed that a mitre would not suit him," and in acting thus he considered himself a true friend to Bruté.[44]

Madame Bruté de Rémur died at her home in Rennes on May 25, 1823. She had lived to a ripe old age; nevertheless, her death was a source of grief to her devoted son in America. The message was delayed in transit and did not reach Father Bruté until early in November. He wrote to His Grace on the ninth of the same month and asked prayers for his dear departed, saying that he was indebted to his good Mother for everything.[45]

At the close of this same year the vice president of the Mountain was deprived of another friend, though separation and not death was the source of this loss. Bishop Cheverus of Boston had received word to return to his native land. He greatly disliked the change, yet he felt it a duty to accept the offer and to devote the remainder of his life to the service of the Church in his own fatherland. Together with the Bishop of Boston went Father Mollevant from Baltimore. He, too, was another loyal friend of Bruté's and the latter grieved to learn of his departure.[46] Upon Bishop Cheverus' departure for France, Bishop Du Bourg of New Orleans wrote to Father Bruté to inform him that his name had been sent to Rome to replace the Bishop of Boston. The humble priest refused immediately and in his simplicity tried earnestly to make Bishop Du Bourg understand how unqualified he was to succeed a man like Bishop Cheverus. In response Du Bourg assured him that either

[43] P. Guilday, *The Life and Times of John England*, p. 574. New York, 1927.
[44] S. Bruté to J. Rosati, 12–17, 1832, St. LCA.
[45] BCA, Case 13–T[41]. 11–9, 1823.
[46] S. Bruté to W. Gaston, 12–4, 1823. CA of A.

his name never reached Rome, or if it had, no appointment would take place.[47]

Archbishop Maréchal received permission from Rome to confer upon Fathers Bruté, Deluol, Damphoux, and Whitfield the degree of Doctor of Divinity. The celebration was scheduled to take place at the Cathedral in Baltimore on January 25, 1824. On January 5, Father Bruté begged His Grace to be excused from accepting the Doctorate. In the same letter he asked permisison to go to France in order to settle his mother's estate and to receive his portion of the inheritance.[48] Evidently the desired permission was granted as he was not among the number at the conferring of the degree. This, however, did not lessen him in the estimation of his confrères. On the contrary, he was admired all the more for his humility. Even the students lauded his simplicity. Mr. McGerry, who was studying at the Baltimore Seminary, wrote to Mr. Egan, a student at the Mountain, saying: "Really I think Mr. Bruté has done well not to accept, for every one knows he has the knowledge of a Doctor." In those days the Doctors of Divinity dressed like the Bishops. In all probability it was this singular costume that Father Bruté wished to escape wearing because its character would have distinguished him from his simple confrères.[49]

In February 1824, Father Bruté accompanied by John B. Purcell left the Mountain, for New York, to sail for France. Purcell was a student from the Mountain, who was destined to complete his studies for the priesthood at St. Sulpice, Paris. Before sailing, Father Bruté was commissioned to conduct a three days' retreat for the Sisterhood in New York. This was accomplished to the satisfaction of all, after which the professor and the student sailed on the *Marmion*, March 1, 1824.[50]

---

47 Bruté Journal, Georgetown UA. Fol. 92, 6.
48 BCA, Case 13–T47. 1–5, 1824.
49 M. Meline,—E. McSweeny, *op. cit.*, I p. 114.
50 S. Bruté to A. Maréchal, 2–24, 1824. BCA, Case 13–T48.

CHAPTER VIII

TEN FRUITFUL YEARS AT THE MOUNTAIN
1824–1834

The *Marmion* came safely to port at Havre de Grace, but no data are extant for the exact date of its arrival. Even Father Bruté's Journal appears rather silent here. Relative to this voyage he recorded but one simple line, "In 1824 travelled to France for Mount St. Mary's."[1] Further correspondence gives evidence of the fact that the voyage was undertaken for several important purposes, of which the primary one was in behalf of the Mountain.

Thus far the Sulpicians had entered into no final agreement regarding Mount St. Mary's. The future of this struggling institution was a problem still pending and awaiting solution. At the request of Father Dubois, Father Bruté endeavored to influence St. Sulpice, at Paris, to accept the Mountain as a preparatory seminary for their French institution. According to this plan it would become a source from which Paris would be recruited with theological students from the New World. This offer was not only declined, but owing to the enormous indebtedness of the establishment St. Sulpice also desired the suppression of the institution.[2] This ill success on the part of Father Bruté to accomplish the primary purpose of his voyage was another trial that passed into his life. However, he did not permit discouragement to conquer him. Bravely and courageously he devoted his attention to the other problems that necessitated his trip abroad.

Upon leaving Paris he spent one day at Vitré whence he repaired to his native city,[3] but the devoted priest

[1] Bruté Journal, Georgetown UA. Fol. 92, 6.
[2] M. Meline,—E. McSweeny, *The Story of the Mountain*, I, p. 130.
[3] S. Bruté to A. Bruté, Easter 1824. Canon Bruté de Rémur Collection. Rennes, France.

was filled with sorrowful emotion as he retraced his steps
to the old home. He knew that the chair at the fireside was
vacant. The one who had shared his joys, the one from
whom he had received his salutary lessons—the fond old
Mother, who blessed him upon his departure for America,
was gone. Nevertheless, he was cordially welcomed by
Augustine and his family who took great pleasure in relating the story of the Mother's holy death. Her departure
was a deep grief for her missionary son, yet there was much
that was consoling regarding the manner in which she died.
Father Bruté was pleased to find in the home of Augustine
the same traditions of faith, the same christian piety that
had characterized the old home which had lately disappeared.[4] Here at the home of his brother he wrote to Archbishop Maréchal. This letter contains the first information
about this voyage. However, the personal character of this
brief message renders it almost unimportant except as an
expression of friendship.[5]

After spending about three months at Rennes, he returned
to Paris. On this occasion, as usual, he sought more than
material favors and took advantage of the visit to make a
long retreat at the solitude of Issy. He chose for his spiritual master, Father Mollevant, who had taught for several
years at St. Mary's Seminary, Baltimore. Father Bruté
made his retreats very regularly and with much exactness.
His notes, recorded at such intervals, give evidence of his
progress in solid piety and of the most intimate union with
God. During this particular retreat he meditated especially
upon the singular graces and benefits that God had bestowed
upon him. Among these spiritual favors he made special
mention of the virtuous priests, who had been his spiritual
directors at different periods of his life. Abbé Guy Carron
was named as his instructor and guide during his childhood.
For the period of his youth during the persecution he
recorded especially two holy martyrs, Fathers Touchet and

---

[4] Abbé C. Bruté de Rémur, *Vie de Monseigneur Bruté de Rémur,*
pp. 237–238.

[5] BCA, Case 13–U[51]. 5–24, 1824.

Sorette. When conditions became more settled and he repaired to Paris to study medicine he chose Father Bourdier-Delpuits for his guide and model. After entering upon preparations for a higher vocation at the Seminary of St. Sulpice, Doctor Bruté confided his interior life to Fathers Emery and Duclaux. As a professor in the seminary at Rennes he was cared for spiritually by Abbé Jean Guéretterie. During his sojourn at Baltimore his directors were Fathers Nagot and Tessier respectively. Father Dubois was mentioned as his confessor at the Mountain. The very thought of God's unlimited mercy in lavishing these favors upon him filled his heart with such unbounded gratitude, thanksgiving, and fear, that he exclaimed: "Oh! what an account will I have to give of such eminent graces."

Father Bruté's memoranda written during his visits at Paris, Rennes, Rouen, and Havre de Grace together with his numerous letters to Augustine and Camille, contain many interesting references relative to his   reunion   with   old friends.   Among the most distinguished of them that he met at Paris was Bishop Cheverus of Montauban; Count de Senft, a former ambassador of Saxony to the French court; the Baron de Heller; the Cardinal Prince de Croy, Grand Almoner; the famous Laennec, who had been his fellow-student at the Medical School; the son of Binet; and his intimate friends, Jean and Félicité de LaMennais.[6]   He also made the acquaintance of Abbé Boisnantier. This distinguished clergyman was a canon of St. Denis and had been nominated to the new See of Gallipolis that was proposed to be erected in Ohio. The colonists, however, had been defrauded in the purchase of the land and in consequence of this unfortunate transaction the new settlement disbanded, and the proceedings relative to the contemplated See were suspended.[7]

[6] S. Bruté to A. Bruté, 7–24, 1824; 8–30, 1824. Canon Bruté de Rémur Collection; J. R. Bayley, *Memoirs of the Rt. Rev. S. W. G. Bruté de Rémur*, p. 56.
[7] *The United States Catholic Magazine*, "A Curious Fact," IV (1845), p. 407; Records (ACHS), XXXVII (1926), p. 29; *The Catholic Historical Review*, IV (1919), p. 415.

Nine years had elapsed since Father Bruté's last voyage
to France. He was happy to observe that the general condition of things was astonishingly different from that of
1815. The country had changed for the better, particularly
in regard to religion. The government seemed firmly advancing in the right course. The mass of the people appeared to be frankly in favor of the existing order of things.
Apparently there was no cause to fear another clash in the
near future. Undoubtedly the nation harbored many impious people, but from all appearances there was also an
incalculable number of just souls. The royal court was
peopled with them. The generous efforts made by all classes not only to repair the rents in the sanctuary but also
to assist the Propagation of the Faith in distant lands was
manifest proof of the religious spirit of the people.

Probably Father Bruté was never more engaged than
during this sojourn, yet in his hurried but accurate style
he made notes of the most impressive changes in his fatherland. Together with these records, he brought back with
him important documents relative to the condition of seminaries, convents, and colleges. According to his statistics,
the ecclesiastical students in their different stages of preparation numbered 35,456. The Sisters numbered 18,644.
The Congregations of Brothers, employed in educating the
poor, were also receiving numerous vocations. Upon this
bright outlook the zealous missionary grounded hopes for
the nation's future. Many of the clergy were advanced in
age, hence the death rate was exceptionally high. The mor-
tuary list for 1824 told 1160, but the ordinations numbered
1363 which was more than equal to the loss. At that
particular time the total number of priests employed was
35,295. France then had a population of 30,000,000 people,
an average of almost one thousand souls to each priest. This
number was far too great, considering the advanced age of
the clergy and the extent of pastoral duty awaiting them.
More than 250 priest were engaged with the various troops
and Father Bruté reported that a wonderful reformation

FATHER

MOTHER

SIMON GABRIEL, BISHOP OF VINCENNES

DOCTOR AUGUSTINE BRUTÉ DE RÉMUR AND HIS WIFE CAMILLE

THE BRUTÉ DE RÉMUR FAMILY

had been effected in many regiments. In addition to these copious notes and documents the scholarly priest succeeded in securing, by purchase and by gift, a cargo of good books among which were some old curious editions of 1476 and 1477.[8]

According to a letter from Mr. Purcell, at Issy, Father Bruté left Paris for Rouen on September 20, 1824, the same day that the remains of King Louis XVIII were transferred from the palace to St. Denis. Mr. Purcell had little opportunity to converse with his former professor because the latter had such a number of things to look after at every moment since their arrival.[9] The missionary left Rouen on September 25 and repaired to Havre de Grace the port whence he was to embark within a few days. The interim was spent with M. Paris, pastor at Notre Dame, where Bruté had the honor to sing High Mass and Vespers on September 26. On the same day he wrote Augustine and family bidding them an affectionate farewell and asking them to bless the good God for the happy days they had spent together. He requested that a Mass be offered for himself and one for his mother and bade them never to forget the suffrages for her to whom he and Augustine were indebted for everything. All were admonished to live wholly for God, for eternity and to offer Holy Communion for his October voyage.[10] He entrusted his will to Augustine, charging him, in case of accident, to send it together with two notes to Bernard Eyquem for Father Dubois at Emmitsburg. The notes should be paid to M. Paris at Havre de Grace. Four days later he wrote Father Duclaux that he would embark on the Feast of St. Remi, October 1. From this letter we learn that he paid for Mr. Purcell's education at Issy but he received nothing for the Mountain and naturally he lamented the lack of interest that St. Sulpice

[8] S. Bruté to W. Gaston, 1–18, 1825. CA of A. Notre Dame, Ind.
[9] M. Meline,—E. McSweeny, op. cit., I, p. 128.
[10] Canon Bruté de Rémur Collection.

seemingly took in Mount St. Mary's.[11] On this occasion, as
during Father Bruté's first visit to France in 1815, his
friends tried to persuade him not to return to America, and
from the following letter we learn that it was with great
reluctance and sorrow that they bade him farewell.

Saint-Brieuc, September 14, 1824.

Dear and Excellent Friend!

   With what lively sorrow I address to you these last lines! You
are going to depart; once again the ocean will separate us! Perhaps several months will pass by ere I receive a word from you!
Oh! How well all this shows us the nothingness of the things of
this earth, and the vanity of all that is not of God! This miserable
life runs on filled with regrets and tears; we meet for an instant
to tell and feel that we love one another; a moment later, we must
speak the cruel word, Farewell!—Well then, yes, Farewell! May
God bless your sacrifices and your labors! Go to spread afar the
kingdom of Christ; work with a new zeal to widen the foundations
of a new church; but in the midst of these distant countries, do
not forget your poor Jean; often place him upon your paten—
and ask for him the grace of strength and light of which he feels
the need more and more.—Rest assured, dear friend, that the remembrance of you will never be effaced from his heart, and that for
life and for death he will be to you, that which he is,

The most affectionate and devoted friend,

Jean de LaMennais.[12]

Not only his friends but also the elements seemed to oppose
the missionary's departure. The winds were against them
and his sailing was delayed to October 4 and again to the
eighth of the same month. He was disappointed yet the opportunity to celebrate Holy Rosary Sunday on land was
gratifying. He said Mass at the Ursuline Convent after
which he assisted at a High Mass in Notre Dame.[13]

[11] S. Bruté to M. Duclaux, 9–30, 1824. Archives of St. Sulpice.
Paris, France.

[12] Abbé C. Bruté de Rémur, op. cit., pp. 287–288.

[13] S. Bruté to C. Bruté, Canon Bruté de Rémur Collection.

After a voyage of thirty-six days, Father Bruté arrived on November 13, 1824, at New York where he was detained for two days by custom officers. In the meantime to relieve Father Dubois of the suspense, he wrote in full the resolutions of their Superior at Paris. The recipient dispatched an answer to reach Father Bruté at Philadelphia, assuring him that while the letter had both pleased and pained, he still loved and respected the writer more than before and only awaited the latter's return in order to carry out a plan. Dubois requested Bruté to stop at Philadelphia and to conduct a three days retreat for the Sisters at the orphanage.[14] Consequently, he arrived at Baltimore on November 24 and at Emmitsburg two days later. Here he found the college rebuilt and was happy to learn that his books had not suffered from the fire, which had occurred during his absence. From thence he repaired to Washington to visit Father Clorivière and other Bretons for whom he had been entrusted with commissions by their relatives in France.[15] Returning from this errand he resumed his classes in Divinity and Philosophy and poured his entire heart into the work. The recent voyage had not abated his interest in the seminary, for the same zeal was displayed in the preparation of the students for their exalted vocations. At this particular date he was preparing two candidates to be ordained at Frederick by the Bishop of Ohio, on March 12, 1825, and five others who were to receive Holy Orders at the hands of the Bishop of Philadelphia on the Sunday after this date. In the preparatory conference Father Bruté stressed especially the obligation of the breviary. After the Holy Sacrifice he considered nothing equal to the unfathomable beauties of the psalms, and he regarded priests as the true successors of David.[16]

This unquenchable thirst in the heart of the learned professor to form new clergy for the Church in America caused

[14] M. Meline,—E. McSweeny, *op. cit.*, I, pp. 132–133.
[15] S. Bruté to A. & C. Bruté, 12–8, 1824. Canon Bruté de Rémur Collection.
[16] S. Bruté to W. Gaston, 3–12, 1825. CA of A.

him to strongly resent the plan that Father Dubois had communicated to him. This plan consisted in the complete transfer of the college and seminary, with all the property and debts, to the Sisterhood in August 1825. Father Dubois wished to withdraw to be rid of what he considered a state of very painful uncertainty. Father Bruté saw things differently. He did not believe the existing uncertainty to be of a nature that would necessitate Dubois' withdrawal or the dissolution of the establishment. Concerning this he wrote to the Archbishop and admonished His Grace of his duty—to examine well whether an end should be put to the good that was being done and to the hopes that existed for the future. He thought that Father Dubois had appropriated to himself the right of deliberating and resolving in a case that seemed to concern all. Nevertheless, Bruté entrusted it to Providence and relied on the good intention and sole responsibility of the Archbishop, yet he had one condition to place before their common Father. Mount St. Mary's housed about 5000 volumes which belonged to the vice president and he wanted it understood that in case the transfer of the property was carried through, these volumes were not to be subject to any claim from creditors. After reminding His Grace of the deposit which he considered too precious not to be disposed of safely, he declined to give further views concerning the case, saying:

I have said enough, I neither change my mind nor can I change that of other people, no, but I grieve . . . . Nevertheless, as to myself, my only doubt is whether I should not be of greater service in France, particularly in Rennes where I have been requested to take the seminary or the Mission Society founded by our bishop. The present superior of the seminary is one of my pupils. Here in America I have succeeded poorly on account of the language. The very fact that our seminary is abandoned by its Superior may be a sign from Providence for me to return to Rennes. At this moment I leave Your Grace to decide before God. If I should stay I leave you also to decide as to the employment of my person. I am ready to go to Philadelphia, New York, South, or wherever Your Grace desires to send me.

A last plea for the preservation of Mount St. Mary's was made in reviewing to the Archbishop the three-fold good accomplished: the college and seminary; the Sisterhood which he considered the finest collection of flowers in the diocese; and the two excellent congregations. Archbishop Maréchal was then urged to visit the Mountain and to judge for himself, leaving the expense of his trip to be defrayed by the vice president.[17]

The transfer of Mount St. Mary's property to the Sisterhood at St. Joseph's did not occur in August 1825 as Father Dubois had planned. Pecuniary assistance reached the Mountain from various quarters, and while the amount was by far insufficient to cancel the entire liabilities, the gifts aided in keeping the institution open. Early in July Father Bruté received a large sum of money to be used in promoting Catholicism in America. Loyalty to the Church and to the Mountain prompted the recipient to expend this wealth for the advancement of the institution to which he devoted his services. The benefactor at this particular time was no other than Charles X whose influence had guided the destinies of France during the reign of Louis XVIII, but who did not come to the throne until September 1824.[18]

As customary the retreat at the Mountain was held during the summer, and we are not surprised to read in Father Bruté's correspondence that he conducted the exercises. Classes were resumed after August 15, and he was again in charge of the seminary. On all occasions he made himself one with his seminarians. He was singularly conscientious in the noble work of training the young clergy. Few have carried on this work of the Divine Master under more disagreeable circumstances and attained a higher degree of success. The occupation in itself was not lightsome, but added to this was the constant fear that the coming day

[17] BCA, Case 13–U[55].
[18] S. Bruté to W. Gaston, 7–23, 1825.   CA of A.

would witness the closing of the establishment and the departure of the students. Father Bruté kept up a continual correspondence with the Archbishop pleading for the salvation of Mount St. Mary's.[19] Everything was confided to His Grace and abandoned to the Providence of God. Nevertheless, owing to the silence of the Archbishop and his slowness to act in behalf of the Mountain, Father Bruté on several occasions suspected His Grace of double dealing. For such transgressions he spared no one not even the common Father of the diocese.[20]

Together with the professorship at the Mountain Father Bruté devoted much time and energy to the composition of numerous articles for the Catholic Press. He contributed to the *Miscellany, The Hartford Catholic, The Shepherd of the Valley,* and *The Catholic Telegraph,* besides several other short-lived Catholic journals. The *Miscellany* was edited by Bishop England, who on account of his numerous duties and lack of material called upon Bruté to assist him as early as August 28, 1825.[21] These two clergymen entertained the highest esteem for each other, yet it was the magnetic attraction of their unlike characteristics that bound them.

Fidelity to God and neighbor was a dominant virtue of this servant of God. He daily sought occasions to perform countless deeds of kindness. On October 3, 1825, a day-laborer fell twenty-five feet from a tree and as the doctor was at a great distance Father Bruté came cheerfully to relieve the poor workman who suffered a dislocated elbow, a double fractured arm, a broken thumb, and a fractured thigh. This eminent physician adjusted the dislocation and the four fractured bones with so much skill and success that the surrounding country was aroused with wonder and admiration for his medical ability.[22] Shortly after this he

[19] BCA, Case 13–W[75]. 11–2, 1825.
[20] BCA, Case 13–P[12].
[21] J. England to S. Bruté, CA of A.
[22] S. Bruté to A. Bruté, 10–3, 1825. Canon Bruté de Rémur Collection.

conducted a retreat for the Visitation nuns at Georgetown; visited the Sisters of Charity at Washington where they were in charge of a school of seven hundred pupils; visited the Carmelites at Port Tobacco and dined with the Jesuits at Georgetown.[23] His charitable deeds were known far and near. Moreover, at this particular time we have placed before us the wonderful excess of charity lavished upon one of his confrères, Father Clorivière, a distinguished character who had served almost nine years as director and confessor to the Visitation nuns at Georgetown. In May 1826 to the great sorrow of all, this worthy priest suffered a stroke which wholly paralyzed his speech. During his illness which continued for more than four months Father Bruté frequently walked from Emmitsburg to Georgetown to assist Father Clorivière in his preparation for death. Often on such excursions Bruté had nothing to eat except apples picked from roadside orchards. As death hovered nearer it was Father Bruté again who spent long vigils at the bedside of the sufferer, repeating again and again in the language they both loved so well, *Mon ami, mon ami! De la croix au ciel!*[24] Father Clorivière passed to his reward on Friday, September 29, and immediately Father Bruté wrote to the Carmelites to solicit prayer for the departed soul. He was pained by the death of every good priest and turning his thoughts again to his one sacred aim in life he bade the cloistered nuns at Carmel pray without ceasing that good priests be granted to the Catholic Church in America.[25]

A marked change took place at the Mountain during the year 1826. Father Dubois, the president, was elevated to the episcopal See of New York, and Mount St. Mary's with all its property was deeded over to Fathers Egan and McGerry who were to occupy respectively the offices of president and vice president. Father Bruté considered this

[23] S. Bruté to A. & C. Bruté, 12–9, 1825. Canon Bruté Collection.
[24] G. & R. Lathrop, *The Story of Courage*. Boston, 1894.
[25] C. W. Currier, *Carmel in America*, p. 415. Baltimore, 1890.

change in government as far from being detrimental to the
institution. In a letter to Judge Gaston he remarked: "Mr.
Dubois is gone to his bishopric. Our boys are as happy as
ever. I am as usual the solitary and servant, teaching
Divinity, Philosophy, and Scripture with the full permission
of our dear Archbishop."[26] Everything at the Mountain
seemed to be progressing, yet misunderstandings were not
wanting. Letters which testify to this are still extant.
Those of Fathers Egan and McGerry addressed to Father
Bruté on January 29, 1827, paint a vivid scene of less sunny
days.[27] About this time the scholarly professor was requested by the Archbishop to revise a History of the Church
written by Reverend Mr. Pise. In a letter dated February
1, 1827, he responded: "I have accordingly done so, and I
am of the opinion that the Work (volume) will prove useful
to all who read it."[28]

The Hogan-Harold schism at Philadelphia had been in
action since 1820. As usual Father Bruté manifested the
same attitude towards it as he had always practised towards
controversies of that nature. He was quick to grasp the
entire situation together with its causes and evil consequences, but he was equally prudent and slow to express
his opinion to others. In 1826 John Hughes, a student from
the Mount, was ordained to the priesthood and stationed in
St. Joseph's Church, Philadelphia. The following year
Harold sank in the waves of the schism and Bishop Conwell
proposed sending Father Hughes to St. Mary's. Immediately the latter confided this proposal to Father Bruté. The
response was penned in the usual frank and sincere style
of his former professor and Father Hughes was advised to
entreat the Bishop not to enforce the transfer until the fatal
articles of peace were actually mended. The young pastor
was also cautioned to adhere strictly to his own private duty

[26] CA of A, 10–8, 1826.

[27] Transcripts in Souvay Collection, Kenrick Seminary. St. Louis,
Mo.

[28] S. Bruté to A. Maréchal, BCA, Case 13–U[68].

and not to encourage visitors who call for the sole purpose of exchanging news.[29]

Following immediately upon this, Father Hughes was practically forced to sign a paper sanctioning the procedure of Bishop Conwell in suspending Father Harold. This paper was no sooner signed than it appeared in the secular press, although a promise had been made that it would be retained at the Bishop's residence. Father Bruté, after reading the scandal but failing to know the singular circumstances wrote Father Hughes a sharp letter on April 23. The recipient's answer of May 27 acquainted the professor with the young pastor's actual position in the case.[30] In all his perplexities during these stormy years, Father Hughes had recourse to Father Bruté, who was a friend too sincere to flatter any one. He knew how to encourage and to warn in the same sentence and he always strove to lead his confrères to remember the more spiritual occupations of their vocation. Controversies with ministers of other denominations were not condemned. He himself contributed his knowledge to some of the most famous ones that were ever conducted. In truth he participated in them to a greater extent than the world will ever know. Nevertheless, he feared lest the excitement of controversy and the applause of men would lead his confrères to neglect their primary duty and grow weak in fervor.

The energetic Bruté had few moments he could call his own. The response to one demand had not left his pen before several others were clamoring for his attention. At this moment Bishop England again pleaded with his confrère to assist the *Miscellany*. On June 9 the Bishop wrote: "Give me all your advice and thoughts fully and freely. I might perhaps differ sometimes from your view but I al-

[29] J. Hassard, *Life of Most Rev. John Hughes*, pp. 58–59, New York, 1886; F. E. Tourscher, *The Hogan Schism and Trustee Troubles in St. Mary's Church Philedelphia, 1820–1829*, Philadelphia, 1930.

[30] J. Hughes to S. Bruté, 5–27, 1827. Old Cathedral Archives. Vincennes, Indiana.

[31] J. England to S. Bruté, 6–9, 1827. CA of A.

ways respect and appreciate it."[31] Evidently the Bishop of
Charleston was anxious to obtain his confrère's assistance
as another letter was sent to the Mountain within the same
week. Accompanying this message was a pamphlet by Mr.
Grimke, one of the state senators. The production was un-
philosophical and the bishop felt it should not be let pass
unnoticed. His Lordship decided that the *Miscellany* would
be the place to attack Grimke and he knew no one more
competent than Father Bruté to prepare the material for
it.[32] The latter accepted the task and spent considerable time
and intense study in preparing material to confute Grimke's
errors, when Bishop England wrote: "I have upon reflection determined to let Grimke alone—but your letters will
be useful to me for a variety of other papers and they shall
be turned to account."[33] In several instances when writing
to others Father Bruté gave evidence of his dislike for such
erratic deeds. Nevertheless, he was too gracious to refuse
his assistance upon the next request.

In unraveling the tangled web of events recorded in the
Bruté-Rosati correspondence, we have come upon an
important incident in the history of the Catholic Church in
America. The young Republic was only a missionary country at that period. Despite this, according to Father Bruté,
the year 1827 marked the beginning of her foreign mission
labor. On November 6, 1827, the thriving Church in
America gave her first fruits to the Orient, when Father
Bellami sailed for China. At his departure he requested
Father Bruté to direct the vocation of a young lady who
wished to become a religious. However, the latter was of
the opinion that she would not fit in the American establishment at Emmitsburg.[34] During this same year the Mountain
Seminary had produced six new priests. Two of this number were sent to New York. Philadelphia received three of

[32] CA of A. 6–15, 1827.
[33] CA of A. 11–12, 1827.
[34] S. Bruté to J. Rosati, 11–21, 1827, St. LCA. St. Louis, Mo.; S.
Bruté to A. Bruté, 12–24, 1827. Canon Bruté Collection.

the newly ordained, and one, a brilliant mathematician, joined the faculty at the Mountain.[35]

At various intervals Father Bruté turned aside from the daily routine and devoted some moments to writing lengthy letters to Augustine and Camille. A goodly number of these messages were personal, an overflow of fraternal affection, admonitions how to live for eternity and to rear their children in the true faith. The outstanding events of the day and news concerning his Breton friends in America were usually imparted in brief lines, and more often in postscripts. Thus he added: "Father Lucas is still successful at St. Peter's Church in Washington, D. C." "I said Mass this morning at the Visitation Convent at Georgetown, for the repose of Father Clorivière." "Trouble continues at Philadelphia between a bishop and a priest. Close your eyes and ears to all that would trouble your faith." "The Archbishop received Holy Viaticum on January 13. He wrote me recently and instead of signing his name Ambrose Maréchal, he wrote 'Ambrose Moriens'."[36]

Early in 1828 Father Hughes took advantage of the good order in his congregation to invite Father Bruté to spend a week with him. A very intimate friendship existed between these two clergymen, and since Father Hughes' departure from the Mountain a continual exchange of letters bound them the closer, if such were possible. The professor especially welcomed the letters of his old pupil for therein he found the soul and character of a true priest. Father Hughes was always interesting and interested. A great work lay before him and to Bruté's consolation his old pupil not only had a work to do but he did it with all his heart.

Father Bruté was not a politician. He maintained that priests should not indulge in such affairs. However, he did take an occasional notice of the campaign in 1828 and lamented the fact that the newspapers contained enough to make the people believe that the candidates for presidency

[35] S. Bruté to J. Rosati, 8–16, 1827, St. LCA.
[36] S. Bruté to A. & C. Bruté 1–1, 1827; 3–19, 1827; 9–13, 1827; 6–3, 1827; 1–27, 1828. Canon Bruté de Rémur Collection.

were giants or monsters.   According to his interpretation
the real patriots were terrified at such exaggerations.   After
the election he notified Augustine of General Jackson's
triumph and Adams' defeat.[37]

An untimely loss befell the Mountain in the late summer
of 1828.   Father Lynch, professor of mathematics, had recently been suffering from ill health.   In the absence of
Father Bruté, the physician ordered the patient to Philadelphia.   Upon being acquainted with this incident the devoted
priest thought it an imprudent step, but knowing that the
orders would be obeyed, he wrote immediately to admonish
Father McGerry to care well for their suffering confrère
whose illness had been caused from insufficient clothing.
The fatherly professor was well aware of the fact that the
rushing American life was not conducive to the virtue of
charity.   Thus he added the following lines to Father
McGerry: "We live in such a hurry and press of business
so as to live very little for one another."   This letter gave
him an opportunity to speak of another momentous necessity at the Mountain.   He urged the erection of a chapel
near the house—more for the priests than for the students.
In France every seminary had its own chapel, and he
prudently stated that if God was sought first, everything
else would follow.   He also encouraged the faculty upon
resuming classes to be mindful of the primary object of the
institution, which was to form true priests for the Church
in America.[38]   Neither medical aid nor the trip to Philadelphia revived the health of Father Lynch.   A letter written
by his confrère contains one line which tells us all.   "We
have just buried our good Father Lynch—a young priest of
real merit."[39]

In the course of the same 1828 we find Father Bruté
faithfully keeping the lead in correspondence with his confrères.   On the death of Archbishop Maréchal he opened

---

[37] S. Bruté to A. Bruté, 7–18, 1828;   8–10, 1828;   12–8, 1828.   *Ibid.*
[38] Original in Souvay Collection, Kenrick Seminary, Aug. 1828.
[39] S. Bruté to M. Le Comte de Menou, Sept. 14, 1828.   Georgetown
UA.   Fol. 92, 6.

communications with Most Reverend J. Whitfield as soon
as the newly appointed Metropolitan was consecrated. The
correspondence, however, remained personal to December
22, 1828. Evidently, His Grace had recently requested the
faculty at the Mountain to resume charge at Emmitsburg
and at St. Joseph's in the Valley. In a brief, though cordial
reply Father Bruté, speaking for the Mountain, declined to
accept the charge. He stated that it was impossible to lay
additional responsibilities upon the already overburdened
faculty. They had recently lost two members of the faculty.
Death had claimed Father Lynch and ill health forced
Father Egan to go to Southern France.[40] Nevertheless,
Bruté's resistance was short-lived and we soon find him
again occupying the office of confessor to the Sisterhood.

Father Bruté had planned another voyage to France, but
early in January 1829 he notified Augustine that Father
Egan's departure for France had frustrated his hopes for
another trip. At that date the Mountain registered one
hundred and forty-one boarders and the faculty was over-
burdened. While he sincerely loved his family, his devotion
to the priesthood and religion was far more intense. Side
by side with academic duties he always kept a watchful eye
on the progress that Catholicism was making throughout
the young nation and he recorded eagerly the arrival of
every missionary. In this same letter he was happy to inform Augustine of the safe arrival of Father Abell, who
brought with him a number of seminarians and two Poor
Clares. He also announced the arrival of the Sisters of the
Sacred Heart, whose intention it was to establish a community in the middle west. The faculty had looked forward
to Father Egan's return, but, within a few months, contrary
to expectation, the sad news of his death reached the
Mountain. This message completely crushed the last faint

[40] BCA, Case 23–G⁴; S. Bruté to A. Bruté, 10–6, 1828. Canon
Bruté Collection.

hope that Father Bruté entertained of seeing his kindred and fatherland in the near future.[41]

Bishop Fenwick of Cincinnati had always taken a lively interest in the northwest country but at this date his health was on the decline, and he realized that the territory assigned to his charge was too extensive for one man to govern and as a result the Church was suffering. Consequently, he appealed to Propaganda on May 12, 1829, urging this august body to appoint an ordinary for the newly erected See of Detroit. He proposed Father John B. Acquaroni, C. M., Reverend Guy I. Chabrat, and Reverend Simon G. Bruté. Thus we find the Father of the Church in Indiana recommended for bishoprics from the north to the south and as far west as the West extended in those days.[42]

Bishop Du Bourg who had resigned the See of Louisiana and accepted the transfer to the diocese of Montauban, France, August 13, 1826, did not forget those who had labored with him in America. Apparently his heart remained with the American missions for he strove to assist them in every way possible. From a letter addressed to Father Bruté, October 10, 1829, we learn that the bishop sent two missionaries from Montauban to Bishop Portier, at Mobile. According to Bishop Du Bourg's orders, these young clerics were to be sent first to Mount St. Mary's and entrusted to the special care of the superior of the seminary where they were to complete their studies and to acquire, besides the knowledge of English, the science of the saints. Owing to the bishop's former episcopal relations with the Church in America, he was greatly interested in the First Provincial Council of Baltimore and gave it much space in his letter saying:

I am presuming that these gentlemen, [referring to the missionaries from Montauban] will find you in Baltimore, at the Council.

[41] S. Bruté to A. Bruté, Jan. 5; May 16; Aug. 14; Sept. 3, 1829. Canon Bruté de Rémur Collection.

[42] V. F. O'Daniel, *The Right Reverend E. D. Fenwick*, pp. 358-9. New York, 1920.

I am anxious to learn what measures of general usefulness will be adopted in this first solemn reunion of ten bishops in a country which in 1790 had but one, and which at the present rate of things will possess fifteen in ten years more. It is necessary to apply a remedy to the inconveniences resulting from the isolated condition of the different churches, to fix a mode of presentation for the vacant Sees and to settle the principal points of general discipline necessary for establishing uniformity. I can see you, my dear Brother, and your active efforts to impress, to the best of your ability, upon this holy assembly a salutary and recollected direction in the venerable documents which should serve as a foundation in its rules. There will result therefrom very much good in which none will rejoice more than I.[43]

Evidently the First Provincial Council convened earlier than Bishop Du Bourg had expected, since it had already passed into the history of the Church in America before this letter reached the Mountain. However, he was correct in his conjectures regarding his confrère. On this occasion Father Bruté served in capacity of theologian to Bishop England, and we are justified in saying that His Lordship could scarcely have selected a more competent assistant. In matters of theology this scholarly clergyman was deep, prudent, and to the point. Every session of the Council found him at his post, but from his letters we learn that he attended none of the social meetings. Writing to Bishop Rosati he said: "During the Council I avoided all the banquets—having nothing in common with American customs—henceforth incapable of beginning to adopt them."[44] That Bishop England was recompensed for his choice and grateful for Father Bruté's services is clearly portrayed in a note in which the bishop wrote: "A thousand thanks for your kindness and aid to me."[45]

Father Bruté had contributed much to the convening of this council. From the time of the assembly of the first

[43] W. Du Bourg to S. Bruté, CA of A.
[44] St. LCA, 12–17, 1832.
[45] H. J. Alerding, *The Diocese of Vincennes*, p. 116. 1883.

bishops of Boston, Bardstown, and Philadelphia, immediately after their consecration in 1810, he was insistent that such assemblies should be renewed from time to time. On more than one occasion he mentioned in letters to the Archbishop the fact that the genial spirit of the first bishops should be renewed and fostered. This wise theologian knew how important it was for the foundation and spread of Catholicism, that the bishops meet and confer as to the proper and uniform rules of discipline to be enforced. Many of the beneficial effects accruing from this Council may be attributed to the prudence and foresight of this theologian.

Years before the convening of this Council many of his confrères were occupying offices in the Church far superior to that of the distinguished superior of the seminary. Father Dubois was Bishop of New York, Father Rosati occupied the See of St. Louis, and an old pupil of the Mountain, Father Portier, was Bishop of Mobile. Father Bruté lived apparently hidden in his Mountain retreat, engaged in that work which he styled the "work of works" —the training of new clergy for the Church. His influence unperceived was reaching out on every side and the entire country was his field of labor. No one particular section especially interested him, and it is safe to state that no human element prompted the motives of his actions. Whatever he planned, suggested, or accomplished was done with that one sacred aim in view, namely laying the foundation broad and deep for Catholicism. Nothing less than the conversion of the entire nation could satisfy this apostolic heart, and comprehending as no other did the agents necessary to accomplish this great work he labored under unequalled pressure. He knew his own natural disadvantages as a missionary,—dislike for appearing in social circles, love of solitude, and a meagre knowledge of English. Father Bruté was a mystic. He was not destined by Providence to labor among savage tribes; yet he was a treasured gift sent by Providence to aid a missionary Church in her days

of need. The greatest need and the one from which the
Church suffered at that epoch more intensely than from any
other was the lack of apostles to preach the word of God.
This was the field in which Father Bruté labored. He spent
the better part of his life in forming true apostles, leaders
of souls, defenders of the Church of Christ. The knowledge
of books and of the science of the saints, which he possessed
in an eminent degree, could not have been utilized to better
account.[46] It is not astonishing then that Father Bruté
watched with strained attention the proceedings of the
First Provincial Council of Baltimore, when the Mountain
was in question. Although far superior in age and ability
to the president of Mount St. Mary's, he respected Father
McGerry's authority and reported to him every move and
attitude of the Council towards the Mountain Seminary.
The future of this institution had never been determined.
It had from the very beginning existed only at the mercy of
Divine Providence, and only for the prayers and secret influence of Father Bruté, the Mountain would have been
crushed at this Council and by those too, for whose good it
existed.[47]

To conclude from the copious correspondence of 1830,
Father Bruté's duties seemed to be mutiplying with years,
yet he was happy to realize that his life for the most part
comprised nothing more than seemingly small, insignificant
tasks. His letters to the Archbishop changed in character
and became almost wholly business-like. On January 29,
1830, he recommended to His Grace the Messrs. Purcell,
Hitzelberger, and McCaffrey for ordination.[48] In another
letter to Archbishop Whitfield, he complained about the im-
prudence displayed by several editors. He objected severely
to the printing of such articles concerning the "Inquisition"
as the April number of the *Jesuit* carried.[49] Every publication in America received judgment according to Bruté's

---

[46] J. R. Bayley, *op. cit.*, p. 55.
[47] M. Meline,—E. McSweeny, *op. cit.*, I, pp. 220–222.
[48] S. Bruté to J. Whitfield, 1–29, 1830, CA of A.
[49] BCA, Case 23–A.–AI.

idea of its worth. The political tone of the *Miscellany*, since the late revolution in France, made him very sad. He was extremely hurt at such treatment from the Bishop of Charleston.[50] At this point we must take into account the fact that Father Bruté was very gentle and affectionate. Consequently, he often took offense at very insignificant words or actions. He was polished and refined to a marked degree and naturally he felt it most keenly when the same treatment was not accorded him in return.

Father Bruté appeared seldom if ever at public celebrations other than religious ones, yet thousands knew him. He had several times refused the mitre, preferring to live in seclusion in a little corner of the seminary. Despite this he filled one of the highest offices in the Church. He was accomplishing the true work of the Divine Master, namely, schooling apostles to be sent out to teach the whole nation. His confrères recognized and admired his profound knowledge of books and many of them sought his assistance. In 1830 Reverend F. P. Kenrick was appointed coadjutor *cum iure successionis* to Bishop Conwell of Philadelphia. On May 7, he invited Father Purcell to the consecration. In the course of the letter he said: "Reverend Mr. Bruté's advice will not be forgotten. His aid in revising my Theology will be most acceptable."[51] When Bishop Kenrick entered upon his vast field of labor as coadjutor of Philadelphia, Father Bruté interested himself with his usual zeal in the good work. He advocated especially the holding of diocesan synods and the establishment of a diocesan seminary. He immediately perceived the utility of Bishop Kenrick's plans to design a course of Theology adopted to the wants of the Catholic clergy in the United States. Long before this date, the prudent professor had detected error in doctrine and morals creeping in under new and alarming forms. He, therefore, understood better than many of his confrères the necessity of destroying these evils at an early date. In con-

[50] S. Bruté to J. Rosati, 3–25, 1830; 11–21, 1830, St. LCA.
[51] F. P. Kenrick to J. B. Purcell, 5–7, 1830, CA of A.

sequence he did more than warmly sponsor the project. He gave most generous assistance to this noble work.

Distance never severed the bonds of friendship with Father Bruté. He was equally as faithful to his friends across the sea as to those in America. From Bishop Du Bourg's correspondence we learn how much this fidelity was appreciated. On May 6, 1830, the bishop wrote:

> I thank you my dear friend, for your attention in giving me from time to time detailed news of your country. You are the only one who procures this consolation for me, one of the sweetest I could desire. I am not very exact in replying which, of course, is due to my pressing occupations, for all the details of my great charge fall on me. But be assured I am none the less grateful.[52]

At this same time Father Mollevant, at Issy, informed his missionary confrère that three young men from Lyons would sail for America on June 20. Two of this number would join Bishop Rosati and the other one was bound for Bishop Flaget's diocese.[53] However, according to Father Bruté the Mountain was not disappointing in its production of missionaries, although its registration had been decreased by new seminaries having been opened in various dioceses. Within the past five years twenty-six of the pupils had received ordination and twenty-eight had become doctors. The legislature of Maryland granted them the right to confer all the degrees except that of medicine. Father Bruté was equally proud of the progress made by the Sisters at St. Joseph's. They numbered seventy-five sisters and novices and had eighteen establishments. He went daily to say Mass in St. Joseph's Chapel and often he was compelled to walk because the snow-storms were too heavy to allow him to travel with a horse. On the Feast of St. Paul, he was forced to wade through snow eighteen inches deep.

[52] Original in CA of A.
[53] S. Bruté to J. Rosati, Aug. 1831, St. LCA.

The winters were very severe yet he assured Augustine that he was enjoying good health.[54]

In 1832 Father Bruté received an appeal from St. Louis to assist the Catholic publication entitled *The Shepherd of the Valley*. This request was granted on condition that Bishop Rosati would not "point out" the author as Bishop England had done on several occasions. In the same reply he enumerated the qualities of a well regulated Catholic periodical. Relative to this he wrote:

> I would insist on the instruction and conversation being of a persuasive, edifying, polished, non-provocative tone. I fear that I myself sometimes yielded to the pleasure of sarcasm or pointed remarks—supposing too easily that this was the better way to proceed. At other times I have stirred up certain matters before the time was ripe to treat them. Our cause is so beautiful and so holy, and then a Journal in the interests of Truth has the same obligation as a sermon from the pulpit.[55]

The dreaded scourge of cholera entered from the North and ravaged the greater portion of the United States during the year 1832. As soon as word reached the Mountain that Baltimore was writhing in the throes of pestilence Father Bruté went to the scene. Upon his arrival he fell victim to a violent attack of intermittent fever which forced him back to the Mountain. After recovering from this siege he returned to Baltimore where he labored in the cholera hospitals until his services were no longer needed.[56] During these alarming days he was kept very occupied, nevertheless, he found time to write many letters, especially to Bishop Rosati. While the sympathetic priest was not indifferent to the desolation and human sorrow that ravaged every home, he was more inclined to view the pestilence from a spiritual angle. In one letter he wrote: "The cholera made poor sinners run to confession like a jubilee

[54] Cf. 8 Letters of S. Bruté to A. Bruté, 1831. Canon Bruté de Rémur Collection.

[55] S. Bruté to J. Rosati, 7–18, 1832, St. LCA.

[56] J. R. Bayley, *op. cit.*, p. 57.

time." At another time he said: "Truly the mercy of God
has made it a time of salvation—a jubilee, amidst such a
terrible visitation and terrors of each family." He also
related that the clergy and the Sisters were of one heart
and one soul for the good of the sick. He admired and
praised the courage of the nuns. In Philadelphia, Baltimore,
and at Emmitsburg they went out to nurse the cholera
patients, while the ministers of other denominations refused
to participate in this labor of love.[57] Father Bruté was
extremely generous in his praise for others, but humility
prevented him from recording his own deeds upon this occasion. However, the numerous letters written at Baltimore
during that particular time testify to the fact that he
labored in that city during the epidemic.

On December 14, 1832, Father Hughes informed his
venerable confrère that a controversy would open in
Philadelphia during the first week of January. Father
Hughes and Mr. Breckenridge, a Presbyterian minister,
were to be the contending parties. The question proposed
for discussion was: "Is the Protestant religion the religion
of Christ?" This controversy was to be ruled by five conditions, of which the second was as follows: "The parties
agree that there is an infallible rule of faith established by
Christ to guide us in matters of religion, for the purpose of
determining disputes in the Church of Christ." The last
condition stated that Reverend Mr. Hughes was to open the
discussion. The minister having subscribed to the contents
of the second condition, Father Hughes decided to open the
debate with the question, "What is that infallible rule?"
After having outlined everything thoroughly in order to acquaint Father Bruté with what he needed, Father Hughes
requested his old master to give him all the aid possible.[58]

From further correspondence of Father Hughes we learn
that he received generous and beneficial assistance from his

---

[57] S. Bruté to J. Rosati, 7–18, 1832; 8–11, 1832; 11–18, 1832.
St. LCA.; S. Bruté to A. Bruté, 9–19, 1832. Canon Bruté de Rémur
Collection.

[58] J. Hassard, *op. cit.*, pp. 126–138.

former professor. Bruté was always profound and it was
difficult for ordinary minds to grasp his lofty thoughts and
explanations. Therefore, on one occasion Father Hughes
was forced to plead for more simple refutations. "Of all
things," said he, "be *clear* for neither myself nor the readers
to whom it is to be submitted possess your intellectual discipline and habits of familiarity with books—and for our
sakes make everything lucid, even to excess." At that date
the controversy had run scarcely one-half the schedule time,
yet as a result Father Hughes was already instructing Bap-
tists, Episcopalians, and Duncanite Presbyterians in the
true Faith.[59] Father Bruté, nevertheless, had his own ideas
and in writing to Bishop Rosati he expressed them very
frankly. He had no use for that type of controversy in
which the publication was divided in such a way that one
week the article was Protestant and the following week it
was Catholic. The time was not ripe for such work. Priests
were too scarce and pastoral duties too heavy to admit labor
that would encroach upon the essential work of the priest.
He, moreover, contended that it would be impossible each
week to supply sufficient material properly digested and well
written. To assert things haphazardly would but weaken
the Catholic argument and prevent the Protestant diatribes
from being refuted. Furthermore, he failed to see the good
that women and especially the Sisters would draw from this
kind of reading. Such material would fill their minds with
curious, impious doubts and cause Rodriguez and the Lives
of the Saints to become insipid.[60]

In the course of the year 1832, Father Bruté drew up a
plan for a volume entitled "Catholic America." Concluding
from the sketch which he sent to Reverend Mr. Deluol,
superior of St. Mary's, Baltimore, we find that this work
would have been written in French. The outline is very
detailed, somewhat complicated, and from the chapter head-
ings it would have been mainly contemporary. Apart from

[59] *Ibid.*, pp. 140–143.
[60] S. Bruté to J. Rosati, 3–18, 1833, St. LCA.

this, the sketch is worth while and it is to be regretted that the project was never carried out during the lifetime of those men whose deeds made up the history of their day. Unfortunately, many of those valuable deeds are lost to us because of the failure to record them.[61]

Through the correspondence of two other clergymen late in 1832, Father Bruté received unwelcome tidings—a slight intimation that he was to be separated from the dear Mountain. As soon as this information reached him that his name had been presented to Rome to fill the See of Vincennes, he dispatched the following letter to protest to Bishop Rosati.

Mt. St. Marie
December 17, 1832.

My dear Lord:—

A first rumor transmitted in a letter of Bishop Kenrick to Mr. Purcell informs me that there is question of myself as Bishop of Vincennes—that it is you and Bishop Flaget who have presented my name. I just returned from saying Mass after this news and I recollect myself a moment to examine the *Will of God.*

I can only love God by doing His Will. I can only save myself by not opposing it—to refuse an office in His Church in which I am a minister, *because* it is painful to me is not surer than to desire and seek something agreeable which is *against His Will.*

Believe me then, that I write only that which seems to me renders this more of an *unhappy nomination for the Church of America than for myself.*

I can write a few orderly lines, teach a class, hear the Sisters' confessions as well as my confrères—it has been my task all my life—but many can be Bishop of Vincennes far better than I and I far worse than the majority of those whom they should have thought of instead of me—for to be a bishop and above all in a missionary country such as this is and to be the first bishop there to begin all that pertains to a bishopric in this country, is a thing

<hr>

[61] *The United States Catholic Historical Magazine,* "Sketch by Dr. Bruté for a Work to be called 'Catholic America'," I (1887), pp. 60–63.

essentially different and for which I believe I do not possess a single one of the necessary qualities, which are the following:

1. To be younger and stronger as Bishop Flaget was when he began in Kentucky. I am fifty-four years of age and last year and this year my health gave way so rapidly that everybody thought I was falling into decline. I have had six or seven attacks of ague from July 1831 to last September, and a melancholy of which necessity alone compelled me to speak to M. McElroy and later to M. Deluol, coming near to what is called *Broken-heart* (useless to speak of the causes) reduced me to this state. M. Deluol had the goodness to make me the offer to retire to the seminary. I consented, but finding myself better and the necessity of my presence here made me desire to remain here provisionally. I could no longer give the ordinary retreat to the young people, even quitted the spiritual reading and their confessions, discontinued all the care of the congregation where I still had my turn in preaching from time to time and singing High Mass. I have also discontinued all confessions and all care of the sick. Since two years I hardly ever go on horseback, not even to the Sisters, preferring to make the two miles on foot—being disabled—Behold what a missionary life demands—so much horseback riding over such a vast territory as these two states and the Northwest would exact from a bishop attached to his first duty—the apostolic life. If I can no longer be the good pastor of our congregation, what kind a Bishop will I be in the West? Could you under the circumstances make a worse choice? Bishop Flaget perhaps had in mind his vigorous Bruté of 1810, but nearly twenty-three years have passed since then. He, too, the vigorous Flaget of those days is no longer thus! And surely I must or am obliged to offer this simple first negative quality—there is need of a priest ten or fifteen years younger than myself—your age, Bishop Rosati, who can begin with ardor and sustain for a long time such a difficult enterprise as a new bishopric. I am the entire opposite of all this.

2. For this faculty of ardor, vigor, and enterprise, it is no longer the same with me. I am broken, crushed, melancholy having become a temptation of which I would never have thought if it were not for its background of pride, susceptibility, and exaggeration (of which you had several incidents at the council) and which I begin year

after year to combat, but always in vain. I possess only timidity
and uncertainty; distrust of men and affairs; reserve and con-
centration which are all opposed to that beautiful and sweet confidence in Providence. I lack that facility of association with men
and of carrying on business which is so necessary to a good bishop
—the common Father and centre of all, his clergy and his people
and even the sectaries and public men of every sort with whom he
comes in contact.

I have been in the seminary for almost thirty years—five years
at St. Sulpice, so secluded. Two years at Rennes, then at Baltimore,
and here since 1810. I live almost the life of a solitary, and when
I find myself for several days at Baltimore I *never* go out into town
(Dr. Chatard excepted). You saw me avoid all the banquets during
the Council. I have acquired none of the American manners and am
incapable after all of acquiring them. Here even, I very seldom
see any of the parents who visit. I am always with my books in my
corner in the third story, or at the Sisters. In this way only I find
myself at ease. I have never learned to converse in English, I lose
the half of it and I am not understood. This situation in which I
have buried myself more and more as it happens to old professors
and directors of seminaries, does no harm to my occupations, which
are the classes, Theology and Holy Scripture; the confessions at
the Sisters, and speaking short, simple exhortations; writing for a
Catholic Journal, and carrying on my correspondence. For a Bishop
of Illinois and Indiana all this is the very opposite of what should
be his true gifts.

3. While I come to speak of the language of the country, Bishop David
will recall to mind that I could not acquire the pronunciation. You
saw this at the Council where, in familiar conversation, I was not
understood. Here and at the Sisters they are accustomed to my
Dutch or French-English. The young men and the Sisters after
some time understand well enough, but visitors lose themselves—nor
am I invited anywhere to preach. At Baltimore after my first
attempts they gave it up—and since 1816, when you came, I being
at the time president of the college, I was never invited to preach
at St. Peter's, nor afterwards. Having lost my teeth at an early
age, and having neglected myself more and more in this regard, I
am incapable of speaking in public. Mr. McElroy never invites

me to Emmitsburg. If Mr. Zocchi invites any one for Easter or
Christmas, he says: *not Mr. Bruté,* no one understands him. And
at Frederick and Hagerstown the same. This object is certainly of
prime importance in a bishop for the West. Perhaps what I have
just said concerning familiar conversation would apply also to business affairs in which I would usually miss the half of it and
especially that which would relate to churches, distribution of buildings, plantations, and purchases. If I would wish to speak about
these things afterwards to my confrères, visiting priests or bishops,
I would mix things up and make them laugh. This of course makes
no difference here because I am free from administrative affairs but
it would be of great inconvenience were this to occur in a bishopric
where everything is to be well begun and well arranged from the
start.

4. This point; business, administration, government of the diocese
   is the principal thing and the principal negative for me. I am
   lacking so much in what is necessary to business and government!
   Without any further examination the following facts will convince
   you of this:

a. Neither at St. Sulpice, at Rennes, nor at Baltimore was I given any
   charge—no title whatever relating to temporal or ecclesiastical
   affairs was ever conferred on me. I have never been chancellor,
   secretary, or Vicar-General. Everywhere that I have been everyone else was preferred before me, and very often men much younger
   than myself.

b. Here the proof has been decisive—Mr. Dubois, when he withdrew,
   gave *the strongest recommendations against me.* Mr. Egan succeeded to everything and he barred me even from the council, stating frankly that nothing could be done with me. The second government under Mr. McGerry was the same. The third under Mr.
   Purcell the same. Only to be vice president; he declared to Mr.
   McGerry that I should not participate in the administration. At
   present I am more of a zero than strangers. I learn from others
   what is going on. It is the same thing at St. Joseph's. When the
   Archbishop and Mr. Deluol appointed me confessor, Mr. Hickey
   distrusted me completely. You will say that I was appointed
   president of Baltimore College for three years, well it is the only
   time that I was superior and then only in a literary way having

nothing to do with the administration. Maréchal, Tessier, and Harent governed the institution and M. Joubert was procurator of the college. Finally, Your Lordship, here is the simple copy of the reply made by Archbishop Maréchal to the Propaganda when ten years earlier I might have appeared less incapable than at present. They consulted him on this same question of a bishopric. "September 4, 1823, The Holy See has asked me if you are a fit subject for an important post. I have just answered that you are etc., etc., (he testifies to my studies and piety) but that you are so light-headed that a mitre would not suit you." I am positive that Archbishop Whitfield has since expressed the same opinion. Archbishop Maréchal reassuring me thus adds: "See if I have not true friendship for you" that is to say by hindering a false appointment which might ruin the only limited good to which I am by nature fitted and consequently, that of the people and the diocese that I might have ten years ago badly administered for its unhappiness and mine.

5. I can only add that such is the unanimous opinion of my confrères here and especially those whom I have trained and having lived with me longer should be better judges. Once they leave here they never come back to give an account of themselves nor do they come back to confession to me but rather to Mr. Purcell and the others.

I have now only to add that I have nothing and am literally poor, except my books which would be useless at Vincennes. I have given up everything even what remained to me in 1824, of the small portion left to me by my Mother in France. I have no vestments but a few common ones. I would be a real burden to everyone without any revenue from my family—no money whatever in the bank— only three hundred dollars without interest in the house here, but this last note is superfluous.

(I am not even a naturalized American. I am French.) Try to choose a young active priest of this country, Mr. Reynolds from Bishop Flaget's diocese, or some one from among your zealous men of Missouri, or of New Orleans, Baltimore, Philadelphia, or one of the Fathers of the Society as Bishop Fenwick of Boston who has done so well. I am the most incapable of all. Above all, practice the great, and this is the only true, rule: an old burgomaster can only be a very poor bishop. Please read carefully and having made this bad choice countermand it both of you. Simon Bruté.

P. S. I have written in God's presence *what is true* concerning myself
and what I believe to be true concerning the necessary requirements which are just the opposite in me: age, strength, horseback
riding, English, spirit and manners of the country, language, conversation, melancholy character, inexperience in affairs, opinions
of those who should know me, destruction of the good which I am
fit for, a badly begun diocese where the Church is very much to be
pitied if it urges forward those bishoprics without providing for
them the proper bishop.[62]

The terrifying cholera appeared again in 1833. Fortunately it did not enter Maryland this time; however, the
southern and the western states suffered intensely under its
cruel ravages. Many fell victims to the pestilence in New
Orleans. Cincinnati, that had suffered the loss of good
Bishop Fenwick on September 26, 1832, again suffered
heavily in this following year. The Bishop of New Orleans
died in September and three Sisters of Charity passed to
their reward during the same year or as Father Bruté said:
"We sent three Sisters to heaven this year." He also
announced that since the reappearance of the cholera, more
postulants than usual entered the Sisterhood.[63]

The Mountain for a second time was to be deprived of
its president to fill a vacant bishopric. In 1833 Father
Purcell was nominated to the see of Cincinnati. Father
Bruté fearing that a change in government at the close
of the academic year would be injurious to the future of the
institution, hurriedly wrote to the Archbishop asking that
the nomination be kept secret for the present and if possible
leave the public to suppose that the following year would
commence under the same president.[64] It was impossible
to keep such news secret. In a letter to Bishop Rosati,
Father Bruté bewailed the fact that the nomination had
been announced to the public; nevertheless, he was among

[62] S. Bruté to J. Rosati, 12–17, 1832. St. LCA.
[63] Cf. 7 Letters of S. Bruté to A. Bruté, 1833. Canon Bruté de
Rémur Collection.
[64] S. Bruté to J. Whitfield, 6–12, 1833, CA of A.

the first to extend congratulations to the bishop-elect and neither one nor two letters were sufficient to convey all he wished to say to the newly appointed prelate. Attached to the second letter was a separate page bearing the following five points of excellent advice:

1. Dimidium facti qui bene capit habet
   resolved to *begin* well—both *piety* and *administration*.

2. For administration—the rule for a parish holds for a diocese—all *eyes* and all *ears* and no *hand* in the first moments—to study the work, the ground, the fellow laborers, the people—*act* and *reform* little, condemn and also approve little—pledge nothing but principles, affection, and good will.

3. Not to be a Mountaineer or of any sectional partiality—not Dominican—not Jesuit—but all to all your clergy—let them all be convinced that in *all* you know but the *priest*.

4. Not to be Irishman, American, Marylander, Kentuckian—nothing— not to enter into party concerns, no, not for the best appearance as v. g. to be at meetings for the affairs of Ireland—or for the Union here—or Nullification—Here all will say of Bishop Purcell:

   "Tous, de pays divers nous sommes et tous pourtant n'avons
   qu'un coeur pour aimer notre bienfaiteur,
   l'ami de Dieu, l'ami des hommes."

   "Errans, il est pour un père
   Méchants il est votre sauveur
   Pêcheurs, c'est votre protecteur
   Orphelins, il est votre mère."

5. They in literature, adopt a model for style, Cicero, Tacitus, or Livy —of the Saints adopt also one, v. g. St. Francis de Sales, as did Bishop Flaget—and so well succeeded.[65]

The same year marks another important event to which Father Bruté's name will always remain attached. The Second Provincial Council of Baltimore convened in October, 1833, and witnessed even a larger attendance than the First

[65] Original in CA of A, 1833.

Council. The superior of the Mountain Seminary, as usual, was interested in several momentous problems. His courage permitted him to present some of these questions personally; others he presented through bishops whom he considered more influential than himself. As early as in the month of May, he suggested a resolution whereby Catholic laymen would give support and endowments to the seminaries.[66] He considered the premeditated suppression of the See of Richmond to be an unmistakable evil and he wished to avert it. Here again he appealed to Bishop Rosati and offered the bishop his notes to use in argument against this suppression. He pleaded that the See be permitted to exist at least until after the next Council which would convene in 1837, saying, "How interesting the future of this country is becoming and how important it is never to make a backward step except in a true necessity."[67]

At the opening of the Council Father Bruté presented the following important propositions in writing. According to his judgment the principal point to examine in the Second Provincial Council is the mode to be established for electing bishops. Until now they had been chosen in one of the five following ways:

1. *Proprio motu.* Some one without authority or warrant suggests a subject to the Holy See. In this way Bishop Concanen, Bishop Connolly, Bishops Conwell, Kelly, and England were appointed.

2. The Archbishop and his suffragans agree upon a person, and such was the presentation of Bishop David as coadjutor of Bardstown.

3. Others have been appointed on the presentation of the Bishop of the diocese, who desired a coadjutor; and in this way Reverend Mr. Blanc was named to the See of New Orleans, which he refused, and Reverend Mr. Chabrat is now for Kentucky.

4. Some have been presented by bishops of other dioceses without the participation of the Archbishop. Thus Bishop Purcell was appointed at the instance of Bishop England; Bishop Kenrick had

[66] S. Bruté to J. Rosati, 5–2, 1833. St. LCA.
[67] St. LCA, 9–17, 1833.

written to Rome in favor of Reverend John Hughes and the Archbishop in favor of Father Dubuisson.

5. Lastly, for the first nomination, that of Bishop Carroll, the Pope
granted the clergy the privilege of electing the bishop, but only for
that occasion, reserving in future the nomination to the Propaganda.

"Rome asks the present Council to lay its wishes before the
Pope for his approbation, as to a regular mode of election
to be observed in future. The Propaganda has stated that
they will not object to grant America election as in
Ireland."[68]

After the departure of Bishop Purcell from Mount St.
Mary's the sole responsibility of the institution rested
upon Father Jamison until February 1834. In a letter to
Rosati, dated March 19, Father Bruté related that a change
of government at the Mountain had just been effected. His
Grace, Most Reverend J. Whitfield, and Father Deluol were
present. Reverend Mr. Butler, the newly appointed president, was given two assistants, Fathers Sorin and Wheelan.
Referring to this same event, one month later, he said that
His Grace with Fathers Deluol and Elder remained five days
to examine everything at the Mountain. Father McCaffrey
was appointed vice president and Father Bruté was forced
to take the title, "Superior of the Seminary." Everything
passed very calmly and the Archbishop was extremely well
pleased with the Mountain.[69]

A few months later the Bulls arrived appointing Reverend
S. Eccleston coadjutor *cum iure successionis* to the Most
Reverend J. Whitfield. On Pentecost Sunday Father Bruté
in the name of the Mountain sent congratulations and
felicitations to this honored prelate. In July he sent a
second letter to Reverend Dr. Eccleston, requesting him to
conduct the retreat at the Mountain Seminary from August
10 to 15. This letter is singular from the point of view

[68] De Courcy—Shea. *History of the Catholic Church in the United
States*, pp. 129–131. New York, 1856.

[69] S. Bruté to J. Rosati, 3–19, 1834; 4–20, 1834, St. LCA.

that it is the first one bearing the signature, S. Bruté, Supr.[70]

The Second Provincial Council of Baltimore had considered questions not only proposed by Father Bruté, but also an important problem concerning him. The erection of a new diocese in the Northwest Territory had been discussed for several years. When the Second Council convened, this same problem was one of the first to receive the attention and approbation of the assembly. Thereupon, the Fathers of the Second Provincial Council requested the Sovereign Pontiff, Gregory XVI to erect the State of Indiana and part of Illinois into a new bishopric with the diocesan seat at Vincennes, Indiana, and to appoint Reverend Dr. Bruté de Rémur the first bishop.[71]

[70] BCA, Case 24–G⁷; Case 24–G⁸.
[71] *Concilia Provincialia Baltimorensia.* Baltimore, 1851. p. 100.

CHAPTER IX

CATHOLICISM IN INDIANA PRIOR TO 1834

Catholicism and civilization, in New France, flourished for two centuries and more before the erection of the diocese of Vincennes. The first civilized nation to explore the primeval forests north of *La Belle Riviere* was Catholic France. She took possession of it in the name of the king and the section formed no mean portion of the French claims in the New World. Hence the territory that now comprises Indiana was under the government of a Catholic monarch from the date of its first ownership by the white man down to the year 1763.

Since the introduction of Catholicism in Indiana, the territory of the present state has passed under the government of various ecclesiastical and civil jurisdictions. Flags of three great world powers have guided and guarded the destinies of the state, each in turn consigning to oblivion the statutes and privileges of the conquered nation and establishing new standards of jurisprudence to regulate the lives of its inhabitants. The same statement, however, cannot be affirmed of the ecclesiastical power. While the territory passed from one ecclesiastical jurisdiction to another, the laws and privileges as a whole remained unchanged since the Roman Catholic Church is One, professing the same faith, maintaining the same creed, laboring for the same universal purpose: the salvation of the masses.

The early missionaries, who first visited the French possessions depended directly on the Holy See. In 1632 the Archbishop of Rouen with the approbation of the Holy See extended his jurisdiction over the country but we have no documentary evidence to substantiate the statement that any one of these first evangelizers penetrated the wilds of Indiana before that date. On the contrary, it is almost incredible to believe that they reached this distant inland sec-

tion at that early date when the land was a veritable forest,
travel almost impossible, dangers numerous, and the deprivation of every convenience beyond present comprehen-
sion.

In 1657 France petitioned the Holy See to erect a bishopric in Canada but desired the Bishop-elect to remain a
Vicar General of the Archbishop of Rouen. After mature
deliberation the Holy See deemed it more prudent to create
a Vicariate Apostolic and to vest the administrative powers
in the scholarly François de Montmorency Laval. The Archbishop of Rouen protested against this and the parliament
of the city defied the authority of the Holy See and forbade
Monseigneur Laval to exercise the function of Vicar Apostolic in New France. Influenced by this opposition the
bishop who was to consecrate François Laval declined to
proceed. The newly appointed prelate was then consecrated
in the chapel of the Benedictine Abbey of St. Germain des
Près, at Paris, Bishop of Petraea and Vicar Apostolic of
New France on December 8, 1658, by the Pope's nuncio.
Upon his arrival at Quebec the following year, 1659, he
found the colony on the verge of ruin. It was suffering
from continual ravages made by bands of Iroquois against
whom the most heroic French settlers seemed ineffective.
Bishop Laval immediately joined the civil authorities in
appealing to the French government for troops to protect
the colony and then turned courageously to his primary
work, the spiritual advancement of the flock. This was not
to be accomplished without difficulty; however, in a short
time he happily succeeded in adjusting matters agreeably
with the Archbishop of Rouen and immediately set about
the organization of his vast diocese.[1]

The Bulls creating the See of Quebec were issued in 1674.
Bishop François de Montmorency Laval was appointed to
the bishopric and continued his commendable labors for
fourteen years. At this period the See of Quebec compre-

[1] Shea, I (1886) pp. 250–261;   A. Gosselin, *Le Venerable François
de Montmorency Laval*, Quebec, 1906.

hended all the possessions of France in North America, Newfoundland, Cape Breton, Acadia, Ile St. Jean, all New France from the Atlantic to the plains of the far West, the valley of the Mississippi, a territory more extensive than Europe. This vast domain east and west of the Mississippi was wholly a French possession and its government was under the jurisdiction of France. The language and customs were French and the priests: the Jesuits and Fathers of the Foreign Missions, who labored in the mission field were French. Who the first white man was that entered the present state of Indiana, and when and where he did so remain still unsettled questions. "As to the date of the establishment by Sieur de Vincennes of the military post which later bore his name, it is assigned in the latest and most decisive inquiry into the subject to late in 1732 or early in 1733."[2] The Old Post maintains a definite and fixed place in American History. It is not within our present field to discuss this feature at length; hence it suffices to say there is but meagre evidence to substantiate the statement that Vincennes was founded in 1702. Truths revealed through scholarly research such as are recorded in the volume entitled *Le Sieur de Vincennes Fondateur de l'Indiana et sa Famille* by Pierre-Georges Roy, are legitimate evidence to disprove the early date, 1702.[3] Mr. P. G. Roy is, on this subject, an authority that historians recognize.

The first recorded fact in the history of the Catholic Church at Post Vincennes, Indiana, was a marriage at St. Francis Xavier, bearing date of April 21, 1749. The entry was signed by Father Sebastian Louis Meurin, S. J.[4] Practical judgment and reason convince us that Catholic ministrations at Vincennes preceded the first registered facts but we have no authority to assign them to any

[2] G. J. Garraghan, (CHR), XV (1930), pp. 351–362. "Earliest Settlements of the Illinois Country."

[3] Pierre-Georges Roy, *Le Sieur de Vincennes, Fondateur de l'Indiana.* Quebec, 1919.

[4] H. J. Alerding, *The Diocese of Vincennes*, p. 56; Records. Old Cathedral Archives. Vincennes, Ind.

specific date. Missionaries were scarce and a resident
pastor would not have been stationed at a mission unless
Catholicism had been established earlier. According to an
account given by the Bishop of Quebec, Father Meurin had
ministered to the inhabitants of Kaskaskia from 1741 to
1748 and from there he departed for Vincennes. If he
labored at Vincennes prior to 1749 no records of his deeds
were preserved. His signature is attached to all records
at St. Francis Xavier's church from the above date to
March 17, 1753,[5] a circumstance indicating that Father
Meurin was the only priest ministering to the inhabitants
at the Old Post during those years. The certificates were
signed also by M. de St. Ange, Lieutenant of Marines and
Commandant for the king at Post Vincennes, indicative of
the close relations maintained at that period between civil
and ecclesiastical power in the mother country, France.

Father S. L. Meurin, S. J., was transferred to Prairie du
Rocher in 1753 and in 1760 he was appointed Vicar General
by the Bishop of Quebec. This transfer wrought no change
in the spiritual order for Father Louis Vivier, S. J., immediately succeeded to Vincennes to continue the care of souls.
All records between 1753 and 1756 bear his signature. He
died at Vincennes, October 2, 1756. The signature of
Father Julian Duvernay, S. J., appears on the register for
the first time on August 28, 1756. He labored zealously for
seven years at the mission of St. Francis Xavier and would
have been engaged in the harvest for many years had foreign agents not closed his successful ministrations and
forced his departure from the Old Post. He was the last
Jesuit missionary to reside at Vincennes.[6]

No civil or political changes disturbed the spiritual administration of these missions until 1763. The long conflict
between France and England for the control of North
America ended in that year, when France by the Treaty of

[5] *Idem*, p. 57.
[6] *Idem*, p. 58; J. Dilhet—P. W. Browne, *Beginnings of the Catholic
Church in the United States*, p. 224. Washington, 1922.

Paris ceded to England Canada and all her possessions east of the Mississippi river. In the previous year the territory west of the Mississippi river had been ceded by France to Spain by the Treaty of Fontainebleau. The ecclesiastical jurisdiction for the present remained unchanged. The diocese of Quebec still embraced the newly acquired Spanish and English possessions. The Spanish authorities on the west side of the Mississippi river resented anything savoring of English dominion and refused to recognize the authority of the bishop of Quebec. Jealousy increased to such a degree that Father Meurin residing at St. Genevieve was at once cited by the Spanish commandant for publishing a jubilee announcement of the bishop of Quebec. Louisiana, or the territory on the west of the Mississippi river, then passed under the Spanish ecclesiastical jurisdiction of the diocese of Santiago in Cuba and remained subject to its orders until 1793. The Indiana country remained subject to the diocese of Quebec. The British authorities raised no question concerning this because Quebec was located within their possessions. But the conspiracy of Pontiac delayed the complete transfer of the Northwest Territory and only in 1765 at the close of almost another three years fighting and negotiating did the British forces take possession of the last French posts in the West.

This delay permitted the French New Orleans Council[7] to enter the unsettled territory north of the Ohio river in 1763, then English territory, and to execute the decree of banishment against the Jesuits. Father Julian Duvernay, S. J., mentioned above, was resident pastor at Vincennes at the time of this hostile act and after his departure the inhabitants of the Old Post suffered the deprivation of all religious consolation for a period of almost seven years.

[7] The order of the Superior Council of New Orleans under which the Jesuits were banished from the missions of Michigan, Indiana, and Illinois preceded by ten years the actual suppression of the Society by Pope Clement XIV. The Society was restored by a decree of Pius VII, August 7, 1814. *Cf. Ill. Cath. Hist. Review*, I (1918–19), p. 62; IV (1921), p. 46; J. Rothensteiner, *op. cit.*, pp. 115–131.

During this interim religious fervor declined and the village was utterly demoralized. In 1767 they sent an account of their spiritual misery to their bishop but, owing to the troubled times, they received no response. Early in 1769 Father Gibault, residing at Kaskaskia, wrote Bishop Briand of Quebec in behalf of these suffering people, saying:

> For the necessities of the different posts of these countries I am almost certain that if your Lordship saw them for himself, he would not hesitate for a single moment to provide for them. There should be two more missionaries, one for the Tamarois twenty leagues from here, the other at Post Vincennes which is eighty leagues distant; disorder there is great, there being no one there to stop it. These persons living in sin nearly all die in despair. I was told of certain deaths the story of which cannot be heard without drawing tears. This portion of your flock is a prey to wolves, especially Post Vincennes where there are many people and much more able to support a pastor than the place where I reside.[8]

The inhabitants of the Post availed themselves of a second opportunity in the following letter to recount their spiritual sufferings to Right Reverend H. M. de Pontbriand,[9] Bishop of Quebec.

> The inhabitants of Vincennes to Bishop
> Pontbriand, asking for a priest.
> April 22, 1769.

Your Lordship:—

The object of this present letter is to beseech you in the name of all the inhabitants of the Post to send us a priest. Our just petitions are more pressing from the fact that we besought you two years ago for a priest and as yet have received no response to the

---

[8] P. Gibault, to J. Briand, 2–15, 1769. Transcript in Benedictine Archives, St. Meinrad, Indiana.

[9] Unknown to the inhabitants of Post Vincennes the Right Reverend H. M. de Pontbriand had died of a broken heart during the war and was succeeded by the Right Reverend J. O. Briand, who was Bishop at the date this letter was written.

letter addressed to you by Mr. Depain. We behold the inhabitants
of Kaskaskia suffering from the same deprivation.[10]

We beg Your Lordship to consider the dangerous state to
which this Post is reduced for the last five years. We are
abandoned and without any priest, a condition that effaces the
ancient principles of religion that we received from our ancestors.
We are unable to inculcate this religion into the hearts of our
children, owing to the misfortune of not being able to give them
the education that would place them in the way of salvation. We
hope that, through the zeal of the pastor whom it will please you
to send us, we may be enabled to place all the children in possession
of the Catholic religion. We pray Your Lordship to be indulgent
enough to send us a priest.

As for our Post, we are able to give you only a very meagre or
faint idea of the misfortunes which befall us because of the little
religion that we have preserved since we have been deprived of the
missionaries who labored in the parish before our present time.
The sad state and the bad disorder causes great evil among some
children. They have no fear of their own fathers, live in ignorance,
and abandon themselves to every vice of which wilful youth is
capable and flee from the path of virtue. This, plus numerous other
inconveniences may be the result of not being able to practice their
christian duties of which they have been deprived for so long a
time. A great number of Christians die without receiving the
Sacraments of Holy Viaticum and Extreme Unction.

The people who have acquainted us with your great love for the
service of God encourage us that you will be attentive to our complaints. We trust you will grant our petitions and send us a priest
who will be able to place us on the right path to a prompt return to
God.

[10] The sufferings in the Illinois country were not however as intense as those experienced by the inhabitants at Vincennes. After
the expulsion of the Jesuits in 1763 there still remained two Recollect
priests, Fathers Luke and Hypolite Collet. The following year Father
S. L. Meurin was permitted to return. He did his best to serve the
missions but it was impossible to reach all. Finally the Bishop of
Quebec in response to Father Meurin's earnest entreaties, sent Father
Gibault as his Vicar General to the Illinois country. Cf. *Ill. Cath.
Hist. Review*, I (1918–19), p. 320.

We offer to defray all expenses incurred by his voyage from Canada and also to pay the person who will bring him to the Post. We realize that you are not ignorant of the number of inhabitants here and the great necessity of a leader to maintain all in the way of salvation. In the meantime we shall pray heaven that our petitions be granted and that you will send us a priest.

With very profound respect, Your Lordship, we are,

Your very humble and obedient servants,

Ste. Marit,

Commander.[11]

The bishop, touched by this humble request, directed Very Reverend P. Gibault, his Vicar General of Illinois and the adjoining country, to take charge of Vincennes. In compliance with this behest Father Gibault repaired to Vincennes late in 1770 and remained two months. He wrote his bishop during this first visit estimating the population at seven or eight hundred inhabitants. He imparted encouraging information regarding the mission and rendered an account of his labors. Marriages that had been contracted before witnesses in the absence of a priest were renewed, baptismal ceremonies were supplied for children who had received lay baptism, and converts were instructed in the true religion. Father Gibault made occasional visits to Vincennes for several years. But the duties of this missionary were too numerous for him to extend these visits beyond a period of a month. He resided successively at Kaskaskia, Cahokia, and St. Genevieve.[12] After the death of Father Meurin in 1777 he was for a long time the only priest in Indiana and Illinois.

For some unexplained reason the Proclamation of 1763 made no provision for civil government in the Indian reserve. The people had neither French nor English law but were at the caprice of petty military tyrants and Indian

[11] Original in Archives at Archbishop's Palace. Quebec, Canada. Etats-Unis. VI, 14.

[12] P. Gibault to J. Briand (1770), Transcript in Benedictine Archives, St. Meinrad, Ind.; *Ill. Cath. Hist. Review*, I (1918–19), p. 81.

agents. The inhabitants became dissatisfied and numerous misunderstandings arose between the French and the English, until in 1770 this complaint assumed the form of a demand for civil government, which was provided in 1774 by the Quebec Act.

Ffteen years after the cession of the Northwest Territory by France to England another civil and political change disturbed the regained calm of Indiana territory. George Rogers Clark captured Kaskaskia in 1778 and took possession of the country in the name of the Commonwealth of Virginia. It was at this place that he met Father Gibault and acquainted him with his plans regarding the Indiana Country. Father Gibault in sympathy with the American cause hastened to Vincennes, where he lent his influence in winning over the people to the American cause. The event was scarcely accomplished when Governor Hamilton with a small force came down from Detroit, entered and took possession of the town in the name of the king of England. This capture was short-lived for Col. Clark returned in February 1779, retook the town from the British. From that date until 1784 it remained attached to the Commonwealth of Virginia. These heroic events make Vincennes one of the most cosmopolitan cities in the United States. She was founded under France, developed under England, became the parent of the American Union in the Northwest Territory and the mother of the five sister states, Indiana, Illinois, Ohio, Wisconsin, and Michigan. Vincennes was also the cradle of American world power for, owing to the revolutionary battles fought on her soil, our western frontier was extended from the Alleghanies to the Mississippi river. After that event the Old Post served as the veritable guardian of the nation's independence on the western frontier until Thomas Jefferson moved our western boundary beyond the Mississippi river to the Rockies.

The various civil and political changes that continually replaced each other to the date of 1784 effected no change in the ecclesiastical jurisdiction. The Northwest Territory continued to belong to the diocese of Quebec. But on June 9, 1784, by a decree of the Sacred Congregation of Propaganda, the newly federated United States became a separate ecclesiastical division, and the Very Reverend John Carroll was appointed Prefect Apostolic. Thus ended more than a century's ecclesiastical attachment of Indiana to the diocese of Quebec. The seven bishops who had occupied the See of Quebec and under whose jurisdiction Indiana territory had passed were: François de Montmorency Laval, 1658–1688; Jean Baptiste de la Croix Cheviere de St. Vallier, 1688–1727; Louis François Duplessis de Mornay, 1727–1733; Pierre Herman Dosquet, 1733–1739; François Louis Pourray d'L'Auberiviere, consecrated in 1739, and died a few days after arriving in Quebec; Henri-Marie de Pontbriand, 1741–1760; and Jean Olivier Briand 1766–1784.

Father Gibault, who for seventeen years had spent himself for the cause of religion in the Illinois country, took up permanent residence at Vincennes in May 1785. According to reports rendered his bishop he erected a new log church, dimension 90 x 42 feet, and then renovated the old building to serve as a presbytery. Prior to his coming the church registers contained only French and Indian names, but as a result of his untiring labors, the Catholic population increased rapidly and many English names began to appear on the baptismal records.[13]

After the establishment of the Prefecture Apostolic of the United States, question arose concerning the ecclesiastical jurisdiction of the Indiana country. A cordial exchange of letters relative to the matter took place between Jean François Hubert, Bishop of Quebec, and Very Reverend John Carroll, Prefect Apostolic of the United States. The case was then referred to the Holy See. Accordingly Rome recognized the territory as a possession of the American Federation and in response, by an Apostolic Brief dis-

---

[13] P. Gibault to J. Briand, 6–6, 1786. Transcript in Benedictine Archives, St. Meinrad; J. Rothensteiner, *op. cit.*, I, pp. 109–144.

patched on November 5, 1789, assigned it to the jurisdiction
of Very Reverend John Carroll. Father Gibault resided at
Vincennes until October 11, 1789. In a letter to the bishop
of Quebec dated May 22, 1788, he enumerates the years of
strenuous labor spent in this dangerous country, recounts
the severe trials that were his daily portion, the countless
sacrifices exacted of him besides the danger he constantly
encountered of being massacred by the savages. In addition
to this he adds his dislike to serve under another bishop
whether it be in the Spanish Dominion or the American
Republic and pleadingly begs his bishop to recall him to
Quebec.[14] Unfortunately he had incurred the displeasure of
the British government by his deep sympathy for the American cause and the Bishop of Quebec writing to Very
Reverend John Carroll on October 6, 1788 said that he could
not prudently consent to Father Gibault's return to the
Province of Quebec. The bishop further stated: "I propose
to give him no employment for the future. Nevertheless,
if you judge it proper to continue him as a missionary, I
ratify in advance all that you may be pleased to ordain
therein, either in regard to him or to other missionaries
now or in future."[15] Consequently he was not only dismissed by the Bishop of Quebec but, owing to the reports
which were spread concerning him, he was looked upon with
suspicion by the Prefect Apostolic of the United States, and
in his old age he was debarred from the ministry in the
field of his life's labor and died in obscurity at New
Madrid.[16]

In the meantime another expedient change in ecclesiastical authority was being arranged. The difficulties that the
Church had to encounter were becoming more numerous
and serious and the clergy realized the necessity of introducing episcopal government into the United States. A

[14] Original in Archdiocesan Archives, Quebec. Etats-Unis. VI, p.
68.
[15] Original in Archdiocesan Archives, Quebec. Etats-Unis, I, p. 1.
[16] *Ill. Cath. Hist. Review*, II (1919–20), p. 90; *St. Meinrad Historical Essays*, I (1928–30), pp. 7–15. St. Meinrad, Ind.; J. Rothensteiner, *op. cit.*, I, pp. 132–139.

committee was appointed to acquaint the Holy See immediately with their decision and to petition for a bishop. The Holy See acted promptly on the petition of the clergy and permission was granted the priests in America to name the place most suitable for an Episcopal See and, for this occasion only, to name the candidate for the new bishopric.

After receiving this message a circular was issued announcing a meeting of the clergy to convene at Whitemarsh in Maryland. The convocation was made in a canonical manner and this synodical assembly was held on the appointed day. Baltimore was the city selected for the new See. The result of the suffrages told twenty-four votes cast for Very Reverend John Carroll and only one besides his own cast in favor of another. When the authentic acts of this assembly reached the Sacred Congregation of Propaganda the Bulls erecting the diocese of Baltimore and appointing Very Reverend John Carroll the first bishop were issued under the seal of the Fisherman's ring on November 6, 1789. The founder of the American Hierarchy was consecrated in the chapel of Lulworth Castle, England, on the Feast of the Assumption, August 15, 1790, by Right Reverend Doctor Walmesley, O. S. B.[17]

Despite the formal decision rendered by the Holy See, the matter failed to be definitely understood and the boundaries between the dioceses of Quebec and Baltimore remained unsettled. On January 29, 1791, a further explanatory document relative to the same question was issued at Rome by the Sacred Congregation of Propaganda signed by L. Cardinal Antonelli, Prefect, wherein the views of the then reigning pontiff were contained in the following succinct lines.

Our Most Holy Father through Divine Providence, Pope Pius VI, declared that according to the tenor of the Apostolic Brief despatched on November 5, 1789, all the faithful living in communion with the Catholic Church both ecclesiastics and lay persons,

[17] Guilday, *Life and Times of John Carroll*, p. 373. New York, 1922.

whether they dwell in the provinces of federated America or in the neighboring regions outside the provinces, as long as they are subject to the government of the Republic, even though they belonged heretofore to some other diocese, will be and shall be hereafter under the jurisdiction of the Bishop of Baltimore, nothing to the contrary availing.[18]

When Bishop Carroll in 1790 found himself the responsible guardian of the Church in the United States his first concern was to supply priests to the numerous settlements which in number far exceeded the reserve of clergy. Under such circumstances he was forced to accept almost any ecclesiastic who presented himself and expressed a willingness to venture into the wilds on the western frontier. After making every possible concession and pressing into service all available ecclesiastics there remained many missions vacant. The departure of Father Gibault from Vincennes caused another three years' vacancy at Post Vincennes. The only opportunities accorded the inhabitants during this period to assist at Mass or receive the sacraments were granted upon occasional visits of travelling priests passing enroute to other destinations. A layman, Pierre Mallet, acted as guardian of St. Francis Xavier's Church until the arrival of another priest. Bishop Carroll had appealed to Europe for clergy and in a letter addressed to Bishop Hubert of Quebec, January 20, 1792, he says: "I await from France in the spring, several ecclesiastics, well selected to serve in the Illinois and at Post Vincennes." He adds, "You will oblige me very much if you will give me a reliable and exact list of the properties owned by your Church or your seminary in the United States. These possessions still belong to you, according to our laws, if you have not dispossessed yourself of them by an act on your part."[19] Bishop Carroll desired to establish order at Kaskaskia and Vincennes regarding some uncertain properties and thereby preserve the honor of both dioceses.

[18] Original in Archdiocesan Archives, Quebec. Etats-Unis, I, p. 3.
[19] Original in Archdiocesan Archives, Quebec. Etats-Unis, I, p. 2.

The Fathers of St. Sulpice at Paris were the first to respond to the mission call. Father Benedict Joseph Flaget, a worthy member of the Society, sailed from Bordeaux in January 1792 and arrived in Baltimore on March 29 of the same year. After spending several months in the Episcopal city he was appointed to Vincennes. Before his departure for the West, Bishop Carroll supplied him with letters of recommendation to General Wayne at Pittsburg, who in turn gave him a letter to George Rogers Clark. Colonel Clark met Reverend B. J. Flaget at Louisville and accompanied him to the Old Post. The zealous missionary arrived at Vincennes on December 21, 1792, after a tedious journey of six months. He found neither comfortable nor modern quarters and the church was in a sadly dilapidated state. It was an extremely poor, log building, sorely neglected, open to the weather and almost ready to collapse. This structure, however, was a veritable thermometer of the spiritual condition of the congregation. Everything in the picture bore a discouraging outlook, yet Father Flaget did not become despondent. True, his heart bled and he was grieved at the present state of spiritual affairs, but he set about as best he could to repair the church and to induce the parishioners to return to their Christian duty.

While formulating plans for the accomplishment of the imperative reform the necessity of which became daily more visible, the good priest was inspired with the happy thought, "a little child shall lead them." He must reach the hearts of the parents through their children. Within a short space of time Father Flaget opened a school, the first of its kind in the village and he himself became the first teacher. The children were taught, over and above the rudiments of secular learning, the principles of Christian Doctrine and the prayers of the Church. A singing class was formed and he taught them many beautiful French hymns which the children sang not only at church and at school but also while engaged in manual labor. Consequently they advanced in piety and devotion and aided Father Flaget in every little way possible to make the services of the church impressive.

Some of the more promising youths were taught how to serve Mass, and the services of the altar were rendered more touching by a group of these pious youths vested in acolyte garb within the sanctuary. The hearts of the parents were deeply moved. They beheld with wonder and surprise the great change wrought in their children and their hearts expanded with a determination not to be outdone by them. Accordingly they flocked to confession in great numbers and frequently appeared at the Holy Table.

Bishop Carroll was highly elated over this spiritual progress and prophesied that marvelous results would rise from out that portion of his vineyard. Writing Bishop Hubert of Quebec on May 12, 1793, he said:

> The villages in the Illinois country and at Post Vincennes, formerly under your jurisdiction, have for several months past enjoyed the benefit of having excellent priests there furnished me from France. I confess to you, dear bishop, that this gives me inexpressible consolation, and I feel convinced that that portion of my diocese will one day be the scene of widespread and flourishing Catholicism. I have urged these gentlemen to labor not only for the salvation of the present generation, but to form permanent institutions.[20]

Father Flaget also employed every available means to improve social conditions among his flock. He encouraged agriculture and domestic manufacturers and purchased a house with adjoining lands for a manual labor school with a view of giving the youth a knowledge of different trades. This project would have met with great success had the days of his service at Post Vincennes not been suddenly shortened. Two years and four months of fruitful labor marked the happy pastoral career of Father Flaget at Vincennes. Much to the regret of Bishop Carroll the youthful missionary was recalled by his superior to fill an office in St. Mary's Seminary at Baltimore. He had fulfilled well the offices of pastor, father, judge, and counsellor to these poor

[20] Original in Archdiocesan Archives, Quebec. Etats-Unis, I, p. 5.

simple folk and they were devotedly attached to him.   To
spare the feelings of his flock he departed secretly in the
latter part of April in 1795.[21]

Apparently Father Flaget left his flock in the path of
virtue but they soon returned to an indolent life when deprived of a missionary and the consolations of religion.
They had lived so long among the Indians with whom many
of them had intermarried, that they had contracted many
of the habits of savages.   They were on the path of decline when Father John Francis Rivet succeeded to the mission.   Father Rivet, another gift of the French Revolution,
was guided by Providence to the assistance of the Catholic
Church in America.   He fled from France in quest of safety
in 1791 and after experiencing the most trying ordeals arrived in Baltimore in 1794.

For several years Bishop Carroll had urged upon the government the duty of caring for the Indians.   He had spared
no influence with President Washington to induce the
military authorities to avail themselves of the services of
the Catholic missionaries for the civilization of the Indians
within American jurisdiction.   The Government declined
to act, on the basis of non-interference in religious matters.
The frequent disturbances that kept the frontier posts engaged in petty quarrels and warfare caused the statesmen
then in power to reconsider the narrow policy first maintained.   Washington recommended to Congress the adoption
of a more helpful treatment of the Indians, a more active
part in their civilization which would teach them the advantages of the Christian religion.   Thereupon Bishop Carroll offered the services of Reverend J. F. Rivet and the offer
was accepted.   A United States commission was issued to
him as "Missionary to the Indians" with a yearly allowance
of about two hundred dollars.

Father Rivet departed in May for his distant mission, St.
Francis Xavier at Post Vincennes and arrived there on
June 12, 1795.   The charge was new to him.   He was full

[21] H. J. Alerding, *History of the Diocese of Vincennes*, pp. 69–73.

of enthusiasm, yet he was practical and zealous. The subject of the conversion, the civilization, and the education of the Indian received thorough study and his conclusions were penned in a lengthy memoir addressed to the Secretary of War and another copy was sent to General Wayne. Father Rivet placed his memoir in the hands of Mr. Arthur St. Clair, Governor of the Territory of Indiana, on October 26, 1795. On the same day he wrote at length to Bishop Carroll, imparting to him a résumé of the memoir addressed to the government, and the detailed information regarding the Indian situation. He made but a cursory mention of the parish, saying, "I continue to attend the parish, awaiting the return of Reverend Mr. Flaget who is anxiously looked for." Intense interest in the great cause abounded in the heart of the zealous missionary and with his ability and keen knowledge of the savage, marvelous results would have been produced had the Government been more gracious in assisting him and the officials less ready to defraud him of the honest salary. In the same letter he complains that the salary for the first quarter had not been paid.[22]

Father Rivet wrote from Post Vincennes on April 30, 1796[23] to Father Neale at Baltimore and again to Bishop Carroll on May 4.[24] In both letters he complained of the lack of interest displayed by the Government in behalf of Indian education. They seemed to ignore his memoir. To Bishop Carroll he exposes for the first time the sad religious condition of Vincennes. Despite his earnest entreaties only forty-two persons of the three hundred and fifty communicants frequented the Holy Table. The laxity resulted not from ignorance for he attested that they were well aware of their duty. He asked Bishop Carroll to address them in a pastoral that would stress particular points, and to insist especially on the necessity of sending their children to catechism instruction. One of the great abuses indulged

[22] BCA, Case 8–BC[4].
[23] BCA, Case 8–BC[6].
[24] BCA, Case 8–BD[2].

in by the inhabitants at that time was that of permitting their children to grow up to their thirteenth and fourteenth years in absolute ignorance of all their duties of religion and then depriving them of further opportunities of receiving instruction after First Holy Communion. He also deplored the uncontrollable passion that the people had for nocturnal dances, but he adds that the custom was so strongly rooted that the priest was no longer allowed to speak on the subject. Rich and poor, old and young, even mother with small infants frequented such amusements. Nor were they satisfied with spending nights at it; the holy days and Sundays at times were spent in dancing. The additional perplexities that Father Rivet submits to his bishop from whom he seeks advice delineate perfectly the lamentable religious state of the white settlers at Post Vincennes.

Father Rivet considered the parish work merely a temporary responsibility, as is evident from the fact that in the Vincennes registers he styles himself "Missionary appointed for the savages, exercising the ministry, for the moment, in the parish of St. Francis Xavier."[25] But it is likewise evident from all his letters that he fulfilled most conscientiously the duties of the commission given him by the United States Government and that he devoted most of his time to the conversion and spiritual care of the Indian tribes. The soldiers at Fort Knox on the Wabash river about three miles from Vincennes also shared in his ministrations. Several of the soldiers were married men. Father Rivet baptized and instructed their children and in time of sickness he hurried to their bedside to administer the last consolations and blessings of holy Church. The good priest has left us no letters that would reveal his success in the holy ministry of souls, but events are books wherein are recorded success and failure, and contemporary with this time we find on records of converts the name of the Hon. William Clark, one of the judges of the Supreme Court in the Territory of Indiana. Upon another occasion

[25] H. J. Alerding, *op. cit.*, p. 73.

we find a distinguished literary man, although an infidel, deeply impressed by the personality of this priest. Volney, who made a tour of the United States, visited Vincennes, which he described as a village of some fifty houses scattered on an irregular prairie surrounded by forests. There he met Father Rivet of whom he speaks in the highest terms as a polished, learned, well-bred gentleman, very kind and tolerant toward all, and whose self-sacrificing efforts for the education of his flock, the Frenchman praises warmly.[26] Such instances, together with the numerous records of marriages, baptisms, conversions, and interments, testify that his success if not recorded in letters was recorded above.

Another inestimable loss befell Vincennes early in 1804. Privations and unremitting labor told early upon the constitution of the self-sacrificing priest so that his life was fast ebbing away. Father Rivet felt that the end was near; still he forced himself along and remained active to the end. On January 31 he recorded his last baptism. He then sent word to his nearest brother priest, Reverend Donatian Olivier, at Prairie du Rocher, to come and administer to him the last rites of holy Church. Anticipating his arrival he wrote out his confession. The Divine Master asked one more sacrifice, and the priest who had travelled hundreds of miles to bring comfort to the dying was denied the same supreme consolation. He sealed his confession addressed to Father Olivier, made a last act of resignation to God's will and expired in February 1804. Father Olivier arrived three days after Father Rivet's demise in time to celebrate his funeral. His death was an irreparable loss to the Bishop of Baltimore and to the inhabitants of Vincennes.[27]

Bishop Carroll was compelled once more to leave Vincennes without a priest. Missionaries from the adjoining states occasionally offered their services but these visits were few. Father Olivier from Illinois attended Vincennes from time to time during the year 1804 and 1805, but from

[26] Cf. Volney. *Tableau du Climat et du Sol des Etats-Unis.* Paris, 1803.

[27] H. J. Alerding, *op. cit.,* pp. 75–6.

July 1805 to April 1806 no missionary visited St. Francis Xavier at Post Vincennes. Fathers Badin and Nerinckx came up from Kentucky arriving at the mission on April 14, 1806, and remained until the twenty-seventh of the same month. This gave all the inhabitants ample opportunity to fulfill their Easter duty. An account of this visit was sent to Bishop Carroll by Father Nerinckx and the contents of this letter proved that the sad state of affairs existing at Post Vincennes described repeatedly by Father Rivet was only too true.

Father Nerinckx returned for a visit to the Old Post early in February 1807, and both he and Father Badin made the same journey of one hundred and eighty miles during the Easter-tide of that year. The former related that they ministered to five hundred people. He described the inhabitants as being very poor, lazy, and extravagant. A number of Miami Indians attended the Vincennes church, which was constructed of wood, and Father Nerinckx baptized several of their tribe on this occasion.[28] These two pioneer missionaries desired to remain longer but not wishing to slight their own flocks to minister to strangers they returned to their home missions. Father Nerinckx continually pleaded with his friends at home to come to assist religion in this section. He urged that each seminary in his fatherland send three priests every six or ten years and after a certain term of service they should be permitted to return to their native land.[29]

Bishop Carroll foresaw the destruction of great good in the Kentucky country that the departure of Father Nerinckx would occasion and he wrote requesting this zealous priest not to go to the Indiana territory. His Lordship intended to send two Belgian Jesuits, Father Francis Malevé and Father Giles Henry, to this neglected region as

[28] C. Nerinckx to his Parents. Fol. 552, 2–11, 1807; Fol. 868, 6–22, 1807. Originals in Musaeum Bollandianum. Brussels.
[29] C. Nerinckx to his Parents. Fol. 552. 5–16, 1806; C. Nerinckx to Father Feydherb. Fol. 552. 7–31, 1807. Originals in Musaeum Bollandianum. Brussels.

soon as other Jesuits arrived from Europe to fill their places at Georgetown. Likewise, Bishop Carroll's Vicar General in the Kentucky country, Father S. T. Badin, wished to keep Father Nerinckx with him.[30]

Inventions and commerce as well as wars in foreign countries brought a flood of emigrants to our shores. This national growth of the United States augmented both civil and religious difficulties and ushered in a multiplicity of problems to be treated not only by the civil but also by the ecclesiastical courts. The Louisiana country that increased the national domain 140% in 1803 passed under the charge of Bishop Carroll as administrator in 1805. A highly checkered career had marked the life of this territory since 1762 and time developed its complexity. Within forty years it had been consigned to four governments: twice, a French possession; once, ceded to Spain; the Stars and Stripes were the fourth to welcome it by purchase within their fold. Ecclesiastical changes were equally varied. From the Quebec jurisdiction it passed under Spanish dominion to the diocese of Santiago, Cuba, in 1763, and then to the diocese of Louisiana, created in 1793 under Bishop Luis Penalver y Cardenas. When the decree of Propaganda confided this additional territory to Bishop Carroll he immediately recommended to the Holy See the erection of four new dioceses and suggested that the sees be located at Boston, New York, Philadelphia, and Bardstown. His advanced age and the increased responsibilities made it expedient that aid be given him and that the vast diocese of Baltimore be divided. The latter projects, however, did not receive the immediate favor of the Sacred Congregation and for various reasons a division of the diocese was refused. Following a more thorough investigation of the situation the recommendation of Bishop Carroll was adopted by the Holy See and on April 8, 1808, the four new dioceses were created. The Bardstown diocese embraced

[30] C. Nerinckx to his Parents. Fol. 552, 6. 8–29, 1807. Original in Musaeum Bollandianum. Brussels.

the States of Kentucky and Tennessee, the Northwest Territory which now forms the states of Ohio, Indiana, Illinois, Michigan, Wisconsin, and that portion of Minnesota east of the Mississippi. The Bulls nominating Father B. J. Flaget the first bishop of the newly erected diocese were received at Baltimore, in September, 1808, but the Bishop-elect was not consecrated until November 4, 1810, and did not reach his see until the following year, May 9, 1811. In the meantime Bishop Carroll had been unable to realize his intentions regarding Fathers Malevé and Henry and consequently they never reached the poor, neglected mission at Vincennes. Father Badin visited the Post in early spring, 1808, and administered to the suffering inhabitants until Pentecost Tuesday. During this sojourn he officiated at the burial Mass of an Indian Chief, whose obsequies were attended by a great concourse of people. At this early date Father Badin thought that Post Vincennes for the Indiana Territory and Pittsburg for Ohio were both in need of a bishop. Father Nerinckx took a broader view of the situation and wrote: "If I were asked for my opinion I would say that each of the seventeen states needed a bishop. Catholics are numerous but they fear to call themselves such because of the heretics." He maintained that:

Each State possessed sufficient extension for a bishopric.

Catholics are already numerous in several States.

The only effective means of developing the Church would be to nominate more bishops.

Then was the opportune time to work for Providence only knew how soon the present peaceful conditions would disappear.

Bishops were needed to command the people, to regulate the lives of the priests, and to preach religion with authority.[31]

Vincennes had now passed from the immediate charge of Bishop Carroll to the jurisdiction of the newly appointed

[31] C. Nerinckx to his Parents. Fol. 552. 2–23, 1808; Pentecost Wednesday, 1808; C. Nerinckx to a friend. Folio 552. 7–26, 1808. Originals in Musaeum Bollandianum. Brussels.

Bishop Flaget yet there was little hope for early improvement owing to the scarcity of priests. Father Nerinckx continued his frequent and lengthy letters to his Belgian confrères begging them for aid, saying:

> Charity presses me to urge you to come soon to the assistance of those thousands and perhaps millions of souls. Every chapter and verse of the gospels urges us to practice this charity towards those poor people.—Vices are very flourishing because there are no priests. The whole country presents a heart-rending and lamentable spectacle. It is deprived of all spiritual consolations. Parents are extremely negligent in regard to their children—many die without Baptism and many grow up to join the ranks of sinners.[32]

In 1812 the Catholics of Vincennes realizing the lamentable condition of their city petitioned their new bishop for a resident pastor. General Harrison, the Governor of the Northwest Territory, residing then at Vincennes, signed the petition. He promised every aid within his power to promote the interests of the mission. For six years this request remained unanswered but not unheard. The bishop could not accede to the wishes of his people because he had no priest to send. Nor did the bishop himself reach that portion of his vast diocese until more than three years after his consecration. Visitations to the missions throughout the states of Ohio and Kentucky filled all the days of his first episcopal years. Then, too, there was another pause in the nation's peace which arrested both civil and religious progress. Hearts and homes were broken; terror reigned in the coast cities; the young Republic was engaged in war. This unsettled condition endangered travelling and retarded success for the worthy bishop who was striving to organize his new diocese. But the venerable founder of the Bardstown See lived near to God and permitted none of these exterior disturbances to frighten or turn him from

---

[32] C. Nerinckx to MM. les Pretres Belgas. Fol. 868, 11. Originals in Musaeum Bollandianum. Brussels.

good. He courageously continued the visitations, rejoicing that his labors were signed with the emblem of salvation. At length the name of his first Western mission—Vincennes —appeared on his schedule. On May 26, 1814, the bishop took leave of Fathers Badin and Chabrat at Louisville and started alone on horseback enroute to the Old Post. He arrived there on the third day, May 28. It would be impossible to give a more satisfactory account of this first visit of a bishop to Vincennes than by transcribing in part what he himself relates in his letters to Father J. B. David.

May 30.—Here I am at Post Vincennes since last Saturday at sunset. Seven or eight young men came to meet me as far as White river, where they remained two days; but seeing that I did not make my appearance on Saturday morning they lost patience and arriving at the village a quarter of an hour before me, had already announced that I was not coming. This little misunderstanding saved me the unpleasantness, and the poor people the trouble of a long premeditated reception. Arrived at the Church I quietly entered, recited a *Te Deum*, and gave a cordial embrace to the kind Reverend Mr. Olivier who had arrived shortly to accompany me to the Mississippi river. In a short time the house was filled with people; all knelt to ask my blessing and to kiss my ring. The old Canadians had taught this ceremony to their children. The joy I felt to see once more those old parishioners was unalloyed. I remember their names and faces with astonishing facility. Many of them shed tears at the thought that I had not forgotten them. I found them as I had anticipated, without religion, without restraint, etc. They had not as yet lost their faith, and a zealous priest in their midst would bring them back without trouble. You cannot imagine what pleasure they find in my company. My room is never empty, and they tender me compliments that would bother Bonaparte himself, as hard as his head is. "Oh! very dear Father," they sometimes say, "if you would only remain with us for a year, we would follow you like lambs, young and old, large and small." I really believe they are sincere and a zealous priest would make saints of them.

June 7.—The longer I remain at this station the more I am persuaded that my presence was necessary throughout this country. Last Sunday, more than one hundred persons received Holy Communion, and eighty-six received Confirmation. Next Thursday and the following Sunday several more are to receive Confirmation as well as the Holy Eucharist, for I follow the same plan I adopted in Kentucky. (To give Confirmation to those only who receive Holy Communion).

The sound of my voice alone, which the old flock remembers well, makes them shed tears. I have very little to do to touch them but this is yet far from converting them. God alone can work this miracle, and I hope He will work it in favor of many.

June 14.—I am still in great spiritual joy and admiration at the thought of the extraordinary fruits which have attended my visit. You could never form an idea of the spirit of compunction and repentance that has overcome the great majority of these good people. The like has never yet happened in any of my Kentucky missions. May God be ever blessed and glorified by it. The demon of petty vanity has breathed many a time in my ear. I hope I have that organ imperfect enough not to hear him. Last Sunday, more than seventy-eight received Confirmation and one hundred received Holy Communion.

After a stay of three weeks, Bishop Flaget took leave of his old parishioners on June 17. He wrote Father David from Cahokia on June 21, describing his journey to this place as a pleasant one. But he added that the present field before him had not as consoling an outlook as that of Post Vincennes. While conditions at the latter place left much to be desired the bishop perceived more lamentable negligence in other missions. This decline was due in great part to the prevailing war spirit.

The visitations being accomplished in Illinois and St. Louis, Bishop Flaget returned home by way of Vincennes. He arrived at Post Vincennes November 12, and remained two weeks with his former flock. During this second visit he twice administered the sacrament of Confirmation, the recipients numbering forty persons in all. According to the estimation of the bishop the parish then consisted of one hundred and thirty Catholic families.[33]

Dearth of missionaries again placed the parish of St. Francis Xavier at the mercy of visiting clergy for another four years. Father Rosati, later first Bishop of St. Louis, accompanied by a Sulpician priest came up from the Kentucky country at Easter time in 1817, and remained several weeks at Vincennes. This afforded the poor Catholics who scarcely ever saw a priest more than once or twice during the year an opportunity to comply with the command of the Church and fulfill their Easter duty.[34] Bishop Flaget accompanied by Father Badin visited Vincennes for a third time in January 1818. They remained two weeks alleviating the spiritual wants of the neglected parishioners and supplying all missionary duties. Shortly after this event Bishop Du Bourg tendered a helping hand to Bishop Flaget and offered the services of four of his priests. The Bishop of Bardstown accepted the offer. These priests were to be assigned to the mission of Indiana and Michigan and were to remain there until Bishop Flaget could make permanent arrangements for the care of these districts.

Accordingly on April 25, 1818, Fathers A. Blanc and F. Jeanjean were appointed resident missionaries for Vincennes. On June 1, 1818, they took their departure from Kentucky where they had been engaged in missionary labors since their arrival from Europe with Bishop Du Bourg. Father Blanc was given charge of the parish of St. Francis Xavier, while Father Jeanjean's charge consisted in founding a college. Owing to misunderstandings that arose among the people the attempt to establish the desired institution failed and Bishop Du Bourg recalled Father Jeanjean the following January, 1819. After three months

[33] These letters were communicated to Father Simon Bruté, by Father J. B. David, in 1814. They were preserved by the Historical Society of Quebec; placed at the disposal of Dom Paul Jausions, O. S. B., in July 1869; translated and published in the *Ave Maria*, V (1869), p. 547 ff., 561 ff., 595 ff.

[34] *Life of V. Rev. F. de Andreis*, pub. B. Herder, p. 145. St. Louis, 1900.

of solitary mission life Father Blanc was joined by a priest of the Congregation of the Missions, Father A. Ferrari.

During the pastorship of Father Blanc, Bishop Flaget accompanied by Father Abell visited the southern portion of Indiana for the fourth time. He stopped at Washington on his way to Vincennes. At the latter place Father Abell preached several times to the great delight and edification of the English inhabitants. After administering Confirmation, the bishop returned by way of Princeton and Evansville where he spent some time performing the usual duties of the holy ministry. Father Blanc continued his missionary labors in the Indiana country until February 1820. He was then recalled by Bishop Du Bourg and sent to New Orleans. During his stay at Vincennes he erected two log churches, one in Daviess country, Indiana, seven miles from Washington, and the other on the Illinois side of the Wabash where a French settlement had been founded twelve miles from Vincennes. Upon the departure of Father Blanc, Father Dahmen, a priest from the diocese of New Orleans, was placed in charge of Vincennes. He too was recalled in November 1821, leaving Vincennes a vacant mission for another two years. Fathers Richard and Brassac from Detroit visited the mission late in 1821[35]

On March 20, 1823, Bishop Flaget ordained Reverend Leo Champomier at Bardstown Seminary and on June 11, appointed him to Vincennes. He was the first priest from the diocese of Bardstown whom Bishop Flaget had been able to place permanently in Indiana. In August, 1823, the bishop went again to Vincennes to settle affairs connected with the residence there of the newly appointed pastor. In going and returning he visited Mt. Pleasant, where he confirmed thirty-four persons. He also visited Washington and two French settlements on the Wabash. On his return he reported that the people at the Old Post wished to have an establishment of Sisters to conduct a school.[36] Vincennes,

[35] H. J. Alerding. *op. cit.*, pp. 88–92; *The Catholic Telegraph,* IV (1835), p. 25.

[36] *Idem*, pp. 92–3; Shea, III, p. 297.

however, grew slowly and the thoughtless spirit of the
people changed but slightly. Father Champomier found
his position a difficult one. Nine months had elapsed and no
provision had been made for the maintenance of their
pastor. He was forced to be content with whatever they
wished to give him and often when mealtime approached
there was not even a morsel of bread in his house. The
cassocks which he had brought from France in 1821 were
falling into shreds and he had not wherewith to buy a new
one. The rectory resembled the stable of Bethlehem and the
church was not even suitable for housing beasts of the
forest.[37] One of the pioneer Journals of that date preserved
the following description of the Vincennes Church.

> Were you to see this edifice which I style a church you would
> doubtless call in question its right to that name, and rather de-
> nominate it a ruined hovel. But I give it that appellation, notwith-
> standing its rough materials, unseemly form, and ruinous condition,
> because it was erected by the Jesuit missionaries to serve as such.[38]

Notwithstanding all this poverty Father Champomier
was happy and in writing Father Badin he begged his confrère to unite in thanksgiving with him for the unhoped for
blessings which the Lord had granted to his labors, saying:

> The greater part of my sheep have approached the sacraments, at
> least that of Penance. There were a great number who had not
> been to confession for twenty, forty and even fifty years. Since
> my arrival at the Post I have declared open warfare on the more
> shameful and scandalous vices at the peril of my life. A number
> of scandalous sinners have been converted, performed public
> penance, and have since led edifying lives. Moreover, fifty Protest-
> ants have made their abjuration.[39]

That same year witnessed another happy change in the
village which at that time had a population ranging from

[37] *Annales de la Propagation de la Foi*, III (1828), pp. 221–2. Paris.
[38] *The United States Catholic Miscellany*, V (1825), p. 236.
[39] *Annales de la Propagation de la Foi*, III (1828), p. 222.

one thousand to fifteen hundred. Four Sisters of Charity from Nazareth, Kentucky, assumed the educational responsibilities of the place and established there an academy and day-school.

This marked success in the spiritual harvest urged the zealous pastor to formulate plans for a new church. The project, however, presented a discouraging outlook. It was impossible for him to build a church unless someone would come to his aid. Consequently, he decided to make their indigence known to the public. His first appeal was addressed to his fatherland through Father Badin. In the meantime while awaiting the response he lived in dire poverty and labored incessantly for the improvement of his flock. At this period Indiana was meeting with a great increase in population, but the poverty of these new-comers was greater even than that of the inhabitants. In earlier years the missionary of Vincennes could keep guard over his flock from the rectory. In one day he could see, if he desired, the greater part of his flock, but those conditions had disappeared. Father Champomier's visitation took him to every part of Indiana and Illinois. These journeys were long and numerous since there were more than forty places to visit. Likewise they demanded copious means but the poor missionary received scarcely forty-five dollars a year. With such scanty revenue how was it possible for him to clothe and feed himself and meet the expenses of journeys that averaged three thousand miles a year? Yet he did it, but he himself scarcely knew how it had been accomplished.[40]

On July 23, 1825, Father Champomier officially placed the following announcement before the inhabitants of Vincennes.

Vincennes offering no suitable place of divine worship, at least outwardly testifying the inward piety of its inhabitants, the Catholics of the town and neighborhood, notwithstanding their

[40] *Idem*, pp. 224–5.

acknowledged poverty, propose to have a neat, if not a splendid, brick church erected in the course of the present and ensuing season. Should their fellow citizens wish to join them in the attempt, or benevolently aid the enterprise, they would gratefully accept of their assistance. Although it is for the celebration of the Roman Catholic worship still all who conduct themselves properly will be allowed admittance, as well as the possession of pews. Sunday next, July 24, 1825, at three o'clock in the afternoon, a meeting of all the members of the congregation, to consult upon the most proper means to carry the project into execution, will take place in the school room of the Sisters. All persons desirous of attending will gratify us in accomplishing their wishes.[41]

This meeting was held and a committee appointed. Preparations for the construction of the building began immediately and various means were used to collect funds. On August 1, 1825, Father Champomier left Vincennes for the purpose of recommending his church to the charity of generous souls at St. Louis and neighboring places in Missouri. Despite the poverty of the country Providence granted the good priest notable success. He hastened back to his flock and after having ministered to their wants he turned his steps towards Kentucky. Both at Louisville and in Scott County the people gave generous alms. Through Father Badin the Society for the Propagation of the Faith in France sent appreciable assistance. Hence by January 1, 1826, the bricks and timbers for the construction of the church were ready and thus far all expenses were defrayed.[42] On March 4, 1826, the *Western Sun* carried the following announcement:

All the inhabitants of Indiana and Illinois must know that on the 30th of the present month, that is on Thursday in Easter week, the corner stone of the Roman Catholic Cathedral of Vincennes will be laid, the ceremony commencing at 10 o'clock A. M.

[41] H. S. Cauthorn, *History of St. Francis Xavier Cathedral*, p. 21. Indianapolis, 1892; *The Western Sun*, XVI (1825). Vincennes.
[42] *Annales de la Propagation de la Foi*, III (1828), pp. 227–8.

The two adjoining States will soon form one diocese, of which Vincennes, being the most central town, will become the residence of a prelate. His beneficence, however, will not be confined to this spot. No! all shall feel the effects of it; Catholic and Protestant shall be the object of his ardent zeal and tender charity. May the earnest prayer of the Saviour of mankind, made to his heavenly Father for all His followers, be heard in our behalf, viz., that they might become one together, as He and His Father were one.... Attend and testify that holy joy which every heart should feel whenever a temple is to be raised to the glory of the Almighty.... It is needless to say the greatest order and decorum are to be observed. May we be able to say, in truth, with a celebrated orator, "That there is not a State in North America which does not testify to the traveler the existence of a Supreme Being," and, moreover, does not proclaim to the eye that the Gospel has reached every part of the union. At present this cannot be said of Indiana; the only temple in it deserving the name, having of late been converted into a ballroom. All are desired to come early, to give time to arrange them in order for the procession.[43]

J. L. Champomier.

The ceremony conducted by Father Champomier and attended by a great concourse of citizens occurred on March 30, 1826.

The cornerstone was a square oriental granite, highly polished on one side, and inscribed under the three symbols of the cross in handsome Roman characters. *Tu es Petrus, et super hanc petram aedificabo ecclesiam meam, et portae inferi non praevalebunt adversus eam.* Aedificata in honorem Sancti Francisci Xaverii, Rev. J. L. Champomier, parochus, 30 Mar., A. D. 1826.[44]

The construction progressed rapidly but from the following letter of Father Champomier to Father Badin we learn that the year 1826 was flooded with trials for the zealous pastor.

[43] H. S. Cauthorn, *op. cit.*, p. 22; *The Western Sun*, XVII (1826). Vincennes.
[44] *Idem,* May 6, 1826.

Vincennes. Jan. 17, 1827.

Reverend dear Father:—

I am to this date the only missionary for Indiana and Illinois. I am always on the go, sometimes in the woods assisting my poor parishioners in procuring timber and sometimes exposed to severe weather and illness on long journeys made in behalf of financial aid. On April 11, 1826, I left for the Eastern States. Our Lord who knew the purity of my designs deigned to accompany me with his grace. Two months after my departure I returned to the scene of my labors, bringing with me two thousand dollars.

After three months of hard work I left on another begging tour enroute to Canada. I crossed the savage country of Indiana where I met a great number of Catholic Indians and I promised to do everything possible to procure for them the aids of religion. I went by way of Detroit where I spent eight days with Father Richard. We mutually complimented each other on the hope of soon seeing a bishop come among us. Upon arriving in upper Canada I fell ill without acquaintances, friends, or money, but I continued on my journey until I could scarcely stand up. I was well received by the Canadian clergy, but I obtained small alms because of the great expense for construction and repair of churches under which these clergymen were laboring. My weakened condition also forced me to leave sooner than I had intended, but I would have died if I had stayed there many weeks longer. My friends in New York and Washington remembered me and offered generous assistance. This last journey consumed three months and four days.

Now I must acquaint you with news more distressing. On October 7, the virtuous and excellent Sister Henrietta Gardiner, whom you knew and esteemed, that worthy superior of my religious, died at Vincennes. She left all her sisters ill. She had vowed herself to the service of her God, for the salvation of her neighbor, and died without the sweet and last consolations of our holy religion.

On November 6, 1826, another disaster occurred. A hurricane suddenly struck Vincennes and swept everything before it. A number of buildings were overturned and among them were the two sides of our church. I learned this news on arriving at Louisville and repeating the words of holy Job, *Dominus dedit, Dominus*

abstulit, sit nomen Domini benedictum, I hurried back to Vincennes.
I realized the necessity of this church, therefore, I did not lose
courage, but trusting all the more in Divine Providence I set to
work again. I shall soon leave for the purpose of collecting in
Missouri, Louisiana, and perhaps Havana. I am,

Your humble servant,
J. L. Champomier, Miss. Apostolic.[45]

With a persevering spirit Father Champomier, upon his
return, had the walls rebuilt in a better manner and the
building was completed sufficiently to be used for services
in the summer of 1827. There was, however, a considerable
debt on the church and the interior remained unfinished
until the advent of Bishop Bruté. Very little was done
towards its decoration and completion during his life. This
was not owing to any want of zeal or interest on the part
of that devout prelate, but solely to a lack of funds.

The *Catholic Miscellany* of 1829 carried an account of
happenings at Vincennes that is worthy of reproduction in
our story. This description of Bishop Flaget's sixth visit
gives the reader a happy view of the spiritual improvement
that was wrought in the village by the zealous labors of their
worthy pastor, Father Champomier.

On the 17th of June the Right Reverend Doctor Flaget, the
venerable Bishop of Bardstown arrived amongst us on his visitation, accompanied by the Rev. Mr. Abell of Kentucky. You are
already aware of the great obstacles which we have met with in
our efforts to build a church. About 4 years ago the Rev. Mr.
Champomier, our pastor, undertook this formidable task, which our
resources could never accomplish; after travelling to several states,
he collected a large sum and saw the walls raised, and the roof
erected, the frames and sashes of the windows made and much
more of the wood-work in preparation, when a storm prostrated
the building and fire consumed the timber; thus was the labour of
a long period made suddenly unavailable. Our pastor did not de-
spond, he again set out, and Providence blessed his efforts; through

[45] *Annales de la Propagation de la Foi,* III (1828), pp. 230–2.

the kindness and charity of our brethren he was enabled to repair our loss. Our church is now one of the finest brick buildings of this portion of the West, perhaps the best building in the State of Indiana. It is built upon the model of the Cathedral at Bardstown; length 115 ft., breadth 60 ft., with five large circular headed windows on each side; a splendid cornice and unbroken roof. The steeple tower does not as yet rise higher than the ridge of the roof. In front there are three gates of entrance, with a fine window over each; all forming a beautiful frontispiece; the brickwork is neatly joined and painted. The interior is as yet in an imperfect state; the floor is laid, but the sanctuary is unfinished. The altar and pulpit are but temporary. The sanctuary is of the semi-circular form with a door on either side leading to small private chapels. There is, however, as yet a considerable debt for which the pastor is liable.

The great bulk of our congregation here is French, and the instructions are usually in that language; when it was announced that Mr. Abell would preach in English after the usual service in the evening, there was a manifestation of pleasure through our population, and the church was crowded. The preacher appeared struck with the contrast between the present and the former state of things in Vincennes, and accordingly, under the full force of his feelings, he addressed his fellow-countrymen to the following effect:—'Beloved Americans. Ten years have elapsed since I had the honor of accompanying our venerable Bishop hither on a previous visitation, and had the pleasure of announcing to you some of the truths of our holy religion on this spot. But under what different circumstances? The wretched hovel which we then called a church could not contain the faithful who pressed forward to partake of the sacred ordinances of the Saviour. In order to afford them that opportunity which the institutions of Heaven required, we were obliged to repress your laudable curiosity, and to exclude you from the morning office, whilst the flock partook of the tremendous mysteries of the altar. After the services in the evening, they with a gratified reluctance withdrew from their own altars to afford you the opportunity of hearing those sublime truths upon which rest their sweetest consolation in time, and their best hope in eternity. But now thanks to the unbounded zeal, the steady perseverance, and the patient industry of their pastor, we find ourselves in an edifice, capable of receiving the child and the stranger. An edifice, whose ample dimensions, like our affectionate hearts, expand to embrace you in the warmth of charity; and thus, by its silent, yet persuasive eloquence, invites us to form but one fold under one shepherd.'

The Bishop published here, the indulgence of Jubilee, and its exercises were very well attended. The deportment of the Catholic body was such as to be called by our separated brethren "a revival." The exercises commenced on Corpus Christi, the 18th of June, and continued eight days.—High Mass was sung at 9 o'clock in the morning on each day, at which there was a sermon; in the evening after prayer and singing there was another discourse: both of those instructions were in French, besides those we had the English instructions.

The Bishop's instructions and exhortations were of the most paternal and kind character.—He gave the Sacrament of confirmation to 172 persons; the number of communicants considerably exceeded 200, several of whom had long been absent from this most important of their religious obligations, and had lived in the habitual negligence of all church discipline, several even in open violation of the laws of God.

It is to be regretted that the visitation took place at the time that our planters are most busy; as several of them and their laborers might have otherwise assisted thereat. Vices which have disgraced those distant settlements are disappearing steadily before the influence of a regular ministry. Intemperance has been almost wholly banished, and men are more reasonably engaged in providing for eternity, than in merely confining their views and exertions to a world which passes away.

Previous to their departure, the venerable Bishop and the Rev. Mr. Abell were publicly entertained by a large body of citizens of all religious denominations. The Bishop remained with us for some time and on Sunday, July 12, he baptized seven grown persons. He is to conduct similar exercises at Washington and at Mount-Pleasant, of which I hope you may receive an account.[46]

[46] *The United States Catholic Miscellany*, IX (1829), p. 70.

In August 1830, Father S. T. Badin at the request of
Reverend G. Richard, the Bishop, and the Indians through
their chief, Pokegon, came to the St. Joseph's country,
Indiana.   He purchased a section of land from the government, built a chapel on the little St. Mary's lake and devoted
himself entirely to the instruction of the Potawatomies.[47]
This same year witnessed another memorable event in the
history of the Church in Indiana.   Reverend Simon
Lalumière, the first native of Vincennes to enter holy orders,
was ordained priest at Bardstown Seminary.   Following
this sacred ceremony he was sent to Daviess county in his
native state as a missionary.   In the following year the
Reverend Leo Champomier, who had labored incessantly
and alone in Indiana since 1823, resigned his charge at
Vincennes and we have no information of his later activities.
Bishop Flaget then appointed the Reverend Lawrence Picot,
who immediately took possession of the pastorship.[48]   On
June 12, 1831, Picot visited Edgar county, Illinois, where he
found 20 Catholic families who had not seen a priest for
six or more years.   At this place several adults received
Holy Communion and twenty children were baptized.
Protestants together with three of their ministers attended
these services.   Thus we learn that at the beginning he
really tried to continue the zealous work of the pastor who
had resigned.[49]

Again the *Miscellany* announces in a quaint yet interesting manner the progress of Catholicism in Indiana.   Once
more we feel justified in preserving the pioneer missionary
spirit by transcribing the article verbatim.

Some few years ago, several Catholic families emigrated from
Kentucky, and settled in the forks of White River. New settlers,
chiefly from Kentucky, but some also from Maryland and other
places, added to their number from time to time. They were occa-

[47] S. T. Badin to L. Cass, (6–3, 1834).   Original in Government
Indian Office, Washington, D. C.   File 1834.
[48] *The United States Catholic Miscellany*, XI (1831), p. 398.
[49] *Idem*.

sionlly visited by priests, sent by the Rt. Rev. Dr. Flaget, Bishop of Bardstown, and three or four times by that pious and venerable prelate himself, whose kindness towards them has been truly apostolic and merits their lasting gratitude. They most ardently desired the happiness of a church, and of a resident pastor; for which purpose a donation of 80 acres of land, having on it some improvements was given by Mr. Wm. Dant and his mother, at a place called the Black Oak Ridge, about six miles from the town of Washington in Daviess County. Yet owing to the scarcity of clergymen and the peculiar circumstances of his diocese, it was not in the good Bishop's power to comply with their wishes; until about a year ago, when he sent them the Rev. Simon Lalumière, a native of Indiana, who had then been recently ordained a priest at Bardstown. This long wished for event was to these comparatively destitute Catholics a cause of general and sincere gratulations. They soon turned their attention to the building of a church, which notwithstanding some delays and difficulties was accomplished in the course of the last month. It is a small but handsome frame building 38 ft. by 28 ft. On Sunday the third inst. it was dedicated to the service of God, under the patronage of St. Peter; on which occasion was assembled a large concourse of citizens of all denominations. The ceremony of dedication was performed by the Rev. Mr. Picot of Vincennes, assisted by the Rev. Mr. Lalumière; after which Mass was celebrated by the former gentleman, and an appropriate and impressive discourse given by the latter. The whole scene was imposing solemnity, and to the Catholics especially, of inexpressible delight. The writer has hitherto witnessed some grand and sublime spectacles, of religious worship, but never before has he beheld anything so soul-thrilling, so awfully divine, as the dedication of a Temple to the Living God! A few years ago the place was the haunt of wild beasts, or the resort of savage hunters. But now truly the wilderness begins to smile, and the alleluias of free republicans and grateful Christians, ascend in ecstasy to their adored Creator.

There are at present within the forks of White River chiefly in Daviess County 102 or 3 Catholic families. Ten of these families have moved here within the last twelve months; being induced to do so, not only by considerations of a religious nature, but also from the beauty of the country, the general fertility and cheapness of the land, the healthfulness of the climate, and the advantage of navigation afforded by both branches of the river. Certainly these are strong inducements to persons disposed to emigrate to this new and rapidly thriving country, but more especially to Catholic emigrants.

It is expected that two other churches will be built in time; one at Mt. Pleasant, nine miles from the Black Oak Ridge where a Protestant gentleman has offered a lot of land for the purpose and further donation of $50 towards its erection; and another at Bog's Creek, seven miles from the new church, where 44 Catholic families reside in one neighborhood. There is also some prospect of having a Catholic church built, in the thriving town of Washington, in the course of some time. The Catholic religion is evidently gaining ground in this quarter, and in other parts of the state also, as will be seen hereafter. Old prejudices are wearing off, as the people are becoming better acquainted with the truth and purity of its doctrines; and there appears already among persons of other denominations a disposition quite favorable to its future growth and progress. The labors of their zealous and worthy young pastor have already produced much benefit to his own flock and have been still further blessed by the conversion of two ladies, —one a Miss Brown whose sister became a convert at the time of the late jubilee; the other a Mrs. Odle, both in the neighborhood of the church, and an old gentleman, a Mr. Neel who lived near Mt. Pleasant. This gentleman had long entertained the belief that the Catholic religion was the only true one; though he never duly embraced it until of late; when he became a professed Catholic; evincing the most edifying sentiments of a lively faith and fervent piety, in which he very soon after died, in the seventieth year of his age.

It is probably known to the readers of the Miscellany generally, that there has existed for several years past, near Bardstown, Ky., a convent of ladies, called the Sisters of Charity, or of St. Joseph. Their great merits were well known to and piously remembered by several of the Catholics from Kentucky; who sensible of the edification and utility to be derived to themselves and their children, from the establishment of a branch of that institution among them, in their new abode built a comfortable house with that view, some time ago, near the spot on which now stands the new church of St. Peter. It is now confidently expected, indeed it is almost certain, that three or four of these meritorious ladies will come out from Kentucky, in the course of a few months to take possession of this new convent. This is an event very generally and ardently desired, not only by the Catholics, but by others also, with a view to the education of their daughters. There are about 40 girls, who will be placed under their care, as soon after their arrival, as they may be ready to receive them.

To the preceding statements it may be proper to add that some time ago the Rev. Mr. Lalumière visited in Shelby County, in the eastern part of this state, four or five Catholic families, who emigrated from Scott County, Kentucky.—They were highly gratified at this visit, not having seen a priest for more than a year before. They attended to their religious duties with becoming piety and devotion. They also, tho at present so few in number, are quite anxious for a place of worship; and a Protestant gentleman offered them a lot of five acres at a place very suitable for the purpose. They indulge the hope and before very long they may be able to accomplish that object, and eventually perhaps from increase of numbers, have a priest to reside permanently with them.

There are several Catholics scattered all over the State; and if we had a resident Bishop, and a few more active missionaries, there can be but little doubt, that our holy religion would prosper still more rapidly, and that you would not unfrequently have to record facts and circumstances, similar to those now for the first time furnished by

A Quondam Carolinian.[50]

The Sisters of Charity from Nazareth, Kentucky, opened a school at St. Peter's in Daviess County in the spring of 1832. These heroic women labored zealously but the humble circumstances of the inhabitants prevented them from appreciating the education and culture that these nuns tried to impart. Consequently their school received but scanty patronage, and they were withdrawn during the following year. In November Bishop Flaget visited St. Peter's. His

[50] *The United States Catholic Miscellany,* IX (1831).

presence was joyfully hailed by everyone, while his apostolic instructions animated and consoled every heart.[51]

Father Picot in company with several guides departed from Vincennes early in September, 1832, for a visit to the Miami Indians. They stopped for several days at Logansport where they found a few Catholic families who hailed with joy the arrival of a Catholic priest. After ministering to the wants of these destitute Christians Father Picot and company continued their journey and reached the Treaty Ground on September 21. Here the priest was received with all the respect due to his sacred office. After the usual ceremonies of introduction to the authorities, the agent of the State, General Marshal, introduced Father Picot to the Grand Indian Chief, who most kindly invited the priest to lodge with him. The council was held three days later and according to the arrangement made by the Grand Chief, his elder son attired in Indian style accompanied the priest to the council. As soon as Father Picot arrived he was waited upon by General Marshal, who placed him by the side of General Tipton and Governor Noble. When all was silent the Grand Chief arose and addressed the Indians as follows:

You see here my children, your father in the black robe; he comes from beyond the Great Lock. He is one of those that always has been recommended to us by our forefathers; he is from that country always dear to them (France), he is the minister of the Great Spirit, of the Master of Life, he comes not to amuse by fiction, but to enlighten by truth; he speaks of nothing but of the Master of Life; he considers every one as his children; he has come for no other purpose, but to teach a good doctrine and a sound moral to all those that will listen to him: he very anxiously wished to see you, and as soon as he has heard you were all assembled in this place, he has started from his residence to pay you a visit, and baptize your children: Now look at him, so that you should know him whenever you see him again.[52]

[51] *The Catholic Telegraph*, II (1833). p. 101.
[52] *The Catholic Herald*, I (1833), p. 43. Philadelphia.

On September 25, Father Picot baptized ten Indian children and then proceeded on the journey towards Father Badin's Indian village which his party reached after several days. At the request of Father Badin the visiting missionary baptized three Indians who had been instructed by their resident "black robe." Then in company with Father Badin, Father Picot visited many families of the settlement and was deeply impressed by the unfeigned piety of the Indians. After several days spent in friendly intercourse Father Picot departed again for Vincennes, a journey that required more than two weeks to accomplish. Over and above the care of his congregation Father Picot travelled more than fourteen hundred miles in 1832.[53] His pastorship, however, was of short duration. He left Vincennes in July 1833. From that time Father Petit, S. J., of the College of St. Mary's in Kentucky and Father Lalumière attended St. Francis Xavier until the arrival of the bishop appointed to that newly erected diocese.[54]

Father Badin continued his apostolic labors among the Indians but the greater number of Christians were on the borders of Michigan, under the direction of the virtuous Belgian priest, Father Deseille. During, the summer of 1834 this excellent clergyman made two excursions among the Potawatomies on the Tippecanoe river. On the first Sunday in May he baptized seventy-six of that tribe and on the first Sunday in September he received sixty more into the Church. To that date Father Badin had expended more than one thousand dollars of his own estate in order to maintain the Indian Mission,[55] and from the following we learn that in return he received no compensation for his arduous labors.

Five months before his death, Bishop Edward Fenwick of Cincinnati, informed me that you had granted one thousand dollars to the three Indian Missions of his diocese, viz., l'Arba Croche, Green

[53] *Idem.*
[54] *The Catholic Telegraph,* IV (1835).
[55] S. Badin to Bishop Purcell. 9–22, 1834. Original in CA of A.

Bay, and St. Joseph to be paid quarterly. He then advanced to me (in Apr. 1832) one hundred dollars on the well grounded presumption that the sum granted would be truly paid and I presume it has been. But for my part, I have received only the sum aforesaid of 100 Dol. although I have expended nearly eleven hundred dollars over and above. I leave it to the Indian Agents and to the citizens acquainted with the case to say whether I have been lax in teaching the Indians the rules of morality, sobriety and industry and to entertain sentiments of peace and unity with the Government of the U. S. especially during the War of Black Hawk. But I may here truly say that neither in the Treaties made with the Indians nor at the payments of their annuities have I received the least compensation for my labors nor for the money I expended to maintain myself and the other members of the mission.

The Treaty of Chicago, An. 1821, entitles the Teacher of the Potawatomi Indians to 500 doll. per an. I leave it to your sense of propriety and justice to determine whether I am entitled from that source to some satisfaction for both, my labors and expenses. I will frankly add that two weeks ago I wrote to Gen. Tipton on this subject.

I have the honor to be with due consideration Sir
Your very obedient and able servant,
Steph. Theod. Badin, Cathol. Missy.[56]

A letter edited in the *Telegraph* and signed "A Missionary" gives us the last written description of Catholic Missions in Indiana prior to the advent of Bishop Bruté. A résumé of these accounts would have demanded less space and time, yet it would have deprived the narrative of that pioneer spirit wherein our honored past glories.

Messrs. Editors:—Having made recently an extended missionary tour through this State, I am reminded of your anxious wish and general invitation to make your paper the medium of communicating interesting details of the progress of our holy religion in the west. Crossing the State obliquely from its western to near its

[56] S. Badin to L. Cass, 6–3, 1834. Original in Government Indian Office, Washington, D. C. File 1834.

northeastern border, I have had renewed occasion to admire the beauty of the country and the fertility of the soil.

The inducements which are offered the emigrants, or actual settlers, are still pre-eminent, while works of internal improvement are either projected or in course of execution, worthy older communities and States of more maturity. Among these may be mentioned, the canal from Fort Wayne to Logansport; and a railroad which has been commenced at Shelbyville, in Shelby county, to extend to the Ohio river at Lawrenceburg.

Our Holy Religion is much known in these parts, nevertheless, great numbers manifest a desire to be made acquainted with its true principles; and Catholics, more or less numerous abound in almost every county. At Rockford, Jackson county, I found a few Catholic families who had recently settled there. I had here, also the unexpected pleasure of meeting a German priest, the Rev. Mr. Ferneding, who was on a visit for the purpose of affording spiritual consolation to his country-men, settled here. Twenty families are expected to join those already located, next spring; so that before long, there will be quite a considerable congregation in this little town. A gentleman here, not belonging to the church, purposes to give two lots for the erection of a church. Previously to his arrival, Rev. Mr. Ferneding had visited a large settlement of Catholics, in Dearborn county. There are in this county upwards of 100 Catholic families, who are preparing a residence for a clergyman to become their pastor. Two hundred persons approached the sacraments at last Easter.

At Columbus, in Bartholomew county, I twice preached to Protestant congregations, who had manifested a wish to hear an explanation of our faith, and said Mass for the few Catholics, some of whom approached the Holy Communion.

In Shelby county near Shelbyville, I said Mass on Pentecost Sunday and remained there a few days administering to the wants of the Catholics, who are augmenting in number both by emigration and conversions, without even making use of the forcing system in case of intermarriage, as our Protestant friends give us credit. Thirty-eight persons approached the Holy Communion, and a lady presented herself for instructions preparatory to her reception into the church. The Catholics of this place expect soon to build a church, and indulge the hope of speedily having a resident clergyman.

Passing through Rush county, on my way to Wayne, I visited a family which had not seen a minister of their religion for years. Several of their children were baptized; and their hearts were gladdened at the visit of a minister of that faith to which they were firmly attached. Continuing my journey, I arrived at Abingdon in Wayne county, where I was warmly greeted by two of our zealous Irish Catholics, who had almost despaired, of seeing a priest among them. The Almighty had at length heard their prayers; and accordingly soon after my arrival the Protestants appeared extremely anxious not only to see the priest but to hear him preach. —Some, who had never before seen one, seemed not a little disappointed at discovering he wore no horns. Having said Mass in a private house, I afterwards preached in the meeting house of the United Brethren. Many attended, and not a few were again disappointed at discovering that our tenets were not so bad as Protestant calumny and distortion would make them. Being by an accident detained here two weeks, the Catholics availed themselves of the time for receiving the sacraments with preparation; and I had the pleasing satisfaction of receiving distinguished converts into the pale of the Roman Catholic Church, which they had discovered to be the true spouse of Christ, by her distinguishing marks; although the one, a Scottish gentleman, of good classic education and strong mind, was educated in the church of England; and the other, a lady, had previously been a Universalist.

One of our good friends had the kindness to procure me a horse, and likewise to accompany me, to seek the residences of our Catholic brethren. In Richmond, a large and beautiful town, where a priest and good school might do much good, I found several. Many approached the Holy Communion, the divine and adorable sacrifice being offered up in a private house. At the request of several gentlemen, I preached in a school-house, on the groundless prejudices that are entertained against our holy religion.

I desired to extend my mission to Fort Wayne and visit the Catholics on the canal, and down the Wabash; but circumstances rendered it impossible for me to do so. You may perceive, however, the great spiritual wants of the Catholics of Indiana; and how inviting is the field presented to the exertions of a Bishop and several priests. If our prayers and expectations in this latter regard should be realized, then will our holy religion flourish, and in every part of the State will arise temples to the true worship of the Most High; then will the sunlight of the true faith dissipate the fogs of infidelity and fanaticism engendered in the dark, filthy, though agitated waters of the Reformation.

A Missionary.[57]

The foregoing descriptions although brief and probably wanting in accuracy portray clearly the condition of Catholicism throughout the State of Indiana prior to the erection of the See of Vincennes. They show that Vincennes was not the only section that gave asylum to Catholics. On the contrary, the entire state was interspersed with embryo Catholic settlements that were craving development and anxiously awaiting the arrival of zealous ministers of the true gospel. These are depicted more in detail in a subsequent chapter by the skilful hand of Vincennes' first bishop.

[57] *The Catholic Telegraph*, III (1834), pp. 278–9.

CHAPTER X

NOMINATION TO THE DIOCESE OF VINCENNES

The creation of new dioceses in the Northwest Territory and the country to the north had been discussed for more than a decade of years before definite measures were taken to establish them. A see at Vincennes was declared essential for the spread of Catholicism throughout that section as early as the year 1825. The bishops on the frontier realized that a multiplication of bishoprics was the only agency competent to direct the spiritual care of the scattered Catholic population and to lead well-disposed non-Catholics to the truth. However, there were numerous obstacles to be encountered. At that missionary period the primary essentials for such development were wanting. Capable men might have been found to govern the new Sees, but the means to sustain them was the vital question. The population was scattered; moreover, it was composed for the most part of foreigners who had never been called upon to lend financial support to Church or pastors. They had emigrated from countries where salary of pastors was regulated and financed by the government. Therefore, Bishop Du Bourg in a letter to the Secretary of Propaganda urged that, before any decision be arrived at in regard to the creation of these Sees, provisions be made for the support of the new bishops.[1]

The diocese of Vincennes, therefore, existed only as a possibility until the year 1832 when Bishops Flaget and Rosati proposed its erection and presented Father Simon Bruté's name for its first bishop. At a Special Congregation of Propaganda on American affairs held on February 25, 1833, this was among the problems discussed; however, at this assembly the proposed See of Vincennes was post-

[1] *St. Louis Cath. Hist. Review.* III (1921), pp. 148–149.

poned for the time, but in case it was erected, Father Bruté was to be chosen its bishop.[2] Thus the problem remained untouched until the Second Provincial Council of Baltimore which opened its sessions on Sunday, October 20, 1833. On October 26, the prelates of this Council proposed to the Sacred Congregation the erection of the diocese of Vincennes and presented for their choice three eminent clergymen according to the following order: Bruté, Blanc, Loras. In a general session held on January 27, 1834, Propaganda discussed the articles proposed by the Second Provincial Council of Baltimore. The coadjutor of Baltimore was named and the vacancy of New Orleans was filled, but the erection of the See of Vincennes was again postponed for three months.

The then reigning pontiff, Pope Gregory XVI, acceding to the prudent and timely petitions of the members of the Second Provincial Council of Baltimore, issued the following Bulls, creating the diocese of Vincennes and appointed Father Simon W. Gabriel Bruté de Rémur, first bishop of the new See, on May 6, 1834.

PAPAL BULL CREATING THE DIOCESE OF VINCENNES

Gregory XVI, Sovereign Pontiff. For a perpetual memorial. Among the very great and weighty cares and anxieties which contiually burden and harass us in the government and administration of the universal church entrusted to us by Divine Providence, the most urgent assuredly is that which regards the state of all the dioceses throughout the entire world: for in us it belongs, in virtue of our supreme power and judgment, to establish them, to determine and change their limits, as times and circumstances, and especially the spiritual good and advantage of the faithful, appear to require it. Since, therefore, by the united suffrages of our venerable brothers, the bishops of North America, it has seemed very fitting, in order to extend and strengthen the Catholic religion in the province or state of Indiana, to erect and establish, with certain

[2]P. Guilday, *The Life and Times of John England*, II, p. 250. New York, 1927.

fixed limits, a new diocese, whose see shall be at the city of Vincennes, we have referred for examination, a subject of so much importance to the congregation of our venerable brothers, the cardinals of the Holy Roman Church, who are placed over the concerns of the Propaganda. Having, therefore, weighed all things maturely, and considered particularly the spiritual good which would accrue to the people of those countries, by the advice and counsel of the same, our venerable brothers, we are assured that the establishment of this new diocese and episcopal see would be very useful.

Of our own will, therefore, and of our certain knowledge, and in the plenitude of our apostolic power, we, by these letters, do erect and establish in the province or state of Indiana, in North America, a new diocese, of which the see shall be the city of Vincennes, from which city the diocese shall receive its title. The extent of the diocese shall be the state of Indiana, and one part of Illinois, the other part to be attached to the diocese of St. Louis, so that the limits of each diocese in the state of Illinois be determined in the following manner: Beginning from the river Ohio, which separates Kentucky from Illinois on the south, directly from Fort Massac, let a right line be drawn through the eastern boundaries of the counties of Johnson, Franklin, Jefferson, Marion, Fayette, Shelby, and Macon, to the Grand Rapids of the Illinois river, which are eight miles above the town of Ottawa, in the county of Lasselle, and hence to the northern boundary of the state, so that the western part of the state of Illinois belong to the diocese of St. Louis, and the eastern part to the diocese of Vincennes.

We, therefore, ordain that these letters are and shall be inviolate, valid, and efficacious; that they have and retain their full power and entire force, and that each and every article specified by us, be strictly fulfilled, and thus, as aforesaid, be without authority judged and defined, by all ordinary judges whatsoever, and even delegated auditors of causes, the apostolical palaces and the cardinals of the Holy Roman church withholding from each and all of them any right to assign a different judgment or interpretation; and that if any such be attempted knowingly, or through ignorance, by anyone whatever may be his authority, the same shall be null and void, apostolic constitutions and ordinances and all other things to the contrary notwithstanding.

Given at Rome, at St. Peter's, under the ring of the Fisherman, the 6th day of May, 1834, and in the fourth year of our Pontificate. For Cardinal Albano.

A. PICCHIONI.[3]

In addition to a partial repetition of the foregoing document the Holy Father in a separate Bull of the same date stating that:

having in mind to make early and felicitous provisions for a new episcopal church and having with fruitful results carefully deliberated with our venerable Brethren, the Cardinals of the Holy Roman Church, in charge of the affairs of the Propagation of the Faith, we have finally directed our minds' eye to you as one, regarding whose virtue, learning, piety, prudence, experience in local condition peculiar to the United States of America, and, above all, regarding whose zeal for the propagation of the Catholic religion, care and prudence both in spiritual and temporal matters, splendid testimonies have been received,

informed Father Bruté of his appointment to the See of Vincennes.[4]

---

[3] C. Blanchard, *History of the Catholic Church in Indiana.* pp. 49–50. Logansport, 1898; *The Catholic Telegraph,* "Erection of the See of Vincennes," III (1834), p. 405.

[4] Dilecto filio Simoni Gabrieli Bruté, Presbytero

Gregorius Papa XVI.

Dilecte fili, salutem etc. Apostolatus Officium meritis licet imparibus nobis ex alto commissum etc. gubernare feliciter. Dudum siquidem provisionem etc. contigerit attentari. Quum igitur per alias nostras similes Literas hoc ipso die datas, quarum tenorem praesentibus pro expresso et inserto haberi volumus novus Episcopatus in Statu seu Provincia Indiana in America Septentrionali satis quibusdam limitibus fuerit a nobis erectus, cuius sedes sit Vincennopolis, qua ex urbe episcopalis eius titulus proficiscitur, Nos ad huiusmodi novae episcopalis Ecclesiae provisionem celerem atque felicem in qua nullus praeter Nos se potest intromittere, reservatione et decreto obsistentibus supradictis, paterno ac sollicito studio intendentes, post deliberationem quam de praeficiendo eidem Ecclesiae personam utilem ac fructuosam cum VV. FF. NN. S. R. E. Cardinalibus negotiis Propagandae Fidei praepositis habuimus diligentem. Demum ad Te qui

These Bulls together with the following congratulatory
letter from His Eminence C. M. Cardinal Pedicini were
mailed to Father Bruté on May 17, 1834, and reached him
at the Mountain on July 22, 1834.

Most Illustrious and Right Reverend Lord!

Our most holy Father, Pope Gregory XVI, acquiescing in the
earnest solicitations of the Bishops of the United States, has decided that a new episcopal See should be erected at Vincennes,
Indiana and he has appointed Your Paternity as the first bishop of
that diocese. I am sending you the Bulls of His Holiness pertaining
to this appointment, at the same time I congratulate Your Lordship
on the episcopal dignity that has been conferred upon you. I am,
moreover, certain, God assisting your labors and zeal, that all
those things which have been ordered by our most holy Father, will
redound to the great utility of the Church in that region. It remains, therefore, that you receive episcopal consecration as soon
as possible, and that you assume the government of the diocese
entrusted to you. Accompanying this letter you will receive a
rescript of the faculties which our most Holy Father deigns to
grant to you. I pray that God may long preserve you safe and
happy.

Your Lordship's

Most affectionate brother,

C. M. Cardinal Pedicini, Prefect

Rome, the office of the Sacred Congregation for the Propagation
of the Faith, May 17, 1834.

The Reverend Simon Bruté

Bishop-Elect of Vincennes.[5]

ex legitimo matrimonio procreatus et in aetate legitima constitutus
existis, cuius apud Nos de morum integritate, doctrina, pietate, pru-
dentia, rerum ad illas regiones Americae Foederatae pertinentium
peritia et in primis Catholicae Religionis propagandae studio ac
spiritualium providentia et temporalium circumspectione praeclara
accepta sunt testimonia oculos mentis nostrae direximus etc.

Datum Romae apud S. Petrum die 6 Maii Pontificatus Nostri anno
IV.
                                         Pro D. Card. Albani
                                         A. Picchioni Substitutus.

(Archivio di Propaganda—Registro dei Brevi, V. 4, ff. 147–148.)

[5] Original in CA of A. Notre Dame, Indiana.

This appointment, humanly speaking, was not in accordance with Father Bruté's desires, yet it was not a surprise since his confrères had continually threatened him with the position. While he had refused it during the preceding year,[6] saying, "I think this place (the Mountain) is where God wishes me to be,"[7] we learn from his correspondence that a presentiment seemed to haunt him continually. In a letter to Bishop Rosati, he said:

> They are threatening me now openly that after Mr. Odin's return which is expected daily that I shall receive my nomination to Vincennes—then it is that I shall be very much embarrassed before our Lord. . . . However, they tell me that you and Bishop David have concurred to present me a second time for this See. . . . Your Lordship, if you deign to write to me soon tell me before God what you think of the nomination with which I am threatened. I remain indifferent as much as I am able but should I not rather insist simply in staying in the place which to me is a veritable treasure and not to undertake those cares which are entirely contrary to my real likes?[8]

One month later in another letter to the same prelate, he wrote:

> I believe that my own refusal is definitely fixed. I tried to remain indifferent and to wish for nothing but the Will of God, but it appears now very evident that if the nomination arrives from Rome, trouble would commence again. Father Odin should have been named from the beginning, but excuse this word if it is indiscreet for I have neither the mission nor the grace to decide for any other name than mine. . . .[9]

Father Bruté was amused shortly after this to read the announcement in the April issue of the *Shepherd of the Valley*, "no disappointment was made as yet for Vincennes."

[6] Cf. Bruté Journal, Georgetown UA. Fol. 92, 6.
[7] S. Bruté to A Bruté, 3–15, 1834, Canon Bruté de Rémur Collection. Rennes.
[8] S. Bruté to J. Rosati, 3–19, 1834, St. LCA. St. Louis, Mo.
[9] S. Bruté to J. Rosati, 4–20, 1834, St. LCA.

Apparently this did not dispel his fear of the office for in writing his brother Augustine he added, "Pray for your poor brother who may be named Bishop."[10] Likewise, further correspondence with Bishop Rosati proves that he was continually urged to accept the nomination, for on another occasion he said:

> As to Vincennes, I am anxious for I received a very pressing letter yesterday from Bishop Flaget, which, plus one from Bishop David the week before, urges me to accept it if I am named and I do not know what to do—that is to say, how am I to know the *Will of God* between these exterior and multiplied appeals and my conviction of my total incapacity. Whereas, if Mr. Odin were named he has evidently all the dispositions required. Please pray that I may distinguish well where truly this *Unique Will* lies—if I did not feel that it is necessary above all to seek it I would not have to deliberate to refuse.[11]

The arrival of the Bulls appointing Father Bruté Bishop of Vincennes caused great alarm among the clergy throughout the East. All who knew him agreed that he was talented, indefatigable, and zealous; but his gentle nature and simple manners had led some to imagine that he did not possess those sterner qualities required for the government of men or the organization and administration of a diocese in a missionary country. At the Mountain practically every member of the faculty opposed the nomination and petitioned against the removal of the superior of the seminary. On July 24, 1834, President Butler wrote in great haste to Father Wheeler at Baltimore, saying: "I must try to calm the panic and counteract the alarms of all.... and endeavor to prevent not the *Will of God*, but what I fear is the proposal of man. Who will attend the Convent? Who will teach Theology? We must have some aged or learned man or what can we do?"[12]

[10] S. Bruté to A. Bruté, 5–23, 1834, Canon Bruté de Rémur Collection.
[11] S. Bruté to J. Rosati, 6–23, 1834, St. LCA.
[12] M. Meline,—E. McSweeny, *The Story of the Mountain*, I, p. 321.

Bishop England voted against Bruté's nomination at the Second Provincial Council and when writing to Dr. Cullen, Rector of the Irish College, Rome, shortly after its adjournment, he said:

> The newly erected See of Vincennes has Bruté, who is one of the best of men, but though my kindest friend, I did my best to keep him out for his own sake and that of the diocese. But I was left in a small minority. Rezé and Kenrick saw so plainly that a party had been formed against anything that I would introduce, that they and I concluded it was better that I should do nothing at this time. However, I sacrificed my feelings and kept charity and affection, and we parted in friendship.

On the following day he added: "Bruté was named for Vincennes quite against my judgment."[13]

In mid-summer of 1834 Bishop England placed the following announcement in the *Miscellany*.

> The erection of the new diocese of Vincennes, comprising the whole of the State of Indiana and part of Illinois, has, we are happy to learn, received the sanction of the Holy See. The Reverend Simon W. Gabriel Bruté, Professor of Theology, in the Seminary of Mount St. Mary's near Emmitsburg, Maryland, has been appointed its first bishop.[14]

Honors may be thrust upon men that at the time appear very unwise, however, on such occasions, noble and learned men never question the direction of Providence. In acting thus they are often given the light to see the wisdom of God in His designs. This was verified in Bishop England. Writing to Bishop Bruté shortly after the latter's installation he said:

> Now, my dearest friend, I was delighted with your account of the Church springing up in the desert. You may be assured, that any-

[13] *Records* (ACHS), "The Church in America," VII (1893), pp. 467, 470.

[14] *The U. S. Cath. Miscellany*, "Diocese of Vincennes," XIV (1834), No. 5.

thing with which you are connected is dear to me. I was for many reasons opposed to your leaving the Mountain and being placed in your present situation. God knows His own means better than we do, and I shall be most happy in finding, as I expect now to find, that I made a mistake in my opposing your removal.[15]

Bishop Kenrick of Philadelphia was another prelate who maintained views similar to those of Bishop England of Charleston. Referring to the American Church and the decisions of the Second Provincial Council of Baltimore in a letter to Dr. Cullen at Rome, he said:

> The greatest evils with which this country has been afflicted are attributed to good men. These good men with the best of intention have procured the elevation of men of virtue, but destitute of the several necessary qualifications. The first cities of the East have had prelates whose imperfect knowledge of the language of the country must make their instructions matter of ridicule rather than of edification. The West is likely to be similarly circumstanced, if the Bishop of Vincennes be selected according to the wishes of the assembled prelates, who in this instance yielded too much to their veneration for the individual.[16]

Within the same discourse, referring again to Vincennes, Kenrick maintained that if the Council had heeded the judgments of Bishop England the assembly would not have witnessed "an old man with the most strange eccentricites of mind, sent in the decline of a life spent in Collegiate exercises to be an apostle of a new diocese."[17]

The Very Reverend John Power, Vicar General of New York, also belonged to the group of those who opposed Father Bruté's nomination. In the course of a letter written to their mutual friend, Dr. Cullen, on July 23, 1834, he said:

> The Bulls of the new Bishop have not been as yet heard of. Believe me when I assure you that the nominations are not what

[15] H. J. Alerding, *The Diocese of Vincennes*, p. 119.
[16] *Records* (ACHS), VII (1893), pp. 289–290.
[17] P. Guilday, *op. cit.*, II p. 533.

they ought to be. Doctor Bruté, they say, is a learned man, but his learning appears to me to be like a lamp in a sepulchre. *Multa tumultuaria lectione devoravit.* In all other respects his conduct is edifying but eccentric.[18]

No one could have been more opposed to this nomination than Father Bruté himself. He knew his limitations better than many of his confrères surmised, yet he did not act on the first impulse; on the contrary, he sought time for reflection and deliberation. He hastened to Baltimore where he made a retreat from July 23 to 27, in order better to enable himself to determine his duty regarding the appointment. At the close of this spiritual exercise he decided to accept the nomination on condition that Bishops Flaget, David, Purcell, and Rosati would insist. He then proceeded to write to these prelates requesting each one to give before God his frank opinion regarding his nomination, saying that he himself was disposed to accept whatever these letters from the West would decide. Father Bruté felt it was too late to talk against the erection of the See as some were doing at the Mountain. Since Rome wished it and the Council had asked for it, he was loathe to believe the Council had made two injudicious requests.[19]

After finishing his letters to the prelates named above he addressed the following to Bishop Chabrat, coadjutor Bishop of Bardstown.

Eternity!!
Auspice Maria.

August 1, 1834. Mt. St. Mary's.

Monseigneur and very dear friend:—

Behold now you are consecrated, ad multos annos! All faith, all love, all holy abandonment. You are saying as Bishop Purcell said on receiving the Bulls which Jesus Christ sent through His vicar on earth. 'I can do all things in Him who strengthens me.' The same orders have reached me. The view of their heavenly

[18] *Records* (ACHS), "The Church in America," VII (1893), p. 469.
[19] S. Bruté to J. Rosati, 7–29, 1834, St. LCA.

origin strikes me quite otherwise than in 1832. I refused without hesitation the first simple nomination, the reasons were so obvious. All things considered I believe now, as I wrote to Bishops Flaget and David and in their heart even to you, worthy and life-long friend, and now by grace like them, that I must accept.

However, no matter how holy and divine appears in the eyes of Catholics and priests the mission received from Rome, and although Bishop David makes it a principle of necessity that I accept, yet since Rome grants time for accepting and since the frequent practice of refusing meets with no reproach, I feel that I am yet free. During this painful suspense I must preserve my peace of mind and seek only the Will of God.

If, after my nomination by the Council, the Bulls charged me in conscience to accept, and permitted no deliberation, I would have promptly obeyed, but since they state I ought to be ready to accept, I think a chance ought to be granted to the new diocese concerning a nomination promising so little for its beginning, and that the opinion should be reconsidered by the neighboring bishops, those who know me so well.

Since the departure of my letter to Bishops Flaget, David, Purcell, and Rosati, the thought occurred to write to you, the young coadjutor, and conjure you to tell me or to tell them, as you would on your death-bed; first, whether it would be better for me to refuse; second, whether there would be any other serious inconvenience than a new delay of six months. I am going to place on the following pages all my reasons. Think awhile, you, the youngest, as I have said, and the one destined to rule for so long the nearest diocese and the one of which Vincennes has been a part until now.

1. Notwithstanding good health, at my age one's strength is diminishing. A little hernia which I have on my right side may come against me in mounting horses, swimming rivers, holding myself properly in the saddle when the currents are rapid. Even though the country is becoming populous, travelling will be frequent and indispensable. Still I have no decisive objection here.

2. My English continues imperfect, the more so since I have lost my teeth. 'They do not understand you,' I am frequently told. This occurs less in the instructions I give than in familiar conversation,

and especially in matters of technical affairs—building, money, etc. My French, too, has suffered.

3. Because of my duty for the past ten years in the seminary and with the Sisters I have lost aptitude in dealing with all kinds of people in the capacity of father, friend, and pastor. I lack the amiability of Bishop Flaget or Bishop David, or Bishop Fenwick, the first Bishop of Ohio, or Bishop Fenwick of Boston. Good will can scarcely supply for the lack of sociability and experience.

4. My application to books, to teaching, to abstraction, and to generalities has deprived me of the taste and aptitude for advancement in a knowledge of the affairs of government, details, accounts—everything required for the material side of the diocese, as of a congregation.... dealings with families, particulars to be remembered on which depends so much....

5. A new bishop should have much intercourse with the non-Catholics who form a large part of the population, to this I am little inclined the same as to magistrates, and I have less idea than any one of the laws and family adjustments of property, and neither taste nor memory for such things. I am without funds, poor as Job, except for my old books.

6. Now see what has been taken from me, books, Sisters, seminary—this last above all. Had St. Sulpice adopted this house I would fear less. But I am an old tree, the rallying post, the pillar of confidence for the young masters as to theology, spiritual reading, a support of the others in seeing me their associate in this seminary work....

7. Now in regard to the necessary virtue. Ah! It is said each should consider himself poorest here. What of exterior mildness? Of temper, so vital in regard to ruling and counseling? Here I am lacking. Yet, sincerely, I dread this fault less than the above reasons. For in carrying out of actual resolutions, I generally find myself on the moderate side. I have had quite often to repress extremes. What is lacking in me is repression of voice, signs of vexation, hastiness in responding, a bad listener,—great faults.

Finally there is a constant reiteration of an impulse that came at the close of my three days' retreat. I find myself saying, 'all things considered, I will accept, if my friends insist, I shall regard it as the best in Our Lord.'

As to the second question, six months' delay for a better nomination. Would it be an inconvenience? Another Purcell or Chabrat would more than compensate for ten or twenty times the delay. Moreover, the idea which I communicated to Bishop David occurs to me again. Could not his Lordship govern that diocese for a time and for its greater good?

See worthy friend, if even with the Bulls in hand I have not considerable reason to hesitate? Undoubtedly the Lord in His mercy manages the new churches of this country but I—poor atom, deserve to be left for a time to my illusion, to lose myself. The Lord will draw His glory from my abasement. I may well be alarmed at the extreme disproportion between accepting and refusing. Then all seems solved, and my friends place themselves on the same side, adding their convictions to those which the above reasons carry, what shall I say? Shall I accept? Truly I know not how to express it. (How to commence, how to justify.) All appears presumption, illusion.

To sum up:

1. The fact of the Bulls, their direct impression, neither sought nor desired.

2. The actual intention, as pure as I can regulate it, even at the hour of death.

3. The voices from the West, from the altar—their grace and light as at the moment of death.

4. My own altar also, even after the most painful uncertainty there is each time a new peace and impulse *to go*.

5. My fear of what another line of Providence may be for this diocese, should I alter this which was made for it not by me.

6. The disproportion of human means for a task so enormous is the same for another as for me. There are a half million souls of various religious belief, with four or five hundred ministers (three hundred and eight in 1830). They have schools of all kinds and money, while we have one priest to care for a thousand Catholics, scattered in that multitude. The Council, however, with eyes wide open asks for a bishop. Rome says let it be.

Oh! what matter who goes, provided he goes with **purity of** intention and entire abandonment.

7. There comes a kind of resolution to go after the manner of the Apostles in the greatest possible simplicity. For each moment the Lord has in view means of grace for me and for all,—the altar, the sacraments, prayer, instruction. What presumption to have lived so little in conformity to the spirit of faith and then to hope to be all at once as Bishop Fenwick, Bishop Egan, and others who have passed away, not to speak of the living!

8. Shall I add the hope of promptly obtaining a good coadjutor and serving him only as a footstool? Yet who am I to be named first bishop,—footstool! Who am I to believe there is importance in accepting and danger in refusing, yes, danger for the diocese. After all, worthy friend, it is for its welfare that I fear to accept or to refuse. Personally, it seems to me fear of accepting is more emphatic, since there are so many arguments and counsels showing that a refusal is safest and surest.

9. Read—Pray—I shall await in peace those letters from the West. I am addressing this to Bishop Flaget in case you should be absent.

S. Bruté.

Should they decide to say: 'Come,' I shall be ready and glad. Should they say: 'All things considered, it would be better to remain,' I shall be ready and even better satisfied.[20]

In the meantime Father Bruté trusted all to Divine Providence and returned to his customary duties. He conducted the retreat for the seminarians from August 10 to 15, and then awaited the responses from the bishops of the West. Within this interim he received a congratulatory letter from Father Hughes, who said:

I have been unusually engaged since I received the news of your elevation to the episcopacy. My congratulations are on this account later, but not less sincere. The place which you have hitherto occu-

[20] Transcript in Souvay Collection, Kenrick Seminary. St. Louis, Mo. Original in Convent Archives. Loretto, Kentucky.

pied seemed to me so important for the Church, that I confess it is with regret I see it vacant. But when I think of the ways by which Almighty God accomplishes His designs, especially in reference to the Church, I can have no doubt but it will be found according to His Will.[21]

Another clergyman who received the announcement with joy was Father Stephen Badin, who at that particular period was laboring among the Indians in northern Indiana. Not being able, for various reasons, to write the bishop-elect he thus expressed his gratification in a letter to Bishop Purcell asking His Lordship to convey his sentiments to the newly appointed.

I have been informed by the *Catholic Herald* that the consecration of the excellent Bishop of Vincennes is to take place on the first Sunday of October in Bardstown where most probably I shall have the opportunity of seeing you....

It may happen that Divine Providence will not permit me to see the Angel of Vincennes; I had intended to write and congratulate him and his diocese on his promotion which has filled me with consolation, but having been uncertain of the place and time where and when he was to be consecrated, and being often destitute either of time or even conveniences in the miserable crowded cabins, where I must lodge in travelling, feeling also frequent fatigues, I have not yet satisfied my heart in presenting him my best respects and assuring him of my readiness to cooperate with or assist him in his exertions to establish and extend the Kingdom of God in his new diocese. Wherefore, I beg of you the favor to communicate these lines to him. I wished to write to him this very night, but it is past twelve o'clock and I must rest in order to continue my excursions tomorrow after Mass.[22]

The bishops in the West differed vastly from the prelates in the East, in their views regarding Father Bruté's nomination. The former considered it a real God-send.

[21] J. Hassard, *Life of Most Rev. John Hughes*, p. 151.
[22] S. T. Badin to J. Purcell, 9–22, 1834. CA of A.

Especially the zealous Bishop Flaget, as we learn from his correspondence, expected marvelous good to come forth from this appointment. After having entertained the bishop-elect for several days he wrote Bishop Rosati as follows:

> During these five days that I have been in the company of this successor of the Apostles I have nothing to do but listen, admire, and bless Providence which attains its ends by inexplicable means, and which would seem to be pure folly in the eyes of the world. The somewhat singular figure of this excellent prelate, the perpetual motion of his fingers, of his hands, of his head, and of his entire body while he converses; the English with an entirely French pronunciation, coming from a large toothless mouth would seem to render him altogether useless for the post which he has been assigned, not to say laughable or ridiculous.—But! mon Dieu, when he celebrates Holy Mass; when he speaks of Jesus Christ, of His love for men, my heart dilates and is inflamed like that of the disciples of Emmaus. I am beside myself. I then hope against hope and I anticipate miracle upon miracle that will be wrought by the venerable Apostle.[23]

Upon the reception of the letters from the Bishops in the West, neither His Grace nor Father Bruté's confrères were able to stay the decision. Immediately he chose October 5, Feast of the Holy Rosary, for the day of his consecration. Bishop Flaget suggested that the event be transferred to October 28, Feast of the two Apostles, Simon and Jude. The bishop-elect then placed the affair in the hands of the bishops in the West assuring them that their decision would meet his approval. Then before preparing to leave his cherished abode he appealed to Right Reverend Doctor Eccleston in behalf of the future of Mount St. Mary's. Father Bruté realized the value of the institution to the future Church in America and he wished the coadjutor bishop in entering upon his new office to give it his serious attention, saying, "to support it, to endeavor to reduce its debt, and to assure

[23] B. J. Flaget to J. Rosati, 9–30, 1834, St. LCA.

its future is an object of sacred solicitude," that devolves at present upon the newly appointed coadjutor of Baltimore.[24] The scholarly priest was so closely wedded to the Mountain and his profession that it was with great reluctance he tore himself away. However, when he perceived any undertaking to be the Will of God he permitted no other consideration to intervene. Therefore, he bade a hasty farewell to the Mountain and the Valley and departed for the West via Cincinnati and Bardstown, never to return again to Mount St. Mary's as a member of its faculty.

[24] BCA, Case 24–G⁹.

CHAPTER XI

CONSECRATION AND INSTALLATION

The newly created diocese of Vincennes seems to have been simply sketched in outline and the details left to Providence to fill in since at the beginning it was wholly destitute of everything necessary to make it an encouraging field for a bishop. Nevertheless, at the call of Christ's Vicar on earth, Reverend Doctor Bruté resigned his position at Emmitsburg where he found manifest evidence of good wrought and to be accomplished in the future, and in the decline of life assumed the arduous duty of founding this new See in the wilderness where everything was wanting except confidence in God. Few pioneer bishops can be named who were ushered into a new diocese so thoroughly shorn of all essentials. The work before him would have been desired by no one and would have been shunned by most of the clergy. Yet a splendid bishopric he would undoubtedly have declined; but to take up his abode in poverty and privation among strangers, to go far from whatever was dear to him on earth were sacrifices dear to his heart. However, this servant of God is not to be judged as having been ignorant of the weighty responsibility that such a task entailed. On the contrary, he was keenly cognizant of the colossal burden that lay before him. This is manifest in a letter written to Right Reverend Doctor Eccleston in which he said: "We preach, worthy friend, the same scandals, the same follies as St. Paul—almost under the same circumstances—fewer pagans—more false brethren—those legions of sectarians and teachers of false doctrines—christians properly speaking without faith and seeing in our faith nothing but one new opinion."[1]

[1] BCA, Case 24–G⁹.

Father Bruté left the Mountain on September 15, accompanied by Reverend Hitzelberger of the Baltimore diocese and Reverend Jury who was returning to New Orleans after having spent several years in the East. Upon reaching Cincinnati, Bishop-elect Bruté and Father Hitzelberger were joined by Bishop Purcell, who travelled with them to Louisville where they arrived on Thursday morning, September 25. Here they were afforded the pleasure of meeting Bishop Flaget of Bardstown and one of his clergymen, Father Ferneding, at the home of Father Abell. Immediately the prelates decided that the solemn ceremony of consecration should take place at the new Cathedral in St. Louis, on the appropriately chosen festival, namely, the feast of the two Apostles, SS. Simon and Jude, October 28. The Bishop of Cincinnati promised to be there and Father Bruté hoped Bishop Rezé of Detroit and Rev. Jeanjean, likewise, would find it agreeable to be present. Here at the home of Father Abell, the bishop-elect wrote to Bishop Rosati begging his confrère to accompany him to Vincennes for the installation which was scheduled for the beautiful day of All Saints.[2]

After several days visit at Louisville these clergymen again dispersed. Bishop Purcell returned home on Sunday, September 28, and on the following Monday, Bishop-elect Bruté proceeded with the Nestor of the Catholic hierarchy of the West to Bardstown. Bishop Flaget was obliged to return almost immediately to Louisville in order to be at Cincinnati for the dedication of Bishop Purcell's new Church—the first German Church west of the Alleghany Mountains—on Sunday, October 5. Thus he was forced to leave Father Bruté to make his retreat under Bishop David. During the brief interim between his arrival at the Bardstown episcopal residence and the opening of this retreat Bishop-elect Bruté visited all the establishments in the Bardstown diocese. On October 5, the first day of this spiritual exercise, the venerable retreatant witnessed the ordina-

2 St. LCA. 9–25, 1834. St. Louis, Mo.

tion of one priest, one deacon, and four subdeacons by Bishop Chabrat, coadjutor of Bardstown. On the same day he wrote again to Bishop Rosati. In this letter he lamented the false statement published in several papers, namely, that his library was a gift to the Mountain, when he had left it there only in trust to be brought to Vincennes when opportunity presented itself, which could not be very soon. The middle West may have appeared somewhat crude in those early days, nevertheless, the inhabitants appreciated books and hungered for education as intensely as the people in the East. *The Catholic Telegraph*, August 8, 1834, announcing Bruté's coming, said: "We long for himself and his valuable library across the mountains, and his aid in the great valley of the Mississippi."

On October 8, Father Bruté wrote from Bardstown to Mother Rose at St. Joseph's, Emmitsburg, to explain his abrupt farewell to the Community and to thank St. Joseph's for all that had been done for him. He made especial mention of the little purse of silver containing almost two hundred and forty dollars, and then requested her to send him the brass crucifix from the confession room. After relating briefly his visits to Nazareth, Loretto, St. Thomas, and St. Mary's, he closed with a short address to Father Hickey in which he thanked him for his gift, a beautiful breviary, and requested this confrère to extend his gratitude to good Doctor Shorb for the gold watch. All were reminded to pray earnestly for the consecration on October 28.[3]

In the meantime Bishop Rezé wrote Father Bruté that it would be impossible to come to his consecration. In the course of the same letter he likewise informed the bishop-elect that the Bishop of St. Louis had, owing to Father St. Cyr's ill health, recalled him from Chicago. This news pained the newly elect and immediately he pleaded for St. Cyr's return because thus far there was no one for Vincennes. In Bardstown he found only Mr. Picot and his confrères advised him to leave this clergyman where he was.

[3] *Bruté—Seton Correspondence*, pp. 399–414. 1886.

After the exchange of several letters, followed by a personal interview, Father Chazelles, S. J., superior of St. Mary's, Kentucky, promised the assistance of Father Petit, S. J., for the installation and a few days following.[4]

At the close of Father Brute's retreat and upon the return of Bishop Flaget, the two prelates in company with Father Petit departed for Louisville where they were joined by Bishop Purcell and Fathers Abell and Hitzelberger whence they left immediately by stage for St. Louis. The remainder of the week of their arrival was spent in preparation for the approaching solemnities. Nevertheless, even in the midst of these days of spiritual delights immediately preceding his consecration there was one care that weighed heavily upon the heart of the zealous bishop-elect. It was the spiritual plight that befell Chicago at the recall of Father St. Cyr. Bishop Rosati was so absorbed in preparation for the dedication of the new Cathedral and other pressing business that it was impossible to discuss this weighty problem with him. However, Father Bruté could not be reconciled to silence on this vital subject and he placed the Chicago situation before the St. Louis prelate in the following written memorial.

The days are slipping by. You are so busy I cannot see you or rather can see you only at times when you ought to be giving that over-burdened head and heart of yours some little repose—I write to you instead.

I beg you to consider seriously before the Lord the case of Mr. St. Cyr and grant me him (or else Mr. Roux or Mr. Loisel or Mr. Dupuy)—but Mr. St. Cyr is already known and esteemed in Chicago.

In this event, (1) I will give him $50 at first and more later on. (2) I will go ahead of him to Chicago immediately after my installation to announce him and to pledge the people my assistance, and I will return there in the spring.

I beg you to consider (1) that the Holy Father who establishes this new diocese, desires that it be encouraged by the neighboring

[4] S. Bruté to J. Rosati, 10–5, 1834, St. LCA.

bishops. Mgr. Flaget grants me Messrs. Lalumière, Ferneding, and Badin—do you grant me Mr. St. Cyr for the space of a year, during which I shall endeavor to obtain some other priests. (2) Be pleased to recall with what zeal and with what respect for the priests of St. Vincent de Paul and the missionaries of Mgr. Du Bourg, I did all I possibly could in 1816, the critical date of yours and Mr. de Andreis' arrival; and in 1819 for his second band of missionaries. No sooner had I consented to accept my appointment, than everything failed me at once,—money, priests to bring along with me, priests already on the ground,—Mr. St. Cyr, Mr. Picot, Mr. Petit, S. J., each for some different reason—money, sisters, everything, and still I am going to be consecrated. Oh! do make an effort and write again yourself to the Archbishop.

If you help to organize this diocese, which you have together created in council, for the Holy Father could not do otherwise than second your desire, within a few years this empty country between yourself and Cincinnati will be filled up—those very important points, Chicago and Fort Wayne—Vincennes will have its Sisters again. Sisters! Ah, Monseigneur, I have done so much to secure them for you. For twenty-five years I have put to use all that I was, all that I had, and now they make me bishop in spite of all reluctance of mine and against my own personal conviction as to the sphere of well-doing in which I should have been allowed to remain.

I have laid before you all my weakness. If you had named a man of talent or enterprise, one made for the place, you might more readily leave him to himself to create his own resources.

But with me the case is quite contrary—even my exterior is against me, as Mgr. Flaget and yourself realize, for there is no dissembling the fact. All this calls for a more generous effort of zeal in the interests of the diocese to which you have together summoned me.

Deign then, to pray and deliberate *in visceribus Christi* and under the eyes, as it were, of His Vicar on earth, who, I am confident, desires only to have his holy enterprise of a new diocese succeed and above all make a good beginning.

The occasion of the dedication of a church in regard to which the Divine Goodness has favored you in so admirable a manner,

when, too, every one comes to respond with joyful efforts to your
simple appeal, will be an auspicious one, I hope, for these simple
lines; it is a child and a subject of St. Louis who supplicates and
the cause, moreover, is such an urgent one. Grant, I beseech you,
the prayer of

                    Your very respectful and devoted brother,
                                             Simon Bruté.[5]

The dedication of the new Cathedral occurred on the following Sunday, October 26. Two days later the learned
Bishop of Vincennes was consecrated by Bishop Flaget of
Bardstown, assisted by Bishop Rosati of St. Louis and Bishop Purcell of Cincinnati.[6] Nearly all the clergy who had
assisted at the dedication of the Cathedral stayed to witness this solemn rite by which a new successor was given
to the Apostles, a bishop placed in charge of a new diocese,
and an eminent prelate added to the hierarchy in the United
States. An eloquent sermon on the divine institution of the
episcopacy was preached by Bishop Purcell on the text;
"Simon lovest thou me more than these?" (Jn. 21:12).
In the course of his remarks, the Bishop established by
several brief but peremptory arguments from scripture and
tradition, the divine institution of episcopacy; expatiated
on the services rendered by the first order of the Christian
Hierarchy to religion, by the vigilance with which, whether
assembled in general council, or in their respective provinces and sees, the bishops detected and proscribed every error,
avoided the profane novelties of words, reduced to silence
the oppositions of knowledge falsely so-called, and faithfully "kept the truth committed to their trust." In proof of
the salutary influence possessed and exercised by the
episcopal body, in the middle ages, for the improvement
of legislation, the extinction of feuds, the diffusing of learn-

[5] Original in St. LCA. G. J. Garraghan, *The Catholic Church in
Chicago.* pp. 77–79.
[6] Bruté Journal, Georgetown, UA. Fol. 92, 6; H. J. Alerding,
History of the Diocese of Vincennes, p. 127; M. Meline,—E.
McSweeny, *The Story of the Mountain,* I, p. 324; J. Rothensteiner,
History of the Archdiocese of St. Louis, p. 513. St. Louis, 1928; *The
Catholic Record,* May 21, 1891. Indianapolis.

ing and consequent amelioration of the condition of the human race, he adduced the authority of Protestant as well as Catholic historians. Finally, after a short but vivid exposition of the virtues which so eminent a station imperiously demands in him who has been raised to it, he concluded with the impressive admonitions in the words of Scripture addressed particularly to the newly consecrated Bishop:

> Have they made thee ruler? Be not lifted up: be among them as one of them. Have care of them. Feed the flock of God, taking care of it, not by constraint, but willingly, according to God; not for filthy lucre's sake, but voluntarily, neither as lording it over the clergy, but being made a pattern of the flock. Pursue justice, godliness, faith, charity, patience, mildness, fight the good fight of faith; lay hold on eternal life, whereunto thou art called, keep the commandments without spot, blameless, unto the coming of the Lord Jesus Christ, from Whom you shall receive a never-fading crown of glory. To Him be honor and empire everlasting. Amen. (Cf. 1 Pet. 5:2–4; 2 Tim. 2:22; 1 Tim. 6:14; etc.)[7]

On the day following this solemn rite the newly consecrated Bishop of Vincennes addressed the faithful of his vast diocese in a pastoral letter that was edifying, instructive, and encouraging.

> SIMON GABRIEL, by the Grace of God and the appointment of the Holy See, Bishop of Vincennes.
>
> To all the Faithful of our Diocese, grace be unto you from God the Father, and peace of our Lord and Saviour Jesus Christ.
> Beloved Brethren:—
> Divine Providence sends me among you as the first Bishop of the newly erected Diocese of Vincennes, through the unanimous call of the Bishops, assembled in council in Baltimore, last year, and the appointment of the common Father of the Faithful, Gregory XVI, the Vicar of our Lord and Saviour Jesus Christ on earth, as expressed in his Bull of the 6th of May last. Unworthy

[7] *The Catholic Telegraph*, III (1834), No. 52. M. A. McCann, *Archbishop Purcell and The Diocese of Cincinnati*, p. 22. Washington, D. C., 1918.

as I am of so great an honor, and of myself unequal to the charge, my only trust is in God, and therefore earnestly calling for your prayers, that I may obtain His divine assistance, I come to be your chief pastor. I come to be a first link in the succession of those who, for ages to come, we do so trust in God, are destined to attend, with their cooperators in a divinely instituted ministry, to your spiritual wants and those of your future progeny.

When you are thus entrusted to our care by the great Shepherd of our souls, the warning of the Apostle of the Nations, to us and our successors in the same charge in the bosom of the Catholic Church is to be received with the sacred mixture of fear and confidence that it necessarily creates—. "Take heed to yourselves and to all the flock over which this Holy Ghost hath placed you— Bishops to rule the Church of God, which he hath purchased with His own Blood."

Saying "yourselves and all the flock," the divine word, my brethren, forcibly marks, that the interest and duty both of the pastors and the flock are the same: to live in the same obedience and fidelity to their Lord and His Church, himself having made it, are inseparable allegiance; to embrace His law, receive His grace, and save together their souls for the life to come. For, my brethren, every day spent on this earth makes us draw nearer and nearer to our eternity, and that judgment of God that awaits every one of us. Amidst all the anxieties and distractions of the present life, a last day is approaching! Death will soon bid us go and leave all the occupations, pains, and pleasures of this world to be shared by other passengers, like ourselves, passengers of a day! Death will soon have called us to "stand at the tribunal of Christ," to receive from Him the sentence of condemnation, happiness, or misery, through that immense eternity. Yes, beloved brethren, let one common interest and purpose cement our union in Christ; to save together our souls. To reach heaven and avoid hell is our common aim, to live a good life and do penance (for who needs not penance?) our common duty. Giving glory to God and cherishing peace with all is our consolation on earth; "faith, hope and charity, these three things," must prove our whole treasure, as they are the only certain pledge of real and lasting happiness.

Such, my brethren, is the whole object and zeal of our union in Jesus Christ. He came to save us on the cross, we will trust and serve Him as our Lord and Saviour—. He taught, first, His divine doctrine, then instituted His Church, to preserve it unchangeable to the end of time; we will, the pastor and the flock, with one heart follow His doctrine, obey His only true Church—the sacraments of His grace; and above all, the Eucharistic sacrifice, we will ever consider as the richest legacy of His love, established by Him for our blessing, therefore, neither to be neglected nor abused —our baptism we will faithfully remember; in penance, through sincere confession and contrition, we will seek the remedy of our sins; in communion, the support and joy of our souls.

Addressing thus our Catholic brethren, we forget not that portion of our flock which unhappy contentions, misleading in time past their ancestors, separated from their common Mother. Happy to see them daily forgetting those times, and inclining, we hope, to come and enjoy with us all the means ordained for our salvation, looking upon us as the only ministers of Christ and the dispensers of the mysteries of God. We will not cease to claim humbly and affectionately from them that confidence from which prejudice or misrepresentations cannot long estrange hearts of good will, men of good sense. Let them be at least convinced that sincere love and respect towards them are duties which we mean never to forget.

As for the interests of society, our magistrates and officers of all kinds watch over them, under Providence and the Will of God, manifested by that of their fellow citizens, sanctions their authority —true religion by the voice of the Apostles having so proclaimed from the beginning—the activity and industry of our citizens are alive on all sides in these so rapidly improving countries, to promote the wonderful blessings bestowed on the land by the Creator. It is religion, however, that most effectually cherishes, supports, and sanctions all the obligations, all the occupations, of good men. Her pastors have them all equally at heart, sharing with their worthy cooperators in all the legitimate joys and sorrows of the flock. Our prayer will only be, that they be all sanctified—for this is the will of God, that both the blessings and trials of the present life, all its labors and all its events, be equally directed by men to secure their reward in the next. To this, faith constantly recalls us; Christian hope points steadfastly; charity refers everything, making it ever tend towards the "one thing necessary," the salvation of our souls.

Your Bishop, beloved brethren, entering thus on his holy duty, begs humbly and earnestly your prayers, and entreats also fervently, the God of mercy to bless you; to fill you with that spirit of peace, charity, and piety, which has the best promises both of the present time and of the life to come. Jesus Christ said "I am the way, the truth and the life"—may He ever find the pastor and the flock His faithful followers, and receive them together in the kingdom of His glory. May He give rest to those who are gone before us,—your departed friends, for whom we shall henceforth unite our prayers to yours, especially at the divine sacrifice.

With you we shall honor the Saints who reign triumphantly in heaven, call for their protection and that of the Angels to whom, says the Divine Word, our Lord "hath given charge over us, to keep us in all our ways." We place our Cathedral under the special protection of Saint Francis Xavier, the whole Diocese under that of the glorious Mother of God, the Blessed Virgin Mary, towards whom it was in all ages the spirit of the Church, that all Christians should entertain the most tender devotion.

Beloved brethren, "we are the children of the Saints," as we pass on earth to go and to meet them in heaven. Permit me, then, to conclude with these few words more of the divine scriptures: "The grace of God and Saviour hath appeared to all men, instructing us, that renouncing iniquity and worldly desires, we should live soberly and justly and piously in this world, waiting for the blessed hope and the coming of the glory of the great God and our Saviour Jesus Christ,.... a people acceptable, pursuing good works.... he who shall persevere to the end shall be saved.... the grace and peace of our Lord be with you."

Given at St. Louis the day after our consecration, 29, 10th month, 1834.

✠ Simon, Bishop of Vincennes.[8]

[8] *The Western Sun and General Advertizer*, XXV (1834), p. 1. H. S. Cauthorn, *St. Francis Xavier Cathedral*, pp. 44–46. Indianapolis, 1892; *The Catholic Record*, May 14, 1891. Indianapolis.

During the octave of the dedication of the Cathedral solemn services were held daily, eloquent and instructive discourses were delivered to large crowds of people, and the entire celebration bore the aspect of a Jubilee. The sermons were delivered by the three Bishops together with Fathers Abell, Hitzelberger, Timon, Smith, Van de Velde, Borgna, Verhaegen, and Petit. The English discourses were controversial while those delivered in French dealt with pious subjects. Bishop Rosati, who was indisposed from the fatigue incidental to the dedication ceremonies together with the cares of his daily life, was unable to preach. Bishop Bruté preached on the eve of All Saints. On this occasion he said: "Tomorrow is the Feast of All Saints— let us first honor their Queen," and he then paraphrased the Magnificat. He also delivered a very inspiring discourse on the subjects of *Heaven* and *Eternity* at the Pontifical High Mass on the following day. On Sunday, octave of the dedication of the Cathedral, Bishop Bruté officiated pontifically.

At noon on Monday, November 3, Bishops Flaget, Purcell, and Bruté together with Fathers Abell, Petit, Hitzelberger, and a seminarian, Mr. Ratigan, bade Bishop Rosati and his clergy an affectionate farewell and departed for Vincennes. The journey by stage required two days and they arrived about noon on Wednesday, November 5. Shortly before reaching Vincennes they were met by a deputation of the citizens consisting of both Protestants and Catholics accompanied by Father Lalumière, who welcomed most cordially their newly consecrated bishop and his worthy guests. This group of men also informed the prelates of the death of Archbishop Whitfield, but they were unable to impart any of the details which would have been interesting and consoling to these clergymen who immediately in the stage recited aloud the *De Profundis* for the repose of their common Father.

The installation took place that same evening. Bishop Flaget addressed the newly consecrated prelate to remind him of his duties. Bishop Bruté also spoke. Both dis-

courses were delivered in the French language, followed by
an inspiring and eloquent sermon delivered in English by
Bishop Purcell. Solemn services with eloquent sermons
were conducted morning and evening throughout the remainder of the week. On Sunday Bishop Bruté pontificated
for the first time in his own Cathedral, assisted by Father
Hitzelberger, deacon; Father Lalumière, sub-deacon; Father Petit, S. J., master of ceremonies. The two visiting
Bishops occupied places in the sanctuary. Bishop Flaget
preached at the gospel in French and Bishop Purcell delivered a discourse in English after Mass. These services
were attended by crowds of Protestants as well as
Catholics.[9] That the entire city took interest in the rare
solemnities we need no further proof that the announce-
ments carried by the two non-sectarian publications edited
at Vincennes at that date. Both read as follows:

> The Right Reverend Doctor Bruté, Bishop of Vincennes, lately
> consecrated in St. Louis arrived at his episcopal residence on
> Wednesday, November 5. He came accompanied by the Honorable
> Bishop of Bardstown, Kentucky, Doctor Flaget, and the Bishop of
> Cincinnati, Doctor Purcell. The installation, according to the
> prescribed forms of the Catholic Church, took place on the evening
> of his arrival; when, after the address of Doctor Flaget to the
> new Prelate and his reply, Doctor Purcell spoke in English to a
> numerous and respectable congregation. Every evening during this
> week at half past six o'clock, an English discourse will be delivered.
> On Sunday a Pontifical Mass will be celebrated by Bishop Bruté at
> eleven o'clock, a. m. at which Doctor Flaget will address the con-
> gregation in French. Vespers will commence at three o'clock, and
> at candle light or about half past six o'clock an English sermon
> will be preached.[10]

The dedication of the Cathedral at St. Louis and the consecration of the Bishop of Vincennes caused much alarm

[9] S. Bruté to S. Eccleston, 11–6, 1834, BCA, Case 24–G[11].
[10] *The Western Sun and General Advertiser*, XXV (1834), p. 2;
The Vincennes Gazette, IV (1834) p. 3; C. Blanchard, *Catholicity in
Indiana*, pp. 55–9.

among ignorant sectarians owing to the fact that the ceremonies were performed with all possible solemnity. At the dedication of the Cathedral when the solemn moment of consecration approached, the drums beat the reveille, three Star Spangled Banners were lowered over the sanctuary, the artillery gave a deafening discharge and the bells were rung. This solemnity was interpreted as "a Popish experiment on the Military of the Country" by S. F. B. Morse in a volume entitled "A Foreign Conspiracy against the Liberties of the Country," published in New York during the following year, 1835, and ignorant calumniators endeavored to seize on this circumstance and affected to see in it the subjection of the temporal power of the country to the Pope.[11] Relative to the installation of Bishop Bruté, a sectarian minister sent to the editor of *The Presbyterian* the following account of: "Popery in Illinois."

> You are probably aware that the Pope had constituted recently all this rich neglected country into a diocese with Vincennes as its designated seat. Yea "the man of sin" has already established himself there and the "mystery of iniquity" is beginning to work in a fearful manner. The newly consecrated Bishop has just arrived with two priests, and taken undisputed possession of the now most important town in the state. · They, it is said, are soon to be followed by twenty sisters who are to take into their hands the training of the daughters of the West. Oh! that the "daughters of Zion" in the East had as much zeal and self-denial as the daughters of the "mother of abominations" and then there would be no more necessity for parents here to "sacrifice" their female offspring to Moloch.[12]

On Monday, November 10, the visiting prelates and clergymen left for their respective dioceses and congregations leaving Bishop Bruté alone with his seminarian, Mr. Ratigan. The bishop then began to study his position. The

[11] *American Catholic Historical Researches*, VI (1898), pp. 187–8.
[12] *Idem*, "Popery in Illinois;" *Ill. Cath. Hist. Review*, X (1927), pp. 83–122. "Morse and Anti-Catholic Movements."

citizens of Vincennes had welcomed him with joy, yet
cordiality and financial support were two vastly different
things. Everything associated with the Catholic population
of that city bespoke extreme poverty. The Cathedral was a
plain brick building 115 feet by 60 feet, unplastered, empty,
destitute even of a place for preserving the vestments and
sacred vessels. There was one simple altar of wood with a
gilded tabernacle, a cross, and six gold candlesticks which
were in contrast with the poverty and destitution of the
place. The Bishop's palace, located near the Cathedral,
resembled a peasant's cottage—a small two roomed house,
measuring 25 feet by 12 feet, scantily furnished, wanting in
many essentials, while comfort was unknown. Bishop Bruté
and Mr. Ratigan were forced to care for the household
duties themselves, because their living quarters were too
small to accomodate a third person. He was even obliged to
buy wood just two weeks after his installation. The trustees
had made no provisions for the support of the bishop;
moreover, they seemed to keep aloof—probably from fear
that they would be unable to support a bishop since they
had found it impossible earlier to support a priest. In scan-
ning the church registers kept by the trustees, Bishop Bruté
discovered that many meetings had been conducted by Fathers Blanc, Dahmen, Ferrari, Chabrat, Champomier, Picot,
and Bishop Flaget, and the minutes revealed that, "for the
most part, the deliberations could be summed up in complaints respecting subscriptions, taxes, contributions, and
other complaints against their priest." He realized that he
stood on the brink of the troubled waters of trusteeism and,
while he awaited these sad conditions to take a definite
turn, he asked for nothing and lived on his small fund which
was sadly decreased by this date. The poor bishop had paid
his own and Father Hitzelberger's traveling expenses from
Baltimore, had given Bishop Rosati fifty dollars to send Father St. Cyr back to Chicago, and paid his own and Mr.
Ratigan's board at Vincennes; whereas, upon leaving
Baltimore he had nothing but the purse, of about two
hundred and forty dollars, donated by the Sisters at

ST. FRANCIS XAVIER'S CATHEDRAL, VINCENNES

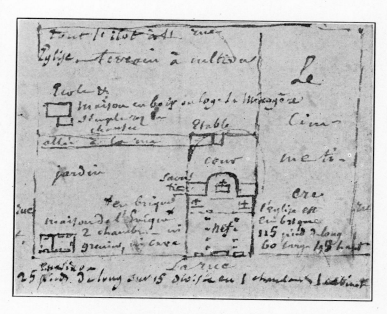

THE OLD CATHEDRAL CHURCH PROPERTY

PEN SKETCHES BY BISHOP BRUTÉ

Emmitsburg. During his sojourn at St. Louis the thoughtful Sisters there procured many necessaries for the poor bishop. Among these items he lists a cassock, rochet, overshoes, and boots.

After pleading with the neighboring bishops for aid the quota of laborers told three clergymen when Bishop Bruté took possession of his diocese. Fathers Lalumière and Ferneding stationed in Indiana were granted by Bishop Flaget and Father St. Cyr stationed then at Chicago was granted by Bishop Rosati for a period of a year. Besides these stations there was Father Badin's mission on the St. Joseph river. The spiritual condition of Vincennes was lamentable. There remained scarcely more than the wrecks of Catholic faith and discipline of the original settlers, or as Bishop Bruté stated it "the *patient* was very ill and very weak." Extreme ignorance prevailed among the people. There was neither seminary, college, religious establishment, nor school. There had been a school at Vincennes taught by four Sisters of Charity from Nazareth, Kentucky, but owing to the spiritual deprivations exacted of them, they had been withdrawn early in 1834. The bishop spoke English only with great difficulty and being alone his labors were rendered all the more burdensome. However, from the moment he took possession of the See he justified the wisdom of his selection as Founder of the new diocese.[13]

The zealous bishop, eager to accomplish every possible good, commenced work immediately. He gave instructions in French after the High Mass on Sundays and he wished to give instructions in English after the Vespers, but it was already so cold in church that only a few women and children attended the services in the afternoon. On November 12, just one week after his installation he commenced the visitation of his new diocese. St. Peter's (now Mont-

---

[13] *The New Record.* "The Diocese of Vincennes," I, p. 2. Indianapolis, 1884; S. Bruté to J. Rosati, 11–18, 1834, St. LCA.; C. Blanchard, *op. cit.,* pp. 56–7; *Brownson's Quarterly Review.* "Discourse on the Rt. Rev. S. W. G. Bruté, D. D., Bishop of Vincennes," III (1849), pp. 195–208; P. H. Clark, *Lives of the Deceased Bishops of the United States,* II, pp. 34–5. New York, 1872.

gomery), near Washington in Daviess County, was the
church privileged to receive his first visit. From there he
went to another congregation seven miles distant and on
November 14 blessed their new church, which Father
Lalumière wished to call St. Simon in honor of the bishop,
but the latter maintained that the Blessed Virgin had yielded the first time when his consecration was transferred
from Holy Rosary Sunday to the feast of SS. Simon and
Jude, and he named the church St. Mary's. From the very
moment of Bishop Bruté's installation, his zealous deeds,
quietly yet forcibly, disproved the Very Reverend John
Power's interpretation of his knowledge—"a lamp in a
sepulchre." On the contrary the words of St. Matthew, "So
let your light shine before men, that they may see your good
works, and glorify your Father Who is in heaven" (5:16),
were practically verified. His intense interest in the spread
of religion was so all-embracing that he wished the knowledge of every new advance effected to be brought before the
public. Hence relative to the blessing of this first small
church and the principal work accomplished during the first
two months of his episcopacy he wrote thus to *The Catholic
Telegraph:*

.... Twelve communions, four baptisms and one marriage marked
the happy day for the pious Catholics of that new settlement. Most
of them came from old Maryland and Kentucky to this country, as
the names of Spalding, Elder, Montgomery, Myles, Young, Smith
&c. bespeak. If things are not yet in their full array at the
Cathedral of Vincennes, still less could be ready for the ceremony
of this humble church, the first effort of new settlers just opening
around the lands of Congress, most of the farms at their first
stage. I would not betray farther their edifying poverty, the procession of little boys in their blue jackets; the roughly hewn joists
and rafters, unplastered walls or ceilings, uncarpeted sanctuary,
nor, the worst, on a very bleak day, the windows left to the poor
protection of some canvass in place of their panes of glass not yet
come from Louisville. Choir and organ being out of question, the
"Melody of the heart" did supply their place. May these hardy

pioneers of better times for their true blessing have a progeny as honest, and as piously inclined successors.

The Catholics of *La riviere au chat*, not visited since Father Petit had been among them, had Mass and instruction from their Bishop. That settlement, twelve miles from Vincennes, is a colony of French families, for cordial and lively dispositions, true to their origin; there the Bishop Flaget was as usual the remembrance of all; "he baptised me," he "married me," "we all loved him," was the cry of the more elderly; and so among the younger ones, the later accounts of that excellent missionary, their last visitor. Some baptisms were administered.

Rev. M. Lalumière had at the same time proceeded to a range of nearly three weeks missionary tour towards *Columbus* and *Shelby-ville;* visiting the Catholic families of those parts, finding some added to their numbers and receiving some into the Church or pre-paring them for it. He found in Shelbyville that they had a few days before enjoyed the presence and ministry of the Rev. M. Badin then on his way to Cincinnati and Washington where important affairs have required his attendance during the session of Congress. M. Lalumière had about the same number of communions as last year. More could have been preparing. In places where there is not a resident pastor, the faithful, when the time of a visit an-nounced to them draws near, and also those who have to travel for their affairs to the places where they know that they will find the priest, ought to make it the principal affair to improve their spir-itual opportunity for which they had often complained at home, that they could not go to meet the clergyman at a distance. Too many with their lively and unshaken faith, remain unaccountably indifferent to the occasions that through the year might more than once present themselves to realize the best graces of Religion.

From *Chicago* the Bishop had the pleasing account of the return of the Rev. Mr. St. Cyr, ordained and sent by the bishop of St. Louis, to that most interesting and rapidly growing town, the southern part of Lake Michigan with which a canal will soon con-nect the Illinois river. He had been recalled to his own diocese, when Chicago with a part of the state of Illinois were attached to that of Vincennes. Our Bishop obtained his return before he left St. Louis after his consecration. A house built on the lot of the church, during the absence of Mr. St. Cyr, was with kind attention, prepared for him. Soon that most promising point may receive Sisters; perhaps have a large college, for in scarcely three years, the town has advanced from a few scattered houses to the astonishing progress of about three thousand souls. Who can tell how much of improvement a few years more may enact for such a place.

South Bend, on the river St. Joseph near the Michigan line, has in its vicinity the establishment of the Rev. Mr. Badin, the Sisters, and the school for the savages. That venerable missionary, called the *proto-priest* of Baltimore, as having been the first ordained in the United States by Bishop Carroll, in 1792, a few years after our American Revolution, shows, after 42 years of labors all over our West: in Kentucky, Ohio, Michigan, and Indiana, all the activity of the most zealous young priest. From South Bend, he visits, occasionally, Logansport and the line of the Canal to Fort Wayne; each time rather a witness to the great good to be done at those important points than actually able to do alone in short visits what would require the habitual presence and utmost devotedness of some indefatigable man or rather of many. Pray, indeed, the Master of the harvest to send worthy laborers into His vineyard, for great is the harvest, and ready; and the opportunity of the works for that canal are urging and actually to be improved.

The *Miamis* having ceded lately much of their lands along that canal and being entitled to have education procured to their youth by the United States, many considerations might induce the Miamis to see it secured to them within this State, some first steps might be taken for enjoying again in this former field of the labors of the Jesuits their happy exertions as missionaries and excellent instructors of youth. The society has, we are told, accepted at the hands of our Holy Father, the special care of the savages our red brethren; may our Indiana grounds, long watered with their sweat and often imbued with their blood, be among the first revisited by them; nay, as education is the great want of our newly settled countries and the best wishes of all good men as they have been repeatedly shown to our bishops, are ready to be fulfilled for every proper undertaking in its favor, may we not indulge the hope that soon our diocese might see the same society add one more col-

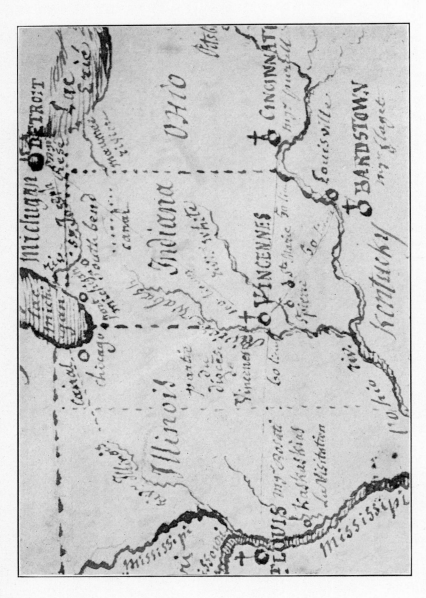

BISHOP BRUTÉ'S MAP OF THE VINCENNES DIOCESE

Taken from a letter to Augustine, February 11, 1835

lege to those they have so successfully established in the diocese, of those of Baltimore, Bardstown, and St. Louis.

We know that our Bishop had in contemplation to visit early his German flock in the congregation of the Rev. Mr. Ferneding and the churches of which the zeal of that good pastor has procured the erection.—He has been so far prevented, as well as from answering other calls that have been made for his visiting or sending clergymen to different parts of his so extensive diocese which has not been so happy as to obtain the blessing secured by Divine Providence to that interesting M'Kenzie's settlement.

I may remark, in general, as I conclude this letter that all seem to welcome the establishment of this new Catholic diocese, all view the settlement of the bishop among us as a thing no less favourable to society than to religion. In every one of the other dioceses this has abundantly proved to be the case. Encouragement to more of immigration; rallying together under circumstances favourable to the welfare and well being of the newcomers; prospects opened to more of activity for many branches of industry; hopes no less generally acceptable to the good sense and religion of the citizens generally for the coming of more of those who devote their lives to the most elevated purposes that faith and charity can cherish; all these edifying things are properly anticipated, viewed, and felt, if it costs an occasional growl to a few of the less favorably disposed, it is truly *for a few;* these parts had never blue laws, blue habits; they are practically, universally on the liberal side. All honors, all trusts, legislative, municipal, and financial lay open to all; our assembly has Catholics amidst its members both in the House of Representatives and the Senate; society numbers them in all its lines of best usefulness and highest respectability, this is no ground for tracts and trash, fair play for religion, peace and prosperity for our country, is the only spirit and motto.

VINCENNES.[14]

The first ordination in St. Francis Xavier's Cathedral occurred on December 22, 1834, when Bishop Bruté con-

---

[14] *The Catholic Telegraph,* "Vincennes," IV (1835), pp. 61–2; cf. *Ill. Cath. Hist. Review,* IV (1922), pp. 255–269; 381–396; *Indiana Catholic and Record,* VII (1916), No. 322, pp. 9–14. Indianapolis.

ferred the four minor orders on Mr. Ratigan. This ordination took place at an early hour at the bishop's Mass. Owing to the extreme ignorance and coldness of the people, for prior to this date only one man and eight or ten women and children had received Holy Communion since the bishop's arrival, he felt that the ceremony would not afford much edification and he conducted it in private. After Mr. Ratigan's ordination he was permitted to handle the sacred vessels and this slightly lessened the bishop's duties. Three days later, on Christmas, His Lordship officiated in the following manner. He approached the foot of the altar garbed in full pontificals. His cross and mitre were carried on a tray by Mr. Ratigan, who then helped him to vest and assisted him during Mass. At Vespers the bishop officiated in cope, stole, and biretta at his throne. From the following account which the bishop himself has left us we are safe in concluding that he was gratified with the results of the day.

Christmas was well attended and after a truly edifying and orderly midnight Mass and some Communions, others took place at the second Mass, at eight o'clock, with those of nineteen youths, making their First Communions, for which they had been prepared during Advent. The Bishop spoke again in French at the midnight Mass, in English, at the last High Mass which had nearly as full a church as the first. Some baptisms took place after it, one of a sensible man lately converted to the Catholic faith.—Solemn vespers with some instruction, and at the end the benediction of the Blessed Sacrament closed the day, during which, much edification seemed to have been received. The full pontifical dignity of our offices could scarcely have been expected to shine forth in all its splendor; either without a sufficient clergy, or in a Cathedral of vast extent, lofty structure, noble form, and strongly built walls; but as yet, as naked and bare, as if just left by the architect and his bricklayers, although covered some six or eight years ago. Still the mitre and the crosier used by the Bishop as he entered the sanctuary, and at his last benediction, have instruction for Catholics wherever they are seen, being viewed as the simple emblems of the authority and office of their first pastors, and of their Apostolical Mission, from the fountains from which all the powers of the ministry incessantly flow through the whole Church of Christ.[15]

Early in 1835 Bishop Bruté sent a lengthy description of the condition and extent of his new diocese to the Bishop of Rennes. Pleadingly he besought his confrère to influence priests in France to come to his assistance in this massive work in America. The poverty-stricken bishop used the reverse side of this letter for a message to his brother. After describing his situation he begged Augustine to send him the following:

> 6 candle-sticks, 20 or 30 inches high; 1 or 2 assortments of altar cards; 1 pair of cruets; ¹silver candle-stick; vestments; surplices; stockings; gloves; cincture; cravat, 2, 3, or 6 Roman Breviaries; 2 missals, better 4; altar clothes, both plain and embroidered; a ring; a pectoral cross (in case I lose mine); a mitre; a crosier (the one I have is gilded wood); oil stocks; a good iron for hosts; a holy water kettle for processions; catechisms and small prayer books; The History of Canada; 2 or 3 dozens of French grammars; a very light chasuble to carry on horseback, and everything else that you would like to send for everything is welcome.[16]

Although the above list embraced a goodly number of necessary articles, seemingly, the bishop had forgotten others that he needed for when writing to Doctor A. Bruté a month later he begged him to procure for him besides a Brother to teach catechism, the following additional articles: "2 very light vestments; 1 rochet (light lace); 1 chalice that can be dismounted; 1 pyx; stocks for holy oils."[17]

In January, 1835, Bishop Bruté received the encouraging news from Father Reynolds that the Sisters of Charity from

[15] *Ibid.;* J. M. Henny, *Ein Blick in's Thal des Ohio,* pp. 46–51. Munich, 1836.

[16] S. Bruté to E. Enoch, 1–13, 1835; S. Bruté to A. Bruté, Canon Bruté Collection. Rennes, France.

[17] S. Bruté to A. Bruté, 2–11, 1835. *Ibid.*

Nazareth, Kentucky, would return to Vincennes immediately after March 25, and would reopen the school on the first Monday in April. In the meantime the school was taught by Mrs. Grandville, an excellent woman whom Bishop Purcell had sent to Vincennes. Nevertheless, these occasional good messages were interspersed with numerous crosses and trials that seemed to multiply along the bishop's path. The winter continued to be extremely severe. The Cathedral, unplastered and without even a stove, was so cold that the good bishop could celebrate only a low Mass for the greater part of the time. It was already February and no provisions for the maintenance of the bishop had yet been made by the trustees. His funds were practically exhausted and he was trying through Father Timon to draw fifty dollars from Baltimore. Back in 1816 when holding the office of President of St. Mary's College, Baltimore, he had through collections raised a fund of $872 for the Lazarist Fathers, but now he felt himself the poorest of bishops abandoned even by those [in Maryland] for whom he had labored incessantly. Despite these conditions he was neither sad nor despondent. After all he wondered what additional joy a priest should seek who had the grace of the morning Mass.

Numerous good priests were needed to further the work of the Divine Master in this new diocese but Bishop Bruté realized that one suspended clergyman was too many. Reverend Mr. Picot had from the very beginning sought admission into the diocese, but acting at the counsel of those who knew this clergyman the bishop persisted in his refusal. Shortly after the consecration of the Bishop of Vincennes Reverend Mr. Picot was canonically suspended by Bishop Flaget of Bardstown. The unfortunate clergyman then became more impetuous than before and persisted in his request to be received at Vincennes. Disregarding the bishop's refusal by letter, he came in person and remained with the bishop for about ten days, but finding himself unsuccessful he finally left as he had arrived—unannounced. Mr. Ratigan also proved to be an unpromising aspirant. He was weak in his studies and likewise in energy, and, consequently, he soon left Vincennes. On this very day another seminarian, Mr. Ruff, arrived from Cincinnati. He was wholly unexpected, although the young man believed the bishop had called him to replace Mr. Ratigan.[18]

These increasing hardships and duties failed to make more than a passing impression on the bishop. He was a soul who thoroughly understood the mystery of Christ and, therefore, did not allow himself to be lost in a multiplicity of details. Writing to Bishop Rosati he said: "Generally my troubles are more on the surface and there is peace in the depth of my heart where dwells a pure and simple abandonment to God alone."

During the severe winter months, Bishop Bruté could not venture on long excursions into his diocese, yet he did not remain inactive but continued his visits to the nearer stations. On January 16, 1835, he was administering to the inhabitants at Cat River, twelve miles from Vincennes. During his sojourn at this French settlement he said Mass in the log house of a poor widow, Mrs. Languedo. Here also he performed the baptisms and marriages, and heard confessions. The bishop left us a graphic picture of the poverty of the place when he wrote:

> They place the best they have on the altar, and with a good intention; two small frames unsuitable on an altar, though indifferent elsewhere; my two ends of candles, used for the first time; they will do for tomorrow, for here everywhere they make use of black lumps of lard, so unsightly, and unfit to place on an altar. The loom on one side, the cask and pot of soap to be made on the other.

The bishop's duties which resembled those of a pioneer missionary on this particular visit were too numerous to permit him to finish the above letter; hence he continued it five days later, saying:

[18] S. Bruté to J. Rosati, 2–4, 1835; 1–14, 1835; St. LCA.

But behold me again at Vincennes! I have a thousand other things
to tell you about this mission. Now, my bed made, and my floor
swept,—which the Bishop no longer does except from time to time,
in order not to forget how!—behold me continuing a little recreation. If I lost myself yesterday in the swamp, it was because I
started too early to visit a sick person eight miles distant on a road
which I could not find alone, and it being only five o'clock in the
morning, after my Mass at half past four, it was but early dawn,
and I met no one. I rode three or four miles, but finding I only
lost my way more and more, I returned to my episcopal city, took
my breakfast, and better directed, I started again about ten
o'clock, and arrived at port.... I prepared the good man who will
not die this time. Then I ate with a hearty appetite their corn
bread, with lard, hot or cold at choice, and drank their coffee without sugar, for one finds this commodity rarely in the interior. When
the provision of maple is exhausted, as was the case at Cat River
where we were three days ago, they make use of honey, but that
too was scarce. The return was very pleasant, the horse travelled
well. My health is excellent.[19]

On February 16, 1835, Bishop Bruté accompanied by Mr.
Ruff went to Edgar County, Illinois, where they remained
until February 25. The missionary bishop received much
consolation from this visit because he found the people more
zealous and devout than the people at Vincennes. On his
return after an absence of almost two weeks there was not a
single confession on Saturday or Sunday except one child
on Sunday evening. The bishop continued to lament the
spiritual infirmities of his people. Adoration of the Blessed
Sacrament was wholly unknown, and many people died
without the Sacraments owing to the fact that the bishop
was either not called or he was called too late.

Over and above these frequent visits to the settlements
nearest the episcopal city, the bishop was occupied with
many other problems essential for the spread and development of the Church. He regretted the fact that Church

[19] *Bruté-Seton Correspondence*, pp. 441–451. 1886.

discipline was not consistent throughout the sister dioceses. Bardstown exacted one day of fast each week during Lent, St. Louis and Vincennes two days, and Cincinnati three days. He wisely maintained that such rulings caused untold difficulties for travellers. At this particular time the bishop was devoting much time to the preparation of his second First Communion class. They were to be admitted to this holy Sacrament on Easter Sunday and to be confirmed on the Sunday following. From the beginning of his episcopacy Bishop Bruté had singular success in making death-bed converts of Protestants. On such occasions he always displayed marked prudence in dealing with convert invalids who were near death.[20]

For a second time within the first year of Bishop Bruté's episcopal administration an unworthy clergyman applied for admission into the diocese. Reverend Mr. Tervoran, a young priest of twenty-seven years, stationed at La Baye in the diocese of Detroit, wished to exchange dioceses and be stationed at (Fort) Wayne, Indiana. Bishop Bruté had heard serious criticisms on Mr. Tervoran and concluding that "the diocese would not be aided by such creatures," he frankly refused the application.[21] Apart from this he sorely needed assistance for Easter and he sent Father Lalumière to Kentucky to obtain Father Petit's services for this occasion. Father Lalumière, however, failed of his purpose and the bishop was left alone for Holy Week. Correspondence confirms the assertion that the Sacred Congregation was cognizant of the dire needs of the Bishop of Vincennes for on several occasions they strove to procure missionaries and money for the new See. During the first year of his administration he received three letters from Rome in behalf of this noble cause. On March 31 the Sacred Congregation wrote as follows:

[20] S. Bruté to J. Rosati, 3–30, 1835, St. LCA.
[21] S. Bruté to Mgr. Rezé, 3–4, 1835;   4–19, 1835, CA of A.

Most Illustrious and Right Reverend Lord!

The priest of God, John Claude François of the Diocese of Verdun in France, sends this letter to Your Lordship. Since he perseveres in his eager desire to enter upon the sacred office of a missionary and since there is, especially in your Diocese, such a scarcity of priests, I have thought that I would do you a favor by sending him to America there to exercise the office of missionary under your direction, he has, therefore, declared his willingness to come to you upon receipt of the money necessary for the journey. Very highly commending to Your Lordship this priest, celebrated for piety, integrity of morals, and gifted with knowledge, I pray that God may long preserve you safe and happy.

Your Lordship's
Most affectionate brother,
J. Ph. Cardinal Fransoni, Prefect.

Rome, the office of the Sacred Congregation for the Propagation of the Faith, March 31, 1835.[22]

Before this letter reached Vincennes, Bishop Bruté wrote the Sacred Congregation giving them another lengthy account of his extreme poverty. He besought this august body of prelates to influence the Superior General of the Jesuits to send priests to his assistance.

The second ordination at Vincennes occurred during the first week in April when minor orders and subdeaconship were conferred upon Mr. Ruff. On Wednesday, April 9, Bishop Bruté ordained this seminarian deacon and intended to confer upon him the dignity of the holy priesthood on Easter Tuesday. The Cathedral being too poor to afford a dalmatic for ordinations Bishop Bruté himself made one. He sewed in the bottom of a chasuble, took off the cross and galloons and used the two large ends of a maniple for the shoulder pieces. In the meantime the bishop found himself too pressed for time to give Reverend Mr. Ruff the necessary attention and therefore found it impossible to ordain on Easter Tuesday as he had planned, and he sent Reverend

[22] Original in CA of A.

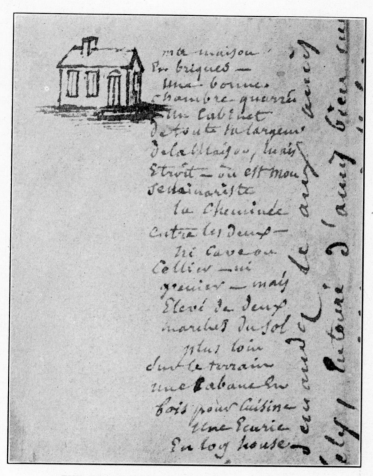

THE FIRST EPISCOPAL PALACE AT VINCENNES

DRAWING BY BISHOP BRUTÉ

Mr. Ruff to St. Louis for his retreat and ordination. The limited time was only an excuse offered to the public. The fact was that Bishop Bruté and his seminarian had had a slight misunderstanding and the bishop wished Bishop Rosati to keep Reverend Mr. Ruff indefinitely.[23]

In a letter written to Bishop Rosati on April 23, 1835, Bishop Bruté announced for the first time his pending trip to Europe. This message reads as follows:

> Now my secret which I can no longer hide from you—I see no other hope for me except *going* to France. I have received from all sides the most pressing invitations—especially from my Bishop of Rennes and from a superior, who assures me very good priests, as well as other succor, if I will come in person. They point out this moment, and I also believe it the voice of Divine Providence. I have decided to leave in July. I hardly hope we can travel together, and I suppose you would rather fear it than desire it knowing how little amiable I am when near!—I but ask your prayers and good advice. We are engaged in a great and a common cause of such a great future, for me what can I hope for this new diocese,—I must go.[24]

The offers thus made to the bishop were too attractive to be rejected. The good bishop, however, decided to visit the whole of his diocese before going abroad, yet he was somewhat perplexed as to the manner in which he would arrange these visits. The congregations were not in a group like those of Maryland, Kentucky, and Missouri; on the contrary, they were located in the four corners at two hundred and two hundred and fifty miles from the See of Vincennes and at three hundred to four hundred miles from one another. He had received pressing invitations to Chicago, [Fort] Wayne, Shawneetown, and to Reverend Mr. Ferneding's parish for after Easter, but owing to the great mileage and the disagreeable traveling it was impossible for him to go in person to each place. Hence the bishop decided to visit the north-west half of the diocese and he dele-

[23] S. Bruté to J. Rosati, 4–23, 1835, St. LCA.
[24] Original in St. LCA.

gated Father Lalumière to visit Columbus, Shelbyville, and several other smaller stations.[25] The report of these visitations might be condensed to fewer words and less space, but in order to preserve the pioneer spirit of the period and to reveal to our present generation the hardships endured by the Founder of the diocese we here insert his own description of the two visitations:

Our Bishop has been absent for nearly four weeks—from the 29th of April, visiting the northern part of this vast diocese; during which time he has travelled more than six hundred miles, five hundred and fifty of which he performed on horseback. On the 23rd of May he returned to Vincennes.

He visited Danville, Chicago, Michigan City, Laporte, South Bend, and two villages of Catholic savages, under the care of Rev. Mr. Deseille, who resides at the first, in Michigan Territory, near the Indiana line; he then proceeded down the Wabash to Logansport, Lafayette, and the numerous towns and villages above Terre Haute.

He has received much information, during this tour, respecting the present state and future prospects of religion, in this section of country; and perceived with pain the great want of spiritual aid in every direction—viewing "the country white for the harvest," and "the laborers so few," so very few, he earnestly prayed on his journey that the Lord may "send Laborers."

In Illinois, while ranging by day, and sometimes by night, over the prairies, with the good man who had kindly volunteered to accompany him, and in Indiana while travelling through the woods, he amply enjoyed the solitude and indulged in the self-communion which it invited; yet amidst the woods and prairies the frequent sight of man-missionary, sent by Providence to "fill the earth," recalled the missionary Bishop to the thought how the earth thus filling for all the purposes of industry and temporal welfare, may be filled also with the knowledge, love, and service of God. The weary, but eager emigrants were seen in the distance; they approached and passed by; men on horseback were exploring the country, or

[25] S. Bruté to J. Rosati, 3–19, 1835, St. LCA.

journeying to the homes they had selected and secured—families with their wagons were pressing forward to those parts which gave promise of rapid improvement, and young mechanics on foot with their light bundles and few tools, cheerful and untired throughout their long journey, passed him by—they passed and were soon lost to sight! It was "the figure of this world that passeth away."

On entering the villages of Illinois and Indiana, you are struck with the indications of rapid growth. For the names of many, you in vain consult the most recent gazetteer—many have sprung up in a single season, Lakeport, for instance, on a beautiful lake eight miles from Laporte.

Everywhere, speculation, in all its forms, bespeaks reciprocal confidence, between the occupants of the lands and those who come, with a view of improving their various advantages, for commerce or agriculture. It would, perhaps, be better if the word "Grocery," in large characters did not so frequently invite the early attention of the settlers. But let charity condemn only abuses! Is not the grocery if properly conducted a very necessary item in the formation of a village?

Hospitality was readily afforded in every house along the road, both in Illinois and Indiana, and in so plain, kind, and cheering a manner as to make the traveller feel perfectly at home. Admitted, welcomed, and entertained without question or inquiry, the discovery of the character of the guest whether a Catholic priest or Bishop made no change.

So little success has as yet attended the efforts of designing men to abuse their credulity and pervert their feelings, that the clergy by simply introducing themselves, in their true character, and not as they are misrepresented, receive the esteem of all good men; all the reputed dangers of popery, inquisitions, and foreign conspiracies, of nunneries and convents notwithstanding. Nay, it is but truth to say, that marks of interest and respect were more than once shown to the age, character, and good purposes of the main traveller; all warning to the contrary being forgotten, amidst the simple accounts he or his companions had occasion to give of the benevolent and sacred object of their journey.[26]

[26] *The Catholic Telegraph*, "Vincennes," IV (1835), pp. 317–318.

Edgar County and Paris revisited.—They were fully reported in February last—Paris is still the same thriving place, with the same expectations of the railroad to Chicago, and presents many attractions to travellers. It has a fine court house. There are as yet but few Catholics in the town, but a large number in the vicinity. They attended during three days at the house of Mr. Bordine, to comply with their Easter duty. On Tuesday afternoon, the Bishop resumed his journey to the north having previously promised that a priest should visit Paris in August. It is hoped that ere long an additional attraction to Catholic settlers in that county will be held out by the establishment of a regular service there.

Georgetown is a fine village. Danville is 10 miles distant from it and is larger and more flourishing. It contains several taverns, two schools, and two or three meeting houses. Here all is activity; and the most sanguine hopes of its future importance are entertained. In this place the Bishop found but one Catholic family. Catholicity, in its true import, is so little known, and vague prejudices against it are so industriously excited, that those who profess it are, in many places, regarded with suspicion for some time; but the people naturally kind-hearted and inquisitive are ever ready for those explanations which, as Mr. Everret lately observed in the legislature of Massachusetts, give quite another aspect to objections. This was exemplified by some intelligent Protestants from Vermont to whom the Bishop offered some of those explanations. He had another opportunity of observing how truth gains upon the candid mind in proportion as misrepresentation endeavors to obstruct its passage.

From this village to Chicago the road lies over vast prairies interspersed with a few patches of wood, and watered by some noble streams, particularly the Iroquois and the Kankakee. This interesting part of Illinois has been well described by Hoffman in his "Tour to the West." The accommodations are as yet what travellers would call indifferent; but who would regard that when the people present so many excellent traits for the present study and future hope of the friend of religion. The Bishop left every place well pleased, fondly believing that the people would easily be reconciled to the "man of sin" of Vincennes, and more easily to the other *sinners* his successors. *Sugar Creek.* Here the Bishop met a physician of Kentucky, returning from the north, and the conversation, turning on professional subjects, recalled many reminicences of the men and schools of France, and the evening passed with much interest to both parties. At bed time the Bishop had to struggle hard to preserve his right to occupy the floor and leave the only bed to the obliging Doctor and another gentleman who travelled with him and who had made their arrangements for the night before his arrival. Two days after this the Bishop had arrived at the house of an excellent family and received comfortable lodging for the night when a Methodist preacher came in who had travelled with his two market wagons; for, as Gobbett says of the successor of Wickham at Winchester, he had family concerns to add to his spiritual affairs.

Chicago, 7th of May. Of this place the growth has been surprising, even in the West, a wonder amidst its wonders. From a few scattered houses near the fort it is become, in two or three years, a place of great promise. Its settlers sanguinely hope to see it rank as the Cincinnati of the north. Here the Catholics have a neat little church. Americans, Irish, French, and Germans meet at a common altar, assemble from the most distant parts of this vast republic or come from the shores of Europe to those of our lakes. Rev. M. St. Cyr is their pastor. They have already their choir supported by some of the musicians of the garrison.— Many of the officers, and a number of the most respectable Protestants attended. The Bishop on his arrival in the diocese had been invited by the Protestants as well as the Catholics of this place to fix his residence among them and felt his gratitude revived by the kind reception he had now received. During his stay he preached three times in English and on Sunday morning administered the Sacrament of Confirmation. On the same day Dr. Chase, the late Protestant Bishop of Ohio, preached in the Presbyterian church of Chicago. The environs of Chicago do not appear as favorable for agriculture as the situation of the town is for commerce; but time and industry may do much for their improvement.

Michigan City at the southeast extremity of the lake is within the State of Indiana. In the town there are many houses in progress and around it industrious settlers are clearing the heavily timbered land and establishing farms which give the place an appearance of great promise. Here there are yet few Catholics.—

Laporte, the county town is already well improved.—At a distance of 8 miles stands Lakeport, on a beautiful lake of considerable extent, from which it takes its name, is the growth of a single season and offers a great field of speculation. At the next tavern the Bishop inquired for Pokegan's Indian people, and went to meet their father Rev. Mr. Deseille, a worthy successor of the *Robes noires*, who now attends the missions of the savages on their old grounds along the St. Joseph's river.

Pokegan's village is a collection of wigwams most of them formed with poles and covered with straw mats, the better buildings are log cabins. The principal of these is the house of God and of His priest. The whole of the lower floor is occupied as a chapel; above, is the apartment of the missionary, with his small table, seat, and swinging bed or hammock.

A partition secures him a record room for all purposes of hospitality and storage. A porch of poles and bark projects towards the garden by which name the worthy man has dignified a little patch of cabbages and potatoes which he can have no thought of improving since his friend must so soon move away. About 600 savages baptised and brought to a state of Christian knowledge and practice the most edifying, would on that spot raise in the heart a desire fully corresponding with that of Father Deseille; that a permanent settlement could be granted to his good people. But that cannot be; all the land is ceded to the United States; most of it sold around them and they must either go beyond the Mississippi—the far west for these most eastern Potawatomies—or be received upon the reserves of their friends farther north in Michigan. This they are trying to effect in order to secure the enjoyment of their religion and the ministry of the missionaries of Bishop Rezé, whose children these Indians of Pokegan were, living just on the borders of Indiana but within the Territory of Michigan.

For the first time among his red brethren, but among a race so well instructed and so well disciplined in the Catholic religion, the Bishop's feelings must have been excited and his mind prepared for new impressions either during those awful moments in which he offered the Divine Sacrifice—a God incarnate, a victim God, the

God of all salvation and love there present—or whilst by an interpreter he addressed the words of eternal truth and benediction to those souls no less immortal, no less angels in human form, whose heavenly destinies it is the province of religion to advance, than any of the most refined and spiritual beings to whose spiritual wants he had administered at St. Joseph's and other places.

They sing their hymns in the Ottawa tongue and recite the Catechism in the same. Many of them used printed books (for all their services had been printed) and they generally have great facility in learning to read and excellent memories to retain what they have learned. They have preserved their traditional attachment to their first fathers, the Jesuits. Some of the oldest of them were baptised by the last missionaries of that order and a few still remembered them. They believe their present good pastor to be of that order and are therefore the more attached to him.

South Bend on the St. Joseph's river; Rev. M. Deseille crossed the Indiana line to accompany the bishop to another Catholic Indian village which he attends.—They passed South Bend a town fast rising in importance, surrounded by good land and situated on the river St. Joseph which will soon be navigable for steam-boats to Lake Michigan.

On the opposite side of the river is the large establishment of Rev. Mr. Badin called St. Mary's of the Lake. The house is on an eminence near a small lake surrounded by a meadow and woods of luxuriant growth. The place is happily situated for different purposes connected with the interests of religion in this part of the country; where there are already a few Catholic families American, Irish, and French. It is the earnest desire of the Bishop soon to see this place redeem its many pledges of extensive usefulness.

VINCENNES.[27]

The Indians of Chichako's Village. From South Bend the Bishop accompanied by Rev. Mr. Deseille went to visit the other village of Catholic Indians above alluded to. A number of the Indians with Chichako at their head met them many miles from the village.—They proceeded in a long cavalcade through the deep forest and numerous morasses; and their guidance was extremely neces-

[27] *Idem,* August 7, 1835.

sary in many of the wild and miry places that led to the ford of the Tippecanoe.—Near the ford they found a camp, at which they were invited to take coffee; which they did sitting upon mats of reed spread upon the ground as if among the Arabs of Moccha; though the coffee might not be brought from so great a distance and the sugar was the produce of their own trees. They had also abundance of excellent molasses. A few miles further on lay the village. The church was built of bark spread over the stakes which formed the sides, and curving rods which supported the roof. A rough hewn cross was raised above it. That simple sign speaks feelingly to the heart of the savage, who knows its meaning, as he approaches the chapel. The same sign meets him again at the graves pointing out the Christian's hope. Alas! for the mistake of those who understand it not; but show anger at the sight.

The evening was spent in pious preparation for the Sunday, which in its turn was spent in a succession of pious exercises. Confirmation was administered to 16 adults, and six children were baptised. A large number of adults were preparing to receive baptism during the stay of Rev. Mr. Deseille among them, which would be some days. Mass was accompanied by the usual singing in the Ottawa tongue and in the afternoon vespers was sung in the same. Those good people evinced dispositions, which excited in the Bishop feelings that were forcibly expressed by Bishop E. Fenwick after his visit to them some years since.

The bishop left them that same evening, parting with much regret from their excellent Father, Rev. Mr. Deseille. Since his return he has learned that, after that worthy priest had spent weeks at Chichako's village constantly engaged in instructing the people, 80 more of those children of nature have become through baptism the children of grace, adopted members of Christ and heirs of His kingdom.

Logansport. Returning home, we pass through flourishing towns and villages, along the Wabash, to Vincennes, of which much ought to be said, but we defer it, until our next tour.

We cannot, however, pass Logansport, without some slight notice. Who can foresee the worldly prosperity promised by its location or the spiritual consolations it is destined to enjoy? The inhabitants are emulous of a share of national improvement and are hastening with admirable efforts to promote it. To this point also religion invites her minister, and directs him to employ his best exertions for her present establishment, and encourages him to hope, for her future advancement. When the Bishop celebrated there the Divine mysteries which were destined from the cross for that place also; when his voice was heard as sent by the Lord Who bled on that cross for America as for the other portions of the world and at His triumphant Ascension said: "Go ye, and teach all nations, and behold, I am with you all days, even to the consummation of the world"—what must have been his impression, on addressing a considerable number of Catholics already assembled in this new settlement, and prepared to erect a chapel, and receive a priest among them. It is the same in the eastern part of the State, along the Erie and Wabash canal, where at the voice of man, permitted by God to be like a second creator; to change, enrich, beautify, and "fill the earth" as his present and future interests may direct, the work of settling and improving is readily progressing. Witness Miamisport and Peru, Wabash-town and Huntington and all-important Wayne. As for Logansport and the line south and west to Terre Haute their time is fast approaching. In many of the places the lots for the erection of churches have already been provided by the zeal of Catholics, nay, in some instances, of Protestants deserving by their friendly and liberal feelings the gratitude of all who can appreciate hearts and minds which the efforts of bigotry to prejudice cannot reach.

Of Fort Wayne, where the church is built and a resident priest located much more remains to be said. Rev. Mr. Lalumière is visiting that range of the country, for the Bishop, who is now preparing for his tour to Europe. The Bishop returned to Vincennes at the end of May, when, owing to the backwardness of the seasons, improvements were just beginning to progress, and was struck with the rapidity of their march. They reflect great praise on the individuals by whom they are undertaken, the public spirit of our citizens displays itself in the increase of substantial brick building which already so much changed the aspect of the town. Many are now in progress at once at different points on the principal streets.

Steamboats arrive and depart daily; six have often been at the landing on the same day.

The settlements are fast progressing and commerce improving all along the borders of that beautiful river which nature has made one of the finest branches of the Ohio, and man is now leading up to Lake Erie, the immense waters of which it will make tributaries to the fortunes of Indiana; as they are to those of New York and Michigan; not to speak of Ohio of which they wash Atlantic-like the whole northern shore. Terre Haute has, already, wonderfully improved the advantages of the Wabash, and is next to Vincennes, the largest town upon its water.

All bids fair in the temporal order of things, both in Indiana and Illinois, to hold henceforth its undeviating course, towards epochs of prosperity, of which it would be difficult to estimate, even for a limited period, the full extent and magnificence. May their spiritual progress be equal to it; and the divine favors for its advancement be no less zealously improved! Unnoticed, almost unperceived, at first, they are, in our days, as in the primitive times of the Church of Christ, left to be valued and cherished or treated with neglect, as human liberty may please to act in correspondence with, or opposition to them. Be it the fervent prayer of all that they may be truly corresponded with! Time is but time, eternity is ETERNITY![28]

The report of these visitations fully acquainted Bishop Bruté with the condition and the prospects of the entire diocese. This knowledge convinced him all the more that he must procure material aid from outside sources if he wished to build successfully and quickly the new diocese committed to his care. True the Leopoldine Association at Vienna had recently granted him 1200 florins and while he recognized it to be an appreciable sum, yet it was but a fraction of what was needed. Immediately he sent to Rome an account of his tour to Chicago and vicinity and wrote the Jesuits personally concerning the one and one-half sections of land near the St. Joseph's river. The scholarly bishop believed this location well adapted for a college. He also wished to obtain French Jesuits to care for the French

[28] *Idem*, August 21, 1835.

settlements at Cat River, Coffee, Logansport and the
Indians of that neighborhood. Moreover, he wished them to
open a college at Vincennes.[29]

On June 27, 1835, the Sacred Congregation sent the following response to Bishop Bruté's letter dated April 2.

Most Illustrious and Right Reverend Lord!

I have received your Lordship's letter written April 2. I am
exceedingly grieved that your diocese suffers from such a scarcity
of priests and I will do everything in my power to relieve this
necessity. In the meantime I have thought to inform Your Lordship that as soon as possible you will receive a sum of money
equivalent to 2000 silver florins from Holland, nor will the Sacred
Congregation fail to aid you in every possible manner in the future.
Moreover, I have addressed myself to the General of the Society of
Jesus to see whether he has any priests of his Society who might
be sent to open a College in your diocese, as Your Lordship desires.
It is indeed displeasing to me that I must inform you that the
Father General has replied that at present he has no priests whom
he can send to your diocese for that purpose. The same Father
General solemnly affirmed that you can even invite to the aid of
your missions the priests of the Society of Jesus who sojourn in
other American dioceses and that they will certainly comply with
the desire of Your Lordship. In the meantime, I pray that God
may preserve you safe and happy.

Your Lordship's
Most affectionate brother
J. Ph. Cardinal Fransoni, Prefect.

Rome, the office of the Sacred Congregation for the Propagation of
the Faith, June 27, 1835.[30]

Scarcely more than eight months had elapsed since Bishop
Bruté's consecration and installation, yet history bears

[29] S. Bruté to J. Rosati, 5–24, 1835; 6–11, 1835, St. LCA.
[30] Original in CA of A.

testimony to the fact that he had already accomplished wonderful work. However, he realized that countless other duties were awaiting his steady hand and courageous heart and he did not attempt to seek rest, but hurriedly prepared for an immediate voyage to Europe.

CHAPTER XII

BISHOP BRUTÉ IN EUROPE
1835–1836

Bishop Bruté had frequently turned to France for help while at the Mountain and used his influence to induce others to come hither or at least to take an active interest in the growing needs of the Church in America. Finding his own diocese in extreme want with no hope of relief he again turned his heart towards his fatherland and prepared to seek for himself and his flock the assistance he had so successfully obtained for others. On July 9, 1835, a week before his departure from Vincennes for France, he prudently secured the property of the diocese by willing it to his successor and appointed Father Lalumière executor.[1] Apparently he allowed himself ample time to reach the port of embarkation, for several weeks were spent with friends along the way; but to the surprise of all he refrained from visiting the Mountain and the Valley. His first stop was at Cincinnati where he visited with Bishop Purcell. Relative to this event *The Catholic Telegraph* gives us the following account.

> The Right Reverend Doctor Bruté, Bishop of Vincennes, left this city on Tuesday last, on his way to France. Notwithstanding the fatigue he has lately endured in the visitation of his extensive diocese and a voyage to Europe which he has resolved to undertake for its interests, this learned and pious Prelate, we rejoice to observe, is in excellent health and spirits. Last Sunday he preached in the Cathedral on the words of St. Paul: "We are fools for Christ's sake" (1 Cor. 10:10)....
>
> In the afternoon, we were favored with an important and highly interesting lecture by the good bishop, on the necessity of acknowl-

---

[1] *The Indiana Catholic and Record,* VII (1916), No. 322, p. 3. Indianapolis; Original Will in Canon Bruté Collection. Rennes, France.

edging and obeying a positive religion, on baptism, and the other
sacramental ordinances. May his fervent discourse and most
salutary lessons be long and faithfully treasured up by all who
heard, and their prayers for his safe return find acceptance with
the God who has chosen him and made him one of the favorite
shepherds of his people![2]

On July 27 Bishop Bruté left Cincinnati for New York
and was escorted as far as Steubenville, Ohio, by Bishop
Purcell who went thither to dedicate the Church of St. Pius.
On his arrival he found, much to his disappointment, that
his old colleague, Bishop Dubois, was away from the episcopal city visiting his diocese. This duty unhappily deprived the two prelates of an interesting visit with each
other. During these days, Bishop Bruté was very active
studying the "conspiracy" of the ignorant sectarians.
Everywhere along the way the prudent bishop recommended patience, peace, and silence, even in proportion to the
excitement of the deluded Presbyterians. He perceived that
there was a profound "conspiracy" among that sect, but his
confidence in God dispelled all alarm and he exclaimed, "If
God is with us who can be against us."[3]

Following a two weeks' sojourn at New York, the port
whence he intended to depart, Bishop Bruté embarked on
the *Rhone,* and sailed at ten o'clock on Saturday morning,
August 8, 1835. Before leaving Vincennes he had appointed
Reverend Mr. Lalumière his Vicar General. Likewise, he
had announced the purpose of his voyage in a Pastoral Letter to his flock, but owing to the fact that he submitted all
material for publication to Bishop Purcell for correction,
this letter did not appear until two days after Bishop Bruté
had sailed. Hence we find the following letter, dated August
10, 1835, instead of the date of his departure from Vincennes.

[2] *The Catholic Telegraph,* IV (1835), p. 317.
[3] S. Bruté to J. Rosati, 8–8, 1835, St. LCA. St. Louis, Mo.; M. A.
McCann, *Archbishop Purcell and The Diocese of Cincinnati,* p. 22.
Washington, D. C., 1918.

Vincennes, August 10, 1835.

Simon Gabriel, by the grace of God and the appointment
of the Apostolic See, Bishop of Vincennes—

To his beloved brethren in Indiana and Illinois—grace and
peace in our Lord Jesus Christ.

Truly Beloved Brethren:—May charity and innocence abound
with all. May prosperity and security dwell in our borders. May
the happiness and contentment, the common zeal for the public
good, and the universal, mutual, good feeling which I have witnessed and shared with gladness of heart since I came to devote the
remainder of my days to your service, forever be fostered by all.

Paul and his brethren in the apostleship said humbly, but most
confidently, when they were visiting or writing to the nations, that
they were sent not by men, but by the Lord; and they called them
whom they thus addressed, their 'children,' or 'brethren,' "according
to the common faith" and the "acknowledging of the truth," for
the "only sake of piety," and of "the hope of everlasting life," with
that unfeigned charity which was in those early days the sign of
their blessed unity in the bond of peace. Their mission, authority,
and true purpose were thus made known, and duly understood.
Our authority, in the succession of time, is but one with theirs.
And thus, with sensible men, it needs no further apology. The
spiritual kingdom of Christ, preparing on earth for its consummation in heaven, "is not of this world." It leaves all sublunary concerns to go their transitory rounds, as the providence of God and
man's liberty may direct them.

'Made of one,' all mankind dwell upon the whole face of the earth
their appointed time; and the 'limits of their habitation' are before
God 'for good or evil,' constituting a temporal order, with an obligation on all, that they act *only for good.* This duty should be the
most acknowledged in a country where the choicest blessings of
the Almighty are bestowed without measure, calling for the most
loving cooperation of all in the promotion of the common welfare.
A glance around us discovers the utmost activity prevailing; men
acquitting, in the most prosperous manner, the primitive mandate,
"fill the earth." And is it not enough to inspire your Pastors, as
yourselves, with an insatiable desire to see the people of this vast

republic, to see our Indiana and Illinois more and more blessed in their independence and industry. What other mind should be in each one of us, but that of contributing to the general and individual happiness, and pleasing God, by pleasing all our brethren in all lawful things.

Such has been, unquestionably, throughout the entire Union, the course of the Catholic clergy and people, no matter from what state or kingdom; at what near or remote period, they emigrated from the eastern world. Hence, from the east to the far west, from the north to the south, of our immense and most beloved country, has been conciliated for us that general favor which the envy, or unreasonable fears and delusions *of a few,* cannot prevent from preserving and increasing among all our fellow citizens; each enjoying in peace the fruit and shade of his own vine and fig-tree, well contented, patriotic, and friendly, under the protection of our free constitution, which equally and impartially extends its blessings to all. Thus secure in our temporal state, we should only think of promoting "the hope of everlasting life," "leading quiet and peaceable lives," as the apostle warns, and our faith directs us.

To cherish in you that spirit and procure that the institutions of our holy religion may extend and display the more among you their usefulness, is our duty. Certainly such zeal cannot be more objectionable in us, than in the ministers of other societies, which being far more numerous, should be less susceptible of admitting pretences against the exercise of a common right; nay more, bound, in a true republican spirit, to protect the pastors and flocks of our own and every other denomination, in its enjoyment.

Must not, beloved brethren, every heart impressed with the excellence and divine authority of the Christian religion, desire to see it extend its blessings to all mankind? It was given for all men and all nations; and in Jesus Christ, there is neither Greek nor Scythian; Roman, barbarian, or stranger; all are the domestics and citizens of the same city. Its spiritual rights and rules belong alike to all, and are to be offered and administered unto them in a manner perfectly independent of the interference of human policy, the civil arrangement of nations, or their differences of languages, institutions, and customs, whatsoever. Convinced that truths, of such plain and obvious bearing, are evident to the minds of all our fellow citizens, we shall ever act confidently, as the line of our duty (responsible as it is in the sight of God) may direct us, for the best interests of our flock; certain of the divine approbation, and not distrustful of the esteem to which we should be thus entitled on the part of upright and reasonable men.

Since it hath pleased the Bishops of the United States to solicit, and our Holy Father to grant the erection of the new See of Vincennes, many have been the favors bestowed upon us by Divine Providence, for which we return all thanks, and invite you to join in the same. These were, however, but humble beginnings, we trust, compared with what we may further anticipate as the blessing of our already numerous, and still increasing Catholic population. In the survey of our wants in the newly erected diocese, it has been easy to perceive how inadequate are our present means to the actual demand; and how many earnest calls from congregations and individuals famishing for the Bread of Life, must be left unanswered, until additional help shall have been obtained, or sufficient time afforded for the development of our own resources. An appeal to the charity of our brethren for this purpose has become necessary, and we have resolved to make it; but to a spirit of zeal and liberality we would first encouarge you. For, beloved brethren, you are convinced that in these new countries, settling as they are on all sides with pledges of the most magnificent prosperity, there can be no more worthy use made of what our Lord grants with so much goodness, than to devote a proper portion of it to secure to yourselves and to your posterity, the blessings of religion.

But although we may trust that zeal will be daily awakening the more in our diocese, as it has happened in those created before it; we are for the present greatly in need to see the Catholic spirit of our sister churches, whether in this country, or in those of the old world, exerted in our behalf, as it has been constantly the case, from the beginning of Christianity, that the more ancient churches should assist the younger, as truly being, in faith and charity, one body in the Lord. Founded in unity by Him to whom the whole earth and the fullness thereof belong, the Catholic Church, is, from her very name, the church of all nations. Remembrance of this one fact is alone sufficient to take away the very idea of foreign interference, in whatever is granted by our brethren at home, or across seas or mountains, as a simple consequence of our being all but one body. On that point, the practice of the apostles, their calls to the faithful, their voyages, their collections of money and means, their missions, and frequent transfer of men ceased not to show how earnestly their Catholic feelings kept alive in their bosoms, the "solicitude for all the churches," and their desire to make them not only pray for, but "help" one another, as far as their abilities allowed, in their various temporal as well as spiritual necessities.

Perhaps, dear brethren, our anxiety not to permit our travels and efforts in behalf of the diocese so recently trusted to us, and as yet, as it were, wholly to be created, to give occasion to any mistake, or misrepresentation, makes us insist too much on these obesrvations; but we are eager to spare the weakness of the weak, and disarm the malignity of the malignant. Painful must it be to Catholics, that their plain, consoling, and elevating sentiments should be misunderstood, and those views of mutual assistance through the different parts of the kingdom of Christ, which is not of this world, simple and amiable as they are, should excite most unreasonable or wicked surmises of foreign conspiracies. The expression of such dishonorable and unchristian surmises, so long unknown in this land of all good feeling, has of late become so frequent and mischievous, that it has become necessary to obviate their bad effects by giving them, as they deserve, on every occasion, a true and unqualified refutation.

When the apostles began that spiritual ministry to all nations, which obtains its glorious continuance amongst us, whether we went in person to the nations, issued orders to them, or received from abroad a reference to their authority, they moved, spoke, wrote, and acted not as strangers and foreigners, but as embracing the whole earth in the same truth, jurisdiction, and grace. So does, to this day, the Church, in the one, same, spiritual commonwealth of Christendom. That commonwealth, in her eyes, has no civil divisions, no civil magistracies, or legislation; these things are of another world, not her own. Christ, "the same yesterday, to-day, and forever," sends and empowers His messengers for the work of the same independent ministry, to-day, as yesterday, and destined to be thus the same until the consummation of the world. The Christian world has no strangers; all are citizens and domestics, not of local households, or of changing faiths, but of that immense, Catholic, and Apostolic Church, that now, as in the beginning, has but "one heart and one soul," of mutual affection, and of common creed.

We thus, as we hope, beloved brethren, express not our own feelings alone, but those of all sensible Americans. It may happen that some, or even many disorderly minds, may be misled to dissent from positions so simple or call in question facts so incontestable as those we have represented to you. Nay, it may so happen, that some editors of papers, miscalled *religious;* and with them a few of the political line, should mistake their duty for the promotion of the peace, order, and real prosperity of this country, as well as for the good of religion; and for reasons best known to themselves, spread with broadcast, the seeds of discord among brethren. We have not to mind their judgment. From the very close of our revolution, to this day, the true judges of what may affect the interest of our country, have in all instances given their practical and most honorable verdict in our favor. Our congress and the legislatures of all our states; our presidents, from Washington, to his present successor; our mayors and magistracy, particularly in our largest cities, far from sharing in the pretended fears of foreign influence, and unfriendly feelings on the part of the Catholic hierarchy and people cease not to bestow on them and their institutions, with the utmost impartiality, all the favors that could be lawfully claimed. They ceased not, besides, to offer to the prelates and clergy all the marks of respect and confidence that could encourage those who knew them not, to cordial intercourse with men whom evil or weak-minded persons misrepresented and reviled; but who are uniformly esteemed, and even beloved, as useful citizens, and most faithful and devoted friends by those by whom they are known.

To conclude, then, beloved brethren; when we leave you for a while, to travel for your best services, and only in compliance with our most pressing sense of love and duty, we entertain no fear for your welfare and peace as Catholics. The public spirit, the laws of our states, and the constitution of our country are, under Providence, sufficient pledges for your security. Only pray that all the good it is our intention to procure, be accomplished;

pray for your Bishop, who will in all his journeying, by sea, or land, hold you in the same remembrance, before God, of earnest prayer.

Before leaving Vincennes, we appointed the very Rev. Mr. Lalumière to reside there principally, and be our Vicar General; besides our authority being sufficiently delegated to him for the ordinary cases of application, the holy co-operation of the bishops of the neighboring dioceses will ever be ready for the spiritual wants that may require it. Wherefore, beloved brethren, whether absent or present in body, with you I shall ever be in mind and in heart, exhorting you, and saying to you with the Apostle, "for the rest, brethren, whatsoever things are true; whatsoever things are just; whatsoever things are holy; whatsoever things are amiable; whatsoever things are of good repute; if there be any virtue; if there be any praise of discipline, think on these things; these things do ye, and the God of peace will be with ye."

Given this 10th day of August, in the year of our Lord, MDCCCXXXV, and first of our Episcopacy.

✠ SIMON GABRIEL,
Bishop of Vincennes.[4]

Owing to contrary winds the *Rhone* was detained for five days in the British Channel and did not come to port at Havre de Grace until Saturday evening, September 5, 1835. Bishop Bruté repaired to the curé's home at Notre Dame du Havre, but his friend of 1824, M. Paris, was no longer there. He had died suddenly while delivering a sermon and his office was then filled by M. Robin. On the following day the missionary bishop celebrated Mass at the Ursuline Convent. After vespers he went to Honfleur to see His Grace, Hyacinth de Quelen, Archbishop of Paris, who had spent several days at Havre but who intended to depart for Paris on Monday. Bishop Bruté was the guest of M. Robin until Thursday, September 10, on which date he repaired to Rouen.[5] From this place he wrote his brother and family

[4] *The Catholic Telegraph*, IV (1835), pp. 373–5.
[5] S. Bruté to A. Bruté, 9–6, 1835. Canon Bruté de Rémur Collection.

begging them not to become impatient with his delay in arriving at Rennes. He assured them of his tender affection but at the same time impressed upon them the fact that God's work must receive his first attention.[6] Eight days were spent at Rouen whence he left for Paris and arrived at St. Sulpice on Saturday evening, September 19. That same night he again wrote to Rennes informing Augustine that the religious articles shipped to him at Vincennes had arrived on the day of his departure. He also promised to be with his brother and family within a few days. On the following day, Sunday, he visited the Solitude —the novitiate at Issy.[7]

It was Friday, October 2, when Bishop Bruté reached his native city, Rennes. Scarcely a month had passed since he disembarked; yet much had already been accomplished. He had visited Havre, Rouen, and Paris, and at each place he was successful in obtaining missionaries and financial aid. He was happy to find his native people so intensely interested in his American diocese. Everywhere the priests cordially welcomed him and daily he officiated at a different church. On Sunday, October 4, and again on the Feast of All Saints he pontificated at the Cathedral of Rennes. Writing to the Mountain on October 12, he said:

I am now at Rennes, where all are very kind to me,—officiating every day somewhere. Yesterday (Sunday, October 11) at the parish of St. Germain, where I was baptized in 1779; made my First Communion in 1791, and returned there a priest in 1808; and I am now at the same altar a Bishop (1835); perhaps tomorrow, a corpse! If not I will soon be at the altar of St. Francis Xavier, Vincennes. Our bishop here is so kind to me. The very next day after my arrival here he went with me to the retreat. He made me conclude it. I gave the last exhortation, said Mass, and gave Com-

---

[6] S. Bruté to A. Bruté, 9–11, 1835. *Ibid.*

[7] The preparatory seminary, the country home, and the novitiate for the Society of St. Sulpice were located at Issy which was three miles south of the centre of Paris. The Society also had there a replica of the chapel of Loretto.

munion to five hundred persons of the six hundred who were in retreat.[8]

The bishop's sojourn at his native city was interspersed with short trips to friends in nearby towns. Hence on October 17, we find him writing from Mans to Bishop Rosati of St. Louis. As usual this note requested a favor in behalf of a grief-stricken family. Bishop Bruté implored the Bishop of St. Louis to locate if possible a certain Mr. Guibert who had settled at Peoria, Illinois, where he established a mill, but whose wife and children at Mans had not heard from him for two years.[9]

Bishop Bruté remained at Rennes and vicinity until the middle of November when he returned to Paris. Upon his arrival at St. Sulpice he was happy to find the following letter awaiting him.

My dearly beloved Lord:

You can hardly know how much good your last letter did for me! I wanted to tell you sooner, but it was impossible for I was so occupied by intricate and pressing business, that it indeed has taken up all my time, minute for minute, without leaving me one. Behold! here I am at Vitré, in the midst of my three hundred children, who let me alone, because it is nine o'clock at night, and I profit by this moment to give you a sign of life and friendship. Your excellent brother has told you how, when he arrived at Ploërmel to *cure* a dead man, he came last week to us; which gave me unbounded pleasure. We passed a delightful evening at the corner of the hearth. Of whom did we speak? I will let you guess; it is our secret; but I can well avow, without indiscretion, that I was touched to the bottom of my soul by the sentiments of piety which this dear Augustine manifested in his every word. I cannot altogether refrain from making this most painful comparison. . . . O my dear Bruté! Must I renounce forever enjoying a happiness similar to yours! Pray, pray, more than ever for the return of him who is so dear to us. . . . I have no news about him;

[8] *Bruté—Seton Correspondence*, pp. 462–3. 1886.
[9] Original in St. LCA.

not more communication between us, and even less than if the one were in Kamschatka and the other in the heart of the African deserts. This is hard indeed!

Pardon me if I burden you with my sorrows; you will render them less burdensome in sharing them with me although it does not depend on you to end or mitigate them.

Farewell my dearest friend and venerable Lord. I embrace you without ceremony but with a most respectful, affectionate, devoted heart. At the holy altar remember poor Jean.[10]

A slight intimation of the religious transformation of Félicité de LaMennais had reached Bishop Bruté before he arrived in France and several times the prudent bishop had warned Félicité in a friendly manner. He had also cautioned his brother Jean, urged him to use stronger measures to lead Félicité from the perilous way. However, on the part of Félicité the counsels of the missionary bishop were badly received, his fears were treated as a chimera and imputed to the ignorance of the times; yet the bishop could not believe that one who had possessed so ardent a faith and burning love was now imbued with doubt and hatred. Therefore, with a heart filled with compassion for the sad state of his former friend, Bishop Bruté departed for Félicité's abode at La Chênaie.

The Bishop of Vincennes was cordially received by de LaMennais, which fact proves he had not forgotten his friend. Unhappy Félicité even assisted at the Mass which Bishop Bruté celebrated on the following morning in the little abandoned chapel; but when the bishop wished to speak of faith, when he touched upon the usual subject of the conversations of their whole life, the silence of Félicité signalized a scepticism which he did not perhaps acknowledge to himself, and painful words were exchanged which embittered this sorrowful separation. Two letters of de LaMennais, published in his posthumous works, portray in bitter terms this last interview.

[10] *Lettres Inédites de J. M. & F. de LaMennais*, pp. 174–6.

Bishop Bruté returned broken-hearted from La Chênaie but he did not abandon all hope. A few days later he made a last attempt to effect the conversion and for this purpose he addressed the following letter to Félicité.

Dear Féli:

Read, at least, this, poor friend, disconsolate with the rest. I beseech you, read!

I come from that holy altar. The Victim there was the same as on Calvary. He who loved you, who still loves you.—*Dilexit me!*—The *mysterium fidei,*—the mystery of faith,—is on that altar, but only the same as on the cross. Jesus Christ the Eternal, consubstantial Son has become man. Your God and mine has loved Féli de LaMennais and the poor Bruté, loved them for eighteen hundred years, even unto death. Thou didst love Him! Dost thou still love Him? Ah! That thou wouldst love Him with an ardent and tender heart! What letters, those in 1809, 1810 to 1815 and later. I still have them.—Neither in heaven, nor on that altar has that Sweet Saviour in any way changed. He loves you. Who am I that I should cease to love you, to wish only to afflict you? No, I wished and ever wish but to serve you. The reproaches of your friend are but those of your Jesus, those of Mary, those of Féli's Guardian Angel. I hope you still believe. But how you forget and forsake them.

You no longer receive, you no longer long for this inseparable Divine Heart. AH! If you still believe, what a solitude, what a void for the soul of Féli! .... I come, poor unworthy man, from receiving Him, from this altar, and from this altar to give Him to this poor afflicted friend to whom I write and address these feeble lines. You no longer receive, you no longer offer up, you no longer immolate this victim for the Church. Priest, always and forever, of that Church which He has acquired by His blood,—*sibi acquisivit sanguine suo,*—You abandon His altars and His sacrifice! .... His friends were confided to you, you have cast them off, you cease to bind them to that Church, to that faith, to those sacraments, their proper heritage. What will you give them instead? Will you be to them another Peter, another Paul, another Mary, another Christ? Another faith than that which was your own? Other sacraments, a new baptism, another penance, another altar, another holy ordination, and new priests, others than were Féli and Jean, and Carron and Tesseyre, and Vincent and Francis de Sales?— All changes! *Nova facio omnia.* I renew all things. Ah! He could say this, and cause the sacrifices of Abraham and Moses to cease, made Himself the Victim, shed His blood, penetrated the heavens, there resides at the right hand—Féli is not such a one, Féli will not accomplish this!.... Ah! that good heart of Féli, that soul ardent with the whole faith but lately all love, where is he now? When shall he return to us? It is he who separates himself from us, leaves us.

We are where he once was, we dwell at that altar, on this rock of Peter, this one baptism, this one faith, *una fides!* He had done so much to confirm us there! It is as it were in His own Name that his friends have quitted Him, since he bound them to Jesus Christ, to His Church, to His altars, when he bound them to himself. O sorrowful mystery, that he could ever detach himself!

Dear friend, always love me, as I love you; but it is between priest and bishop, but without being able to abolish our character, you destined for the sacrifice and I myself with the right to appoint to this sacrifice, and cause that astounding miracle of the divine consecration and transubstantiation to place Jesus Christ on the altar, by other hands as well as yours; in order that in the Faith of the Church they go and carry her teaching, which is that of Jesus Christ, not that of man, or of genius or of the imprudent man who believes himself to be such. Oh! What is he but man without the divine promises? It is from 1809 that I judge, from your faith in 1809, and from your heart as it was then and years after: of our *cor unum in unica fide Christi et Ecclesiae Catholicae, Auspice Maria.* Of this heart which was but one with my own in the sole faith of Christ, and of the Catholic Church under the patronage of Mary.

God alone and our eternity,

S. Bruté.[11]

[11] Abbé C. Bruté de Rémur, *Vie de Monseigneur Bruté de Rémur,* pp. 280–3.

After a month of zealous labor in Paris, Bishop Bruté departed for Lyons arriving there on Saturday evening, December 19. During his sojourn in this city he was the honored guest of M. D. Petit, pastor of St. Francis de Sales' Church. Here as elsewhere the untiring servant of God was occupied every minute. On Sunday following his arrival he officiated pontifically at St. Francis de Sales' and was invited to dine at the Archbishop's palace. On December 21, he visited the seminary and the council of the Association for the Propagation of the Faith. Bishop Bruté remained in this city for the Christmas-tide solemnities and was happy during his stay to meet two old friends with whom he had attended the Seminary of St. Sulpice. While sojourning in this city he also visited the famous shrine of Notre Dame de Fourvieres, which overlooks the city, the relics of St. Irenaeus, the first church of the Christians, and the Sisters of the Sacred Heart, at whose convent he celebrated Mass on the Feast of the Circumcision. From Lyons he intended to go to Vienna, return by way of Rome, arrive at Rennes on the last of March and repair to Havre de Grace after Easter.[12] Writing to Bishop Rosati on January 3, he said: "I shall probably be at Rome in February or March. I intend to pass through Vienna. My only desire is to place myself and the new diocese in the heart of the Holy Father and to visit the tomb of the holy Apostles." Having learned that a colony of Sisters of St. Joseph were to leave Lyons for St. Louis, Missouri, on January 4, Bishop Bruté accepted the invitation of Father Cholleton and attended the ceremony of profession and investing on Sunday, January 3. He entrusted the Sisters with the above mentioned letter written the same day to Bishop Rosati, commending

the good Sisters of St. Joseph who unite their zeal and charity with that of the worthy Father Cholleton, with whom I visited them this morning and received the vows and vestitures of a large number of subjects. I was very much edified by that holy house.

[12] S. Bruté to A. Bruté, 12–21, 1835. Canon Bruté de Rémur Collection.

I could not see them go towards your shore without seizing the opportunity of expressing to you my most respectful attachment.[13]

Circumstances forced the Bishop to change his plans; for, relative to the continuation of this Journey, *The United States Catholic Miscellany* stated:

> The good Bishop of Vincennes has celebrated solemn High Mass in several places in France, and explained the necessity of aiding our missions. He has especially in Lyons, by his preaching and explanations, excited very ardent zeal and increased activity in the cause of the missions. He has engaged the services of some priests and was to have left Lyons for Germany on Monday the eleventh of January.[14]

However, Bishop Bruté again changed the route of his tour and according to the following extract of a letter written three days later we find him at Geneva enroute to Rome.

> This morning, 14th January, I had the happiness of offering the Holy Sacrifice of Mass, where once was the capital of Calvinism, in the parish church of St. Germain, in which are now to be seen 7000 Catholics, four priests, and eight Sisters of Charity, although there were no more than a few hundred Catholics in the city in 1803, when liberty of conscience was granted to them at the epoch of the annexation of Geneva to France. The rest of the Canton is exclusively Catholic. The children of Calvin, or rather of Socinus and Servetus, have lost even the shadow of their Protestant faith; nor yet have they become more liberal to their Catholic neighbors, to Anglicans or Methodists, reserving the right of fellowship only for Unitarians and Deists. For, observe, they have lately dedicated a statue to Jean Jacque Rousseau, and the professor of Theology was *one of the subscribers*. Oh! what a chaos of principles; the downward path of rationalism!![15]

[13] Original in St. LCA.
[14] *The U. S. Catholic Miscellany*, "The Rt. Rev. Dr. Bruté," XV (1836), p. 295.
[15] *The Catholic Telegraph*, V (1836), p. 133.

From Geneva Bishop Bruté repaired to Florence where
he spent Sunday, February 21. At this place he was the
guest of M. de Senft, who at the time of Bruté's last trip
to France in 1824 was president of the Association for the
Propagation of the Faith. In a letter to his brother
Augustine he commended the piety of M. de Senft, saying he
had not met such virtue and goodness since he had left
Lyons. On this particular Sunday he celebrated Mass at
the Carmelite Monastery of St. Mary Magdalen. The Eternal City was his next destination. From there he wrote
Augustine on February 28, reminding his brother of the
fiftieth anniversary of their father's death. On Monday,
February 29, the bishop was received in private audience
by the Holy Father, Gregory XVI. Kneeling before this
saintly pontiff he asked his blessing first to be a good bishop
as in 1804 he had knelt before Pius VII, and asked his blessing to be a good priest. Gregory XVI received him affectionately, conversed with him for a long time concerning
the American missions, spoke with sorrow of Félicité de
LaMennais, and allowed him to depart only after offering a
rich donation for his diocese.

In this blessed city, the centre of Catholicism, Bishop
Bruté strengthened himself more in his faith, in his love,
and in his respect for the Church and its supreme head.
Through his profound erudition, as well as by the virtuous
simplicity of his manners, he won the admiration of the
most remarkable men of that epoch, such as the Cardinals
Angelo Mai and Mezzofanti.[16] He also renewed his acquaintance with Cardinal Fesch. When yet a cleric at St.
Sulpice he had been appointed to serve the Cardinal's Mass
at the Tuilleries. Cardinal Fesch presented him with four
costly paintings and from Cardinal Mai he received two
cases of valuable books.

While at Rome Bishop Bruté drew up a document containing a general retrospect of the Catholic Church in the
United States to the month of March, 1836. He submitted

[16] Abbé C. Bruté de Rémur, *op. cit.*, p. 290.

to the Sacred Congregation a number of readjustments that he considered necessary for the development of Catholicism in the United States. At the Second Provincial Council of Baltimore in 1833 he was openly opposed to the suppression of the See of Richmond and he now grasped the opportunity to advocate the restoration of this See and to propose Doctor Paul Cullen, Rector of the Irish College, Rome, for its bishop. Likewise, he was much chagrined at a rumor of the day which stated that Bishop England of Charleston was to be transferred to the See of New York.[17] He also proposed verbally and in writing the name of Very Reverend Doctor Power, Vicar General of New York, to Cardinal Fransoni, for coadjutor to Bishop Dubois of New York.[18] In addition to the foregoing readjustments Bishop Bruté wrote the Sacred Congregation concerning the increase of bishoprics and the hierarchy in the United States. At that date the Catholic population of our young republic numbered two million two hundred thousand.[19] The influence of the Church upon non-Catholics was constantly increasing but the chief obstacle to the progress of the Church was the want of priests. This hindrance, according to Bishop Bruté, could be decreased only by a multiplication of bishoprics.

Unfortunately his time was short and he could not remain in Rome long enough to satisfy his piety and his thirst for knowledge. He departed from the Eternal City on March 17, and arrived at Turin five days later. From a letter written to Augustine on March 23, we learn that at this place he was the guest of the Archbishop. After a several days' visit he repaired to Vienna where he had some acquaintances, and where he desired above all to thank the charitable Leopoldine Association, which had sent him aid for his new diocese. He was well received, courted by the nobility, by the learned and the pious, and treated with

[17] P. Guilday, *The Life and Times of John England*, II, p. 238.
[18] J. Cardinal Farley, *The Life of J. Cardinal McCloskey*, p. 112. New York, 1918.
[19] *John England's Works*, III, p. 227. Reynold's Edition. 1849. J. Murphy Co. Baltimore.

signal respect by the Imperial family. The Empress of
Austria and Prince Metternich, in particular, took the live-
liest interest in his accounts of the American missions, and
loaded him with favors. But the missionary bishop says in
his notes that he found himself much bewildered in the
midst of such honors and very much out of place in the
courts and among the grand personages with whom his office
and the object of his journey brought him in contact. He
made but a passing stay at Vienna.[20]

After this mission was accomplished, Bishop Bruté betook himself to Paris and established his general quarters at
the Seminary of St. Sulpice. Here as at the Seminary of
Rennes and all other seminaries that he visited, he edified
masters and pupils by his simplicity and self-denial. Whenever he appeared in one of the courts for recreation the
seminarians all gathered around him and requested him to
tell them about his missions. This was not difficult for him
to do as his mind and heart were filled with the subject,
and he did it in such an attractive manner that he gained
several missionaries for his cause. The zealous bishop's
singular simplicity, as depicted in the following anecdotes,
contributed much towards gaining the seminarians' affection. Upon his arrival at St. Sulpice while ascending one
of the stairs he found two seminarians in a hopeless predic-
ament. They were struggling under the weight of a box
which they wished to carry to their room. Owing to the
steep stairs and the insufficient strength of the two clerics
little advance was made towards accomplishing their task.
The bishop offered his assistance, took the box at one end
and did not let go until it had reached its destination.
Charmed by this amiability, but believing him to be a
country curé, accustomed to little ceremony, they thanked
him and asked his name. Great was their confusion upon
learning his title, but the humble bishop immediately
assured them that he was accustomed to hard labor and that
he was happy to have rendered them so small a service.

[20] Abbé C. Bruté de Rémur, *op. cit.*, pp. 290-1.

On another occasion a seminarian, M. B. Petit, from Rennes, seriously injured his foot in trying to help extinguish a fire. Bishop Bruté being a skilled physician dressed the wound every day and kissed the foot with a religious respect that inspired all present with a holy admiration. A cleric remarked one day that M. Petit was about to lose the nail of one of his toes. "As to this," answered the bishop, "when we built the church at Emmitsburg, and I performed the functions of a common workman, so many stones fell on my feet that now I have not a single nail left. One can live and work without them." From personal observation the seminarians learned that this servant of God while solicitous for the health of others took very little care of his own health. One day he fainted in their midst and scarcely had they carried him out of the hall than he asked for his hat and departed for the Convent of the Sacred Heart where he had promised to say Mass and preach.[21]

Bishop Bruté found remarkable grace and favor among his fellow countrymen and during his sojourn at Paris he was in great demand as celebrant at religious services. He officiated at a different church almost daily. On May 15, he celebrated Mass in Loretto Chapel, Issy, and on Pentecost he officiated at Sacre Coeur.

The missionaries accepted for the Vincennes diocese began to report after the middle of May, and to date of May 19, seven from outside Paris had already arrived at St. Sulpice. On Trinity Sunday three seminarians for Vincennes were ordained to the priesthood at St. Sulpice. These missionaries were of different nationalities, yet they possessed but one heart and one soul and were prompted by one desire, namely, to labor for the salvation of souls. When they met each other for the first time they affectionately embraced each other like brothers.[22]

Two priests, Celestin de la Hailandière, and Maurice de St. Palais, in this group of missionaries were destined one

[21] *Idem*, pp. 285–7.
[22] S. Bruté to A. Bruté, May 16, 19, 21, 1836, Canon Bruté de Rémur Collection. C. de la Corbinière, L'Indiana, p. 464.

day to succeed Bishop Bruté to the See of Vincennes. The former, born at Combourg in 1798, moved with his parents to Rennes where he received his secular education. He studied for the sacred ministry at St. Sulpice, Paris, and was ordained to the priesthood on May 28, 1825. After ordination he was stationed at St. Germain's Church, Rennes, where he served as assistant until 1836 when he decided to accompany Bishop Bruté to America. The latter, M. Maurice de St. Palais, was born on November 15, 1811, at La Salvetat, in southern France. His parents were of noble birth, hence young Maurice received the best in education that Paris could offer. After completing with honors his secular education he entered the Seminary of St. Sulpice and was one of the group of three ordained there on Trinity Sunday, 1836. However, it was not without difficulty that Bishop Bruté obtained this young priest. Madame de St. Palais exerted all her maternal influence to soften the heart of her son and to prevent this cruel separation; seeing that her supplications were ineffectual, she had recourse to His Grace, Hyacinthe de Quelen, Archbishop of Paris, and begged him to use his authority to retain her son whom she was willing enough to give up to the Church but whom she did not have the courage to allow to depart for foreign missions. In response to this request Archbishop de Quelen wrote:

> Affairs have taken such a turn that it is impossible to make the Bishop of Vincennes withdraw, for he came to France and Europe to seek help in money, ornaments, sacred vessels, books, and chiefly in priests for his new diocese. Sacerdotal charity is Catholic like the Church. It is the dispersion of the Apostles and the zeal of the missionaries which has converted the world. There are in yonder America souls awaiting the generosity of a mother whom the Lord will know full well how to console, in the loneliness of her last moments.

After such an answer, Madame de St. Palais no longer refused her son to the Lord but with pious resignation acquiesced in the sacrifice which God demanded of her heart. This sacrifice was the more keenly felt, since the poor mother never again beheld her son in this world. Nevertheless, it would have been difficult for the Archbishop of Paris to resist the simple but weighty arguments of Bishop Bruté and still more the charm with which God's grace had stamped his features.[23]

Among the worthy missionaries who returned with Bishop Bruté to America we find the names of M. Comte du Merle, M. Julian Benoit, M. Anthony Parret, M. Louis Neyron, M. John Corbe, M. Bernard Schaeffer, M. Louis Mueller, M. John Vabret, M. Stanislaus Buteux, M. Maurice Berrel, M. Vincent Basquelin, M. Michael Shawe, and M. Benjamin Petit. The good bishop brought over twenty missionaries on his return voyage, all of whom were for his diocese with the exception of two. However, he fails to list the names of the remaining five.[24] There were other students whom Bishop Bruté accepted but he left them at St. Sulpice to complete their studies. Among this number was Right Reverend Francis A. Bessonies, who in a letter to Reverend Edmund Schmitt recounted his meeting with the bishop as follows:

.... I went to meet him as he was coming out of the chapel of Loretto at Issy to offer him my services for his new diocese. I will never forget his answer. He threw his arms around my neck, and said: "My dear child, I am so glad to see that there is a prospect for a new altar to be raised in my dear Indiana. But you will have hard times; you may be lost, and have to stay all night in the forests, *a la belle etoile*." My answer was, I would like that. "You are my man," said he, "you are accepted. I will send for you in three years." This took place in May 1836 just before he returned to America. He had with him a dozen or more priests or students. One was the late lamented Bishop de St. Palais, just ordained. Also the late Mgr. Julian Benoit not a priest yet at that time. Also Louis Neyron for a long time parish priest of New Albany, who

[23] Abbé C. Bruté, *op. cit.*, pp. 291–3.
[24] C. de la Corbinière, *op. cit.*, pp. 463–4.

died a few years ago at Notre Dame. Also Fathers Parret, Buteux, Corbe, Comte de Merle....

.... Bishop Bruté's appearance was that of a saint and such he was. People were tearing off his cassock to get a relic and it is said he performed miracles....[25]

On May 29, the date of their departure from Paris, Bishop Bruté wrote the Sacred Congregation at Rome. He informed this august body of the marked success of his voyage and again suggested the erection of more dioceses in the United States. Then at Rouen, enroute to Havre, the bishop expressed his gratitude in the following letter to the Leopoldine Society for its noble and generous benevolence.

Rouen, May 30, 1836.

Your Grace:

It is impossible for me to leave the shores of France without assuring you of my heartfelt esteem and deep gratitude for such an abundance of kindness and assistance given me during my stay in Vienna.

Twice I have already enjoyed your great benevolence which enabled me to do so much for the beginning of the new diocese of Vincennes, i. e. twenty individuals embark with me from Havre on the first of June.

I left Paris yesterday and this evening I leave here from Port Diese. All the individuals appear to be very apt because I chose from a large number who presented themselves, only those who had the very best recommendations. Eleven of them are priests, two deacons, two subdeacons, three who have received minor orders and two very promising students. I possess, furthermore, a goodly supply of ornaments, books and other church goods. I regret that those which I received in Vienna were toll barred at Strassburg and can, therefore, arrive here only after my departure from Havre. Nevertheless, the remainder will promptly follow me. How grateful I am to the esteemed persons who have so generously provided for the shipment of them. I venture upon my departure to beseech

[25] F. Bessonies to E. Schmitt, 3–14, 1893. CA of A. E. Schmitt Collection. Notre Dame, Indiana.

Your Grace especially to remember the diocese of Vincennes at future distributions. The great number of my companions, namely those twenty whom I took along and among whom are only two missionaries for another diocese, will render your support very necessary. The Propaganda in Rome would do scarcely anything and the Society in France centers its special interest in the Missions of the East which likewise are very deserving of the same.

I and my missionaries recommend ourselves to your prayers and remain,

Faithfully and gratefully yours,

✠ Simon, Bishop of Vincennes.[26]

This band of missionaries embarked on June 1, 1836, on board a merchantman sailing from Havre to New York. The passage was remarkably stormy and lasted fifty-two days. On one occasion the tempest was so violent that the passengers believed the vessel would be engulfed. They fell on their knees and Bishop Bruté gave them general absolution. Immediately he said to them: "My children, fear not, it is a ruse of the devil, we shall not perish."[27]

An eye witness who accompanied them on this voyage gives a description of Mgr. Bruté's actions on this occasion in the following words:

Nothing could surpass his kindness and attention to all during the voyage from Europe. He had obtained a special permission from His Holiness to celebrate Mass on board the vessel; but the passage was so tempestuous that we could rarely enjoy that consolation. We had thirty days continual storms. We were nearly all very sick. The good Bishop alone was calm, as when seated in his own library,—sharing all the inconveniences of a protracted voyage—and bad accommodations,—neglecting himself and attending with unwearied solicitude to the wants of every one. Night and day was he beside the berths of those whom sickness rendered incapable of assisting themselves. Even the poor deck passengers

---

[26] *Berichte der Leopoldinen-Stiftung Im Kaiserthume Oesterreich,* X, pp. 22–23. Vienna.

[27] C. de la Corbinière, *op. cit.,* p. 464.

(most of them Dutch) had a large share of his good offices. Amidst
all this, he found time to write a great deal, prepared an immense
quantity of matter for his European correspondence, and held from
time to time the most interesting conversations on the political and
religious state of America, and particularly on the field of our
future labors. The most minute circumstances regarding the
Western missions were familiar to him. His comprehensive mind
grasped the whole at a single glance, and his habits of analysis,
aided by a powerful memory, enabled him to retain all that was
valuable.[28]

Bishop de St. Palais completed the description by relating
the following incident which he says

bears the stamp of that holy eccentricity sometimes observed in
the saints, which to the outward world looks like an absence of
mind on their part, but which to an attractive observer is indicative of the run of their thoughts and the preoccupation of their
heart. On board of the vessel he never failed to wake up every
morning and call to meditation the priests and seminarians whom
he had recruited—and whom he joyfully led to the wild regions of
the West to labor with him in God's work. They had a cabin all
to themselves, that they might be free and on the way prepare to
become missionaries. Now the mode which he adopted to awaken,
after the *Benedicamus Domino* which was not always effective in
rousing them, was to sing before each bed the following strophe of
a sweet hymn to the Blessed Virgin: *Virgo Dei Genitrix, quem
totus non capit orbis, In tua se clausit vicsera, factus homo.* And
to repeat it until the sleepy one actually got up. In this manner
he permitted himself to infringe on the hour of the great silence.[29]

The merchantmen came safely to port at New York on
July 21, 1836,[30] and Bishop Bruté with his band was happy
to disembark. The custom officers demanded several days
to examine all the baggage, hence it was impossible for

[28] M. Meline,—E. McSweeny, *The Story of The Mountain*, II, p. 374.
[29] *Ave Maria*, "Audran Reminiscences," III (1867), p. 330.
[30] *Berichte der Leopoldinen-Stiftung Im Kaiserthume Oesterreich*,
X, pp. 23–27. Vienna.

them to depart immediately. In the meantime the bishop
was occupied with placing several of his men and arranging
their traveling to these various destinations. Two priests
were sent from New York to the northern part of the Vincennes diocese, Reverend Bernard Schaeffer to Chicago and
Reverend Louis Mueller to Fort Wayne. The remaining sixteen then departed with the bishop for Philadelphia. Upon
their arrival eleven of the group were left to enjoy the
hospitality of Bishop Kenrick, Messrs. Hughes, Fresnaye,
Hurley, and McDonnell while Bishop Bruté took the remaining five to Maryland and left them at Mount St. Mary's to
study English.[31] As this was his first visit at the Mountain
and the Valley since his consecration all were much excited
and happy over his coming. The first two days of August
were given to this visit and Bishop Bruté left on the eve of
August 3, for Philadelphia via Gettysburg. Upon his return the eleven missionaries were divided into two groups.
Three were sent via Pittsburg to bring the heavy baggage
down the Ohio river. The remaining eight accompanied
the bishop to Louisville via Cincinnati. Reverend Louis
Neyron was left at New Albany to care for the Catholics
at this place and vicinity. Another was left at Louisville to
await the arrival of the baggage and to take the stage on the
following day, while six departed with the bishop for Vincennes and reached their destination on August 20, 1836.
Upon their arrival Bishop Bruté found the following encouraging letter awaiting him.

Most Illustrious and Right Reverend Lord!

I have received Your Lordship's letter written May 29, which
also informed me that on June 1, you were entering upon your
journey to return to America. I was pleased to gather from the
same letter that a considerable number of priests and ecclesiastics
had determined to accompany you to your diocese. I hope, likewise, that all will be worthy and that they will answer to the expec-

[31] S. Bruté to J. Rosati, 8–21, 1836, St. LCA. *Bruté—Seton Correspondence*, p. 466. 1886.

tations of Your Lordship and to that of the Sacred Congregation. I will not neglect to see to it that the remaining 500 scutes, promised to you as an aid by the Sacred Congregation, are paid to Your Lordship in America. What you have written in regard to increasing the number of bishops in the United States of America seems to me very opportune, but this matter of great importance will be treated when the Sacred Congregation will examine the decrees of the next Provincial Council of Baltimore which is to be held during the coming year.

I pray that God may preserve you safe and happy.

Your Lordship's
Most affectionate brother
J. Ph. Cardinal Fransoni, Prefect

Rome, the office of the Sacred Congregation for the Propagation of the Faith, June 25, 1836.[32]

Bishop Bruté had been absent from his see for thirteen months, yet the missionary activities which he had begun in the diocese were not dormant during this interim. The untiring clergymen were toiling laboriously in their respective places; Father St. Cyr at Chicago, Father Ferneding at New Alsace and Dover, Father Lalumière at Vincennes and vicinity, Father Ruff at Fort Wayne, Father Deseille among the Indians in the north, and Father Claud François (who was sent to the Vincennes diocese by the Sacred Congregation and who met Bishop Bruté on the way as His Lordship was enroute to the port whence he sailed for Europe),[33] labored at Vincennes until December 1835 when the Vicar General, Father Lalumière, transferred him to Logansport. The good accomplished by these devoted priests afforded the bishop no small pleasure and encouragement upon his return.

[32] Original in CA of A.
[33] *Annales de la Propagation de la Foi*, VIII (1835), p. 320.

CHAPTER XIII

CROWDED YEARS OF EPISCOPAL LABOR
AUGUST 1836—AUGUST 1837

A year spent in distant travels, in recruiting worthy apostles to further the Kingdom of Christ in a new land, was a strenuous task accompanied by untold sacrifices. Happily for the diocese of Vincennes Bishop Bruté never permitted difficulties to intimidate him. He did not belong to the category of travelers who evaded hardships. On the contrary, he met them cheerfully, bore them patiently, and sought neither rest nor vacation as a recompense when they were ended. His actions were ever characterized by a fervent zeal and an intense enthusiasm to establish firmly and rapidly the word of God in all parts of his extensive diocese. Therefore, upon returning to Vincennes with his select volunteers he did not delay, in entering upon the task before him. The future prospects afforded the bishop much consolation, but it was a consolation abounding in gratitude to the Giver of all blessings as portrayed in the following excerpt of a letter written to Bishop Rosati on the day after the return to Vincennes:

Here I am at Vincennes since yesterday evening, my heart continually affected, moved by gratitude towards God for this year of voyages without accidents and the results whereof seem such good promises. What consolation could I go to see you but Madame Dolahan tells me that you yourself intend to come soon. Likewise, Bishop Purcell, who is up near the lakes, has left me several lines to inform me that he would if in any way possible take his return route through Vincennes. I have written him to make this happy event possible. What an agreeable surprise would be this meeting of the three brothers.

I arrived with six of our gentlemen of whom three are priests. One was left at Louisville and will come with the next stage. Three

[MM. Buteux, Shawe, and Petit[1]] follow us by way of the Ohio with the heavy baggage to be unloaded at Evansville. I say heavy baggage but a bell and an organ would have increased its weight to advantage. But let us thank God for that which we have received and be resigned to do without many things. At least I have the happy consolation of having obtained worthy subjects who will be very useful, I hope, when they know the language. Five of them remained in Maryland for this purpose. One was stationed at New Albany. Two went from New York to the north—one to Fort Wayne, the other to Chicago, a German and a very good priest who with the worthy Mr. St. Cyr will admirably establish this Church now become so important—without forgetting that the good to be hoped for depends on your own heart. Oh! we shall have an understanding about all this at our next meeting.[2]

At this moment Bishop Bruté again visualized the future. New creations—churches, schools, and religious foundations rose before him and in spirit he beheld the enormous good that would be effected by the virtuous band who accompanied him to America. In writing ten days later to Bishop Rosati he said: "My young Missionaries are learning English, *Ad Majorem Dei Gloriam,* and will use it a long time after my death. I have indeed great hopes." Success had crowned his fatiguing travels, nevertheless, the good God had reserved for him sufficient crosses in the form of vital problems that demanded skilful solution. But Bishop Bruté was not selfish or self-centered. While he anxiously sought to build and to fortify his own diocese as securely as possible he had time to console his confrères who were struggling beneath the burdens of their own respective Sees. Thus in the same letter he sympathized with Bishop Rosati in his financial difficulties, exhorted him to greater hope, firmer trust in Divine Providence, and entire confidence in the holy Will of God. These two prelates especially were very intimate and although Bishop Bruté after a year's

[1] Cf. Letter of S. Bruté to J. O'Riley at Pittsburgh, 8–31, 1836. Souvay Collection, Kenrick Seminary, St. Louis, Mo.
[2] S. Bruté to J. Rosati, 8–21, 1836. St. LCA. St. Louis, Mo.

absence was much concerned about visiting several distant
stations he willingly offered to remain at home until September 24, or even October 8, to accommodate the Bishop
of St. Louis, who wished to visit Vincennes.[3] This visit was
not long deferred for Bishop Rosati spent the first days of
September, Sunday included, at Vincennes, and Bishop Bruté
courteously sent Reverend Celestin de la Hailandière to accompany the visiting bishop on his return to St. Louis.[4]

Thanks to the unfeigned gratitude that permeated the
life of the Bishop of Vincennes we are not lacking authentic
accounts of his episcopal labors. Besides sending news of
every new undertaking to his clergy and neighboring bishops, he addressed lengthy accounts of their labors to his generous friends abroad. The following letter written to the
Most Reverend Archbishop of Vienna illustrates his fondness for detailed descriptions as well as his gratitude to
benefactors and whole-hearted solicitude to obtain like assistance for adjoining dioceses. Possessing a literary style
singularly his own, the bishop was also gifted with the happy faculty of thanking for past favors and of asking for
further aid in practically the same sentence. This, too, was
done in a manner free from embarrassment as is borne out
by the following letter.

Vincennes, Sept. 5, 1836.

Your Grace:

I am unable to express my feelings which rise up to God, as do
your merits and those of so many who labor solely for the glory of
the Church.

I sailed from France on the first of June with nineteen* missionaries, among whom were ten clerics—some with major, some with
minor orders, and nine other candidates for the priesthood, and
arrived in New York on the twenty-first after a difficult and dangerous voyage. It was a long time before we received our baggage

[3] S. Bruté to J. Rosati, 8–31, 1836. St. LCA.
[4] S. Bruté to Dr. Bruté, 9–8, 1836. Canon Bruté Collection, Rennes,
France.
* In this enumeration the Bishop does not take into consideration
the lay brother who accompanied him to America.

from the *port*. Then we journeyed to our present location, over 800 miles away. We have been here two weeks with the exception of some missionaries who have already been appointed. Among those who were appointed are two that speak German; namely, the Reverends Mueller and Schaeffer. The first mentioned is stationed at Fort Wayne and the second in Chicago on Lake Michigan. Father Neyron is stationed nearer to us, namely at New Albany, where there are also Germans whose language he understands fairly well and in which he will probably perfect himself. The missionaries who came with me are young priests whose talent and ability were highly recommended by their Bishops and of which I too am convinced, and I look forward to great fruit from their labors if they remain faithful to their resolutions. During the four months that we have dwelt together my confidence has been daily strengthened that, after learning the language so necessary for the missions, they will make themselves very useful and have great success. The most of our laborers had difficulty with the language but they speedily overcame it.

In Philadelphia I found that the money which had been sent for me by the Leopoldine Society in 1835 was in the hands of my correspondent.

Our excellent friend, Mr. Schwartz (consul of the American States in Vienna), promised me that this money from the Leopoldine Society should henceforth be sent directly to me, which method seemed to be just as secure and simpler.

As regards the cause of the enormous expense for the Diocese of Vincennes at its beginning, I wish to recall the oral description to which your Grace as well as the Very Reverend Nuntio gave so much attention and which I also left recorded. Reverend Dubuisson (a Jesuit who visited us here last year) wrote to me before my departure from Munich that he had read this report and confirmed it. It treats of the present dire necessity and of the vast, inestimable future of these arising churches in the United States. From its pages the Leopoldine Society may see also that their rich contributions for the Diocese of Vincennes, for which I thank God, will by no means suffice, and that this Church cannot be made self-sustaining in this new country where people are still continually coming and going, and are, therefore, very poor and will be for a long time.

Likewise, this Diocese is as important in its location as in its extent, since it is nearly one-third as large as France. The Holy See had long wished its establishment but as finances were lacking Divine Providence placed it under your protection.

After serious reflections I found that it would be more advantageous to the propagation of the Faith to use the capital instead of the meager interest of the sum, and thus gain the advantage of placing many good laborers in the field at once. I did it; but already the first expense of our journey across was very great, although I got our passage rather cheap—450 francs per person. The cost of the preparations, as well as the long stay of all with me, fell mostly to my expenses. Also those who go to the missions, as well as those who have already gone, will long need our assistance in their poor and scattered mission-stations. And neither can we renounce your indispensable support for the growth and reputation of church and schools in order becomingly to inspire the fear of God and give no occasion for comparisons with sects, whereby our good reputation would suffer and weak souls would lose courage; as also for supplying many a church with the equipment necessary for divine services. It is impossible to give a complete description immediately upon my arrival; but I hope that Your Grace and the members of the Association will remember the representation and the description of this Diocese and the importance of my present situation, as well as the amount of money that I must obtain for its beginning, should a division be made before you receive another account from me. It seemed to me the best manner of expending the money received was to obtain zealous and virtuous missionaries.

My good esteemed neighbor, the Bishop of St. Louis, Rosati, is with me at present and will remain two or three days. As we were talking about our needs he bade me delineate his wants also; and I must testify that his diocese, although more advanced than mine, has made very good use of the first subsidies, but in reality is still in straitened circumstances. I do not hesitate, therefore, to recommend him to the pious efforts of the Leopoldine Society as one of our most worthy Bishops.

The consciousness that I have given you a true testimony of my colleagues, and among them, of the one in Cincinnati, is a great consolation to me, and I rejoice anew while I heartily and confidently recommend to your noble and magnanimous sentiments the need of Bishop Rosati as well as my own wants.

Your admirable care for the Church across the sea has earned the most beautiful and heartiest gratitude.

May Your Grace not withdraw from me in a foreign land that benevolent kindness which, alas, I could only too briefly enjoy in your company and in that of the excellent Nuncio.

Remember in your prayers your humble

✠ Simon, Bishop of Vincennes.[5]

This letter shows that the bishop sought material wealth solely for the promotion of God's kingdom here below and not for exterior pomp or personal comfort. He realized the spiritual good that could be drawn from material means and he used them so as to secure the most beneficial results. Again this lengthy communication depicts his thoroughly spiritual character. While this letter is mendicant in nature, it is permeated with the thought of God; commencing, as we observe, with outpourings of gratitude both to the good God and to his benefactors and closing with a petition for spiritual succor.

The first months following his return to the episcopal city were unusually crowded ones. It required much time to settle affairs at Vincennes and to respond to the petitions of his missionaries who were requesting him to visit them at an early date. Those at Fort Wayne, having received no response to their first message, dispatched a joint letter revealing their poverty and intimating scandals perpetrated by a certain Reverend Mr. O'Bierne who was stationed at Logansport. Bishop Bruté seldom acted without due deliberation, hence lack of leisure often prevented his immediate decision on serious problems. At length the bishop succeeded in drawing up a list concerning the order of his pastoral visits. Responding at this time to Reverend François and Mueller, who were stationed at Fort Wayne, he said:

[5] Berichte der Leopoldinen-Stiftung Im Kaiserthume Oesterreich, X, pp. 23–27. Vienna.

I would like to tell you just now, *exactly* the time of my visit. I cannot, however, state whether it will be in this fleeting month or later on. I arranged with Reverend Ferneding to go first to his church in Dearborn County, at the corner of the diocese towards Cincinnati, which plan would hardly allow us to commence with you. I would prefer to go from there to you, rather than pass your place to Dearborn County. Reverend Friends, I have but to repeat to you that your poor bishop is but *one* for a diocese as extensive as the third part of France or all Italy—though on arriving here he would fain be everywhere *at once*—in Chicago, for instance, at South Bend, and meanwhile not be too long absent from the new Seminary here, having only a few subjects capable of furthering the work.

Ah! I am very happy to be able to rely on such good priests and true apostles as you are for all, still it requires a little patience united to confidence in God and abandonment to His Providence before we can move forward in good order, which blessing, I humbly trust the Lord has in store for us. Courage then, thrice courage and an increase of forbearance and zeal. Ah! how unfortunate are not those blind ones who pretend themselves priests without realizing the sacred duties of their noble calling. The trouble is that *even* after a sincere and true consecration it remains yet for us to watch over self as St. Paul says openly he was doing, lest from a good priest or a bishop one die a reprobate.... Still we must have more pity than indignation for those awful falls.

Your poverty charms me and I would like to be in your place. However, we must remedy it in as far as we are able. Enclosed please find a small remittance for personal use. At the approach of winter use it for the most pressing and the best as good brothers, and about your trunk, do not worry, dear Father Mueller, it is safe, but unfortunately, still in Pittsburg. All the luggage has been stopped on account of the drought of the Ohio; all the sources are obstructed, no water until heaven sends some rain. Dear friends, let us be patient and ever adding to our spiritual treasures. As soon as we shall have received the goods we shall forward them to you with the trunk and all the articles you asked for the church. With regard to the funds you need for building, it would be impossible for us just now to spare them. You realize that the amount

allotted us by the two Associations is a mere help. Here, I dare not
do a thing, and the work stands as Father François knows—in
brick and joists. Again, I say, let us renew our patience, too happy
if we are enabled to roof it for the winter. Not being aware of
what you need most I cannot think of anything better to do, than to
enclose one hundred dollars. I trust it will reach you safely. At
this beginning of our episcopal career it is not easy for us to know
what is most pressing and best to do.[6]

The brief comment on unfortunate priests, in the above
reply, is not to be interpreted in terms of a compromise.
Bishop Bruté would have been the last prelate to have tolerated such procedure. On the contrary, the contents of
this joint letter caused the prudent bishop serious deliberation for he fully realized the disagreeable problem that confronted him. At that period the tie that bound the clergy
to a particular diocese was very loose and consequently, we
find them moving from one vicinity to another. Nevertheless, the Bishop of Vincennes was cognizant of the responsibility and after weighing well the charges brought against
this offending clergyman he immediately took measures to
forestall further abuse of the sacred ministry within his
territory. Hence he wrote again two days later to Father
François and bade him to carry out the following orders:

1. To take up residence at Logansport and assume charge of its parish
   and the country as far north as Lafayette inclusively. To receive
   with simplicity and moderation whatever be offered him by sober
   men. The Bishop said: "I never accept from drunken men." If
   necessary, to buy a horse at a moderate price from one of these
   three gentlemen, Messrs. Laselle, Murphy, or Comparet, for anyone
   of those would accept the Bishop's obligatory note which he would
   insert at the close of his letter.

2. To tell Rev. Mr. O'Bierne to return immediately to Vincennes, or
   for the present the bishop withdraws from him all faculties. [This
   second part however was left to Father François' judgment.] In

[6] S. Bruté to C. François & L. Mueller, 9–13, 1836. CA of A.
Notre Dame, Ind.

case the reports concerning O'Bierne be exaggerated or since his illness there be a change for the better, then orders to return were to be given without speaking of a cessation of his priestly functions. In either case Rev. Mr. O'Bierne was forbidden to accept any further personal donations over and above the amount necessary for his sustenance.

3. Read this together with the most worthy Father Mueller and both of you arrange for the best. We must put an end to those scandals and worthily prepare here the future of our Church.

Obligatory Note.

I, Simon, Bishop of Vincennes, pledge myself to pay the price agreed by the Reverend Mr. François, for one horse and saddle.

Vincennes, Sept. 15, 1836.[7]

The missionary clergy and the citizens of Vincennes seemed to vie with each other to obtain the first services of the bishop. The clergy pressed hard for both spiritual and financial assistance, while the town awaited most anxiously the fulfillment of the bishop's educational designs, in view of which they placed the following announcement in their local paper:

> It gives us pleasure to learn also that our worthy citizen, Bishop Bruté, is putting matters in train to establish a college in this place. His great success in establishing St. Mary's College at Emmitsburg, Maryland, and his eminent popularity as a learned and good man, gives us the fullest assurance that his labors will not be unavailing. With these advantages, healthy and pleasantly situated as our Borough is—easy of access by water a considerable portion of the year, and by stages from almost every direction nearly the whole year, we cannot see why this should not become one of the most desirable places in the west to educate the youth of the country.[8]

[7] S. Bruté to C. François, 9–15, 1836. CA of A.
[8] *Western Sun and General Advertizer*, XXVII (1836), p. 3. Vincennes.

While the learned Bishop desired to comply with the wishes
of his episcopal city at an early date they remained without
further development for practically another year. A letter
to Bishop Rosati refutes the statement that the desired College was opened in 1836. On December 6, 1836, Bishop
Bruté wrote:

> I am delaying the opening of a college in order to send more
> clergy to the missions. I await my five missionaries in Maryland
> to assume the educational activities of the diocese. I myself teach
> school on Saturdays and Sundays after Vespers—gratis. It would
> be more agreeable to me to have a regular school but I must keep
> my good clerics at their English and Theology.[9]

And again in the course of the same letter he said: "We
have not as yet announced the college or have we built it.
We have three pupils and they speak of a few others but
I am waiting for winter to pass." Added to this delay in
the educational field the bishop intimated the fear that the
Sisters' school, reopened in the spring of 1835, would again
be suppressed. Continuing his letter to Bishop Rosati he
stated:

> The Sisters of Nazareth intend to open a hospital in Louisville.
> I fear losing the four we have here because the School at Nazareth
> is large and the Community receives but few subjects. I am pleased
> with those stationed here. They have nine boarders and several
> others are expected. If this school is suppressed I shall appeal to
> Emmitsburg to supply us with Sisters.[10]

He makes mention again of this topic three weeks later
saying: "I am threatened that I am going to lose my Sisters' school. . . . they are going to be recalled to Nazareth."[11]

The pressing affairs for the general welfare of the diocese
kept the bishop at Vincennes or within close proximity and
thus prevented him from visiting the more remote stations

---

[9] S. Bruté to J. Rosati, 12–6, 1836, St. LCA.
[10] *Idem.*
[11] S. Bruté to J. Rosati, 12–27, 1836. St. LCA.

at an early date. This caused him no small anxiety as he had planned to see all his missionaries before winter. He was much disturbed at receiving no news from Chicago and begged the Bishop of St. Louis to inform him if he had heard from there. Conditions at Fort Wayne were no less alarming. According to the latest report Father Mueller was very ill due to the cold weather and his poverty-stricken dwelling. Previous to Father Mueller's coming to America he had spent seven years in Rome and four years in Africa. Consequently, he had not experienced a cold winter for eleven years and his physical constitution was no longer accustomed to rough climate. This illness grieved the bishop who knew there was not one missionary to spare. Since their arrival on American soil the zealous shepherd had labored hard to prepare his clergy for the missions and from all appearances success was granted to even the first months. Three missionaries, namely, Fathers Schaeffer, Mueller, and Neyron had been placed before they arrived at the episcopal city. Early in September, Father de la Hailandière was appointed pastor of the Cathedral and Father de St. Palais, who made rapid progress in the English language, was stationed at St. Mary's near Father Lalumière. Father Corbe was placed in charge of a French settlement that was established on the Cat River twelve miles from Vincennes. The Catholics of *La riviere au chat* had been visited by Bishop Flaget and Father Petit, S. J., prior to the erection of the Diocese of Vincennes. At the advent of Bishop Bruté this settlement was one of the first to receive his services, for early in 1835, when writing to *The Catholic Telegraph* he said: "the Catholics of *La riviere au chat* had Mass and instruction from their Bishop." This colony possessed no church at that date or if they did the structure was too dilapidated to be used, for the bishop tells us that he said Mass in the log house of a poor widow, Mrs. Languedo. Deeds recorded show that in 1836, Louis Tougaw conveyed to Bishop Bruté of Vincennes one acre for a church lot and on April 3, 1836, Mr. Pierre Menard of Kaskaskia deeded to the same bishop one hundred acres of woodland on the

Cat river in T. 2, N. R. 1, W. The bishop was very appreciative of this donation and made mention of it in all his correspondence. At that particular time, it was their intention to found a village at the ferry crossing, to erect a church on the heights above and to name the place Corbeville.[12] The last desire was never realized. The place retained the name of *La Riviere au Chat* for two years and since 1838 it has been known as Francisville and St. Francisville.

In the midst of these numerous urgent duties and just at a moment when the bishop could scarcely give a thought to any movement beyond his own diocese, he found the struggling Church in the Middle West attacked by erroneous writings. The October number of the *Western Messenger* (Unitarian) printed in Louisville, Kentucky, contained a letter in which the celebrated Unitarian Minister, Doctor Channing of Boston, condemned Popish Christianity with all its synods, creeds, and forms, as mere rubbish of barbarous ages and triumphantly introduced *pure deism* to his readers. This letter on Catholicism which later was reprinted and circulated in pamphlet form was an elaborate production of inconsistencies, absurd pretentions, and palpable contradictions. Bishop Bruté read the article and he was quick to perceive its underlying principles. Its foundation stones were nothing more than the theory of rationalism and deism as advocated by Voltaire, Diderot, Rousseau, and Payne. The bishop having lived through the horrors and evils of that era in his native land, naturally possessed a keener knowledge of this theory than Doctor Channing could ever hope to acquire. With faith, truth, and knowledge far in the ascendency over the would-be "star of the East"—Doctor Channing—the scholarly bishop in three lengthy treatises, analysed and refuted the Unitar-

---

[12] S. Bruté to A. Bruté, 9–8, 1836. Canon Bruté Collection; S. Bruté to C. François, 1–25, 1837. CA of A.; S. Bruté to J. Rosati, 10–15, 1836. St. LCA.; J. Taggart, *Historical Sketch of St. F. X. Catholic Church, St. Francisville, Illinois.* 1908; *The Catholic Telegraph,* IV (1835), pp. 61–2. *Bruté—Seton Correspondence,* pp. 441–51. 1886.

ian's Essay on Catholicism so completely that only the prejudiced and the ignorant remained to congratulate "the pride of Boston."[13]

Late in November, 1836, Bishop Bruté visited Father Ferneding's two parishes at New Alsace and Dover respectively.* To that date this was the most distant visitation made since his return from France. Several hurried excursions had been made to less distant stations as St. Peter's, St. Mary's, Terre Haute, Cat River, and New Albany, but

Grogan's home

[13] *The Catholic Telegraph*, V (1836), pp. 389–90; 398–9; 406–7. Cincinnati, O.

* While Bishop Bruté's extant correspondence and the documents give no intimation to that effect, a parish chronicle records an earlier visit to these settlements:

In 1835, the diocese of Vincennes having been established, Father Fenerding invited the Bishop, Rt. Rev. S. Bruté, to bless the church. The Bishop promised to do so, coming over Madison on steamer to Lawrenceburg. The important question was, how to bring him to New Alsace, fifteen miles west of Lawrenceburg. A meeting was called. Mr. Balthasar Hamerle promised to furnish the horse, but how about the wagon. A Protestant owned a one-horse wagon, covered with canvas, a committee was sent to the owner of the wagon. Mr. Miller, the owner said, you may have my wagon but my horse will draw it and I will be the driver. This was gladly accepted.

On the day appointed, the committee went to Lawrenceburg to meet the Bishop. He arrived at 1 o'clock a. m., and two clerics were with him. They brought the Bishop to the hotel, refreshments were offered him and a bed. The Bishop refused both and rested on two chairs. At daybreak the journey to New Alsace started. From Lawrenceburg to Guilford the Bishop and clerics said the breviary. Mr. Mueller had an eye on the Bishop, watching him closely. Later he remarked "that if the Bishop was not a saint, he could not believe there was one."

Arrived at New Alsace, the Bishop repaired to the church. Father Ferneding had the children there for instruction. Among them was a blind boy, whom the Bishop noticed. Father Ferneding told him that the boy was blind. Bishop Bruté went to the boy, laid his hands on his head, saying: *"Mon Dieu, Mon Dieu,"* blessed him and gave him a gold cross.

After Confirmation the Bishop proceeded to Dover. Returning he was met on Tanner's Creek Hill by some members of New Alsace congregation. Mr. Louis Gutzwiller was good on the violin. When the Bishop came near, they sang "Grosser Gott" in the woods. The Bishop was so touched at this solemn hymn, that he dismounted from the wagon and coming to the singers, with tears in his eyes, shook hands with them, saying: "Such good people must have a pastor." Before leaving the Bishop promised to contribute $500.00 towards the building of a brick church. On his way East, he sent $150.00 toward purchasing a chalice and vestments, the balance was sent later. Cf. *St. Paul's Church, New Alsace, Indiana*. New Alsace, Ind. 1928.

duties were too pressing to permit the occupied prelate to be absent on lengthy journeys. The congregation at New Alsace numbered one hundred and fifty German families while Dover was composed of about ninety Irish families. These two places fortunately had received the regular services of Father Ferneding for more than two years and, consequently, much had already been accomplished. St. Paul's Church property at New Alsace dates back to 1832 when twenty acres of land was deeded to Bishop Purcell of Cincinnati, who in turn deeded it to Bishop Bruté after the erection of the diocese of Vincennes. Dover was established earlier, dating back to about 1825. It was then known by the name, Cross Roads McKenzie Settlement and St. John's Church property consisting of two acres deeded to the Bishop of Cincinnati in 1826[14]

Owing to the nearness of these places to Ohio, Bishop Bruté took advantage of the opportunity to visit Bishop Purcell and spent two days at Cincinnati. This visit, however, was prompted by more than mere pleasure. He desired to obtain the services of Bishop Purcell for the ordinations that were to take place on the fourth Sunday in Advent at St. Francis Xavier's Cathedral and hoped the Bishop of Cincinnati would accompany him on his return to Vincennes. His plans met with disappointment. Fathers Montgomery and Junker were away on a business trip to New Orleans, Father Badin had gone to Cleveland where Father Dillon had died and Bishop Purcell was left alone. Under those conditions it was impossible for him to comply with the wishes of Bishop Bruté who left Cincinnati on November 25 and returned alone to Vincennes. Following this disappointment the Bishop of Vincennes sent to St. Mary's, Kentucky, for Father Petit, S. J. However, his Superior found it impossible to spare him and this left the bishop alone to give the retreat and prepare the candidates

---

[14] S. Bruté to J. Rosati, 12–6, 1836. St. LCA.; S. Bruté to S. Eccleston, 11–25, 1836. BCA. Case 24H.3; J. H. Alerding, *History of the Diocese of Vincennes*, p. 376; St. John's Parish Records, Kelso, Indiana. Dearborn County Courthouse Records.

for ordination. The retreat opened on the third Sunday of Advent and closed on the fourth Sunday with ordinations which elevated Benjamin Petit, Charles Dumerle, and Anthony Parret to the rank of subdeacon and Rev. Michael Shawe to deaconship.[15] While the retreat was in progress the bishop received a most distressing letter from Father François, at Logansport. Luckily their baggage, which had been detained since July, owing to low water in the rivers, arrived at Vincennes on the same day and the untiring bishop immediately hastened Fathers François' and Mueller's trunks on their way via Terre Haute and Lafayette. Then in a hurried letter he sent the suffering missionary a check to alleviate his most pressing needs. The bishop bade him not to take employment, but rather to engage in giving a few lessons in French. Likewise, the good priest was instructed to reclaim all that had been promised him for marriages, funerals, and masses; moreover, to accept whatever the parishioners offered on other occasions. Bishop Bruté never loved money for money's sake, yet he maintained that it was wrong and did an injustice to the missions to refuse money for services.[16]

Bishop Bruté, when a simple priest was most exact in the observance of the rubrics and when functioning in the capacity of professor in the major seminary, strove earnestly to impress this obligation upon his charges. Again when elevated to episcopal dignity he beheld the necessity of uniformity in Church discipline throughout the new republic. Upon his return from Europe he made another attempt to solve this problem. These points were discussed at length especially with the Bishop of St. Louis. Early as October 15, in a letter to Bishop Rosati he said: "The fast on Wednesdays and Fridays of Advent is a practice in Maryland but not a general law of the Church. Would it

[15] S. Bruté to A. Bruté, 12–21, 1836, Canon Bruté Collection; S. Bruté to C. François, 12–15, 1836. CA of A.; S. Bruté to S. Eccleston, 11–25, 1836. BCA. Case 24H.3; S. Bruté to J. Rosati, 12–6, 1836. St. LCA.; H. J. Alerding, *op. cit.*, p. 226.

[16] S. Bruté to C. François, 12–15, 1836. CA of A.

not be better for us not to adopt it here in the West?"[17]
Then to forestall in his own diocese any rubrical mistakes
during the coming year he placed an order for one dozen
ordos early in December. The printers were delayed and
this order failed to reach the bishop even in January for
when writing again on the twenty-seventh of the month he
said to Bishop Rosati: "No ordos—I have written our
gentlemen to do their best in good faith. We have made
three errors here since Epiphany although I have the regu-
lations pinned up in the sacristy."[18] Bishop Bruté had written twice to His Grace at Baltimore but failed to elicit a
reply. Then in a third letter he said:

> I have written you twice but received no response. A few lines
> from you occasionally would encourage one here in the West. If
> you foresee important questions for the coming Council please let
> me know. I have several in mind and rather difficult ones too—
> dealing especially with the general discipline, for example, the fast
> in Advent. Wednesdays and Fridays are scheduled in the Ordo,
> but Cincinnati, Bardstown, St. Louis, and Vincennes do not observe
> it.[19]

The scholarly bishop had figured prominently as a theologian in the two preceding Councils and now that he was a
member of the hierarchy he anxiously awaited the announcement of the third meeting of this august body. In
the meantime the Vatican Librarian, Cardinal Mai, sent a
letter saying: "Mr. Wm. Jackson has been delegated to
send your Lordship two cases of books—one hundred and
fifty volumes, and the money, promised by the Sacred Congregation last March, will be sent as soon as they are able
to bear the expense." The Cardinal likewise added: "We
shall retain a lasting remembrance of your virtues and we
are confident there will be a rapid spread of religion under
your leadership in those regions." Another letter arrived

[17] S. Bruté to J. Rosati, 10–15, 1836. St. LCA.
[18] S. Bruté to J. Rosati, 1–27, 1837. St. LCA.
[19] S. Bruté to S. Eccleston, BCA. Case 24H.3.

from Rome and was written by Father J. McCloskey at the Convent of St. Andrea della Valle, informing Bishop Bruté that he was sending the four paintings that Cardinal Fesch had promised.[20]

On December 23, the seminarians began to decorate St. Francis Xavier's Cathedral for the coming festival of Christmas. The devoted prelate described it as a veritable Bethlehem, but, in a letter to Augustine he assures his brother that the nudity of the structure will be quite forgotten after his clerics have accomplished their plans.[21] Then writing to Bishop Rosati two days after Christmas he said:

> We spent a better Christmas this year than when I used to pontificate all alone. I assisted pontifically at the mid-night Mass which was sung beautifully by Father Buteux and several good voices in the sanctuary choir. They sang the Gloria and the Credo. The people wished to take charge of the remainder with their clarinets and our hand organ. I pontificated on Christmas Day at the High Mass.[22]

In this same letter Bishop Bruté protests against the date appointed for the Council. A letter from Father Deluol announced the opening of the Council at Baltimore for April 14, 1837. This was too soon after Easter and he requested the Bishop of St. Louis to procure a change, a more suitable date rather nearer to Pentecost.

The wintry blasts did not stay the zeal of the energetic Father of the diocese or keep him at home within the episcopal city. Early in the new year 1837 he resumed his visitations of the nearby stations. On January 2, he left Vincennes at three o'clock in the morning in an open carriage enroute to Terre Haute and the neighboring stations of Thralls, and Paris, Illinois. He remained there for the

---

[20] Cardinal Mai to S. Bruté, 8–20, 1836. CA of A. S. Bruté to J. Rosati, 12–6, 1836. St. LCA.; M. Meline—E.McSweeny, *The Story of the Mountain,* I, p. 356.

[21] S. Bruté to A. Bruté, 12–21, 1836. Canon Bruté Collection.

[22] S. Bruté to J. Rosati, 12–27, 1836. St. LCA.

feast of Epiphany during which time he assisted and encouraged Father Buteux whom he was placing in charge there.[23] Life in this place was but a repetition of the sufferings and privations experienced by the self-sacrificing missionaries at every new foundation, yet this new beginning added another picture to the scene of their poverty and the bishop realized that success would be unattainable unless further financial assistance be granted the diocese. In view of this he penned another lengthy letter to his benefactors in Austria. This was the second account sent since he returned from Europe but the first one written in a missionary's hut. The contents of this message could be reduced to less space but any attempt to do so would detract from the spirit which prompted its writing.

January 6, 1837.

Your Grace:

For the benefit of the Leopoldine Society, as also to show our gratitude, I shall give you a candid report of our efforts and arrangements in the establishment of the new diocese of Vincennes.

Eager to accomplish as much good as possible, I exercised great prudence in distributing the missionaries whom I had brought with me to these scattered districts in order to establish missions and congregations where it seemed most convenient for Catholics to settle and contribute to the erection of Churches.

I sent some Missionaries to visit the more remote regions; others I took with me to my bishopric in the state of Vincennes, or rather to the city by the same name, which has 3000 inhabitants, and where they are to establish a seminary and college.

I sent some to the state of Maryland to obtain a higher education, in order to become more efficient; two were sent to the seminary and college at Baltimore, and three to the seminary at Emmitsburg. At their departure I exhorted them to be models to those entrusted to their charge, in economy, obedience, in sciences, in their training of the youth, in their guidance to knowledge, to piety, and to have constantly before them the great and ennobling work of the

[23] S. Bruté to A. Bruté. 1–1, 1837. Canon Bruté Collection.

Church to which God has called them, that with this view in mind they might advance the more rapidly and return as useful members.

The number of pastors in the Diocese, with the exception of five who are in the different seminaries, of whom one is a priest, three are deacons, and one a lay-brother qualified to take charge of a school, are apportioned as follows:

1. In Fort Wayne Father Mueller, who has most of the Germans in his mission.

2. In Chicago Father Schaefer, who, likewise, very laudibly directs the Germans.

3. At the same place Father St. Cyr, whose guidance of the French and Americans is also very praiseworthy.

4. In the county of South Bend Father Deseille has charge of the conversion of the Indians or Savages.

5. In Logansport Father François is also in charge of the Indians.

6. Terre Haute and the regions near Paris in the state of Illinois are assigned to Father Buteux.

7. Father Corbe has charge of St. John on the Cat river.

8. & 9. At St. Peter's and St. Mary's on the White river are Fathers Lalumière and St. Palais.

10. At New Albany and the Knobs resides Father Neyron.

11. At Kelso Father Ferneding has charge of two large congregations of Germans.

12. At Vincennes resides Father de la Hailandière as pastor of the Cathedral of St. Francis Xavier. He makes his home with me. Next to our house is the new Seminary in which there are three subdeacons and two deacons.

Thus the clergy of the missions now consists of thirteen priests. These, with the Bishop, make the number fourteen who daily offer up the Holy Sacrifice of Mass. Besides these, there are five deacons, three subdeacons, and one lay brother, making the entire number twenty-three who serve the Lord. At the founding of the Diocese in the year 1834 there were only two priests here.

There is but one large church in the Diocese and this is here at Vincennes; the other twelve are built mostly of wood and are very small.

There were very great expenses to contend with; first the traveling expenses from France for twenty persons, next the voyage from Havre to New York. The greatest expense, however, is the upkeep of the missions and the supplying of the necessary equipment.

We are very moderate and simple in our daily food. Like the ordinary people we drink water at our noon-day meal, and tea or coffee for supper; never wine or other alcoholic beverage. A prominent gentleman, who believed that we as Frenchmen were in need of wine, presented us with a barrelful; but I had it sold and the money laid by, as contributions from our mission friends are always greatly appreciated.

Disbursements are constantly necessary for the erection of Churches, and first, for the purchase of land upon which conveniently to build. Thus the expenditure for five such places amounted to 2000 florins, which I paid through my missionaries, besides 2000 florins for the fitting out and upkeep of the mission itself as also for the support of the priests from the time of their arrival in the Diocese until their appointment. The expenses for the seminary and the priests who reside with me are double that amount. Lastly, for the five whom we left in Maryland the annual expenses run over 1000–1200 florins.

Thus you have an account of my expenditures and at the same time of my efforts in establishing the new missions of this new Diocese for the advancement of the good cause. I beg you to believe the Bishop who has recently been so kindly received, as every other description would be incorrect and insufficient to give the Leopoldine Society an accurate view of the administration.

I send you this letter (unworthy of your hands) written in the mission station on the banks of the Wabash, 70 miles from Vincennes, where I live in the huts of the Mission-Station Thralls, near the city of Terre Haute, to which I have come to celebrate the feast of Epiphany. I find here very pious Catholic families, especially immigrants, whom I put in charge of the Parisian priest, Father Buteux. You would certainly be interested in an exact description of the little log cabin which serves Father Buteux as a home and also as a house of prayer; but, lest I ramble too far, suffice it to say that his cabin is a perfect resemblance of the holy stable at Bethlehem; and for this reason it is very consoling both for him and for me—all the more so since we hope that such a humble beginning may in time expect a greater blessing. May God give us His grace and fertility of soil.

As regards the missionaries among the Indians and Proselytes, I refer to my former oral and written communications and to those of Father Deseille. In this wilderness where I am writing my heart is filled with gratitude as I think of the kindness and benevolence of the members of the Leopoldine Society. However, I will close; begging God fervently for you in my prayers and thanking Him for all.

✠ Simon,
Bishop of Vincennes.[24]

On Monday, January 23, 1837, the first tree was felled for Father Corbe's church at Cat river. Bishop Bruté was present and presided at the ceremony which opened with public prayer after which the bishop assisted by Mr. Chapeau cut the first tree. Then a great number fell on all sides. It was a festive day for the settlement and the bishop tells us "all were happy."

The bishop had travelled hundreds of miles since September. To this date he had visited Terre Haute, New Albany, and Cat river each three times and made several trips to St. Peter's, St. Mary's, and to Dearborn county. However, he could not remain away long enough to visit the more remote places because the seminary continually recalled him and he considered the two deacons and three subdeacons too precious a hope to be neglected. Thus he was forced to direct and encourage his missionaries in the north as best he could through correspondence. The latter part of January witnessed the bishop's lenten pastoral on its way to all missions. Chicago had already appealed for dispensation from abstinence on Wednesdays. Distress there was general and while the bishop still retained Wednesday

[24] *Berichte der Leopoldinen—Stiftung Im Kaiserthume Oesterreich,* XI, pp. 27–31. Vienna.

he decided to yield to their entreaties if further complaint arose. In the midst of such varied and laborious occupations we do not marvel that correspondence with his colleagues was seemingly neglected. Nevertheless, had it been possible for them to have visualized his actual position no one would have considered himself forgotten by the Bishop of Vincennes, as did Father J. Hughes (later first Archbishop of New York), when he sent Bishop Purcell the following message on January 2, 1837.

> How is our good friend Bishop Bruté coming on? The care of all the churches (that are to be) has banished his old friends from his recollection. I used to receive an occasional letter from him, which was always an occasion of delight as well as of edification; but of late he has forgotten me. I see, however, that he does not forget the Pope of Boston—Channing. It does me good to read his pieces in the Telegraph.[25]

The tremendous question that occupied the bishop's thoughts at this moment, aside from his numerous episcopal duties, was the coming Provincial Council of Baltimore. The four years that intervened between the Second Council and the Third in preparation witnessed not only an appreciative growth of Catholicism but also an alarming growth of anti-Catholic bitterness. The burning of the Ursuline Convent at Charleston; the dedication ceremonies of St. Louis Cathedral interpreted as a "Popish experiment on the Military of the Country;" the installation of Bishop Bruté at Vincennes, interpreted as the establishment of the "Man of Sin" and the "Mystery of iniquity" in the Illinois country; the publication of Rebecca Reed's and Maria Monk's vile attacks on convent life, and M. Granville's diabolical romance, *Peep to the Valley thru the Grate of a Confessional,* were some of the black deeds of bigotry that mar the history of this period.

[25] J. Hassard, *Life of Most Rev. J. Hughes D. D.,* p. 172. New York, 1886. Shea, III. p. 646; S. Bruté to C. François, 1–25, 1837. CA of A.

Bishop Bruté realized that a powerful antidote must be prepared to counteract this fanaticism and he looked forward to the Provincial Council as the only trustworthy laboratory wherein this compound could be produced. He maintained that great benefits would accrue from a reunion of Bishops. There were so many designs of God to which each one would bring his own special grace. According to the scholarly bishop's predictions there were numerous considerations that would greatly influence the long future but some were more pressing than others. After pondering the situation most carefully Bishop Bruté was thoroughly convinced that the interests of the future Church demanded a Metropolitan See in the West and the erection of new sees with the appointment of more bishops and coadjutors ready to aid or to succeed as needed. In view of this he advocated replacing Richmond in the American hierarchy; elevating Natchez, Nashville, Little Rock, Pittsburg, Peoria, and Natchitoches to episcopal sees; appointing a coadjutor for New York; and placing the new Metropolis at St. Louis or New Orleans. Concerning the new Sees his preference was Natchitoches to Natchez owing to the fact that it was nearer Texas where several unfortunate scandals were then damaging the cause of religion. Each of these points was a chapter for examination. In addition to the foregoing articles the bishop suggested that the Council come to an agreement concerning uniformity in Church discipline, e. g., in the matter of fasting. They should adopt one rule for the East and one for the West. However, this did not exhaust his list of topics to be treated by the Council. He further maintained that no prelate conversant with the spirit of the day would deny that the subjects of newspapers, colleges, mixed marriages, religious societies and their confessors, vows of religious, ecclesiastical property, and the Association, both here and in Europe, for the propagation of the Faith were not mature for discussion. Concerning the vows of religious he begged to differ from suggestions afloat that novices should not be admitted to vows before they reached their twenty-fifth year. This was making in-

dividuals wait too long. Then regarding the establishment
of new sees he was so firmly convinced of their tremendous
importance and so anxious to impress this truth on higher
authority that he courageously wrote to the Sacred Congregation on January 26, 1837, concerning this affair.[26]

January 28 brought a letter from Bishop Purcell replete
with thanksgiving for the complete victory that God gave
him over Campbell in the religious debate held from the
thirteenth to the twenty-first of January. This intelligence
was most gratifying to the Bishop of Vincennes who lived
but to labor for the triumph of our holy Faith. The letter
also contained news from St. Joseph's Valley, Emmitsburg.
The very name alone sent a thrill of joy to the heart of its
former director. Nevertheless, this information was a surprise. Three Sisters, Samuel Ann, Beatrice, and Mary,
with Father Hickey's consent were departing to enter the
Visitation Cloister at Kaskaskia, Illinois. While the bishop
knew that the church authorized the passage from an in-
ferior to a superior order of perpetual vows he thought it
best to encourage stability towards the first vocation. On
the following day Father Lalumière left for St. Louis and
New Orleans on a collecting tour for the benefit of his
church. Bishop Bruté recommended the worthy cause in a
letter to Bishop Rosati asking that the good priest be granted permission to carry out his noble purpose.[27]

Owing to the great distance between Baltimore and the
West, together with the pioneer travelling facilities Bishop
Bruté was constantly uneasy about the convening of the
Council at such an early date after Easter. He wrote Archbishop Eccleston in January to acquaint him with the time
required to travel between the two places, saying: "The
stage requires two days from Vincennes to Louisville, and
two more from there to Cincinnati, plus three or four days
from there to Wheeling, and two days from there to Baltimore. This is the trip not including a stop at each place

---

[26] S. Bruté to J. Rosati, 1–27, 1837; 2–10, 1837; 3–11, 1837. St.
LCA.; J. Cardinal Fransoni to S. Bruté, 4–25, 1837. CA of A.
[27] S. Bruté to J. Rosati, 1–28, 1837; 1–29, 1837. St. LCA.

A LETTER OF BISHOP BRUTÉ TO ARCHBISHOP ECCLESTON, FEBRUARY 16, 1837

where I have business." No reply to the above was received and after the elapse of a month and upon the receipt of a letter from Father Badin of Cincinnati, he wrote His Grace as follows:

A letter from M. Badin received at this moment says, 'It will be next to impossible for Bishop Purcell to attend the Council if it be held so soon after Easter.' I myself wish to conclude plans for my return by way of the north visiting Fort Wayne, South Bend, and Chicago; hence please notify me at once regarding the exact date. I received no response to my letter of January 18, and this lack of communication is painful.[28]

The following day brought the desired information—a letter from His Grace containing the definite date and the list of questions proposed for discussion at the Council. Responding five days later the humble prelate wrote:

I thank Your Grace for the letter received on February 17, which settles the date for the Council. I shall arrive a few days earlier as I wish to ordain our two deacons and bring them back as priests. I can more easily do that before the Council because my visit to the north has been announced to the priests as taking place after the Council. My absence makes things so difficult for those whom I leave and to whom I am still so necessary. My position is so different in this new foundation from all the other dioceses.

As for the questions and nominations, *Deus providebit!* On many I have but vague notions, and in knowledge and prudence to deal with them I am lacking still more.

This Council! This Council! How it preoccupies the mind and heart. Let it do so above all at the altar for now truly, *Pietes ad omnia utilis est.* What wisdom is needed! What poor blind men we are to forecast such a future with our means. To me it all seems a dream. Neither creator nor ruler,—I cannot put two thoughts together, and for every step to be taken here I see so much for and against! Alas! this condition is what I am bringing you

[28] S. Bruté to S. Eccleston, 1–18, 1837. BCA. Case 24H⁴; 2–16, 1837. BCA. Case 24H⁵.

for my contribution—and all of yours put together are not worth much more after all. Let us pray much.[29]

Evidently this coming Council was studied more intensely by the Bishop of Vincennes than by any other members of the hierarchy. Perhaps others even judged him to be too solicitous about the general good; nevertheless, his interest was not centered on the whole province to the degree of neglecting his own episcopal territory. His deeds render testimony to the truth that he labored as devotedly during these days as he had done previous to the announcement of the Council. Multiplied duties received his attention. Especially was the good prelate much concerned about conditions at Chicago and the Sisters' School at Vincennes. Bishop Rosati in a letter dated February 23, 1837, informed Father St. Cyr that he wished him to return to the St. Louis diocese before Holy Week. This intelligence was a painful blow to the Bishop of Vincennes who had no one to replace Father St. Cyr and hoping against hope he wrote Bishop Rosati as follows:

> I fear that it will be too late and impossible to ask that Mr. St. Cyr remain a while longer in Chicago—however, see how many priests you have my good bishop—already thirty-one and four more whom you are going to ordain.... As to the chalice which he has in Chicago, if M. Lalumière has not yet taken back those that were sent to St. Louis to be guilded you might keep one of them and Mr. St. Cyr could leave his own in Chicago.[30]

The above plea proved to be ineffective and for reasons not stated the Bishop of St. Louis found it impossible to comply with his colleague's wishes.

The school proposition at Vincennes was another source of trouble that caused the care-worn prelate much anxiety at that date. Regardless of his oft repeated entreaties the

---

[29] S. Bruté to S. Eccleston, 2–22, 1837. BCA. Case 24H⁶; S. Brute, to A. Bruté, 3–18, 1837. Canon Bruté Collection.
[30] S. Bruté to J. Rosati, 3–11, 1837. St. LCA.

Superiors at Nazareth were determined to withdraw the four Sisters stationed at Vincennes. Consequently, he wrote to St. Joseph's, Emmitsburg, on March 13 and begged Mother Rose and her council to come to his assistance. Four days later he was joined in this appeal to St. Joseph's, Emmitsburg, by a retired colleague, the worthy Bishop David, who wrote Mother Rose as follows:

Feast of the Dolors of the B. V. M., 1837.

Bishop Chabrat will start from here for the Council on Wednesday after Easter Sunday. I will persuade him to pay you a visit, though he appears anxious to make as short an absence as possible. But he will be in company with Bishop Bruté, who will certainly visit you. This good prelate is much distressed about his school, as the Superiors of Nazareth are determined to withdraw the four Sisters who are at Vincennes. He will solicit you for some to replace them. I hope you will not refuse that favor to one who has served you so long, so faithfully, and so fruitfully. I don't approve of the resolution of the Sisters of Nazareth, but, I have now no control or influence over them. There is a good deal to be done in that new diocese. If he can obtain nothing, he will be compelled to form a new society out of the wreck of old ones. He is so holy that I hope God will direct and bless him.[31]

Evidently this project had an extremely slow development. Bishop Bruté was held in suspense for months before he received a definite reply. Despite this the prelate remained wholly abandoned to God's designs. He realized that only a patient man could speak of victory; hence he cheerfully watched many other events pass into his administration before the Sisters arrived from Emmitsburg.

Early in March the Reverend Michael Shawe completed his course of studies for the sacred ministry under the scholarly Bishop Bruté and was ordained by him on Passion Sunday, March 12, 1837. He was the first priest ordained in St. Francis Xavier's Cathedral at Vincennes. Two weeks

---

[31] *Bruté—Seton Correspondence*, p. 476. 1886.

later on Holy Saturday, March 25, the Reverend Anthony
Deydier at the age of forty-eight years was ordained priest
in the same Cathedral. These events were genuine
sources of true joy for our missionary prelate. However, for each newly ordained subject there were scores
of stations contending for his services. Father Shawe's
first missionary labor was performed at Evansville where
he was sent shortly after ordination in company with the
Vicar General, Father de la Hailandière, to communicate
with the Catholics and to obtain a lot whereon they might
build a Church. Judge Law of Vincennes had promised
Bishop Bruté a lot in Evansville for Church purposes. The
two clergymen discovered that Judge Law's property lay at
too great a distance from the inhabited part of the city to
be convenient. Consequently, the proposed donation was
not effected and the two clergymen returned to Vincennes.
Likewise, Father Deydier's first missionary work was accomplished in Evansville where he was sent by the bishop
early in May, 1837. After several weeks he, too, left for
Vincennes. In November he returned to the scene of his
first labors and took up permanent residence.[32]

Bishop Bruté left Vincennes on Easter Monday, March
27, 1837, enroute to Baltimore to attend the Third Provincial Council. He stopped at New Albany to visit Father
Neyron and then proceeded to Louisville. Here at the home
of Father Reynolds he met Bishop Chabrat, coadjutor of
Bardstown, and in company with this prelate he departed in
a stage coach on March 30 for Baltimore via Cincinnati and
Wheeling. While crossing Ohio the Bishop of Vincennes
was forced to share the driver's seat. Exposed thus to the
bleak winds he contracted a severe cold that developed later
into the fatal malady that robed him of life. Upon their
arrival at Baltimore Bishop Bruté in company with Bishop
Purcell departed for Emmitsburg where on Saturday,

---

[32] S. Bruté to A. Bruté, 3–18, 1837; Canon Bruté Collection; S.
Bruté to J. Rosati, 3–11, 1837; 3–16, 1837, St. LCA.; *Bruté—Seton
Correspondence*, pp. 474–5. 1886. H. J. Alerding, *op. cit.*, pp. 226;
265–7.

April 15, he ordained the Reverends Julian Benoit and Vincent Bacquelin to the holy priesthood.[33] The two prelates returned again to Baltimore in the afternoon of the same day.

The Third Provincial Council of Baltimore opened on Sunday, April 16, 1837. A Pontifical Mass was celebrated by Archbishop Eccleston and the sermon was delivered by Right Reverend Francis Patrick Kenrick, Bishop of Arath and coadjutor of Philadelphia. At the end of the Mass the pontifical oath was administered to Bishops Bruté, Blanc, Chabrat, and Clancy, who had been elevated to the hierarchy since the last Provincial Council which convened in 1833. The first public session was held on Monday afternoon, April 17, followed by daily sessions until the close which took place on Sunday, April 23. Nine Sees including the Metropolitan See were represented. On this occasion Bishop Bruté was assisted by his consulting theologian, Father Peter Richard Kenrick, later Bishop of St. Louis.

The Fathers of this Third Council petitioned the Holy Father to erect episcopal Sees at Nashville, Natchez, and Dubuque. The decrees of this Council dealt with ordinations, the support of aged and infirm priests, ecclesiastical property, church music, collection of money by priests outside their dioceses, uniform observance of the Roman Ritual. Likewise, it forbade the clergy to bring ecclesiastical cases before the civil courts, adopted the Ceremonial prepared by direction of a former Council as the uniform ritual for the Church in the United States, consented to the abrogation of Easter Monday and Pentecost Monday as holidays of obligation and with the abstinence on Wednesdays in Advent. The final decree dealt with the convocation of the

---

[33] *Memorial Volume of St. Mary's Seminary, Baltimore*, p. 51. Baltimore, 1891; H. J. Alerding, *op. cit.*, p. 226; M. Meline,—E. McSweeny, *op. cit.*, I, p. 362; Shea, III, *op. cit.*, p. 646; *Bruté—Seton Correspondence*, p. 475. 1886. S. Bruté to J. Rosati, 3–16. 1837. St. LCA.; S. Bruté to A. Bruté, 3–18, 1837. Canon Bruté Collection.

next Council which was to be held on the fourth Sunday after Easter in 1840.[34]

A brief investigation of the subjects acted on by the Fathers proves that the Third Council of Baltimore treated only a limited number of the articles which Bishop Bruté considered urgent and important for the progress of religion. Many of his views were never considered until years after his death. From a letter written to Bishop Rosati on April 24, 1837, we detect manifest dissatisfaction on the part of Bishop Bruté over the proceedings of this Council. He maintained that its good was too limited. According to his estimation a Metropolitan See for the West should have been provided immediately. Likewise, the silence on the part of the Council regarding Pittsburg and Richmond was censurable, while the erection of Dubuque was premature. He held Bishop Rosati especially responsible for this last erection which was suggested, decided upon, and the candidates chosen in less than five minutes. Bishop Bruté believed that a committee should have been appointed to investigate this frontier section as to geographical position, civil administration, conveniences, and relations to neighboring sees before a new diocese was created. He had always been confidential with Bishop Rosati, consequently, he expected similar treatment to be accorded him in return and he was grieved because the Bishop of St. Louis had not consulted him or even intimated the above plan to him prior to their meeting in Council. From this same letter to Bishop Rosati we learn that this turn of affairs caused the Bishop of Vincennes to be reticent on other points which he thought should have received comment in the Council.[35]

Bishop Bruté did not return by way of his northern missions as he had planned. At the close of the Council Archbishop Eccleston and the bishops present repaired to Frederick, Maryland, where they participated in the con-

[34] P. Guilday, *The Life and Times of John England*, II, pp. 377–400. New York, 1927; Shea, III, pp. 444–5; 646; *Concilia Provincialia Baltimorensia*, pp. 121–156. Baltimore, 1851.

[35] S. Bruté to J. Rosati, 4–24, 1837. St. LCA.

secration ceremonies of St. John's Church on April 26, 1837. From there the Bishop of Vincennes returned to the Mountain for his Eudist colony and the two newly ordained priests. These five in company with their bishop who really was too ill to travel departed for Vincennes via Cincinnati. A short rest was taken at the latter place whence on May 6, 1837, Bishop Bruté sent a detailed letter to Propaganda. The contents of this letter deal essentially with the same objections regarding the proceedings of the Council which he had given expression to in the letter to Bishop Rosati on April 24. He urged the erection of Pittsburg and named Father John Hughes as eligible for the office. He also maintained that Doctor England should be transferred to New York; Richmond should be replaced in the American hierarchy and that the vast distance separating the East from the Middle West demanded a second ecclesiastical Province in the United States.[36]

The health of the bishop was not improved by the brief rest at Cincinnati and he experienced much suffering on their homeward journey. At New Albany, on board the *Shelby* enroute to Evansville, he wrote again to Bishop Rosati and addressed it to Cincinnati hoping to reach him there as he returned from his prolonged visit in the East. At this writing the indisposed bishop was worried over conditions at Chicago and he pleaded again with the Bishop of St. Louis to grant him Father St. Cyr until he had an assistant to send Father Schaeffer, saying:

> I have not been urging you earnestly enough or with confidence in our Divine Master to yield to Mr. St. Cyr's wishes and my own, at least for a few months longer. I am so sick that I do not think that I shall be able to go to Chicago to see my worthy Mr. Schaeffer. I have had much consolation in seeing them so well disposed to help one another—and you see from Mr. St. Cyr's detailed letter that the responsibility of two thousand Catholics is in question....

[36] P. Guilday, *op. cit.*, II, p. 400.

Be so good as to take this last remark into consideration—do it, I implore you. . . . not for me but for the great common cause.[37]

Upon Bishop Bruté's return to the episcopal city he was deluged with information concerning the foundation of new colonies, the increase of immigrants, and the growth of earlier settlements. Together with this intelligence came the urgent requests from various stations for a priest to visit and to administer to their needs. The devoted prelate was sorely perplexed for he knew not where to turn for aid. His quota of priests was limited and some of those were too deficient in the English and German languages to labor fruitfully among any but their own nationality. It was then that the Bishop of Vincennes wrote to Doctor Keane, Vice President of the Irish Seminary, to obtain English speaking clergymen. Should this elicit a favorable reply he knew it would require months to accomplish the project, and what was to be done in the meantime? Evidently Bishop Rosati failed to respond to Bishop Bruté's letter written on board the *Shelby* at New Albany, for before another fortnight elapsed he wrote again to his colleague at St. Louis, pleading for Father St. Cyr in the following pathetic words: "Ah! Monseigneur, grant me all you possibly can, I have no second priest to send to Mr. Schaeffer for those two thousand, perhaps at present, three thousand Catholics, so amazing a thing is this deluge of Catholic emigration."[38]

The health of the bishop continued in a critical condition; consequently, the weight of his burden was becoming more intolerable. He was not able to undertake the long journey to the north, yet he considered a further delay detrimental to the northern missions. Therefore, in company with Reverend Mr. Petit he left Vincennes on Monday, May 29, enroute to Logansport where they arrived seven days later. His plans were to have Father François accompany them to the Chichakos village on the Tippecanoe river and the Meno-

---

[37] S. Bruté to J. Rosati, 5–8, 1837. St. LCA.
[38] S. Bruté to J. Rosati, 5–19, 1837. St. LCA.

minee village on the Yellow river, two large congregations under Father Deseille's care. However, upon their arrival at Logansport he was confronted by startling intelligence. Owing to false accusations Father Deseille had been recently expelled from the Indian reservations and retired to South Bend. The numerous sacrifices experienced by this servant of God among the Indians were known to the bishop who fully appreciated the worth and labors of such a noble character. In view of this he changed the entire route of his travels, decided to forego the visit to Chicago and repaired at once to South Bend to see this zealous missionary. Several days were spent in conversing on pious subjects which edified and consoled good Father Deseille in his trouble. Bishop Bruté and Reverend Mr. Petit then proceeded southeastward to Fort Wayne where three days were spent in Father Mueller's company. Thirty persons were confirmed at this place. At the close of the three festive days the bishop in company with Father Mueller and Reverend Mr. Petit visited a colony of Germans near Fort Wayne and then repaired to the Miami reservation twelve leagues away. Here in an Indian hut the good bishop wrote a detailed account of the trip and Father Deseille's sorrow to his brother Augustine.[39]

Since the arrival of Father Deseille at the Indian village, Pokegan, Michigan, in 1830, he had labored incessantly among the Indians both in southern Michigan and northern Indiana. Nevertheless, as every good work suffers persecution so did the labors of this untiring servant of God. Prejudice against Catholicism was highly prevalent in those days and the unstable character of some of the tribe served as instruments in the hands of the bigots. Authorities acknowledged that the Indians controlled by the Catholic priest were more orderly than those under direct rule of an agent, nevertheless, contentions arose over payment of annuities to the Catholics of the tribe. Not being able to

[39] S. Bruté to C. François, 5-25, 1837. CA of A.; S. Bruté to A. Bruté, 6-21, 1837, Canon Bruté de Rémur Collection; S. Bruté to J. Rosati, 7-9, 1837. St. LCA.

deprive them openly of their equal rights, the officials devised a scheme which would exteriorly justify them in curtailing the meager annuities. Early as August 7, 1835, Col. A. C. Pepper, Indian Agent at Logansport, wrote to Father Deseille and accused him of trying to prevent the future departure of the Potawatomies. The devoted missionary was absent from Pokegan, visiting other bands for about two months hence he did not receive the above letter until early in November. On the tenth of the same month he responded to Col. A. C. Pepper and explained definitely that his labor among the Indians and his personal interest in the race dealt not with their temporal concerns.[40]

Before the first letter had been received and answered by the missionary priest, the Commissary General of Subsistence had written to him on November 3, 1835, addressing his communication to the office at South Bend. Father Deseille never sent to this station for mail, consequently, the letter reached him only after a long delay. These false accusations, however, were too weak to intimidate or deter him from good and he responded to this letter in the following frank and fearless terms:

Near Bertrand, Berrier Co.
Dec. 28, 1835.

To the Commissary General of Subsistence.
Sir:

I did not receive your letter of November 3 before the 19th day of the current month, December, it being directed to the office of South Bend where I never sent for letters there being some offices much nearer home, viz. Bertrand and Niles.

In answer to which I have the honor to observe to you that I wonder much at being the object of such unpleasant accusation though I can not remember that I ever have given any real occasion for it. Since 3 years that I occupy a missionary station amongst the Poutauwatomie Indians of the St. Joseph reserve, I never mingled myself in any concerns about their lands or other affairs with

[40] L. Deseille to Col. A. C. Pepper, 11–10, 1835. Original in Government Indian Office. Washington, D. C. File 1835.

the Government and my endeavors were only directed towards their mental and moral improvement and this has been in so far a constant line of conduct for me that I never went out to any treaty or payment nor was I ever present in any of their Councils.

Concerning the Indiana Indians it was only since 18 months that I first began a missionary excursion among them with the consent and approbation of their former agent, General Marshall. There I observed the same line of conduct and I have had no further relation than with the band of Makos, Menominee and Chichakos. Two of them made last winter, a treaty with their agent by which it was stipulated (as it is reported to me) that they should settle all in one village.... This treaty was made 6 weeks before I had any thoughts of a treaty and much less of settling in one village, from which it appears that this idea is not of my invention.

What now belongs to the accusation of exhorting the Indians to build a church-house this is a mistake too. The real fact is this, those Indians being at a distance of between 40 or 60 miles from my home I could not reach them oftener than twice or 3 times in a year and finding themselves obliged to travel that distance, for coming some times to church they often expressed to me their wish to have a church-house at their village. I could not but approve it but I deemed it useless being convinced that it was not possible for them to stay much longer in that country without being protected by the laws against encroachment of the Whites and for this reason I would not take one step to begin and after several repeated solicitations I told them that I did not see any possibility for them to remain in this country unless they should get from their great father the President the favor of being subject to the laws as white people and this I did not tell them before I had ascertained myself that the intention of the Government was not to remove all the Indians to the West but rather to extinguish their nationality. So I was told by persons in office whom I supposed to be well acquainted with the proceedings of the Government.

I hope, sir, this will be enough to convince you that it is a great mistake to say that I have ever exhorted the Indians to oppose themselves against the intentions of the Government or what is worse not to comply with the engagements or stipulations towards

the same. This I can not qualify otherwise than a very bad calumny. If further proofs should be wanted I could indicate several
Whites, who are in the habit of frequenting my meetings which are
always public.

That the generality of the Indians feel a strong opposition to the
removal to the West is a fact to which several could and may have
concurred but all are absolutely independent of my proceedings and,
therefore, I do not consider it my task to enumerate them here.

With great respect your most humble servant,

L. Deseille.[41]

At this same period Father Lalumière, Vicar General
of the diocese, was trying to recover the amount due
Indiana for the education of the Indians. The government
had stipulated the sum of two thousand dollars per annum
for the Indian missions but up to that time Indiana had
not received her share of the appropriation. Therefore,
Father Lalumière wrote Mr. John Law, who had gone to
Washington, D. C., on business, to look into the matter and
request the one in charge of the affairs to deliver the amount
due Indiana to Mr. Law for Bishop Bruté or Father
Lalumière, who was in charge during the bishop's absence.[42]
The above petition failed of its immediate purpose and
Indiana again received no share of the Indian Instruction
Fund. The following year, March 21, 1836, Father Deseille
took up the question again with Col. A. C. Pepper at Logansport. The missionary priest had been advised by a letter
from Mr. Gibson, Commissary of Subsistence dated January
22, 1836, that the Indians of the reserve Menominee, Much-
kah-tah-mo-way, had obtained from the General Government the special favor of remaining undisturbed upon their
reserve for as long a time as they desired. In view of this
the Indians desired Father Deseille to establish a school on
their reservation in the spring for the instruction of their

[41] L. Deseille, to the Commissary General of Subsistence, 12–28,
1835. Original in Government Indian Office, Washington, D. C. File
1835.

[42] S. Lalumière to J. Law, 12–30, 1835. Original in Government
Indian Office. Washington, D. C. File 1835.

children. Immediately, he applied to Col. A. C. Pepper for permission to found this school and requested that this Agency should obtain an appropriation for the purpose from the Indian Instruction Funds. Should the latter be impossible Father Deseille intimated that he felt disposed to undertake the work gratis. The missionary was confident that the Agency would permit him to continue the moral and religious instructions of the Menominee, Chichakos, and Ash-kum because all had received the same favor by a rescript of the Secretary of War dated January 9, 1836.[43] Nevertheless, his hopes again were blighted upon the reception of the following brief note:

Indian Agency,
Logansport, Indiana,
April 18, 1836.

Sir:

Your letter of the 21st of March is at hand, in answer to which I have to request that you will take no steps towards the accomplishment of the objects indicated in your letter, before you furnish me with a copy of the letter referred to by you from the Commissary General of Subsistence, as well as a copy of the rescript of the Secretary of War noticed in your letter. I am not advised of the grant of any such special favours as you mention and cannot comply with your request before I shall be instructed to do so by the proper Department.

Yours respectfully,
A. C. Pepper, Indian Agent.[44]

Contrary to the refusal contained in the foregoing message an allowance of three hundred dollars was granted on April 19, 1836, towards the support of the Catholic Indian Missions in Indiana. This appropriation for the year beginning April 19, 1836 to April 19, 1837, was paid to Bishop Bruté who conscientiously used the sum to continue the

---

[43] L. Deseille to Col. A. C. Pepper, 3–21, 1836. Original in Government Indian Office. Washington, D. C. File 1836.

[44] A. C. Pepper to L. Deseille, 4–18, 1836. Original in Government Indian Office, Washington, D. C. File 1836.

labors of Father Deseille and his aged interpreter, Mrs. Campeau among the Potawatomies along the Tippecanoe and Yellow rivers.[45]

In the spring of 1837, Col. A. C. Pepper ordered Lewis Sands, assistant Indian agent at Logansport, to repair to the Indian country for the purpose of determining their attitude towards the future removal westward. On May 11, 1837, Lewis Sands wrote to Col. A. C. Pepper assuring him that he had executed the orders. He reported that all prospects bade fair for an early emigration. All the Indians were aware that their lands were sold to the government and they were to remove to their new homes, save a band that resides near the Yellow river and are under the influence of a priest. After visiting the priest, Father Deseille, Lewis Sands decided that the missionary was influencing this band to believe that they had not sold their reservation and that it would remain theirs as long as they lived. Lewis Sands informed Col. A. C. Pepper that unless this missionary's influence be curtailed they must expect to remove only a portion of this band.[46] Thereupon, Col. A. C. Pepper submitted this intelligence to C. A. Harris, Commissary of Indian Affairs, with the suggestion that he write and inform Father Deseille that such conduct was a violation of law and rendered him liable to its penalties.[47]

Three days later Col. A. C. Pepper wrote to Father Deseille and charged Lewis Sands to deliver this letter in person. Apparently Pepper had confirmed the accusations in the three days intervening between the letter written to Harris and the one addressed to the missionary. In the former he stated that he had not been able to prove by anyone but Indians what he believed to be true concerning the priest, while three days later he wrote and accused Father

[45] S. Bruté to C. Harris, 6–25, 1838. Original in Government Indian Office. Washington, D. C. File 1838.

[46] L. Sands to A. C. Pepper, 5–11, 1837. Original in Government Indian Office. Washington, D. C. File 1837.

[47] A. C. Pepper to C. Harris, 5–13, 1837, Original in Government Indian Office, Washington, D. C. File 1837.

Deseille of having told both the Indians and the white men that the treaty negotiated with the Yellow river band of Potawatomies was a fraud practised by the government. Father Deseille was requested to exhibit to Lewis Sands all evidence of his citizenship in the United States. If he declined to do this he would be proceeded against as a foreigner. In either case he would be removed from public lands on which the Indians resided. Col. A. C. Pepper then repeated: "You are, therefore, hereby notified to quit the aforesaid public lands within three days, and to cease holding any talks or councils with the Potawatomies of Indiana whatever."[48]

On May 20, 1837, Lewis Sands reported that this letter had been delivered in person and that Father Deseille had no evidence to show but acknowledged he was a foreigner and not entitled to citizenship in the United States. Furthermore, he was convinced that he had not the right under the law to remain longer on the public lands on which the Indians reside and he agreed to remove within the time mentioned—three days.[49] Ten days later A. C. Pepper sent the report of the above interview to C. Harris, saying:

> Mr. Deseille obeyed the order to leave the public lands on which the Indians reside and when he left the Indians he told them he would visit the Bishop of Detroit who would obtain from the President of the United States authority for him to return and live with them as heretofore.

The above remark of Father Deseille to the Indians caused A. C. Pepper to question the authority of his own action and he requested C. Harris to inform him whether his course as explained by the reports and correspondence referred to above could be sustained by the laws of the United States and the authority of the Indian Department.[50]

[48] C. A. Pepper to L. Deseille, 5–16, 1837. Original in Government Indian Office. Washington, D. C. File 1837.
[49] L. Sands to A. C. Pepper, 5–20, 1837. Original in Government Indian Office. Washington, D. C. File 1837.
[50] A. C. Pepper to C. Harris, 5–31, 1837. Original in Government Indian Office. Washington, D. C. File 1837.

After traveling more than six hundred miles on horse-back Bishop Bruté returned to Vincennes. There, a letter awaited him from the Bishop of St. Louis informing him of Father St. Cyr's departure from Chicago on April 17, The Bishop of Vincennes was reconciled to the course of events and wrote Bishop Rosati as follows:

> Nothing remains for me, Monseigneur, but to thank you with all the effusions of my heart for all the good that Mr. St. Cyr has accomplished in Chicago during his long stay granted by you, and I do not murmur in any wise against his recall. I bless this excellent priest and before God I shall never separate him from the pastorship of a parish truly created by him and where I hope that his memory will be perpetuated for a long time in order to encourage this new flock to persevere and his successor to increase still more the great amount of initial good that has been effected.[51]

This abandonment to divine Providence was not to pass unrewarded. In less than a fortnight Father O'Meara, an Irish priest, joined the diocese of Vincennes and Bishop Bruté at once sent him as assistant to Father Schaeffer at Chicago.[52]

Episcopal duties had multiplied during the bishop's absence, consequently, the month of July was an exceptionally busy one. To Father François at Logansport detailed orders were given to increase the Church property by purchasing the lot examined by the bishop on his recent visit there. If the owner should refuse to sell it for five hundred dollars the bishop pledged to pay the additional one hundred dollars. Father François was also instructed to continue the subscriptions otherwise they would be forced to abandon the mission. The bishop then continued in his usual fatherly strain saying:

> Write and tell me all your needs and I will see to them. You did not tell me whether those good people made a collection for

---

[51] S. Bruté to J. Rosati, 7–9, 1837. St. LCA.; *Ill. Cath. Hist. Review*, II (1920), pp. 323–7; J. Rothensteiner, I, pp. 552–564.

[52] S. Bruté to J. Rosati, 7–29, 1837. St. LCA.

you upon your return or whether Mr. D—remitted the five dollars for the burial. Excuse details, I dislike them as much as you do but they are indispensable and a serious duty for us. You see what consequences would follow both for you and me if we neglected them. We must work without human respect. It is the same for the building of your church; you must busy yourself about it and interest everybody else in it.[53]

At this date the settlement at Jasper, Indiana had a Catholic population of twenty families. Father St. Palais, who was in charge of St. Mary's near Washington, accepted also the care of this place and visited it occasionally from Daviess County.[54] Another parish was founded in the same month when on July 18, 1837, Bishop Bruté appointed Father Shawe resident pastor of Madison. In the official appointment which was made in writing the bishop said:

> At the moment I have nothing particular to recommend to you only try with your usual gentle and effective manner to make the best impression and beginning that you can in Madison—just in opposition to the spirit of Presbyterianism which is now tearing asunder the city's foundations.[55]

On July 19, 1857, the bishop furnished Father Shawe with the following official permit authorizing him to solicit and to accept contributions:

> We authorize by the present lines the Reverend Michael Shawe to receive the contributions and offerings he may obtain for erecting a church at Madison and the other sacred purposes trusted to him by his Bishop.
>
>   19th July, 1837
>   Simon Bruté, Bishop of Vincennes.[56]

Father Shawe repaired to Madison and began the work as-

[53] S. Bruté to C. François, 7–15, 1837. CA of A.
[54] S. Bruté to J. Rosati, 7–29, 1837. St. LCA.
[55] S. Bruté to M. Shawe, 7–18, 1837. CA of A.
[56] Original in Georgetown University Archives, Fol. 92, 6. Washington, D. C.

signed to him. At the beginning his flock was small but under his fruitful labors it grew and developed into a numerous congregation. The old Masonic Hall was used for divine services during 1837 and 1838 until the church was completed.[57]

Since the beginning of 1838 the Superiors at Nazareth, Kentucky, had insisted on selling their property at Vincennes and withdrawing the four Sisters. To this Bishop Bruté objected strongly. Finally an agreement was entered into which settled the affair for the moment. Bishop Bruté purchased the property paying them $1,300 for the land and the house which was in a bad condition. Much to the regret of the Community at Nazareth only two Sisters were recalled. They were to leave Vincennes on August 11. The remaining two teachers, Sisters Sebastia and Rosalia, were given permission to leave their Community and to remain at Vincennes where they were to found a branch establishment. This agreement was decided upon out of veneration for the virtuous bishop and not because of any dissatisfaction in the Community. The two teachers were pious, holy women but the bishop doubted their ability to found an institution. Therefore, he wrote again to Mother Rose at Emmitsburg, on July 19, 1837, begging her to send three Sisters to join the two or rather, vice versa, the two were to join the quota from Emmitsburg, for the rule and dress of the Emmitsburg Sisters would be adopted and one from that Community was to be installed as the Superior of the new Community.[58]

This simple record closes Bishop Bruté's episcopal career for the year, August 1836 to August 1837. One year had passed since he returned from Europe with his select band of missionaries. Though the bishop still suffered from the want of an adequate supply of priests these twelve months show a considerable growth in the diocese. The bishop cer-

[57] C. Bilger, *History of St. Mary's Parish, Madison*, p. 2. Madison, 1915.
[58] *Bruté—Seton Correspondence*, pp. 482–7. 1886.

tainly had much to rejoice over, little to regret, and, while his desires for the future were numerous, his accomplished deeds proved him to be far from an unprofitable steward in the service of the Great Master.

The month of August differed slightly from the preceding one. New phases of old problems were ushered in and additional duties arose and disappeared giving the days an appearance of true complex variables. All demanded the bishop's attention and although his health was critical he found himself master of but few leisure hours. Early in August Father Schaeffer sought his advice concerning unrubrical practices which had crept in during Father St. Cyr's pastorate: marriages, baptisms, and churching of mothers in private homes, marriage without exacting or referring to confession, funerals never held from the church, and other practices. A week later the devoted prelate wrote Bishop Rosati informing him quite explicitly concerning this laxity in the observance of the rubrics. This, however, was brought to the knowledge of the bishop out of zeal for ecclesiastical discipline and not as a depreciation of the worthy founder of the Church in Chicago. In the course of the same letter he informed his colleague regarding Mr. McCosker, a suspended priest of Chambersburg, Pennsylvania. Recently, this unfortunate priest had passed through Chicago, said Mass, collected large sums, and then departed, as he said, for the diocese of St. Louis. Bishop Bruté said:

> I thought it was my duty to notify you of this. I had lost sight of this unfortunate since 1834. We shall need to use great prudence in this case on account of his character which is so hidden. I would like to see him return to his native country. Perhaps he will find salvation in your diocese just as Messrs. Jamison and Wiseman. May St. Vincent de Paul save all the poor wanderers who go astray! I have two here who worry me to death, Mr. Keegan, who wants to study medicine, and Mr. O'Bierne.

The spiritual poverty of these ecclesiastics was thrown into bold relief by the zealous bishop's request to make a retreat under the direction of Bishop Rosati.[1]

[1] S. Bruté to J. Rosati, 8-11, 1837. St. LCA. St. Louis, Mo.

Notwithstanding a small number of unworthy clergymen, who grieved the bishop, religion was progressing rapidly within the diocese. There were now fifteen priests on the missions and several with the bishop at Vincennes for whose edification he requested Father Hughes to stop with him on his way East from St. Louis. In the episcopal city itself, owing to the zeal of the pastor, Father de la Hailandière, the bishop had the consolation of confirming one hundred children at the Cathedral on August 10. Then on August 20, he confirmed a class of eighty-three persons in St. Mary's Church at Black Oak Ridge. Another manifestation of religious progress was the announcement of a college that was to open in the fall at Vincennes.[2]

This new institution, founded by the bishop, was to be conducted by the Eudists who had returned from Mt. St. Mary's in May. The citizens at Vincennes knowing Bishop Bruté's educational abilities had looked forward to this establishment since his appointment to the newly erected See of Vincennes. However, it was impossible for him to grant their desires at an earlier date. In a lengthy article entitled, "The Catholic College of Vincennes," the local paper stated:

> The exercises of the College will commence on the second of October next. Virtue as well as knowledge being the object of a sound education, the discipline of the College will be mild and parental, but all its rules properly maintained. Boarders will not be admitted more than fifteen years old, or less than ten, nor from other institutions without proper testimony.
>
> As for the religious exercises of the house, the pupils will all attend (good order requiring it) without interfering with their liberty of conscience. The course of instruction will embrace successively, all the branches of classical education, competent teachers are secured.

[2] S. Bruté to J. Hughes, & S. Bruté to J. Rosati, 8–8, 1837; St. LCA. *The Catholic Telegraph*, VI (1837), p. 342.

Terms.

Boarding, tuition, mending, and washing per annum $100.00

Bed and bedding, if furnished by the institution .... $ 8.00

Stationary can be furnished by the institution at the current rate.

Medical attendance unless parents prefer to pay the expenses incurred by sickness .... $ 3.00

First six months to be paid in advance, the rest quarterly in advance.

Day scholars, per quarter in advance .... $ 5.00

No deduction will be made in consequence of a student leaving the College before the expiration of the quarter, except in the case of sickness or expulsion.[3]

Bishop Bruté's invitation to Father Hughes was graciously accepted for on August 22 he wrote to Bishop Rosati that Father Hughes had preached twice to his seminarians and had proceeded on his journey eastward that day. At the moment urgent business did not permit the bishop to accept his colleague's cordial invitation to St. Louis for the retreat. Instead he was sending Father de la Hailandière to return the valuable volumes loaned by Bishop Rosati. He requested that this priest be instructed how to proceed in the event of a bishop's death, especially in regard to the transmission of ecclesiastical property.[4]

Early in September the missions of Perry and Dubois Counties received Bishop Bruté's attention. In company with Father Benoit he visited Rome on the Ohio river on September 3. Very few Catholics were found at that place, but eight miles from there at St. Mary's on Oil Creek they found forty families and ten miles north of Rome they found twelve families that met at Cassidy's Settlement. From this vicinity they crossed over into Kentucky and called on Fathers Coomes and Wathen to express appreciation for their devoted services. These two clergymen together with Father Durbin had often ministered to the scat-

---

[3] *The Western Sun and General Advertizer*, XXV (1837), p. 4. Vincennes; *The Catholic Almanac*, 1838. Baltimore, 1838.

[4] S. Bruté to J. Rosati, 8–22, 1837. St. LCA.

tered Catholics in southern Indiana. Crossing the Ohio again into Indiana they traversed a section of Harrison county and then proceeded to Jasper, in Dubois County, where they found a large foundation of German Catholics. This colony had purchased land for more than one hundred families and of this number forty families had already arrived. Descriptive of this visit Bishop Bruté wrote:

> I cannot express the great sorrow I experienced when, on visiting the Jasper Mission, I celebrated the Sacred Mysteries in presence of a great number of German Catholics but was unable to impart to them the saving words of our holy religion. After Holy Mass I wept bitter tears, raised my hands to heaven and told my sorrow to my God. But greater was my grief when I saw several of the people shed tears because (as those who spoke English informed me) there was no one to break the Bread of Salvation for them (Jerem. 4:4).

After having travelled about two hundred miles on horseback the Bishop left Father Benoit at Rome and returned home alone. Upon his arrival at Vincennes on September 16, he planned another missionary tour to Chicago, but to the disappointment of the bishop this plan was again frustrated. A second anxiety was the silence of St. Joseph's, Emmitsburg, to his request for Sisters and on September 25, 1837, he wrote urging that the Sisters be sent before inclement weather made travelling disagreeable.[5]

The ever increasing missionary activities, the burdens of the episcopal office, and failing health urged the bishop to make a formal application to Rome for a coadjutor on August 24, 1837. The earliest available information on this action is contained in a letter to Bishop Rosati, dated September 21, 1837, in which he stated:

[5] S. Bruté to C. François, 9-16, 1837, CA of A. Notre Dame, Ind.; S. Bruté to Fr. Wathen, 8-27, 1837. CA of A. Notre Dame, Ind.; *Bruté—Seton Correspondence*, pp. 491-3. 1886. *Berichte der Leopoldinen-Stiftung im Kaiserthume Oesterreich*, XII, p. 39.

I have written to Rome and submitted the following three names, Father Petit, S. J., of St. Mary's College, Kentucky; Father de la Hailandière, Pastor of the Cathedral at Vincennes, and Father Reynolds of the Bardstown Diocese. The first they will refuse me although I have written to Father Roothaan, General of the Jesuits. The second knows little English and makes no effort to acquire it, but each of the three are more capable than I am of advancing this poor diocese.[6]

It was characteristic of the Bishop of Vincennes that notwithstanding the crying need for priests he was slow to receive foreign applicants. Moreover he repeatedly assumed the responsibility of cautioning his colleagues. Reverend Eugene Kopesky, who fled from the political upheaval in his native land, stopped with the Bishop of Vincennes enroute to New Orleans. His host advised him to go first to St. Louis and make a retreat which would afford him both a mental and a physical rest. A week later Father Peyson from Avignon applied for admission to the Diocese of Vincennes. Although he presented authentic documents and was permitted to say Mass, the bishop sent him on probation to the seminary at St. Louis before employing him. Ten days later he wrote his colleague at St. Louis as follows:

I received a letter yesterday from Pére Ladaviere at New Orleans, which obliges me to warn you and the seminary about Mr. Peyson in stronger terms than I have already done. The letters received from the Fathers in France assert that he is a questionable subject.

In the same letter he warned against Mr. Gueret who had forced an exeat for Vincennes from the Archbishop of Paris. An individual professedly sent by the Carthusians of Switzerland similarly engaged the attention of the bishop.[7]

[6] P. Card. Fransoni to S. Bruté, 12–14, 1837. CA of A.; S. Bruté to J. Rosati, 9–21, 1837. St. LCA.
[7] S. Bruté to C. François, 10–11, 1837. CA of A.; S. Bruté to J. Odin, 10–5, 1837. St. LCA.; S. Bruté to J. Rosati, 9–18, 1837; 9–26, 1837; 10–6, 1837, St. LCA.

On October 6, 1837, Bishop Bruté received from Father François the sad intelligence of Father Deseille's death. This intrepid missionary was ministering to the Indians at Pokegan village where he had presentiments of his approaching death. When he took leave of them on September 21, he remarked that probably they would see him no more. Upon his arrival at South Bend he was indisposed. The second day his condition was more critical and he gave orders to dispatch messengers to Logansport and to Chicago for a priest. The messengers returned three days later; both priests were too ill to travel. In the afternoon of the same day, September 26, Father Deseille feeling the approach of death had two attendants carry him into the chapel at four o'clock where with profound devotion he administered Holy Viaticum to himself. In less than one hour after returning to his cot the good missionary expired, invoking the sweet names of Jesus and Mary and with a most placid smile on his countenance.[8]

The worthy pastor of Chicago, Father Schaeffer, survived Father Deseille only six days. We have the bishop's own account of his death in the Annals of the Leopoldine Association where he wrote:

> With sorrow I report that I have already lost an excellent co-worker by death. Reverend Bernard Schaeffer from Strassburg, who accompanied me on my return to America in 1836 and whom I sent to Chicago immediately after our arrival. He was able to preach in German, English, and French, and on account of his fervor and unwearied zeal for the salvation of souls he was beloved by all. To the great grief of all who knew him he died on October 2, the Feast of the Holy Guardian Angels.[9]

The death of these two faithful priests brought sorrow to the paternal heart of the bishop. Upon receipt of a de-

---

[8] *Ave Maria*, I (1865), pp. 474–5; *Berichte der Leopoldinen-Stiftung im Kaiserthume Oesterreich*, XII (1837), pp. 33–7. Vienna; S. Bruté to J. Rosati, 10–6, 1837. St. LCA.

[9] *Berichte der Leopoldinen-Stiftung im Kaiserthume Oesterreich*, XII (1837), pp. 33–7. Vienna.

tailed report he gave expression to these sentiments in a letter to François in which he said:

> You can imagine how the details of our dear confrère's death affected me, and the sorrow and admiration aroused by all that followed this beautiful death—a death not less touching or less regretted than that of Father Schaeffer. As a Christian these deaths have left upon me an impression of deep and sincere resignation; but as a bishop and with such a dearth of missionaries it has brought upon me very deep affliction. A third death is that of Mr. Gottofrey who came with us in 1836, but returned to France for his health six months later. He, too, died the death of a saint.[10]

The Good Master was mindful of the bishop's holy abandonment in these severe losses for the vacancies in the ranks of the clergy were soon replaced. This made it possible for him to send pastors to the fatherless flocks. Reverend John Plunkett, a student from Mt. St. Mary's Seminary, and Reverend Benjamin Petit, one of the band who accompanied the bishop to America in 1836, were elevated to deaconship on Saturday, September 23, 1837, and were ordained to the holy priesthood by Bishop Bruté, at the Cathedral on Saturday, October 14, 1837. Father Petit was sent at once to South Bend to resume the work of Father Deseille. Father Plunkett remained at Vincennes for a short time to minister to the missions in that vicinity. Before winter he was sent to assist Father Shawe at Madison.[11]

The bishop's visitation schedule had registered 700 miles on horseback during the months of June and July, and 600 miles for August and September. This outdoor life seemed at the time to strengthen him but as soon as he remained in the house he again experienced the same bronchial trouble. His strength was on a constant decline and his condition was becoming alarming. Therefore, with the hope of restoring his impaired health he left Vincennes the week fol-

[10] S. Bruté to C. François, 11–29, 1837. CA of A.
[11] *The Catholic Telegraph*, VI (1837), p. 372; H. J. Alerding, *History of the Diocese of Vincennes*, p. 351.

lowing the October ordinations and in company with Reverend Mr. Parret he repaired to St. Mary's at the Barrens, Perryville, Mo., for three or four weeks rest.

This brief cessation of episcopal labors gave him ample time to make a detailed survey of both the Vincennes and St. Louis dioceses. He took an inventory of all that had been accomplished and drew up plans for furthering religious conditions within them. At that time his episcopal see embraced 53,000 square miles, a territory greater than one-fourth of France. It was, therefore, not astonishing to find the budding congregations founded at great distances from one another. Of the twenty-five counties in Illinois that belonged to Bishop Bruté's diocese there were only three, namely, Cook, Edgar, and Lawrence that had a chapel. Nine counties, namely, Cook, Clark, Iroquois, Crawford, Wabash, Edwards, White, Gallatin, and Vermillion had been ministered to during the bishop's travels, but the remaining thirteen had never seen a priest. He had never been able to visit the very southern part of Illinois, Fort Massac and Shawneetown, and two and one-half years had already elapsed since his last visit to Chicago. In Indiana there were chapels or stations in twenty-seven counties and the devoted prelate had visited the greater number of those stations. Nevertheless, this left a remainder of more than fifty counties, and some of the more populated ones, without priests and chapels, and the bishop had not been able to visit these places for the last three years. The bishop himself was amazed at these conditions and in his astonishment he exclaimed:

Were I Pope I would have no difficulty in placing two more bishops—one in Indiana and the other in Chicago. Then in ten years, 1847, and in another ten years, 1857, there would be greater and more beneficial good accomplished than if all this immense territory is left to my weak hand.

The enfeebled prelate had written to Propaganda on August 24, beseeching the Sacred Congregation to grant

him a coadjutor and now after an investigation of his neighboring diocese he maintained that Bishop Rosati not only
needed a coadjutor but he should also petition for an episcopal see in Arkansas. At that time the Diocese of St. Louis
comprised 163,000 square miles or more than three times
the extent of the Vincennes Diocese. While the work that
had been accomplished in the past twenty years was admirable, for then (1817) neither Illinois, Arkansas, nor
Missouri except the eastern portion was scarcely in existence; now (1837) all was above the power of a single
bishop. Bishop Bruté thought it almost incredible for one
bishop to extend his care to a diocese larger than four
times the whole kingdom of Naples.

Further scrutiny of the St. Louis Diocese revealed that
out of the forty-two counties in Illinois, only ten had been
visited by Bishop Rosati or his priests. This left thirty-two
without spiritual care. Of the thirty-two counties in Missouri, only twelve received clerical services leaving twenty
to the mercy of God. They were able to care for only four
of the twenty-three counties in Arkansas, leaving nineteen
counties without spiritual attention. This examination
showed that Bishop Rosati and his clergy were able to care
for only twenty-six counties out of the ninety-seven counties
then within the diocese, while they were forced to neglect
seventy-one counties or more than two-thirds of the entire
diocese. At that epoch, however, emigration followed the
rivers and consequently much of the above territory was
uninhabited.

After preparing these statistics the thoughtful bishop began to devise methods that, if employed, would improve this
condition. He then had more than twenty priests in the
Diocese of Vincennes. The college faculty, strong in ability,
were few in numbers: one priest, one deacon, and one
Eudist lay brother. The sisterhood numbered only two
members. "Behold my two grains of mustard seed," exclaimed the bishop. He himself was weakening rapidly and
realized that his days were declining yet he was anxious

to introduce workable methods that would continue in an effective manner the work of the Divine Master indefinitely after his labors were ended. In view of this he suggested establishing the traveling missionary band and formulated a code by which they could be governed. Independent of the congregations and stations these missionaries were to visit on a circuit of three, six, or twelve months, and preserve for the Church the dispersed Catholics wherever they were found. These Catholics were gradually to be formed into groups, then into centers, and finally into new congregations. When the latter period of development had been attained, their charge would be given to a newly ordained priest.

These missionaries would not occupy themselves with the Indians, but only with the interior and extremities of the diocese—portions which the bishop considered their immediate charge. They were to arrange with each other and divide the territory in such a manner that the same priest would visit the same sections in order to follow up the initial good effected. Likewise, the missionaries were to be extremely exact when leaving a place to indicate the date and place of the next meeting. They, too, were to be very punctual as to time and place. In case one could not keep the next appointment he was to inform a confrère who would supply in his stead and even though it were only a deacon, he could instruct, baptize, register new catechumens, and assign the new date and place of the next meeting.

The prudent bishop suggested that a portion of the financial aid given by the Propagation of the Faith be used for the maintenance of the traveling missionaries. It was his object to provide the means of salvation for as many souls as possible. He maintained that if they waited until regular parishes could be formed before giving aid to the scattered Catholics a goodly number of them would perish. The bishop completed his plans for the traveling missionaries' activities by saying:

There remains now but to choose a good director, two or three assistants and determine on the distant centres where they will begin work, such as Peoria, Shelbyville, Vandalia, and Springfield. While leaving much to the initiative and zeal of the missionaries themselves, who will try from year to year to develop and improve the work, we can, however, incorporate in our plan the experiences of the early missionaries of these localities.[12]

After spending several weeks at the Barrens and with Bishop Rosati, the two prelates went to visit Kaskaskia. The Bishop of St. Louis left there on November 9, and repaired to the Barrens to prepare and have everything in readiness for the consecration of the new stone church at the Seminary on Sunday, November 12. Bishop Bruté was cordially invited, and, moreover, had promised Bishop Rosati that he would be there. On Saturday Mr. Pierre Menard took the bishop on his departure from Kaskaskia in his cart to the ferry, but they arrived too late, the boat had already traveled a mile up the river. Another attempt was made to reach the boat at a point up the river where it made a second stop. This too was a failure. The bishop could have left Kaskaskia on the following morning before daybreak and reached the Barrens in time for the solemnities but Providence intervened. The bishop had learned that both priests were gone from Kaskaskia and the Convent of Visitandines would be without Mass if he departed. Consequently he remained, said Mass, gave Holy Communion to the nuns at the Visitation convent, and exhorted them to pray fervently for all at the Barrens. Descriptive of this visit, Sister Mary Barber recorded:

.... It was to this little chapel the saintly Bishop Bruté used to steal, and pass hours before the Blessed Sacrament. We often met him going along in silence and on tip-toe, without raising his eyes or stopping to speak to anyone, his breviary under his arm.[13]

[12] S. Bruté to J. Rosati, 10–28, 1837; 10–29, 1837. St. LCA.

[13] *Records* (ACHS), XIII (1902), p. 221; S. Bruté to A. Bruté, 11–12, 1837. Canon Bruté Collection. Rennes; S. Bruté to J. Rosati, 11–12, 1837. St. LCA; *Bruté—Seton Correspondence*, pp. 493–4. 1886.

The bishop returned home on Saturday, November 25, after an absence of five or six weeks. He was obliged to be in Evansville on the following Thursday and then return immediately to transact important business at Vincennes on Saturday. Father Neyron visited the bishop at Vincennes on November 29, and imparted a bit of unwelcome news. Mr. Ratigan had come to the Knobs during the Bishop's absence and after preaching to the congregation he departed from New Albany for St. Louis. His intentions were to join the St. Louis Diocese but if Bishop Rosati should refuse he would return to seek employment at Vincennes. Bishop Bruté wrote asking Bishop Rosati to persuade Mr. Ratigan not to come because he would never accept him. In the same letter he took occasion to inform his colleague of the conduct of Mr. McCosker whom he had forbidden to minister in the Diocese of Vincennes. This unfortunate man continued to remain at the canal going only to the sick who were in danger of death giving as excuse his right to absolve *in extremis*. While the poor bishop realized the desolation of the 1500 souls employed on the canal without a pastor he would not consent to employ a hypocrite. On that very day another rambler, Mr. Healy, sought employment from Bishop Bruté. This clergyman had been in Charleston, in Maryland, and in Philadelphia. Upon being sent away by Bishop Kenrick he went to Ireland in July. He returned again only to find himself refused at Philadelphia, Pittsburg, and Cincinnati. Then he proceeded to Vincennes where his tears and supplications were, likewise, ineffective for here, too, the bishop refused to accept him and warned his colleague at St. Louis that if Mr. Healy called there it was not he who sent him thither.[14]

Spontaneously the bishop discharged the disagreeable duties first but their number was not in the ascendency. A goodly number of the thirty letters that awaited his attention contained pleasing information. From Father Petit he learned that this young priest had thrown himself, heart

---

[14] S. Bruté to J. Rosati, 11–29, 1837. St. LCA.

and soul, into the work among the Indians. In response the fatherly prelate warned him to be prudent in all, saying:

> These people will not be successful in having the law repealed. Whatever may have been its origin—however faulty or dishonest even—if the fault lay in the documents upon which the law was based then above all, we should, as Father Deseille said, refrain from meddling in what is not in the line of our duties.

Father François' letters communicated interesting news concerning large numbers of recent immigrants and the discovery of more Catholic families in the southern part of his district. In responding to him the bishop urged that the good work be continued but Father François should not attempt to care for Indianapolis. He would authorize Father Bacquelin, who was only twenty-five miles distant, to care for this mission. The poor priest was then assured of further assistance from the general funds, and a collection among the bishop's friends in the East. Then by way of consolation the bishop wrote:

> Do not be discouraged; God will help. You say that you need nothing for yourself. You are always too modest in your demands, but do not wait until you experience actual suffering before appealing to the heart of your poor bishop. What I have belongs to all. I am simply the administrator of the kindness of our good friends in France.[15]

Notwithstanding the thirty letters that awaited the bishop on his return from St. Louis he truly suffered to find no letter from St. Joseph's, Emmitsburg. This suffering was the keener because of his recent visit to the flourishing institutions in the neighboring diocese where he had learned from Bishop Rosati that Emmitsburg was sending Sisters to Cape Girardeau, a small village far more insignificant than Vincennes which now seemed to be neglected. Nevertheless, the two good Sisters who had remained were continuing the school in the most edifying manner. Bishop

---

[15] S. Bruté to C. François, 11–29, 1837. CA of A.

Bruté visited and examined their school on Friday, December 1. They had seven boarders, thirty day scholars, and three candidates for the Sisterhood. Unknown to the bishop good news was on its way. Mother Rose's letter arrived on December 15, saying, "On November 24, it had been decided that Sister Benedicta Parsons and Sister Mary Margaret Cully were to go to Vincennes."[16]

These two Sisters in company with four others destined for New Orleans left Emmitsburg on December 11, 1837, enroute to Vincennes, a journey that required more than two weeks. They stopped for a short rest at their establishment in Cincinnati. At this place they received a letter from Bishop Bruté wherein he stated that owing to his precarious health the physician had ordered him South for the winter. He welcomed the Sisters and assured them that the Vicar General would care for their needs until his return. They had no further hope of seeing the bishop until his return, but much to their agreeable surpise they met him upon their arrival at Evansville. He again welcomed them and bade them not to open their school until he returned.[17]

Prior to Bishop Bruté's departure from Vincennes he conferred the holy order of deacon on Reverend Mr. Parret of Clermont, and ordained to the priesthood a member of the college faculty, Reverend Maurice Berel, Eudist, of Rennes. He then placed Father de la Hailandière in charge of all diocesan affairs and directed his clergy to have recourse to the Vicar General during his absence. He requested Father François to take the proper care of his own health and to keep an eye on young Father Petit in the north who was not accustomed to our hard winters, adding: "With priests so devoted, so zealous, so full of the love of God and souls there remains to me only the duty of cautioning them to preserve their health." To Bishop Rosati he recommended Father Buteux who wished to collect at St. Louis. This priest had three churches in his district, name-

16 *Bruté—Seton Correspondence*, pp. 495–502. 1886.
17 *Ibid.*, pp. 502–3.

ly, Terre Haute, Paris, and Thralls Station.   He also announced the arrival of another seminarian, Mr. J. Kelly, and made known his decision to accept two more who had recently made application.[18]

Enroute to New Orleans Bishop Bruté stopped for a brief visit at Natchez where he learned to his sorrow that Father Hayden had refused the bishopric.   To his horror he also learned that McCosker had been there making money out of his impious deceptions.   Bishop Bruté maintained that hell seemed to be conscious of the good that was in preparation and filled with rage played the infernal trick of sending McCosker to Natchez to prepare the way for Father Hayden precisely because it was he whom Bishop Kenrick had sent to replace this unfortunate man at Chambersburg.[19]

While at New Orleans in quest of health the bishop again spent much time studying the spiritual condition of the United States.   At that epoch its situation was unique in the Church;   therefore, he concluded that too much stress could not be placed on the nomination of new bishops.   Conditions demanded that this period should receive the highest norms of faith, sound doctrine, and unfeigned fervor, but progress was not to be calculated by the merits and indispensable service of any one individual.   In order to fulfill more fruitfully his obligations towards this progress he had applied to Rome on August 24, 1837, for a coadjutor and Rome responded on December 14, that the Sacred Congregation would carefully consider the matter.   The truth was that Rome left it to the judgment of Archbishop Eccleston and the other Bishops whether the Bishop of Vincennes should have a coadjutor and who it should be.   The first name presented had been refused by the Society.   Bishop Bruté could not understand why a concession could not be made and give

[18] S. Bruté to C. François, 12-4, 1837. CA of A.; S. Bruté to J. Rosati, 12–25, 1837. St. LCA.; *The Catholic Telegraph*, VII (1838), p. 29.
[19] S. Bruté to S. Eccleston, 1–22, 1838. BCA. Case 24I¹; S. Bruté to J. Rosati, 1–20, 1838. St. LCA.

him the Jesuit, Father Petit, since St. Ignatius himself had permitted that the patriarch of Abyssinia should be taken from among his first associates. Moreover, the greater number of ancient bishops had been chosen from the regular clergy, and also a goodly number of the Popes. Then, too, the above ruling had been deemed proper under circumstances that were not as demanding as were those of this period which marked a singular epoch in the history of the Church in America. Here was to be found an entire continent populating by leaps and bounds and the whole territory threatening to be wholly protestant or rationalistic as Bishop Bruté wrote: "unless the occasion and crisis, the only chance and moment, *Now*, be not improved to the very best; for there can be *no too great* liberty of best choices. What will become of the religious Orders or Congregations if they produce no bishops or if indifferent selections be the only ones they permit to the Pope and Bishops."

Bishop Bruté believed the Jesuits were rendering an injustice to the Church by refusing to permit their subjects to become bishops. He realized that the interests of the immense future demanded of the hierarchy as an essential point of their duty that they found the episcopacy on firm ground. Nothing too much could be done to gain that point. He saw the future good that would accrue from having English speaking prelates to govern the dioceses and in refusing him Father Petit they were denying him a clergyman who had the two primary essentials, namely, knowledge of English and customs of the country.

Prior to this three bishops in the United States had been chosen from among the Jesuits ranks. Two were consecrated before the bann of suppression was lifted, but Bishop Fenwick was chosen later. In the sixteen dioceses existing at that time the Jesuits numbered fifty-seven priests out of a clergy of 422. Many select secular priests had entered their ranks and Bishop Bruté believed it not more than worthy of the charity and zeal of the Society to grant at least occasionally some return to the bishops. Again the

Bishop of Vincennes realized that it would be difficult to dispense with a member who held an important office such as provincial, professor, or rector, but Father Petit was employed mostly in mission activities. Nevertheless, since the refusal he would be satisfied with the second candidate, Father de la Hailandière, and personally also with the third, Father Reynolds, but he knew that some of his respected colleagues objected to the last name. Exemplifying again the spirit of holy abandonment he said:

> I leave the whole affair to our Lord, but once more what will become of the true meaning of the maxim *Ad Majorem Dei Gloriam,* if the interest, so fundamental of the Episcopate, of the Apostolate of the foundation of Churches holds but a secondary place.
>
> I have had but one ambition ever since I came to this America, namely, to see Religion prosper—the Church prosper—for they are not two things but one. Now I dare not demand that it prosper my own way for others would have the same right to demand the same. I am cognizant of my faults of ignorance, or partial judgment, of wrong decision in many cases, more than I could be of the actions of others, especially, of my Superiors, hence let the Will of God be declared by them.[20]

Taking inventory of spiritual conditions did not occupy the entire sojourn of the Bishop in the South. On the contrary, he was quite active. On January 31, 1838, he went to Mobile to visit Bishop Portier. Relative to this visit Bishop Blanc wrote Bishop Purcell:

> Our Brother of Vincennes, has now been nearly three weeks at Mobile, and has not, so far, been benefited by the change, in consequence of the weather that has been uncommonly bad with us. I expect him back here in a few days.

Bishop Bruté's primary purpose in this visit was to arouse interest for the poor sections of Indiana and secure

---

[20] S. Bruté to S. Eccleston, 1–22, 1838. BCA. Case 24I¹; 2–20, 1838. BCA. Case 24G²; 3–9, 1838. BCA. Case 24I²; S. Bruté to J. Rosati, 1–20, 1838. St. LCA.; P. Card. Fransoni, to S. Bruté, 12–14, 1837. CA of A.

the assistance of his colleague for Father Buteux who was
then collecting in the South for his new Church under construction at Terre Haute. How well he succeeded may be
determined by Bishop Portier's personal gift of two hundred
dollars. In New Orleans the venerable prelate visited the
various Communities, the Hospital, and the Asylum, assisting the priests with the confessions or supplying for Mass.
On March 9, he accompanied Bishop Blanc to St. Michael's
where they spent several days visiting the Boarding School
of the Madames of the Sacred Heart. The day following
their arrival Bishop Blanc at the advice of his visiting colleague baptized a non-Catholic student, thirteen years old,
who had been taken critically ill on the preceding day. Bishop Blanc then departed for the Assumption parish where a
Confirmation class awaited him on the following day. Bishop Bruté was happy to remain at St. Michael's and assist
the favored girl who expired during Bishop Blanc's absence.
From this place the Bishop of Vincennes wrote His Grace at
Baltimore recommending Father Plunket, assistant to Father Shawe at Madison, who desired to make a collection
in the Metropolitan city in behalf of their church. Madison
on the Ohio* between Cincinnati and Louisville seemed to
be very promising and was at that time one of the largest
towns in Indiana. Several families from Baltimore, well
known to Bishop Bruté, had settled there. Father Shawe
had succeeded in obtaining a lot by donation from Mr.
McIntyre, a Presbyterian, and was building the first church.
The bishop also announced his return to Vincennes for the
end of that month.[21]

On March 25, 1838, Bishop Bruté in company with Father
Buteux of Terre Haute and Father Van de Velde of St.
Louis were on board the *Louisville*. The first two were en-

---

* Named by Bishop Bruté at the season of summer, *La Belle Riviere
sans Eau*,—The Beautiful River without water.

[21] A. Blanc to J. Purcell, 2–18, 1838. No. 200. CA of A.; *Bruté—
Seton Correspondence*, pp. 504–510; 580–2. 1886; S. Bruté to S.
Eccleston, 3–9, 1838. BCA. Case 241²; S. Bruté to A. Bruté, 1–31,
1838. Canon Bruté Collection. Jefferson County Courthouse Records.

route to Vincennes via St. Louis, while the third was returning to St. Louis with six or seven students from Louisiana.
The happy bishop wrote a detailed letter of the interesting
voyage to his brother Augustine. He left nothing untouched
and dwelt at length on the beautiful rivers in our Middle
West, the passengers on board, and the customs of the day
after which he exclaimed:

> Ah! my dear one. I behold the beauties of earth and sky. I
> have seen the Emperor Napoleon, I have seen the Empress and the
> Archduke of Austria. I have seen two Popes and the grandeur of
> two centuries, but what is it all in comparison to the joy experienced
> by a priest at the altar or a good Christian at the reception of
> Holy Communion.

From a letter begun on board the *Louisville*, March 28,
continued at St. Louis, March 31, and finished at Vincennes
on April 2, we are informed that Bishop Bruté arrived at
St. Louis on March 29 and spent two days with Bishop
Rosati before returning to Vincennes. While his health
was better he still insisted that Archbishop Eccleston obtain a coadjutor for the diocese because he was too feeble
to attend to all the needs of his see. This, however, was
suggested not through a spirit of self-seeking; the afflicted
prelate was willing to remain active but his territory was
too extensive for one man to govern. In the same letter he
strongly advocated the creation of a new see in Arkansas.
This again testifies to the loyal spirit of his disinterested
labor.[22]

The bishop arrived home on April 2 and was happy to
be among his missionaries once more. His health had improved and he manifested exceptional interest in the diocesan activities. The first important question to be adjusted
was one concerning the new Community. The two Sisters
of Nazareth who had remained at Vincennes refused to
unite with those who arrived from Emmitsburg and, decid-

[22] S. Bruté to A. Bruté, 3–25, 1838. Canon Bruté Collection; S.
Bruté to S. Eccleston, 3–28–31, 1838. BCA. Case 241⁴.

ing they could not be foundresses themselves, consented to ask reentrance at Nazareth. Bishop Bruté wrote to Nazareth and also to Bishop Chabrat and requested that these two good souls be received again with charity. In an immediate response both Bishop Chabrat and Father Reynolds wrote that the two Sisters would be received with joy at their Convent. They departed at once in company with a friend of the bishop and arrived at Louisville within two days.[23]

This problem solved the bishop then proceeded to arrange for a school. His plan was for a Boarding and Day School, with a separate Free School. There were only two Sisters and the house they occupied was poor, small, and dilapidated. Despite this the Sisters were hopeful. They were willing to undertake the work and to obtain more Sisters from Emmitsburg provided the bishop would increase their accommodations. In view of this he exchanged the property purchased from Nazareth for more spacious grounds nearer the Cathedral. It was a valuable corner lot with an extensive garden; hence, far superior to the place they then occupied. The lot contained four buildings which would afford ample accommodations for the Academy, Boarding and Day School, and the Free School. The principal building was a two story brick house containing four large rooms. A few steps from this building was another one story brick house, containing two rooms. At the north corner of the lot about twenty paces from the other buildings was an old frame house containing five rooms. A blacksmith's shop, separated from the other buildings by a fence, made the fourth. The principal building was converted into the Boarding and Day School, and the blacksmith shop was fitted up for the Free School.

The citizens of Vincennes welcomed heartily this new addition to their educational system and the local paper, *The*

---

[23] *Bruté—Seton Correspondence*, pp. 519–20;   S. Bruté to J. Rosati, 4–12, 1838.   St. LCA.

Western Sun and General Advertizer, announced with much pride:

> Bishop Bruté and his friends have offered, for some months past, to the inhabitants of Vincennes, the use of a free school for boys, kept by able and efficient teachers; success has attended the effort, and we rely on Providence to continue the same with increasing benefit for the youth. We have made arrangements to secure one also for girls, and they will be taught by the Sisters of Charity of St. Joseph's who have lately taken the place of their esteemed Sisters of Nazareth.
>
> To contribute to the utmost of our abilities, to the good of the Borough of Vincennes, and county of Knox, has been for years past the object of the Bishop and his friends. They have done it without interfering with the exertions of others. So much room exists for doing good, and gradually developing all the best prospects of Vincennes, that all who try to do it in proportion to their means, and through a proper use of them, can but rely on the good sense of the community for approbation and encouragement.
>
> The school announced for the girls is already partially in operation, but it will soon be carried on in a more extensive plan.[24]

The Sisters obtained permission from their Superiors to teach the same branches of education taught at St. Joseph's, Emmitsburg. In the Boarding and Day School, besides the usual English branches, French, Music, and needle work were taught. The poor children in the Free School were taught the English branches and the French Catechism, as the bishop wanted them to learn the latter in their mother tongue.

After the exchange of many letters between Vincennes and Emmitsburg and much pleading on the part of the Bishop, Father Vabret, and the Sisters, Mother Rose finally made it possible to send two more Sisters to Vincennes. The school grew rapidly. In less than six weeks the Boarding and Day School numbered forty pupils and the Free School registered eighty poor children. Owing to the oppo-

[24] *The Western Sun and General Advertizer,* XXIX, (1838), p. 3.

sition of the people the Sisters were forced to keep the Free School separate from the boarders and day scholars or forfeit the good that could be done the rich as well as the support of their own home. The Bishop left all arrangements of the school to the Sisters affirming that they knew more about those things than he did; nevertheless, at the beginning he helped them along financially and shared with them whatever he had until the success of their school rendered this assistance unnecessary. The Free School for girls, conducted by the Sisters of Charity, was partially financed from the proceeds of a three days' fair given by the ladies in which all, even Protestants, were very active for its success. A sum of four hundred dollars was realized.[25]

Although laboring under corporal infirmities, the consequences of hardship and exposure the zealous bishop resumed on April 27 the visitation tour of his diocese. He proceeded first to Washington, Daviess County, but finding Father Lalumière's new brick church unfinished he went to St. Peter's, six miles distant, where he administered Confirmation to thirty-two persons on Sunday, April 29, 1838. From this place he sent a detailed letter to St. Joseph's, Emmitsburg, and availed himself of the opportunity to petition the Mother to send more help to Vincennes. On Wednesday, May 2, in company with Father Shawe and a layman he left for The Knobs, eighty miles distant. This district he described "as a most beautiful hilly country." A double forked creek flowed at a distance of one and one-half miles from the church. There were no bridges, thus everyone traveling that route was obliged to wade the streams. Upon reaching this spot, much to the venerable prelate's surprise, a good stout Irishman carried him across both streams and then returned for Father Shawe. The layman, who accompanied the clergyman, was ready to wade the stream but the Irishman bade him wait and he carried him in like manner. At this place Father Neyron awaited the Bishop to confirm

[25] *Bruté—Seton Correspondence*, pp. 532–8; 541–5. 1886; *The Western Sun and General Advertizer*, XXIX, (1838), p. 3. Vincennes; *The United States Catholic Miscellany*, XVIII (1838), p. 91.

a class of sixty-three persons, among whom were many recent converts. This solemnity occurred on Sunday, May 6, and the bishop was happy to note the singular coincidence of three generations—a grandmother, aged eighty-two years, her daughter and granddaughter, confirmed on the same day. He also rejoiced to see where formerly a small log building was the only temple of God, now a new brick church commenced two years ago stood completed on the site, while the congregation had almost doubled in numbers. This church, named Assumption, was built on a grant of seven acres of land, destined to afford ample space for a cemetery, school-house, and presbytery. At this early date, Father Neyron had already succeeded in establishing pious confraternities for the practice of devotion and mutual edification.

From The Knobs the bishop went to Madison where Father Shawe was building a stone church ninety feet long and fifty feet wide. Three days were spent at this place in the course of which the bishop met several of his old friends who formerly resided at Baltimore. The congregation was rapidly increasing and everything bade fair for a prosperous parish in the future.

On his return to Vincennes the venerable prelate stopped at New Albany where on Sunday, May 13, a class of thirty-four received Confirmation. This was encouraging for both the Bishop and Father Neyron inasmuch as formerly predjudice against Catholicism had been rampant in this town. Father Neyron had succeeded in obtaining lot No. 3 on Upper Market Street, from Daniel Dwyer and his wife. This property was deeded to Bishop Bruté on July 3, 1837, but the erection of the first church in New Albany was deferred until the following spring, 1838.

Following this visit the bishop returned home just in time to preside at the First Communion of a class of thirty-four and to administer Confirmation to a class of fifty on the third Sunday in May. Early in June he travelled to Dearborn County but Father Ferneding's church was not completed, therefore, he was obliged to delay the blessing of it as well as the sacrament of Confirmation. A second visit was made to Father Neyron at the Knobs, likewise to Washington, St. Peter's, and St. Mary's whence he returned home after an absence of more than two weeks. During this same time Father Lalumière was visiting in the north at Chicago, and along the canal where he was successful in suppressing a riot that was raging among the Irish laborers. One riot had previously taken place, and unfortunately, much blood had been shed. His presence, with a commanding appeal to their faith, made the laborers instantly disperse. He exhorted them to behave as true Irishmen, and true Catholics, worthy of the country of their adoption. All who witnessed the scene gave great credit to Father Lalumière's exertions and, likewise, commended the excellent disposition of the people. The Bishop was much surprised to learn that Father Lalumière had found nearly three hundred families at Joliet. New appeals were coming in constantly for priests, but the perplexed bishop had no one to send them. The settlement at Jasper now told forty-six families; while Father de St. Palais visited them once a month, their zeal and piety made the bishop solicitous to obtain a permanent pastor for them.[26]

The Germans seem to have had a preference for the Diocese of Vincennes. At that period one-third of the immigrants were Alsatian. To Bishop Bruté's sorrow he had only four priests who thoroughly understood the language. He realized the critical position of those people who could speak the German only and he was doing all in his power to procure priests to relieve the needs of these newcomers entrusted to his care. Generally these people purchased large tracts of land and established in groups. In this way

[26] S. Bruté to J. Rosati, 6–20, 1838. St. LCA.; S. Bruté to C. François, 5–27, 1838. CA of A.; S. Bruté to A. Bruté, 6–21, 1838. Canon Bruté Collection; *The Catholic Telegraph*, VII (1838), p. 301; 316; *Bruté—Seton Correspondence*, pp. 519–23; 532–7; 1886; *American Catholic Historical Researches*, XV (1898), p. 87; *The United States Cath. Miscellany*, XVIII (1838), p. 91. Floyd County Courthouse Records.

entire German parishes or villages were formed, such as
Jasper, Indiana. Another early colony, similar to Jasper,
was the recent Picquet settlement founded by Joseph Picquet
from Strassburg, in company with Ferdinand Hartrich, and
Etienne Laver at Ste. Marie in Jasper County, Illinois, about
forty miles from Vincennes. Here they purchased 13,000
acres of land late in October 1837 and by June 1838 they
were hopeful that their colony would soon number one
hundred and fifty families. A goodly number of Germans
had already settled in Madison. Father Schneiderjans visited this station at the end of June 1838 and reported to the
bishop that he had heard confessions and gave Holy Communion to two hundred.[27]

Bishop Bruté had exercised great prudence in obtaining
land for Church purposes in every promising settlement.
This alone necessitated great expenditures for in many
places the priests were not fortunate enough to receive land
donations but were forced to pay high prices for suitable
locations. The maintenance of the clergy on the poor missions and all were poor in those days also required much
cash. To these were added the expenses of the missions
among the Christian Indians. Struggling under such financial burdens it is not astonishing to learn that the funds
often ran low. The Leopoldine Society and the Association
for the Propagation of the Faith distributed appreciable
sums from time to time for which the bishop was grateful,
nevertheless, with the most prudent management these gifts
were not sufficient to defray all expenses. On May 21, 1838,
Bishop Bruté acknowledged and thanked the Leopoldine
Society for the receipt of 6000 florins for which he received
in exchange $2,900. While these donations may appear

---

[27] *Pastoral-Blatt*, No. 3, p. 34. March, 1924. St. Louis, Mo.;
Records (ACHS), XLI (1930), pp. 122–4. Philadelphia; *The U. S.
Catholic Miscellany*, XVIII (1838), p. 91; *The Catholic Telegraph*,
VII (1838), p. 316; *Berichte der Leopoldinen-Stiftung im Kaiser-
thume Oesterreich*, XII (1838), pp. 38–9; S. Bruté to C. Bruté ,7–16,
1838. Canon Bruté Collection.

large for those days they were extremely small in comparison to the work that was to be accomplished.[28]

The government, too, had failed in its duty towards the
Indians. They had granted on April 19, 1836, an annual
appropriation of three hundred dollars for the instruction or
education of the Indians in Indiana. The amount was paid
for one year and then was discontinued. Bishop Bruté cognizant of this injustice wrote to Hon. C. Harris, Superintendent of Indian Affairs, on June 25, 1838, reminding
him of their neglected duty. He reviewed in detail the
faithful labors of Father Deseille, his perseverance in the
noble work until death, and the salutary influence he wielded over his baptized flock which numbered more than one
thousand. His Christians were faithful observants of the
law of the country and all the white people in the vicinity
testified to the fact that Father Deseille's Indians were
strikingly better than any of the other Indians. The bishop
likewise informed the Superintendent that this heroic labor
did not cease at Father Deseille's death which occurred on
Sept. 26, 1837. He was immediately replaced by another
priest, Father Petit, who had faithfully and successfully
continued the work during these seven months. The bishop
believed this statement sufficient to entitle them to the
amount designated and to urge the government to remit the
delinquent appropriations. At the close of this testimonial
he added the following certificate which had been requested
by the government officials.

I do now certify that the whole of the allowance of $300 for the
Catholic missions among the Potawatomies of this state of Indiana
was wholly expended for the purpose mentioned, besides a larger
sum out of the funds of the Church added by me.

Simon G. Bruté, Bishop of Vincennes.[29]

Vincennes, 27th June, 1838.

[28] *Berichte der Leopoldinen-Stiftung im Kaiserthume Oesterreich,*
XII, pp. 37–41.

[29] S. Bruté to C. Harris, 6–25, 1838. Original in Government Indian
Office, Washington, D. C. File 1838.

Together with the above letter he sent to C. Harris the following lengthy inquiry which is self-explanatory. In order to give our readers a clearer knowledge of his disinterested zeal for souls we quote this inquiry in its entirety.

Vincennes, Indiana.
June 25, 1838.

Sir:

I submit as a matter of inquiry whether the Indians who have been formed by their Catholic missionaries Mr. Deseille and M. Petit to the best moral habits of the civilized life, in point of their marriages, parental and filial relations and duties, relations of justice, and strict honesty among themselves and towards their white brethren, habits of strict temperance and decency, reverence of the laws of the country so as to make them excellent citizens, resolved besides so to use labor and industry whether in farming or exercising useful arts that can make them independent and above all the allurements of idleness and want to trespass against morality, whether I say such Indians could be permitted to remain upon lands not yet sold if they have any acknowledged to be such, or on lands that they would buy and secure in a regular manner for their own occupancy living there under common subjection to all our laws and common equal protection by them.

Their desire so to remain, becoming regular and good citizens, is strengthened by a motive that might be considered as the best pledge for their fulfilling every proper expectation for their being indeed good citizens and persevering to improve the more in their civilized condition, viz., by their resolution to be as they are admitted by all to be now, exemplary Christians regularly organized under a form of religious worship and pastorship, assisted in the usual Catholic way by those whom the Bishop of Vincennes could send them as he has done so far, as ministers of their religion and persuasion.

So far examples of such a state of things has existed in different of our states, and in particular, as for Catholic Indians become part and parcel of their population we might allude to the Penobscot Society about Norridgewock in Maine.

Should the inquiry lead to a favouring the petition of our Indians for remaining among our citizens, in what manner ought they to propose that it be granted them.

The present respectful inquiry has seemed to imply in itself not only the good of our friends, but that of our state that, all balanced and considered has not better citizens than they would be to expect from great many of those who are every year considered as a valuable accession to our population a most sober, moral, religious, inoffensive, and exemplary set of men, of good heart, reflecting mind, and most tractable temper seems a fit object of interest and good hope in the state once permitted to be a part of us.

Very respectfully, Sir, Your humble Servant

✠ Simon G. Bruté, Bishop of Vincennes.[30]

The bishop did not stand alone in his demand for justice; there were others who maintained the same principles. Among this number was Judge Law, of Vincennes, who considered it his sacred duty to support the Bishop in this appeal for the Indians' honest rights, and in view of which he sent the following letter together with Bishop Bruté's to Hon. C. Harris, on June 27, 1838.

Vincennes, Indiana
June 27, 1838.

My dear Sir:

Enclosed you will find the communication from my good friend, the Catholic Bishop of Indiana and Illinois, relative to his mission among the Potawatomies and a certificate (as you requested) showing the application of the $300 heretofore granted by the Government—of course items of such an account, or receipts could not be expected. This certificate I presume will be satisfactory to you. I have no doubt it has been *well* and *faithfully* expended for the purposes for which it was originally granted. The allowance ceased as you perceive on the 19th April 1837. One year's allowance would be due on 19th April last—and another commencing on that day for 1838 would seem due.

[30] S. Bruté to C. Harris, 6–25, 1838. Original in Government Indian Office, Washington, D. C. File 1838.

The Mission since the grant was made, and the money expended as appropriated by the Government has been continued at *the expense* of the Bishop solely.

Of the good effects of the Mission, both as to the habits, manners, and morals of the Indians, cannot be doubted. Should not this grant be continued until the Indians are removed? I think so. The policy cannot, I trust, be doubted. You will see the progress made from the Bishop's letter. The other communication, you will see in relation to other matters—how far the Bishop's views coincide with the Government I cannot say of this you are a better judge than I am—relative to the continuance of the grant of $300.—and the payment for the year 1837—I cannot doubt. Write me your views, which I may show the Bishop.

With high regard, Your obedient servant,
John Law.[31]

If Hon. C. Harris responded directly to Bishop Bruté's appeal, his secretary failed to file a duplicate or the Indian Bureau Archives failed to preserve it. Judging from the following brief response in which the officials' intentions were communicated to Judge Law, it is more probable that the bishop's letters were never answered.

August 2, 1838.

Sir:

I have to acknowledge the receipt of your letter of June 27th with the enclosure from the Bishop of Vincennes.

The information, that has reached this office from its agents, shows that M. Deseille exerted himself on several occasions to dissuade the Indians from removing, as measures then and now believed to be for their benefit, and more recent advices impute similar proceedings to his successor. For this reason, and for that also of their probably speedy emigration, it is deemed improper to continue the allowance from the civilization fund.

H. C. Harris.[32]

[31] J. Law to C. Harris, 6–27, 1838. Original in Government Indian Office, File 1838, Washington, D. C.

[32] C. Harris to J. Law, 8–2, 1838. Original in Government Indian Office, File 1838. Washington, D. C.

While the above decision was an injustice to honest labor, the bishop considered it too small a matter to disturb his peace. He trusted to Providence to care for them as it had done in the past and made no further application for government assistance.

On June 30, 1838, Bishop Bruté left Vincennes again on another extensive visitation tour. He went first to Lawrence county, Illinois, on the Wabash where on July 1 he blessed Father Corbe's new church, at St. Francisville. After the blessing of St. John's Church he administered Confirmation to a class of thirty-four. From there he returned again to Madison by way of the Ohio river, where he met Father Shawe who accompanied him via Lawrenceburg to Father Ferneding's parishes at New Alsace, Dover, and Blue Creek.[33]

Pioneer congregations celebrated the blessing of a church and the visitation of a bishop with the greatest possible solemnity and it required no eulogy on the part of their clergy to induce them to prepare for such events. On this occasion the above congregations prepared to receive Bishop Bruté with every possible mark of respect. Everyone who could procure a horse joined the cavalcade enroute to Lawrenceburg, on June 6, to meet and conduct him to New Alsace. At the distance of one-half a mile from the presbytery another large procession on foot carrying flowers and banners and accompanied by a choir awaited in eager expectation his coming. Unexpected circumstances caused his delay and night intervened without permitting these good people to welcome their bishop in the manner they had desired to receive him. Bishop Bruté in company with Father Shawe arrived at New Alsace at nine o'clock on the following morning, July 7. In the afternoon of the same day the bishop and his companion visited St. John's Church at Dover. Father Shawe delivered a learned discourse in English to a numerous assemblage of Catholics and Protestants. The subject of his sermon was the necessity of worshipping God

[33] S. Bruté to A. Blanc, 7–15, 1838. CA of A.

in a manner and form which He Himself had ordained and which was shown to be only that of the Catholic Church. Many, Catholics and non-Catholics composing his audience, were moved to tears and all wished this zealous priest to favor them with frequent visits.

The blessing of St. Paul's Church at New Alsace took place at nine-thirty o'clock on July 8. This was followed by a solemn pontifical Mass in which the piety and devotion of Bishop Bruté edified all who were present. He was assisted by five priests. The Very Reverend Father Henni, Vicar General of Cincinnati Diocese, addressed the congregation in the German language. He congratulated them on their good fortune in possessing a church for the worship of God, but he warned them at the same time, that all this would be profitless if they, themselves, failed to become the living temples of God and to manifest in their works the evidence of a sincere and heartfelt conviction of their faith. He also admonished his audience to lay aside all that had hitherto caused contention and advised them of the necessity of this reconciliation using as his text the Gospel of the day, "If therefore thou offer thy gift at the altar, and there thou remember that thy brother hath anything against thee;" etc. (Matt. 5:23).

After Mass Bishop Bruté confirmed more than one hundred persons. He prefaced this sacred ceremony with an impressive sermon in which he admonished them to be strong and steadfast in the Faith. Following the ceremony of Confirmation Father Shawe addressed the congregation in the English language. He explained chiefly the ceremonies of the day. The services then closed after having continued for more than four hours. Owing to his weakened condition the bishop found it impossible to remain until the close. He was forced to leave the church during Father Shawe's discourse.

Early on the following morning the venerable prelate in company with Fathers Ferneding and Henni repaired to Blue Creek fourteen miles distant to bless St. Peter's Church, a promising congregation which was occasionally visited by Father Ferneding, where four tracts of land to the extent of 55 acres had been donated to the bishop. Here again the happy farmers left their harvest fields and swelled the procession that went out to meet and to accompany their bishop and his attendants to their little frame chapel. The blessing of the church was followed by the Holy Sacrifice, during which the whole congregation continued to sing devotional hymns in their *Mutter Sprache*. The ceremonies ended with a brief discourse delivered by Father Henni.[34]

From this place Bishop Bruté went to Shelbyville, one of Father Bacquelin's stations. In order to reach Indianapolis enroute to Shelbyville he was obliged to share the driver's seat in the public stage with dark, threatening clouds overhead. "Five minutes after his arrival, a storm burst for the benefit of the driver and the nine persons in the coach who not only had no room for the old man [the bishop] but also tried to prevent the driver from giving him a place at his side, saying the stage was overloaded." It was night when he passed through Indianapolis and he could do no more than baptize two negroes. At Shelbyville the bishop found only twelve persons for Confirmation.[35]

Terre Haute was the next place to welcome the bishop. He arrived there in the evening of July 14 and confirmed a small class of four persons on the following morning. Then in company with Father Buteux who was in charge of these stations he proceeded to Thralls Station—St. Mary-of-the-Woods—where he administered Confirmation on the Feast of Our Lady of Mt. Carmel, July 16, to fifteen persons. Both said Mass at St. Mary-of-the-Woods on this feast and then returned to Terre Haute. At this place he was happy to find Father Buteux's new brick church rapidly building on

[34] *The Catholic Telegraph*, VII (1838), pp. 301–2; S. Bruté to J. Rosati. 8–16, 1838. St. LCA.; S. Bruté to A. Bruté, 7–16, 1838. Canon Bruté Collection; Franklin County Courthouse Records.

[35] S. Bruté to A. Bruté, 7–11, 1838. Canon Bruté Collection; S. Bruté to C. François, 7–23, 1838. CA of A. S. Bruté to S. Eccleston, 7–23, 1838. BCA. Case 241⁵.

lot No. 1, acquired, according to records, on January 12, 1837. The walls were already raised to the cornice and everything necessary for its completion was provided. New churches were more precious than gold mines to the devout bishop and on such occasions his joy was imparted to friends far and near. Thus in a letter commenced at St. Mary-of-the-Woods and finished at Terre Haute in the course of the same day, Camille Bruté, his sister-in-law, at Rennes, was given a hurried but accurate sketch of this Church. Another pen-picture of the same church was sketched in a letter to Bishop Blanc. On July 17 the bishop and Father Buteux crossed over into Illinois to visit the third church built by Father Lalumière which was situated at Paris Prairie. Here the bishop conferred the sacrament of Confirmation on eight persons. The venerable prelate had been traveling constantly now for three weeks and he felt the necessity of getting back home. Hence from the latter place he proceeded homeward, arriving there on July 19 accompanied by Father Ferneding, who had visited the German settlement of Mr. Picquet in Jasper County, Illinois. His presence afforded the German Catholics of Vincennes an opportunity of receiving the sacraments. On Sunday, July 22, he preached at Mass in the German language and after Vespers he gave a second instruction. He then proceeded to Jasper and Evansville to care for the spiritual needs of the German Catholics at these two places. The German population was growing rapidly in the episcopal city and the bishop was doing all in his power to procure for them a more regular attendance. Likewise, measures were being taken to erect a church on the lot given for that purpose by General Harrison when he last visited Vincennes. On the following day the bishop wrote Father François and described in brief terms his recent extensive tour, saying: "this is but a preparation for my visit to the North. My health is always precarious, but better, Courage a thousand times, my good friend. I see the seeds of an abundant harvest." His stay in the episcopal city was short. On July 24, he left again to visit Mt. Carmel,

Coffee, Shawneetown, and other stations in Southern Illinois, that had never received a visit from their bishop.[36]

Under these laborious visitations the venerable prelate was continually weakening and he felt the need more and more of having a coadjutor. Archbishop Eccleston had written to him the preceding January but since then the poor bishop had heard nothing more concerning a coadjutor. He, too, had written a second time directly to Rome but received no response. Believing it quite impossible to continue in this manner he wrote His Grace again late in July begging him to insist on this necessary help being granted:

> In the meantime I go on as well as I can with a task which is too heavy for me with my failing health. I am unable to face such a burden and I'm always threatened with a more serious relapse when these journeys are made during the cold and rainy weather. Since the month of May I have in a radius of 150 to 160 miles, administered the Sacrament of Confirmation ten times, and blessed three churches. These journeys would make about 1450 miles in two and one-half months. By stages 780 miles; by steamboat 502 miles; the remainder on horseback and on foot. The motion would not inconvenience me were it not for the change in temperature and the morning dews. One does his best but health suffers—there is the continual changing of beds, from bad to worse is the only alternative. Bishop Flaget gave me but five years to live and I am now finishing the fifth—Please think of my coadjutor.[37]

[36] *The United States Catholic Miscellany*, XVIII (1838), p. 91. Charleston, S. C.;   S. Bruté to C. François, 7–23, 1838.   CA of A.; S. Bruté to A. Blanc, 7–15, 1838, CA of A.;   S. Bruté to C. Bruté, 7–16;   1838.   Canon Bruté Collection;   S. Bruté to S. Eccleston, 7–23, 1838.   BCA.   Case 241[5];   *The Catholic Telegraph*, VII (1838), p. 316. Cincinnati;   Vigo County Courthouse Records.

[37] S. Bruté to S. Eccleston, 7–23, 1838.   BCA.   Case 241[5];   *The United States Catholic Miscellany*, XVIII (1838), p. 55.

With the month of August 1838 we enter upon the last year of the apostolic labors of Bishop Bruté. We have followed him on lengthy visitation tours traversing, since May, a distance of more than 1600 miles, visiting the Catholic centers in the southern and central portions of his immense diocese, as far north as Indianapolis. Then scarcely had he returned from the last of these missionary expeditions when he planned a still more extensive journey to the north. This, however, could not be undertaken until the latter part of August, owing to important proceedings at Vincennes. The diocese now numbered twenty-four priests and six seminarians. Through the zeal of the bishop six churches had already been erected in his diocese and twenty-three more were in the process of building. Within the episcopal city a diocesan seminary, a college for seculars, a free school for boys, an academy for young ladies, and a free school for girls had been established in the brief space of less than four years. During this time the venerable prelate toiled laboriously to found and to finance the above establishments, while he himself used an unfinished Cathedral of four bare walls without a substantial sanctuary, sacristy, or campanile.[1]

From the above brief survey we realize that the welfare of the Church was the one object of the bishop. That he considered himself bishop of the diocese embracing 53,000 square miles and not merely bishop of Vincennes, the episcopal city, is manifest in his great effort to provide churches for as many Catholic settlements as possible before he attempted to complete the Cathedral. Scarcely could it claim the name, owing to the severe poverty existing everywhere; nevertheless, it was under roof and there was ample space for the congregation to assemble and with that the bishop made himself contented until other stations received provi-

---

[1] *Berichte der Leopoldinen—Stiftung im Kaiserthume Oesterreich,* XIII, (1839), p. 7. S. Bruté to A. Bruté, 8–2, 1838. Canon Bruté Collection. Rennes.

sions for housing the congregations assembled for divine worship.   In order to facilitate and to accomplish more efficiently the work of erecting churches he visited his clergymen frequently, assisted them in the selection of sites for buildings, and planned ways and means to raise money to defray the expenses.   From his youth he abhorred debts and now when occupying the bishopric he preferred to beg rather than to permit his clergy to contract debts.   This frequent intercourse with his priests also gave him a thorough knowledge of their dispositions and abilities which enabled him the better to direct each one in the labor entrusted to him.   How well the venerable prelate succeeded in this apostolic charge may be inferred from the amount and quality of work accomplished.

It is evident that Catholicism had already made rapid progress within the diocese when Bishop Bruté concluded that his Cathedral was next in rank to receive attention. His health continued poor and from his knowledge of medicine he knew that life for him was but a matter of time.   Consequently, he was the more anxious to complete the Cathedral and make it worthy of its name.   From his correspondence we learn that the work was begun in the summer of 1838 and over and above numerous other duties the management of it required much of his time.   In a letter to Father Shawe, giving his reasons for withholding several favors at the moment, he added:

> Besides, we are completely upside down with our Church repairs. The Sanctuary unroofed, the nave and aisles a forest of scaffolding for the plastering, then the steeple is to be got up—the wood already cut at St. Francisville, and soon to sail up our proud Wabash, and go and tell the skies, not a lie, as the tall column in London, but the true love of Vincennes for the honor of God.[2]

In connection with the supervision of this material structure was another task, spiritual in nature, but none the less important.   Reverend Mr. Parret had completed

[2] J. R. Bayley, *Memoirs of Rt. Rev. S. W. G. Bruté*, p. 96.

his preparatory studies and awaited ordination to the holy priesthood. August 15, Feast of the Assumption of our Blessed Lady, had been designated for this solemn ceremony and Bishop Bruté considered it his sacred duty to conduct the young cleric's retreat. In a letter dated August 16, 1838, he related to Bishop Rosati that at last work on the Cathedral had been begun and at that date the sanctuary was uncovered for the purpose of repairing the roof and adding a belfry. When he arose on the vigil of the Feast the sky was dark and heavy. He trembled for the ordination ceremonies on account of the condition of the Church. Nevertheless, on the eve of the beautiful day the high altar was prepared in the roofless sanctuary as there was no other convenient place. The solemnity began on the following morning at six and lasted until eight o'clock. The sky continued very heavy but the wind sustained the clouds until one hour after Mass when the rain fell in torrents. Evidently the work on the Cathedral progressed at no great speed for in another letter to Bishop Rosati, dated January 4, 1839, he mentioned that the church was half plastered, the belfry begun months ago, and much space was still occupied by the cumbersome scaffolds.[3]

Prior to this date the bishop had not been able to devote much time to study over and above teaching in the seminary, but having at last been successful in establishing his educational plans at least in miniature institutions he felt entitled to the use of his library. Early as July 23, 1838, he had written Mr. Frenaye to look after the transportation of his library from the Mount where he had left it four years ago, but now on August 15, 1838, he wrote the Mount officially requesting that his library should now be sent to Vincennes, "his holy spouse—her dower." In the same letter he listed certain books that the college might keep in payment for Father Vabret, Reverend Mr. Berel, and Mr. Berel a lay brother, the St. Gabriel's College faculty, who

---

[3] S. Bruté to S. Eccleston, 8–9, 1838. BCA. Case 24I[7]; S. Bruté to J. Rosati, 8–16, 1838; 1–4, 1839. St. LCA. St. Louis, Mo.; H. J. Alerding, *History of the Diocese of Vincennes*, p. 226.

had been trained there for Vincennes. The impoverished bishop had been asked several times to pay the bill but he did not have the cash. It was but just that he endeavored to show in the following lines that he might have been considered to have had some claim on the Mountain.

> During my twenty years and more there I had neither salary nor pocket money. I procured from Charles X of France six hundred dollars, and then four hundred through M. de LaMennais and others. I gave the students, I can say, more than one thousand theologies. I always paid my own traveling expenses and freight on books. The loan of my library for these last four years ought to pay what I owe for those students.[4]

Whilst engaged in these manifold labors the untiring prelate still found time for visits to nearby congregations. His correspondence with the Archbishop of Baltimore reveals that he visited St. Peter's, Daviess County, on August 9, and again on the twentieth of the same month. Both letters informed Archbishop Eccleston of his failing health which was rendering him more and more incapable of the tremendous episcopal burden. In the latter he insisted again on being given a coadjutor and suggested the same three names of Fathers Petit, S. J., de la Hailandière and Reynolds, to which he added:

> Act on these recommendations, beloved and respected Metropolitan, and if with my colleagues, who are superior to me before God, you procure any other name that His providence will have ordered, any one from His adorable hand through your agency will please me and will be more able than I am to carry on His glory and kingdom in this part of His Church.

On the following day, August 21, he administered Confirmation at St. Mary's whence he returned to Vincennes to prepare for the journey to the north.[5]

[4] S. Bruté to S. Eccleston, 7–23, 1838. BCA. Case 24I[5]. M. Meline —E. McSweeny, *The Story of the Mountain*, I, p. 383.
[5] S. Bruté to S. Eccleston, 8–9, 1838. BCA. Case 24I[7]; 8–20, 1838. BCA. Case 24G[10].

Pursuant to plans formulated more than a month before Bishop Bruté left Vincennes on August 22, enroute to the northern part of his diocese where he would visit Joliet, Chicago, Michigan City, Laporte, Niles, South Bend, and Logansport, and then return by way of Indianapolis, Vernon, Madison, Louisville, and Bardstown. Before reaching the future metropolis on Lake Michigan where he arrived on the night of August 29 the bishop stopped at Joliet and then spent several days in ministering to the neglected Catholic laborers on the Illinois Canal where he shared the hospitality of their poor shanties. Descriptive of this visit Bishop Bruté wrote on August 30 in a letter to Mother Rose:

Chicago, one hundred and fifty miles north of Vincennes, on the Lake Michigan, southwest corner; a city of seven or eight thousand,—largest in the diocese. Alas! so small a wooden church where I have just celebrated the Divine Sacrifice, though we have near a thousand Catholics, they tell me;—one priest, Mr. O'Meara, —I had a second, Mr. Schaeffer, our Lord recalled him to heaven, I hope.

Arrived yesterday night from the line of the works of the Illinois canal. I will spend till Sunday here planning and devising for my successors. Also, so little of genius at plans!—unless our Lord himself pity such an immense *avenir* that I know not how to begin well! I dream of Sisters here—but how so? Col. Beaubien offers lots, etc. Very well—but Sisters?

A small wooden church, not sufficient for the fourth part on Sunday; and yet most (as usual) of our Catholics, are of the poorest; and the few, better off (as usual too, in our West), so eagerly busy at the great business of this West, growing rich, richer, richest;—too little ready, when the talk is only of lots, interest, and estate in Heaven; or of placing in its Bank on earth, by hands of the Church, and that poor Bishop, the cashier of said Bank, in this part of the world, who could sign bills of millions of eternal acquittal, etc., etc. Well Mother! tell me how I will succeed to spirit our busy Chicago to build a good, large, brick church. Another man,—yes, some proper man might succeed, not this unworthy Simon.

But enough! I must go to meet Mr. O'Meara, and devise plans. I would take more pleasure to speak of the shanties where I lived, and have done some duty these few days past; but now I am in the city, and owe myself as well to the city as to the shanties.[6]

On Friday, August 31, the missionary prelate wrote Archbishop Eccleston and described his present tour along the Illinois canal and at Chicago. Likewise, he informed His Grace of Col. Beaubien's promised donation to the Church, namely, two lots situated in the most promising part of the city. The same gentleman had also contributed four hundred dollars towards the erection of a new church. Bishop Bruté was kept extremely occupied during these days planning for the future church in this growing city but there were no Confirmations in Chicago on the occasion of this canonical visitation or if there were the pastor, Father T. O'Meara, neglected to record the ceremony. The fact that Bishop Bruté failed to make mention of it in his correspondence is sufficient evidence that Confirmation was not administered during this visit. Nevertheless, four infants claimed the honor of having received baptism at the hands of the devoted prelate. Francis Bush and Adam Sheinegar were baptised on Saturday, September 1, 1838, and Gwenthlean Kinzie and Margaret Gahan received holy baptism on Sunday, September 2, 1838.[7]

During his sojourn among the canal laborers Bishop Bruté had opportunity to make a thorough study of the immediate and remote causes of the factional riots—between the Corkonians and Connaught men, or as they were also called "Far-ups" and "Far-downs"—that had demanded the presence of Father Lalumière in this district several months previous. Striking at the root of this evil he wrote

[6] *Bruté—Seton Correspondence*, pp. 546–554. 1886; S. Bruté to J. Rosati, 8–16, 1838.   St. LCA.;   *St. Louis Cath. Hist. Review*, I. (1919), pp. 201–214; G. Garraghan, S. J., *Catholic Church in Chicago*, pp. 103–104.

[7] Baptismal Register in St. Mary's Church, Chicago. S. Bruté to S. Eccleston, 8–31, 1838. BCA. Case 241[8];   *Ill. Cath. Hist. Review*, III (1920–1), p. 423. Chicago.

Bishop Hughes from Chicago begging him to devise some
means of deterring emigrants when they first landed in
New York from enrolling themselves in these associations,
to discover their leaders, and "to find some way to their
conscience." This request was effective and found expression in a pastoral issued by the coadjutor Bishop of New
York, in which these associations were condemned.[8]

From Chicago Bishop Bruté proceeded to Michigan City
whose site four years previous had been marked by a few
houses but at this date had already grown to a considerable
size. Pushing on from there via Laporte and Niles he
reached South Bend on the morning of September 5, the day
following the departure of the Indians from Twin Lakes.
The visits at the last three places had been very brief and
afforded the traveling bishop no opportunity for rest. Owing to an appointment at Logansport he resolved to rush
away from South Bend in the same manner. Hence upon
entering Father Petit's little cabin he addressed him in the
words, "My son in an hour we start for Logansport." Then
forthwith the paternal-hearted bishop began to lavish upon
his young priest every possible consolation. Father Petit,
the *Robe Noir*, remained calm but his soul was crushed.
Since his ordination to the holy priesthood, October, 1837,
he had labored indefatigably and successfully among the
Indians and the Catholic Americans of northern Indiana
and southern Michigan. But it was especially in the midst
of the Indians where simplicity and frankness prevailed that
he loved to exercise his zeal for souls. He loved his dusky
children of the forest and in return they amply reciprocated
his unfeigned affection. Although he had not the leisure to
make special study of their language he succeeded after
several months in mastering it sufficiently to dispense with
the interpreter for confessions and ordinary conversations.
He was especially successful in effecting numerous conversions having on one occasion baptized 102 Indians within a

[8] J. Hassard, *Life of Most Rev. J. Hughes*, pp. 258–9; *Works of|
the Most Rev. J. Hughes*, I, pp. 318–319. New York. 1865.

period of two months. During the missionary career of
his predecessor measures had already been taken by the government to remove these Indians to reservations farther
west and the dread of these plans being effected had been
the constant fear of Father Petit.

Frequently Father Petit gave expression to these fears
in his correspondence to his Mother at Rennes. Early in
1838 he said: "This mission is threatened by an approaching destruction; the government wants to transfer the Indians to the other side of the Mississippi. I live between
hopes and fears, but then I place my hopes and fears in the
hands of the Lord." Three months later on April 4, 1838,
he wrote:

> I have a sad perspective of my Indian Mission soon being de-
> stroyed, and it is like a dark cloud to my present life.... Those
> christian souls will dry up without the aid of the Sacraments which
> they approach with so much love, when they are left to languish
> under an unknown sky where I their Father shall be unable to
> follow them. I shall do all in my power not to abandon them. If
> they leave I wish to accompany them as far as the Jesuit Missions
> on the Mississippi.... God alone knows how my heart grieves.

When writing his fond Mother again on July 9, 1838, he
informed her that:

> As long as the Indians remain in Indiana I shall be, I believe,
> their Missionary. Their attachment to me and I to them is stronger
> than ever today. Yet some days the fear comes upon me that I
> shall see this Mission destroyed. Ah! were I but free! When they
> go to the Mississippi, they would not be without a priest!

Suddenly, on August 30, 1838, the government commenced
collecting the Indians at Twin Lakes Encampment and Father Petit's fears became a realization. By night the officers
had succeeded in gathering about one hundred and seventy.
At the close of the third day, September 1, the enrollment
had reached seven hundred and fourteen. Two days more
were spent in preparation for the departure which took

place at nine o'clock on Tuesday morning, September 4. In the meantime Father Petit assembled them once more, offered the Holy Sacrifice of Mass, and divested the small chapel of its ornaments. After a heart-rending farewell he departed. Shortly after this, under pretence of a council the Indians were surprised and made prisoners of war. The officials then wishing to use the Catholic missionary as a police force invited Father Petit to accompany them, but he responded that it was impossible to accept the invitation without permission of his bishop, who had already refused him in order to prevent suspicion at connivance of the ecclesiastical authority to the rigorous measures taken by the civil power. It was at this moment that Bishop Bruté arrived at South Bend and bade Father Petit be ready to accompany him to Logansport.

After the brief respite of an hour at South Bend, Bishop Bruté in company with Father Petit resumed his travels enroute to Logansport. Along the road they met other travelers who acquainted them with distressing intelligence concerning the poor Indians. As a result of having been goaded along in the heat and dust for a distance of twenty-one miles on the first day several had died from the effects, while fifty-one were unable to resume the journey on the following day, owing to illness and a lack of transportation facilities. Consequently, these were left to follow later, while the others proceeded on their route. A distance of nine miles was traveled on the second day. Scarcity of water and food in the country together with the heat and dust retarded the progress of the emigration. On the third day a distance of seventeen miles was covered bringing the suffering Indians on the evening of September 6, to the encampment decided upon in the immediate vicinity of Logansport.

The knowledge of all this suffering and misery pierced Father Petit's heart with intense grief. Finally on the morning of September 7, Bishop Bruté after earnest prayer and deliberation granted the intrepid missionary leave to follow the emigrants on condition that he would return upon order or as soon as another missionary replaced him. The desolation of exile was transformed into genuine happiness at the appearance of Father Petit at camp. Men, women, and children rushed out to greet him and to receive his priestly blessing, while the non-Catholics present looked on in great astonishment. The "Black Robe" was permitted to come and go everywhere at liberty and General Tipton himself acknowledged that the missionary's power in camp was far superior to his own.

On Sunday morning, September 9, 1838, Bishop Bruté assisted by Fathers François and Mueller blessed the new church, erected on one of the tracts of land acquired by the pastor of Logansport. The venerable prelate was obliged to shorten the ceremony on account of his failing health. Father Benjamin Petit celebrated Mass at camp on this day. In the afternoon Bishop Bruté accompanied by the above clergymen visited the camp and administered Confirmation to twenty Indians who had been prepared by their missionary on the previous day. Father Petit, in a letter to his Mother, described this celebration as a grand triumph for the Catholic Faith. The whole city of Logansport was at the camp and everybody was equally astonished and edified at the admirable piety of the Indians. Bishop Bruté, who was much affected by this touching scene, has left us the following account:

Mr. Petit was invited to say Mass on Sunday in the midst of the camp under a great awning which shaded the altar. In the afternoon I myself visited the good Indians. A crowd of people composed of Catholics and Protestants from the city, was in attendance and no one grew tired of admiring the spirit of recollection and resignation of those true Christians. As I approached, Mr. Petit came first and knelt for the blessing, then all received it kneeling on the road that led to the tent. Following this ceremony they took their places very orderly and some with books and others by heart, sang Vespers in the Ottawa language. I recited the Oration and delivered a sermon which a young interpreter translated with great intelligence and piety. Then they intoned the *Veni Creator* in Ottawa and after the first verse I proceeded to administer the sacrament of Confirmation. The confirmed numbered twenty. How much did we regret that so many were deprived of the same grace owing to their early departure. I closed the services by giving Benediction. Then whilst we recited the rosary in common I accompanied Mr. Petit into the tents of the sick, where one received Extreme Unction and another received Baptism; both died that night.

An account of this celebration was likewise recorded by Judge Polke in his "Journal of an Emigrating Party of Potawatomi Indians, 1838." "The priest formerly attached to the Catholics among the Potawatomies asked and obtained leave to say Mass today and perform the ceremonies of his Church in camp. The rites are now being performed."[9]

Bishop Bruté and Father Petit departed from Logansport on Monday morning September 10. The missionary went north to South Bend for his necessary baggage, while the bishop proceeded southward and alone on his visitation route. Short visits were made to Indianapolis, (North) Vernon, Madison, and Louisville, whence he went to Bardstown to assist at the celebration on the following Sunday. Father Richard P. Miles who had been nominated to the new see erected in Tennessee by Pope Gregory XVI on July 28, 1837, received episcopal consecration as the first Bishop of Nashville in the Cathedral of Bardstown, Kentucky, on Sunday, September 16, 1838. Bishop Flaget had gone to Europe, hence Bishop David was chosen to be consecrator. Precarious health forced him to decline the invitation and

[9] *Indiana Magazine of History*, XXI (1925), p. 318; *Annales de la Propagation de la Foi*, XI (1838), pp. 382–400. Lyons; *The Catholic Historical Society of Indiana*, Bulletin No. 2. pp. 5–6. Indianapolis 1927; Abbé Bruté de Rémur, *Vie de Monseigneur Bruté de Rémur*, pp. 298–302. Rennes. 1887; S. Bruté to J. Rosati, 8–16, 1838. St. LCA.; *Ave Maria*, I, (1865), pp. 518–521. Notre Dame, Ind.; L. Esarey, *A History of Indiana*, I, pp. 377–85. Fort Wayne, 1924; J. Rothensteiner, *History of the Archdiocese of St. Louis*, I. pp. 677–688; Cass County Courthouse Records.

thus Bishop Rosati became consecrator assisted by Bishops
Bruté and Chabrat. The prelate of Vincennes described this
occasion as "Bardstown's glorious day." It was indeed a
memorable day for every Christian present, but its special
significance was immensely greater to a prelate of Bishop
Bruté's calibre—possessing as he did a heart steeped in a
love and a knowledge of our Lord which no books or pondering could give him; which could be gained only by living
in His company. The early morning services marked the
close of a successful retreat which had been conducted at the
Cathedral. Six hundred received Holy Communion on this
occasion. In a letter to Mother Rose at Emmitsburg, Bishop
Bruté said this solemnity

> was followed at nine o'clock by the consecration of Bishop Miles,
> a Dominican Father from Maryland: forty-seven years, looking
> so venerable as Bishop Rosati looked, too, consecrating him for
> Nashville, Tennessee. Pray, pray indeed, for the founders of the
> Church in this far West, that a share of the immense blessings you
> enjoy in the East be granted them.[10]

On Monday following this celebration the Bishop of Vincennes departed for his episcopal city where he arrived on
Wednesday after having been absent from August 22 to
September 19. He had travelled alone more than nine hundred miles. Of this distance three hundred miles had been
traversed in open stages or rather *char-a-bancs* without
tops. Upon his return the feeble prelate was exceedingly
prostrated. Health was rapidly failing him. At Logansport he had been forced to shorten the ceremonies when
blessing the church, and, likewise, at the consecration of

---

[10] *Bruté—Seton Correspondence*, pp. 553–4. 1886; *Annales de la
Propagation de la Foi*, XI (1838), p. 400. Lyons.; Shea, III, p. 608;
V. F. O'Daniel, *An American Apostle*, p. 58. Washington, D. C. 1923;
The Father of the Church in Tennessee, pp. 256–7. New York. 1926;
J. H. Lamott, *History of the Archdiocese of Cincinnati 1821–1921*,
p. 353–4. New York. 1921; P. Guilday, *The Life and Times of John
England*, II, p. 399. New York, 1927; *The National Pastorals of
the American Hierarchy*, p. 120. Washington, D. C. 1923; B. J.
Webb, *The Centenary of Catholicity in Kentucky*, p. 174. Louisville,
1884.

Bishop Miles he was too ill to remain in church during Father Timon's sermon. Such tremendous labors as he had been engaged in were far beyond his physical ability and it was utterly impossible for will-power to carry him along much farther. Pleadingly and beseechingly he had in numerous letters made known his wants and begged his Metropolitan to secure a coadjutor for Vincennes and now to find on his return that the Archbishop's prolonged silence continued, he was overwhelmed with sorrow for his suffering Church. Patiently he bore the grief for another fortnight and then poured out his heart again to the cold-hearted Metropolitan, asking him: "Kindly read this attentively."

Your Grace,

On September 15 I had the honor of writing to you from Bardstown—a brother, somewhat disappointed, to his brother; a colleague to his Metropolitan. I have, however received no answer.

It is the heart that complains, but still more do business affairs suffer. First of all, the naming of a coadjutor is of prime importance to this diocese. (My health is in question.) These long journeys exhaust me and are shortening my days. I have already travelled about 4000 miles since the first of May, and more than 900 miles from August 22 to September 19. Our territory is very extensive.

A steamboat carries you, My Lord, to Norfolk, or the railroad to Richmond, or to Winchester which are the most distant places you have to visit in your diocese. This diocese contains from fifty-two to fifty-four thousand square miles and the missions are located at the further extremities, while the roads for hundreds of miles are such as you have never travelled for ten miles. Travelling in Maryland even twenty-five years ago was like a Berlin or French stage compared to our western accommodations. Therefore, I repeat, my health enters into the questions to be considered as well as the spiritual and temporal administration, and the transmission by testament of our extensive church property.

Your ecclesiastical property is distributed among yourself, a body of trustees, the Jesuits, the Sulpicians, the Sisters of Charity, the Carmelites, and the Sisters of the Visitation; while here all rests upon me—more than fifty or sixty different sites, several of which are of considerable value—(more than 1500 acres of land, in 80–160 and 300 acres lots—others of 40, 7, 4, etc.)   All is on my shoulders, according to the canon of the first Council, notwithstanding the fact that I objected to the security and advantages of this system.   It is regrettable that between two States and twenty-two counties the deeds cannot be obtained of a uniform kind, and, assuredly, if there are good ones, there are also bad ones.   Then, in Illinois, if the taxes are not paid within the year the property is sold.   That happened to me once, in the case of a lot;   imagine my embarrassment at the time.

This affair of a coadjutor, so long expected, has become, shall I say it?—hateful and ridiculous.   Father Petit at the Jesuit College in Kentucky has been refused me (Father Petit himself did not refuse).   Father de la Hailandière is obliged to return to France soon, for at least a year, and how am I alone to attend to this immense trust?   Not a single one (Yes, one,—M. Lalumière— he alone) of the members of our clergy is naturalized, nor has even taken the first steps towards naturalization, nor would they wish to do so, even if I desired it.   Half of them are like myself (as I had been those 25 years in Maryland)—no exeat, permission *ad revocationem des evêques.*

My Lord, what are the reasons for refusing me a coadjutor? I have here none of those reasons that exist in New York.   Bishop Rosati has the promise of obtaining one whenever he wants one, but he has not the urgent need of one that I have in regard to ecclesiastical poverty.   This responsibility is divided in his diocese the same as it is in yours.   Two religious orders make up about two-thirds of his clergy while my clergy are all secular priests. Likewise, he has two religious Communities of women, while the only one I have is depending entirely on me—(the Sisters' lots consist of almost an entire square, facing on three streets.)

I have lost no time in acquiring lots and land on every side because I thought I owed this to the future Church and the intentions of the two associations, the German and the French.   However, I greatly desire to have a coadjutor in order to make everything secure, and Father Petit and Father de la Hailandière, to whom I owe the half of these acquisitions, are refused me—I am answered neither by you nor by Rome.

My last letter from Cardinal Fransoni is dated July 22, and is in answer to a letter of mine written from New Orleans on January 17. It contains not one word on this important subject— nor on Texas, concerning which I wrote a powerful appeal, with Bishop Blanc—(but they have taken care of Texas—hence it matters little whether they spoke about it in my letter)....—the only answer I get is that concerning the two "cases of conscience"....

Kind and respected colleague deign to reply.[11]

The above correspondence paints a vivid picture of the neglected prelate's condition and the colossal burden that he was forced to bear practically alone. Nevertheless, this was not all. Other trials appeared as soon as he had returned to Vincennes and the bishop was sorely tried from all sides. Father Vabret, President of St. Gabriel's College, fell ill; the doctors pronounced his case lung trouble and ordered him south for the winter. Then in behalf of the interests of the growing diocese the bishop deemed it expedient to send Father de la Hailandière, his Vicar General and quasi-coadjutor, to Europe to procure more missionaries and financial aid. This meant the loss of important assistance to Bishop Bruté and he admitted in a letter to Bishop Blanc that Father Vabret's illness had subjected them to great difficulties at Vincennes, but he added: "with God's help I shall face them."

Before these two clergymen had sailed for the South, the one to remain there for his health, the other enroute to Europe, there came a call for priests to be dispatched at once to the Illinois canal. Fathers Benoit and Plunket were immediately rushed to the scene, 250 miles distant where to their sorrow they found the alarming epidemic even more dreadful than the messengers had announced. A malignant

[11] S. Bruté to S. Eccleston, 10–8, 1837. BCA. Case 24I⁶; *Bruté— Seton Correspondence*, p. 553. 1886.

fever was raging throughout the line of works and claimed many victims daily. This proved to be a very laborious mission for the two priests. During their sojourn at the canal they were called upon to attend between six and seven hundred people who succumbed to the disease.[12]

In the meantime the venerable prelate began to experience trials of illness among his clergy. Father O'Meara was prostrate at Chicago. Father François came from Logansport early in October to visit the bishop and fell ill at Vincennes where he was obliged to remain until the sixteenth of the month. Upon his departure Father Corbe from Cat River arrived at the Bishop's house for a visit and he, too, took ill and was forced to remain at Vincennes until October 29. At this date the epidemic had already reached Fort Wayne and Father Mueller informed the bishop that fifty of his parishioners had been carried away by the fever. These alarming statistics caused the bishop to be much disturbed about his priests along the canal and, likewise, at Logansport, Fort Wayne, and Shelbyville. However, encouraging news was received from Father O'Meara at Chicago. He had recovered from the siege of fever and was busily occupied with the foundation of his new stone church. He was happy to inform the bishop that this foundation 85 x 45 feet was already raised above ground. Father Petit also sent His Lordship an edifying letter from Quincy, Illinois, and assured the bishop that all was well with him.[13]

After a few weeks' cessation from the lengthy visitation tours the bishop believed his health to be much improved. Consequently, he resumed his classes in the Seminary, took Father Vabret's class in French at the Academy, and assumed the parochial work of Father de la Hailandière at the Cathedral. Thus with the help of Father Berel, vice president of the College, and Father Parret, he was able

[12] S. Bruté to A. Blanc, 10–20, 1838. CA of A. Notre Dame, Ind.; S. Bruté to J. Rosati, 11–3, 1838. St. LCA.; M. Meline—E. McSweeny, *op. cit.*, I, pp. 383–4.

[13] S. Bruté to C. François, 10–17, 1838; 10–29, 1838. CA of A.

to do the work of the absent Fathers. While his interest in the teaching profession never waned he realized that his educational foundations could not be conducted successfully for any length of time under such a sparse faculty. In view of this and the future of his diocese he wrote his bosom friend Abbé Jean de LaMennais at Ploërmel requesting him to send a colony of Brothers of Christian Instruction to take charge of the schools at Vincennes. Together with his letter—his last to de LaMennais—he sent another addressed to Augustine Bruté beseeching him to entrust to Father de la Hailandière all that he wished to send the poor Bishop of Vincennes, but he forbade his brother to send anything for personal comfort.[14] The good bishop allowed himself no comfort or privilege which he could not share with others. His spirit of poverty was admirable and his charity was universal and unbounded. All that was poor and uncomfortable he reserved for himself and it was a common occurrence for the generous prelate to deprive himself of his linens to bestow them on the sick and indigent. Often Bishop Bruté returned home without a shirt, and he never permitted any one who called upon him for alms to go away empty handed. On such occasions, contrary to the usual practice, he did not give the worn and castaway garments, but the best clothes he possessed.

Although Bishop Bruté's health seemed at times to be improved, he himself knew that it was fast failing him. This, however, did not deter him from active good or cause him to lose interest in the general welfare of Catholicism in America. Since the previous winter he had kept a watchful eye on the new Republic of Texas whose religious status was guided by hirelings disguised in shepherd's attire. Within the confines of the entire state there were only two clergymen and these were priests who according to canon law would have been regarded as non-functioning. They said Mass daily because they were supported by the people, but

[14] S. Bruté to J. de LaMennais, 10–20, 1838; S. Bruté to A. Bruté, 10–21, 1838. Canon Bruté Collection.

they gave no instruction and heard no confessions; lived with their household, and were veritable stumbling blocks to the little faith that still survived in the hearts of the poor people. Early in the year Bishop Bruté had collaborated with Bishop Blanc in sending to the Sacred Congregation a detailed account of existing conditions in Texas. Rome, too, had heeded the advice and ordered measures to prohibit the evil but Bishop Bruté foresaw those measures to be too mild. A Visitor's power was far too limited to be able to crush the evil, whereas a bishop would possess faculties to exterminate the evil without further delay. Since Rome had failed to recognize his interest in Texas the venerable prelate wasted no further time writing the Sacred Congregation, nevertheless, he continually advised Bishop Blanc how to proceed and also kept in constant touch with the Reverend Visitor-Father Timon. Upon reading an interesting letter from the latter and desiring to do all in his power to end the undesirable condition he wrote at once advising Bishop Blanc as follows:

> Send a short and precise letter to Rome with a little map of Texas on the opposite page (here is a little map) and give in ten or fifteen lines a complete summary of our political situation of unalterable independence which is already recognized by France, England, etc., so that Rome will send us a bishop immediately or at least a Vicar-Apostolic. To wait or to rely upon the Bishop of Monterey would be to ruin everything.

Undoubtedly the establishment of a Vicariate Apostolic in Texas, July 16, 1841, is to be ascribed in part to the interest and continued agitation of Bishop Bruté.[15]

Turning from this regrettable condition we find the bishop's heart gladdened by the return of Father Benoit from the plague-stricken canal region. A few days later he

---

[15] C. Deuther, *Life and Times of Rt. Rev. John Timon*, pp. 68–9. Buffalo. 1870; Fitzmorris, M. A. *Four Decades of Catholicism in Texas, 1820–1860* p. 45. Washington, D. C. 1926; S. Bruté to A. Blanc, 10–31, 1838; 1–26, 1839. CA of A.; S. Bruté to J. Timon, 12–7, 1838. CA of A.

wrote Bishop Blanc to inform him that this good priest would visit New Orleans shortly after Christmas in behalf of his church, St. Mary's, Perry County, on the Ohio. In the same letter he expressed his appreciation for the generous charity lavished on two other priests of the diocese, Fathers Lalumière and Buteux, and prophesied that rich blessings in return would descend upon New Orleans.

> In twenty or thirty years after my death you will say: "I wish that this poor Bishop of Vincennes could see this change and development—it is owing to the charity shown to him.
>
> Father Benoit is this good priest(from St. Mary's, near our Rome, on the Ohio, and Troy) whose letters I read for you last winter. His devotedness touched me deeply. God has blessed him— granted him consoling conversions of Protestants and also Catholic families who had fallen away.

Moreover, favorable news was received from Father Petit the misionary who accompanied the Potawatomies to their new home. Writing on November 13, 1838, from Osage River in Kansas, the Black Robe gives his bishop details of the journey which ended on November 4, and their meeting with the Jesuit, Father Hoeken, to whose missionary zeal these Christians were entrusted. Portions of this letter deserve a place in our narrative.[16]

> Monseigneur:
>
> To fulfill the promise you exacted of me when, at Logansport, I received your parting blessing, I must render Your Lordship an account of our long and painful journey. The very day you yourself started for Bardstown, where you were called upon for the consecration of a new Bishop for our America.... I took the road to South Bend to procure my little necessary baggage. Whilst I awaited the public conveyance at the hotel, a traveller advanced and presented a sketch in crayon which seemed good and which represented the ceremony of Confirmation in Camp—the altar at the

---

[16] S. Bruté to C. François, 11–9, 1838. CA of A.; S. Bruté to A. Blanc, 11–15, 1838. CA of A.

foot of a great tree, the linen draperies, Monseigneur, Mr. Mueller and myself, a young interpreter and all the Indians with grave demeanor, pious and so solemn. Several questions were asked concerning their language, habits, and traditions. I started and arrived at South Bend on the 11th, towards noon. I spent a part of the evening hearing the confessions of the sick who had asked for me.... Next morning I started again for Logansport; I counted upon joining the emigrants at least at Lafayette but such speed was made that I met my Indians at Danville, only. They were walking on the right bank of the river and the stages' route followed continuously at the left. Several times I strove to obtain a conveyance to carry me and my baggage to Danville, but to no effect. Finally, we had to move on to Perrysville where, leaving my luggage behind me, I profited by the kindness of a Catholic, Mr. Young, who offered me one of his horses and accompanied me as far as Danville....

It was Sunday, Sept. 16. Scarcely had I arrived when a Colonel came along to look for a favorable camping-ground. Shortly afterward I saw our poor Christians, walking in file, surrounded by soldiers who hastened their march under a burning sun, at noon, in the midst of clouds of dust, followed by the transport wagons in which were found thrown pellmell several sick persons, children and women too frail to walk. They encamped half a mile without the city where soon I joined them. I found the camp as you, Monseigneur, had witnessed it at Logansport; a scene of desolation— the sick and dying on all sides. Mostly all the children, overcome by the heat, had fallen into a complete state of languor and extenuation. I baptized several new-born babes—happy Christians— whose first steps will lead from this land of exile to the heavenly abode. The General to whom I presented myself, expressed his satisfaction at seeing me and, by unexpected condescension, he rose and offered me his chair—the only one in the place. That night was the first I spent in a tent. Next day the Indians were hustled into transport wagons, the horses were mounted. At the moment of departure, Judge Polke, Chief Leader, came to present me with a horse which the Government rented of an Indian for my use on the road. The Indian, at the same moment, came up to me and

said: "Father, I, I give it to you, saddle, bridle and all!" We
started for another encampment where we were to be allowed a
few days' rest.... When we quitted the camp, we left behind us
six graves under the shade of the cross. There, the General dismissed his small army and he, too, left us....

Soon we found ourselves on the great Illinois prairies, from one
camp to another under a burning sun and without any shelter. The
prairies vast as the ocean and the eye seeks in vain for a tree; not
a drop of water there. It was a veritable torture for our sick, of
whom some died each day from fatigue and misery. We began
evening prayers in common, and the white men, attracted through
curiosity, were astonished to find so much piety in the midst of so
many trials. Our evening exercises consisted of a chapter in
Catechism, prayer, and a hymn, *Je mats ma confiance*, which I en-
toned in the Indian language and which was repeated by the whole
audience with an impetus that these new Christians bring to all
acts of Religion....

Sunday morning the Indians attended the Holy Sacrifice. I
preached on the Gospel of the day, recommended the recitation of
the rosary during the route. Then I folded my chapel, lowered the
tents, and mounted once more. Ordinarily we did not travel on
Sunday, consequently Mass was preceded by morning prayers and
Catechism, followed by the rosary. In the afternoon another reunion took place for Catechism. Vespers was sung in the Indian
tongue, the rosary followed, then evening prayer and a short
sermon....

I could not but feel elated during the trip, with the attentions
of the Catholics. When we encamped near a town where there
were some, they came to see me, invited me to breakfast the next
day before the start, and indeed did all in their power to manifest
their joy at seeing a Priest. A few days' journey from the River
Illinois, I was stricken with fever; an old Frenchman came to me
in camp and made me promise, by force of pleading, to take a
few days' rest at his home. Next morning he introduced his wife,
he had brought a conveyance for me—but the fear to find myself
once more far behind the emigration crowd and the difficulties which
would result, made me give a decided refusal. Hardly had we
arrived in Naples, where we crossed the Illinois, than a Protestant,

married to a French Catholic, from Vincennes, hearing that a sick priest was among the emigrants stationed there for two days, came to offer his house. I accepted, and, thanks to the great care lavished upon me, the fever was cut short. I boarded the public wagon at Naples and started in advance for Quincy, in order to end up my cure by a few days' respite in that city. There I met a German priest, Mr. Bricksweide, and a German congregation, who received me with a welcome hard to be imagined. I was also well received by some American Catholics and by several Protestants—the wealthiest of the place—who offered me hospitality.

Upon the arrival of the Indians at Quincy, the inhabitants who compared this emigration with preceding ones, could not help but express their surprise at the modesty of our Christians, their tranquillity, and their general demeanor. . . .

As we marched along the left bank of the Mississippi, the heat was excessive, the weather sultry, the water bad. On the opposite bank the temperature was cooler, sometimes even cold, and the change produced a salutary effect upon the health of the Indians. In Missouri, we had scarcely any sick. The Indians were permitted to hunt on the route; from Illinois to the Indian territory was a fine hunting-ground abounding in deer, quails, and pheasants. But it was our misfortune upon approaching the assigned country, to find out that game became more and more rare and the woods more and more scarce. . . .

At a day's journey from the Osage River, Father Hoeken, S. J., came to meet us. He speaks Potawatomi and Kickapoo. He announced his intention to leave the country of the Kickapoo, where he resided and to establish himself amongst my Christians. Hence, Monseigneur, your aim and mine are achieved. This young Christian Mission, in the midst of anxiety, exile, and the ravages of epidemics, receives every possible aid from Religion. The sick are anointed, the ground where they are buried is blessed, the faith kept and the practices of religious duty are accomplished. Even in temporal sorrow and want, the one whom the Indians call their Father has had the consolation to give assistance. And, now once more in the hands of the able Jesuits, they need not regret the violent blow which severed them from our country, as they say, where their fathers rest. You wished, Monseigneur, for the Glory of

God and the salvation of these Christians—I looked for nothing else. Let us hope your wishes will be fulfilled. Starting September 4, we arrived November 4. The number of Indians at the departure was 800. Some escaped; about thirty died. I believe the number did not exceed 650 at the arrival.

Awaiting the order from Your Lordship that will separate me from my children. I am, etc.[17]

Late in October Bishop Bruté's valuable library arrived from Mount St. Mary's but he was somewhat troubled to find it considerably depleted. More than half of his books bore no mark of ownership and, therefore, the Mountain seemed to experience great difficulty in distinguishing them from the college library and it required several months to settle matters satisfactorily. The venerable prelate wished the Mount to accept books in payment for the three students who had been trained for Vincennes, but evidently the president wanted the bishop to pay cash. The two parties concerned seemed to enter into no satisfactory conclusion when finally on December 12, 1838, the bishop wrote: "Simply send me the bill." At the same time in addition to what he had already told of his claim to the Mount he recalled other sums of money paid by himself.

$150 to Baltimore for the first students sent thither from the Mountain. $600 paid to St. Sulpice for those students who went to France from the Mountain and who, upon their return, rendered valuable services to their Alma Mater; besides the expenses of their journey which I collected from friends. My journey to France from the Mountain in 1824, I paid myself. I gave Father Dubois $1,700 reserving the right to take back $300 if I left the College, or if it should be discontinued, but I never asked for the money and left it to the College, and accepted only the clothing, like the other missionaries whom we always clothed on their departure. I served 20 years and more without any salary; drank water, and walked to spare stage-fare; never made Niagara or other travels though I had often wished to visit Montreal's old

---

[17] *Annales de la Propagation de la Foi*, XI (1838), pp. 400–8. Lyons.

library and archives. We sent seventy or more priests to the different dioceses and the most of them we educated without any money from their bishops.

The College then sent him a bill for $416. The bishop acknowledged a $200 indebtedness but called for arbitration on a larger sum. Reverend Mr. Butler was chosen arbiter in the case and decided that the charges for the three students from Vincennes be reduced to $382. Bishop Bruté accepted the verdict but Providence again came to his assistance by sending a charitable lady, Miss Emily Harper, to pay the bill.[18]

This ingratitude on the part of the Mountain certainly pained the generous bishop intensely. Not only was he forgotten where so many claims demanded recognition but also in higher circles and in matters of greater moment, his just demands were ignored. He depicts this emphatically in a letter to His Grace on the Feast of the Presentation, November 21, 1838.

> I could not take a better day to chide you again—for I would wish to do so, very gently under the auspices of Mary, since we are both servants of this kind Mother and, under her direction, I would like to obtain some explanation of your silence for more than two months after my letter from Bardstown, and the two others written after, and the silence previous to that—in fine, almost the whole year.
>
> There were, however, very serious reasons, why I should have had an answer, while I cannot imagine one, which would have caused you to refuse to write to me. I beg of you once more as our Metropolitan, to let me know your decision in regard to the cases which I submitted to you, for example, the request I made to have a coadjutor—it seems to me that this subject called for some correspondence. Do write a short letter at least to your colleague.
>
> I fear that you do not even care to take my letters from the mail, hence I have entrusted this one to a mutual friend who is, likewise, a man of great discretion. I call to your attention this time only

[18] M. Meline—E. McSweeny, *op. cit.*, I, pp. 384–5; 390–1.

one important question, that of a coadjutor. It has been a cause of great anxiety to me and of contradictory resolutions which would have been settled by the long expected letter from you and from the Propaganda.

Finally I made up my mind, and, without further delay, what I should have done at an earlier date, I did without any further intelligence on the subject of this coadjutorship. I sent M. de la Hailandière to France. My Lord, I would have too much to write on this subject, so I hasten to beg you to send an answer to your colleague and old friend. I ask it in the presence of our Lord and under the auspices of Mary, this very day.

P. S. With all trust in Providence under Superiors, both you and the Sacred Congregation, who abandoned me entirely to that Divine Providence without any regard to the letters, which apparently they do not deem worthy of notice. I do not understand this silence, and I am doing my utmost to judge no one, but really, the simplest rule and the one that our good M. Emery insisted upon, in regard to correspondence, is that every letter, even that of a servant, demands an answer. I have certainly been much better these last two months, and if I would have had rest I believe I would have been cured—but I am, like my missionaries, at my post. I am no better than my brethren, provided I finish my course I am not making my life more precious than myself. The cause of my ill health remaining, I may die at any time, as I have been warned. With all the responsibility of a first foundation resting on my shoulders, I considered it advisable to ask for a coadjutor.

I have done my duty in asking for one, and am still doing it by insisting .... to treat your suffragan thus, is not, to my mind, the duty of a Metropolitan. A too wide extended Metropolitan See causes him overwork and fatigue. I believe it would be better to divide it, but in the meantime, will you not answer my letters and correspondence, my dear archbishop?[19]

This obvious neglect on the part of the Metropolitan urged the bishop to take up the affair with his colleagues in the West. It finds expression in letters to Bishop Rosati

[19] S. Bruté to S. Eccleston, 11–21, 1838. BCA. Case 241[10].

on December 4 to 18, where he complains that notwithstanding eight or ten letters written to Archbishop Eccleston he has received no reply. He confirmed this in correspondence to Bishop Blanc when on December 14, he said:

> I seem to be in bad grace with our dear Metropolitan, though the cause is unknown to me. He has suppressed all correspondence with me, though I cannot recall giving him any reason to do so. After waiting eight months I complained to Bishop Rosati when we were at Bardstown for the consecration of Bishop Miles, 'Our Metropolitan does not like to write' was his answer. At Bardstown I wrote on September 16, 1838, a most fraternal letter asking for a reply. In another month I wrote from here and in the last three months I have written at least three or four letters without receiving an answer. A real mystery of nearly a year's duration and towards one who has been the servant of Maryland, Baltimore, and the Mountain for twenty-five years and who when he was a simple priest was treated very differently by the predecessors of this worthy Metropolitan—one of my own children at St. Mary's. I received three times as many letters from Archbishop Carroll and ten times as many from Archbishop Maréchal as from our present strange Metropolitan.

This was not spoken through irritability, heartlessness, vanity, or otherwise. Bishop Bruté loved, esteemed, and respected Archbishop Eccleston, but he added: "If he finds it too tiresome to correspond with us that, in my opinion, will confirm the necessity of forming a Metropolis in the West so that the interests of our future Church here be more actively looked after."[20]

Despite the fact that Bishop Bruté was left to bear the burden alone when scarcely able to be active, he was constanly occupied with a multitude of duties characteristic of a pioneer prelate's days. He filled the offices of professor and director in both the seminary and the academy and performed the varied duties exacted of a missionary pastor.

[20] S. Bruté to J. Rosati, 12–4, 1838; 12–18, 1838. St. LCA.; S. Bruté to A. Blanc, 12–14, 1838. CA of A.

Regardless of the hour, the distance, or the weather he responded promptly and cheerfully to every sick call and it happened often that those to whom he administered the consolations of religion were not nearer death than the prelate who attended them. The Good Master, whose flock he tended, was not unmindful of the manifold sacrifices made by the suffering shepherd for the salvation of souls and according to the following accounts, that were related by eye witnesses, our Blessed Lord on several occasions deigned to give visible evidence of His pleasing recognition.

One stormy day the feeble prelate was called to attend a sick person living on the opposite side of the Wabash river in Illinois. He prepared without hesitation and departed immediately with his guide. Upon their arrival he prepared the happy Christian to meet his God and after administering to him the sacraments they again departed on their homeward journey. Owing to the continued downpour of rain, all at the episcopal residence were in consternation to see His Lordship traveling in such weather and upon his return they strove hurriedly to relieve him of his wet cloak and to offer him dry clothing. Great was the surprise of all to find the good bishop's cloak perfectly dry.

On another occasion the virtuous prelate was summoned one bitter winter night to attend a dying man who lived several miles from the city. Cheerfully the bishop responded but after having walked a short distance through the deep snow his guide began to complain and then roughly refused to proceed farther because his feet were stiff and numb with cold. The bishop who was fervently reciting his beads interrupted his prayer long enough to request the guide to walk in his footsteps. Heeding this request the man's suffering ceased immediately and he continued the trip with inexpressible willingness.

The inexhaustible zeal for souls that burned within the bosom of Bishop Bruté did not permit him to visit only those parishioners who called for him; on the contrary, he frequently went in search of those who had strayed from the flock and strove to bring them back within the fold. All were his friends, regardless of race or nationality, but the poor and needy were his favored children. Heaven only can recount the number that he befriended and aided especially during the cold winters. This charitable apostle was often seen making his way from hut to hut in the poorer section where he found many a hovel without fuel and the occupants shivering with cold. After speaking a few cheerful words which always contained some timely counsel he took leave only to enter another cabin that was even more destitute. Before nightfall he would be seen directing teamsters with loads of wood to these lowly cabins and the suffering occupants could be heard blessing the name of their "Angel of Mercy." On more than one occasion he purchased all the wood at the market and then was seen escorting as many as five and six wagon loads along the street at one time, directing them to different homes. This was not an occasional practice of the bishop but a common one during the winter seasons.[21]

Notwithstanding the fact that these multifarious labors were far too colossal for a declining prelate, letters testify to the continuation of Archbishop Eccleston's prolonged silence on the subject of a coadjutor for Vincennes. In the midst of this trying situation Bishop Bruté did not abandon his post. On the contrary, he abandoned all to divine Providence, continued his labors in the episcopal city, visited his clergy in the vicinity, and through correspondence guided the labors of the most distant missionaries. At this particular time he wrote frequently to advise Father Shawe how to proceed in the midst of the various difficulties he had to encounter when engaged in the erection of the first Catholic church in Madison. On one occasion he bade the worried priest to appeal to Fathers Ferneding and Schneiderjans, assuring him that a collection throughout these settlements would probably afford him fifty or one hundred dollars

[21] H. S. Cauthorn, *St. Francis Xavier Cathedral*, p. 52; **Page** Family traditions. Vincennes.

toward his church. Shortly after this he offered to send Reverend Mr. O'Reilly, after Christmas, to care for Madison while Father Shawe would go to Canada for the purpose of collecting for his church. The venerable prelate did not fail to remind his zealous missionary that God is always mindful of his many sacrifices; moreover that he is not alone in sufferings, losses, and trials:

> You see my dreadful losses in place of success. The good priests, my hope, die. Priests, most troublesome, come and go. Likewise the seminarians, the good go; for example Mr. Dumerla, while the bad pierce the heart that cherished and fostered them. But what of it, ... it may be the personal gain of the bishop and the priests if they do not succeed to benefit the diocese or a particular mission. But for all that we should neglect nothing.

Again he wrote: "Judge if your old Bishop is in trials with plastering, steeples, farms, houses, buildings, arranging deeds, etc." to be managed alone.[22]

At this date the scholarly prelate was also much concerned about establishing the authentic date and name of the early foundation at Vincennes, before it would become impossible to retrace them. Consequently, he wrote a very detailed letter concerning this subject to Bishop Signay of Quebec and begged him to entrust the work to one of the zealous priests residing near the archives of the Mother Church of our West. Not only was he anxious to establish the origins of the inaugural mission in his new diocese but he also wished to preserve the noble deeds of the early missionaries who labored in this territory. This task he entrusted to Father St. Cyr in a letter where he enumerated the early Jesuits and designated St. Louis, Belleville, and Quebec as places fruitful in material.[23]

[22] S. Bruté to A. Blanc, 1–8, 1839. CA of A.; S. Bruté to J. Rosati, 1–4, 1839; 1–11, 1839; 1–15, 1839. St. LCA.; S. Bruté to C. & A. Bruté, 12–27, 28, 29, 1838. Canon Bruté Collection; S. Bruté to M. Shawe, December 1838. CA of A.

[23] S. Bruté to J. Signay, 11–20, 1838. Original in Quebec Cathedral Archives. Etats-Unis. Vol. VI, p. 80; S. Bruté to J. St. Cyr, 1–13, 1839. St. LCA.

On September 24, 1838, Bishop Bruté had written to inform the Leopoldine Association of Father Kundek's arrival. In the same correspondence he promised to send a report of his last extensive visitation tour as soon as his health would permit. More than three months had elapsed since then and the feeble prelate still found it impossible to keep his promise. However, on January 19, 1839, he dictated a lengthy report which acquainted the above Association with all the proceedings and progress of his advancing diocese. He described in detail especially the settlements founded by the Germans. At this date Father Kundek was stationed at Jasper, Indiana, where he was rendering admirable service in the German congregation which numbered already more than eighty Catholic families. The appreciative bishop predicted a successful future career for this worthy missionary, who was not only able to direct his own compatriots but, having mastered the English language very quickly, he was also preaching and instructing in English.

The venerable prelate was no less satisfied with the work of Father Czackert, who sent by Father Passerat of Vienna, for the Picquet Settlement, threw himself heart and soul into his work and was the first priest to reside among the colonists at Ste. Marie.

> During the first years of the new settlement, priests from Vincennes, Indiana, visited Ste. Marie from time to time attending to the religious needs of the colonists, till in 1839, Reverend Peter Czackert, a Redemptorist, was given to them as residing pastor.

Besides working for the colonists, Father Czackert extended his zeal to the surrounding missions. Bishop Bruté in this same report of January 19, 1839, to the Most Reverend Archbishop Milde of Vienna, said:

> We have also the pleasure of receiving Father Czackert, who was sent to us by the Reverend Father Passerat in Vienna. He has already visited two parishes, that at Evansville and another more thickly populated one at Mt. Carmel, and has strengthened them with the consolations of religion. He is now intent on estab-

lishing a house for the Redemptorist Fathers in the colony of Mr. Joseph Picquet. The good Catholics there are very glad to have priests who speak their Mother-tongue, as heretofore I was in a position to send them only missionaries of another tongue, whom they did not understand.

Father Czackert also ministered to the faithful of St. Joseph's a hamlet of fifty inhabitants in German Township, Vanderburg County, nine miles north of Evansville, where he said Mass in a private house. He was the first priest who is known to have visited the district of St. James' congregation in Gibson County, Indiana. He, likewise, labored at St. Philip's also a hamlet of fifty people, eleven miles from Evansville.

Bishop Bruté, likewise, eulogized the labors of Fathers Mueller, Ferneding, and Schneiderjans in the north and southeastern sections of the diocese. He recounted the number of priests laboring on his missions, endeavored to show that this number was too few for the constant increasing population and tried to influence his benefactors to induce more German priests to pursue a missionary career.[24]

Early in November before Bishop Bruté had received the news of Father Petit's arrival with the Potawatomi Indians at the Osage river, he sent a message to recall him to Vincennes. This letter did not reach the missionary until December 23, 1838. Fever and fatigue caused by the laborious journey engendered a serious illness from which the poor missionary suffered during his entire sojourn on the Osage. The fever had left him only three days before the arrival of the bishop's letter which informed him of the absence of Fathers Vabret and de la Hailandière. Immediately Father Petit decided to return and arranged his departure for January 2. After traveling 150 miles on horseback in company with an Indian the suffering priest found

[24] *Berichte der Leopoldinen-Stiftung im Kaiserthume Oesterreich,* XIII (1840), pp. 1–10. Vienna; *Pastoral-Blatt,* LVIII (1924), p. 35. St. Louis, Mo.; *Records (ACHS),* XLI (1930), pp. 122–4 Philadelphia.; H. J. Alerding, *op. cit.,* pp. 228; 290; 293.

it impossible to continue the journey. The Indian sent his horse back to the reservation and tied the other one to the stage which carried them to Jefferson City where they remained for one day. The remainder of the distance to St. Louis was traveled in an open wagon amidst rain and very bad roads. At St. Louis Father Petit was welcomed as a brother by the Jesuits, who procured medical attention for him at once. After three days strength seemed to be reviving and he, therefore, entertained hope of being able very soon to return to Vincennes. On January 18, he wrote from St. Louis informing Bishop Bruté of his condition and his whereabouts. This letter was delivered by the Indian guide enroute to Logansport. Consequently, Bishop Bruté looked forward to welcoming his dear missionary back to Vincennes at an early date, when much to his surprise and grief the alarming news was received, on February 10, that Father Petit's condition was hopeless. Then four days later the grief-stricken bishop received the message of this good priest's death which had occurred on February 10, 1839. A solemn Requiem Mass was celebrated at the Cathedral on Monday, February 18. The bishop was assisted by five priests. The whole parish was in attendance and many non-Catholics were present at the sad ceremony to hear Bishop Bruté's touching eulogy.[25]

These trials and sorrows failed to wrest the feeble bishop from his post where he labored daily after physical strength had begun to decline. On February 20, he rode forty miles to visit the Picquet Settlement where he remained for two days. This was his first visit to Ste. Marie and he was greatly edified by the good Father Czackert and his 130 parishioners. Another source of consolation was the labor of Father Piesback who recently came from Cincinnati and

[25] *Annales de la Propagation de la Foi*, XI (1838), pp. 382–400. Lyons; *Ave Maria*, I (1865), pp. 518–21; *The U. S. Cath. Miscellany*, XVIII (1839), p. 310; *The Catholic Hist. Society of Indiana*, Bulletin No. 2 (1927), p. 6; S. Bruté to A. Blanc, 3–17, 1839. CA of A.

established another German congregation in Jasper county, Illinois.[26]

Clouds and sunshine seemed to vie with each other to claim the closing days of the feeble prelate, for trials and consolations followed in close succession. The tear-dimmed eyes were still moist from the loss of Father Petit when Father Berel, vice president of the St. Gabriel's College, lay dangerously ill. The afflicted prelate administered the last rites of Holy Mother Church and with a calm, yet sorrowing heart he recited the prayers for the dying, when suddenly the young priest grew better and was spared to his bishop and the diocese. Then from a letter to Bishop Blanc we learn that a second consolation was afforded the feeble prelate on April 12.

> Father Vabret arrived here last night, entirely recovered and overwhelmed, as also Father Benoit, by your goodness. I received the box containing the seven stoles. The fact that you shower us so constantly, so abundantly, and so patiently, with so many marks of affection and interest, touched me deeply. I cannot help but bless you with all my heart, for all that you do for our priests, for Vincennes, and for all the diocese.[27]

Bishop Bruté had frequently lamented the absence of priests to provide for the spiritual wants of the numerous German emigrants in his extensive diocese. At this time it was undoubtedly a happy consolation for him to find Father Kundek, stationed at Jasper, so willing, active, and efficient. At Easter time this zealous missionary ministered to the Germans at Vincennes, and Picquet Settlement. In the absence of Father Deydier who was on a collecting tour in behalf of his church, Father Kundek also visited Evansville and vicinity. After this missionary expedition of 250 miles

---

[26] S. Bruté to A. Blanc, 2–23, 1839. CA of A. S. Bruté to J. Rosati, 2–21, 1839. St. LCA.

[27] M. Meline—E. McSweeny, *op. cit.*, I, p. 392; S. Bruté to Fr. Elet, 3–19, 1839, St. Louis University Archives; S. Bruté to S. Eccleston, 3–22, 1839. BCA Case 241[11]; S. Bruté to A. Blanc, 4–13, 1839. CA of A.

the good priest was again with his own congregation for the feast of Easter. Then on April 21 we find him at New Albany, where he preached in French and German, and after visiting various mission stations he tells us: "On May 4, I preached to a mixed congregation on the White River, perhaps under the same tree under which a few years previously the Indians had gathered to offer sacrifice and worship to their deity."[28]

Scarcely had these consolations appeared on the horizon when another trial crushed the bishop's heart. Reverend Mr. O'Reilly who supplied at Madison during Father Shawe's absence in Canada had upon the latter's return mysteriously disappeared. Much to the surprise of all he suddenly appeared at Logansport where he again commenced his former reproachful life. Bishop Bruté exercised all patience and forebearance towards the poor unfortunate man; his person was spared—his bail and debts paid, but to no avail. As a last resource the bishop was forced to suspend him. Mr. O'Reilly, then, in open rebellion continued to exercise his priestly functions causing a schism within the diocese. Bishop Bruté then notified his colleagues and placed the following announcement in the *Telegraph:*

> A suspended priest, Rev. M. O'Reilly, is now exercising the functions of the holy ministry in the Diocese of Vincennes, without power, or authorization. We give this earnest warning to all the faithful of our diocese, to beware countenancing him, and beg them to heed this notice of their Bishop.[29]

Difficulties of this character experienced by Bishop Bruté found an echo in the east, whence Bishop Hughes sent an appeal to his former professor for material needed to prepare lectures on the trustees troubles. In his usual thorough manner Bishop Bruté supplied the desired information. He

[28] *Berichte der Leopoldinen-Stiftung im Kaiserthume Oesterreich,* XIII (1840), pp. 10–22. Vienna.
[29] *The Catholic Telegraph,* VIII (1839), p. 158; S. Bruté to C. François, 4–30, 1839. CA of A.; S. Bruté to J. Rosati, 3–18, 1839. St. LCA.

drew up a catalogue of the principal schisms and disorders
that had arisen from the trustee system in this country.
On Holy Thursday, March 28, 1839, this information and a
number of pamphlets together with a letter of prudent
council were sent to the coadjutor of New York. In a subsequent letter, dated April 19, he rejoiced at the success of
the lectures and the good effect of the pastoral letter of
Bishop Dubois.[30]

While the physician had warned the declining prelate
several months previous that his condition was serious and
death could claim him at any moment, he continued his episcopal activities. His resolute will and fervent zeal seemed
to triumph over the painful disease which was consuming
his ebbing live. As the spring of 1839 advanced he continually grew weaker, yet he ventured to plan another journey of almost a month's duration. On April 18, 1839, he
wrote Father François at Logansport:

> I intend to absent myself for a few days. I am going to Wash-
> ington, then to Mt. Pleasant, to see Father St. Palais, then to Father
> Neyron, afterwards to Bardstown, and finally, perhaps, to Madison.
> I shall be home before Pentecost, if God grants me life or re-
> animates my health which has been much impaired these last three
> weeks.[31]

A three-fold motive prompted this last visitation of Bishop Bruté. He hoped it would prolong his life, secondly, he
wished to assist and encourage his clergy at these different
stations, while the third and most essential one was to make
a retreat at Bardstown. From the last motive, which he
confided to no one save Bishop Rosati, it is evident that he
knew this journey would be his last one. While thus engaged at Bardstown his solitude was interrupted by a letter from Father Vabret informing him that the schismatic
priest—unfortunate Mr. O'Reilly—was still exercising his
sacrilegious ministry and taking the wages of his iniquity

[30] J. Hassard, op. cit., pp. 197–8.
[31] S. Bruté to C. François, 4–18, 1839. CA of A.

from the poor deluded people, his own compatriots in Father François' district, while the latter was quite ill from the effects. Thereupon, Bishop Bruté wrote Father François encouraging him to be "of good heart and not to mind that unhappy man. We can do no more now than humble ourselves before God and pray that this first calamity of open schism and rebellion (in our diocese) may have its end." After sending the following Pastoral for the laity of Logansport and vicinity, the bishop continued his retreat realizing that he had accomplished all within his power to end the evil.

Beloved Brethren in Christ,

Since we have made known to you by your own pastors and even in the Catholic papers, as our monition was already printed in the *Telegraph* of Cincinnati that the Rev. Mr. O'Reilly has no powers to exercise the functions of a Catholic priest in the diocese nor in any other until he may have his faculty restored, your faith and your conscience forbid you to permit him any functions among you— He cannot say Mass or you be present at it without an enormous sacrilege; his pretended absolutions are equally null and mere sacrileges and his preaching mere art, of schism to which you cannot listen without being partakers of the same. This is all well known to that unfortunate fallen priest, and he cannot insist on his present criminal course but against the cry of his own conscience, to which we supplicate our Lord, as Head of this diocese, and under him his vicar on earth, our Holy Father, that he may at last listen. We have exhausted towards him all length of forbearance and patience before we would lay him, as he now is placed, under full suspension; his crime in his present course is the greater for it; separate then entirely from him as it is your only Catholic duty and salvation, and do not aggravate his sins by using in any way his sacrilegious, false, and worse than useless ministrations. A man that does not listen to the Church, you know it, is no more to you as our Lord tells you, but as a heathen, and if he was used himself to teach others so, when he lived as a true Catholic and priest, when he turns a schismatic, a contumacious and disobedient man, suspended and deprived of all faculties as a priest, he is but the more guilty whom all the faithful must, for their only mercy to him, carefully avoid to encourage in his revolt and sacrileges.

We do charge your true pastors so to appeal to your faith and warn you of the present situation of Mr. O'Reilly and earnestly remind you of your duty as Catholics towards the Church and your Bishop and father in Christ.[32]

From Bardstown Bishop Bruté went to Madison where he arrived very ill on Saturday, May 4. To add to his misery Father Shawe was absent visiting Father Ferneding at New Alsace and the poor suffering bishop scarcely able to support his feeble body was called upon to attend three distant sickcalls. On this occasion he administered the consolations of religion to souls who were not as near death as he himself. After this mission was accomplished the bishop left by boat for his episcopal city via Evansville. While on board he conceived an ardent desire to see Bishop Rosati and the clergy of St. Louis. Consequently, he decided to prolong his journey for another week and instead of landing at Evansville, he continued westward and landed at Kaskaskia from where he wrote the Bishop of St. Louis several days later, on May 10. He spent a week at the Visitation Convent and with an intimate friend, Mr. Pierre Menard. Following this he departed for Vincennes where he arrived in a completely exhausted state on Friday, May 17. He realized that as far as physical strength was concerned he had lost more than he had gained,[33] but from the spiritual viewpoint it is not to be questioned that he added stores of wealth to his already princely account. The bishop's life had always been strangely divided between restless, zealous, all-embracing activity and deep and fervent contemplation wherein he filled the hours with God's sweet absorbing Presence, His invigorating company, and the joy of His friendship. In other words Bishop Bruté was a

[32] S. Bruté to C. François, 4–30, 1839. CA of A.
[33] S. Bruté to J. Rosati, 5–10, 1839; 5–22, 1839. St. LCA.

genuine mystic whose life depicts a union of holy action and divine contemplation. However, the latter had been given precedence during this last journey which ends the devoted prelate's active labor beyond the episcopal city. Reluctantly we now stand in readiness to witness the deeds of his last mortal days that will place the seal on his beautiful apostolic career, which in success ranked second to none, though measured in time it was all too brief.

CHAPTER XIV

LAST ILLNESS AND DEATH

The apostolic career of Bishop Bruté did not terminate with his last visitation tour. During the brief period of life that was granted him after his return to the episcopal city he was occupied for the greater part of the time with diocesan affairs. On Pentecost Sunday, May 19, he administered Confirmation at the Cathedral in the afternoon although he was too ill to pontificate in the morning. His continued debilities prevented him from offering the Holy Sacrifice during the following week and he was living in happy anticipation that he would not be deprived of this privilege on Trinity Sunday. Happily his desires were realized for we read in *The Catholic Telegraph:*

> On Trinity Sunday he celebrated the thirty-first anniversary of his first Mass, being assisted on that occasion by two of his clergy, who supported him at the altar, whilst he offered the divine sacrifice with a heart overflowing with love, and lips that breathed the spirit of piety. They who had the happiness to attend him on such occasions can never forget the ardent devotion, with which he performed that sacred office.[1]

For the bishop life continued to be an alternation of trials and consolations. He was much concerned because the symptoms of Father Vabret's former illness were again apparent and in his solicitude for the president of St. Gabriel's College he took precautions to lighten his labors. Coincident with the above concern the venerable prelate was consoled by the submission of Reverend Mr. O'Reilly and his reconciliation on condition that he leave for New Orleans. In his solicitude for this erring priest he wrote

[1] *The Catholic Telegraph*, VIII (1839), p. 238.

Bishop Blanc requesting him to facilitate Father O'Reilly's return to Europe.[2]

These official duties and the knowledge of his approaching death failed to disturb his peace of soul. This is manifest in a letter written to his brother, Augustine, on May 29, in which he stated: "My health is failing fast. My days are vanishing, but every day my heart experiences greater joy at the unremitting progress of the Church. Although I should like to remain a little longer I am resigned to the Master's Will." Like sentiments were expressed to Bishop Rosati on June 6.

> I am growing weaker, so much so that I have resolved to receive the Holy Viaticum on the morrow.
>
> I am in peace, but the solicitude of the uncertainty of my succession occupies me, troubles me—and to leave my priests without advice and temporal and spiritual direction—for myself I would not inconvenience any one of my colleagues. But for the affairs and our priests—this new diocese wholly in creation and all the proprietary on me alone—this disquiets me. I dare not write a more express desire—Divine Providence.
>
> A change has taken place these two days, especially today. I do not hope for any improvement or do I await Mr. de la Hailandière. In eight or ten days there may be a widowed church here.
>
> Deus et omnia, Auspice Maria.[3]

The attending clergy were cognizant of the bishop's critical condition and the president of the college sent an urgent appeal to Bishop Rosati requesting him to come at once. On the following day Bishop Bruté rallied sufficiently to give directions for his funeral and to make final provisions for the temporalities of his diocese. Although he was no longer able to carry on his own correspondence he still continued to direct the affairs of his diocese. On June 13

[2] S. Bruté to J. Rosati, 5–22, 1839. St. LCA. St. Louis, Mo.; S. Bruté to A. Blanc, 5–22, 1839. CA of A. Notre Dame, Ind.
[3] S. Bruté to A. Bruté, 5–29, 1839. Canon Bruté Collection Rennes; S. Bruté to J. Rosati, 6–6, 1839. St. LCA.

he dictated a letter delegating Father François to adjust misunderstandings that had arisen between the pastor and the flock at Fort Wayne.[4]

We have repeatedly had occasion to allude to Bishop Bruté's frequent and urgent requests for a coadjutor. It was, however, not in the designs of Providence to grant the bishop the consolation of witnessing the realization of this unquestionable need. Notwithstanding this the bishop received intimations from Archbishop Eccleston to the effect that Father de la Hailandière's appointment was probable and that he awaited daily the official announcement. Despite the archbishop's expectations the bulls appointing Father de la Hailandière, which were issued on May 17, 1839, did not reach America before Bishop Bruté's death.[5]

Unto the close of his life the appreciative bishop was mindful of his benefactors and he responded to each gift in a letter abounding with gratitude and blessings. At this date he was no longer able to give the Leopoldine Association a lengthy description of his progressing diocese, therefore, he bade one of his clergy, Father Kundek, write his benefactors a detailed account of the recent mission activities within his see. Before the intrepid missionary had time to complete this task, Bishop Bruté received another gift of 5000 florins. On June 21, the dying bishop dictated a brief but grateful reply to his worthy benefactors at Vienna.[6] His gratitude also found expression in letters to his colleagues and his faithful priests. He announced to them his reception of the last sacraments, encouraged them in their zealous labors, and solicited prayer for the repose

[4] S. Bruté to J. Rosati, 6–2, 1839. St. LCA.; S. Bruté to C. François, 6–13, 1839. CA of A.; M. Meline—E. McSweeny, *The Story of the Mountain*, I, p. 393.

[5] S. Bruté to S. Eccleston, 6–7, 1839. BCA. Case 241[12]; Cardinal Fransoni to S. Bruté, 6–25, 1839. CA of A.; M. Frenaye to F. Kenrick, 6–24, 1839. *Kenrick—Frenaye Correspondence*, Villanova, Pa. 1916.

[6] *Berichte der Leopoldinen-Stiftung im Kaiserthume Oesterreich*, XIII (1840), pp. 9–10.

of his own soul.[7] From among these letters we here insert his last words to Father Ferneding, who was stationed at New Alsace.

Vincennes, June 21, 1839.

My dear Father Ferneding:

I have been so low that I received Holy Viaticum and Extreme Unction. I continue in extreme weakness. Pray much for me. Let the work of God go on zealously. Men are nothing. Father de la Hailandière will return in August or September. For the present Father Lalumière is our Vicar-General. Father de la Hailandière returns with some good men, some from Alsace. My good friend, God will bless our dear diocese. Happy each of us, if we do our best for it. I am so weak. I cannot dictate any more. (Then following in his own handwriting.) Your devoted friend and bishop, asking your heart's prayers for a good death and the repose of my soul.

✠ Simon G. Bruté, Bishop of Vincennes.[8]

With true fraternal affection he thought of his brother and wrote him a last message on June 16. Therein he reminded Augustine that notwithstanding the fact that their fields of labor had been widely separated here on earth they had remained tenderly united in Christian affection as faithful sons of their most worthy Mother. He blessed Augustine and in his heart all the members of his brother's family. Likewise, the good bishop begged Augustine to remember him to all their relatives whose prayers he solicited and bade his brother to continue to assist Father de la Hailandière and Vincennes as he had done in the past for whatever aid was granted was given for the love of God.[9]

We are not to infer from the foregoing that the attention of the bishop was wholly engrossed in the material affairs of his diocese and of his friends; other things were

---

[7] S. Bruté to S. Eccleston, 6–22, 1839. BCA. Case 241[13]; S. Bruté to A. Blanc, 6–23, 1839. CA of A.; S. Bruté to J. Rosati, 6–17, 1839. St. LCA.

[8] Transcript in CA of A.

[9] S. Bruté to A. Bruté, 6–16, 1839. Canon Bruté Collection.

uppermost in his mind. Eternity had been for him a living reality throughout life. Eternity was ever in his heart, on his lips, and incessantly flowed from his pen. In fact it was the sacred keynote of the bishop's life. It was this thought of Eternity that prompted him to address a spiritual testament to his diocese eight days before his death.

LAST ENTREATY TO ALL

Vincennes, June 18, 1839.

I recommend to all the faithful of the diocese to persevere above all trials in the Divine faith and in the only true, Catholic, apostolic Church the Church of God on earth, having the doctrine of Christ from the days of Peter (and the apostles), to his present successor Gregory XVI and to the end of time.

As there is no other name under heaven through which we may be saved, but the name of Jesus, so it is to His Church that He has trusted the doctrine, and graces and conditions of that salvation. Faith, obedience to the Church as to Himself,—for so He commanded—the divine sacrifice, the pure victim really present, the reception of His Body and Blood in the Holy Communion; the other sacraments, Baptism, Penance, Confirmation, Holy Order, holy anointment of the sick, and Matrimony, dignified as a sacrament in the true Church, profaned out of her bosom and its unity broken, by divorce.

But may the children of the Church remember that faith cannot save them without works, nor the grace of the sacraments reach their souls without the requisite conditions and preparation. "Be ye holy because I am holy, said the Lord."

As for our brethren unhappily misled by their ancestors into so arbitrary and contradictory ways, all the result of mere private opinion, they are dearly present to my heart, and I entreat them to reconsider how impossible it is that so many sects, whether the later or the older of them, should have been made by Christ His true Church; they all rather conspire to destroy it, even Baptism, the Divinity of Christ, and the fear of hell. I entreat them in the charity of Jesus Christ to consider how inconsistent is their situation, how insecure are their self-assumed conditions of salvation, knowing that Christ says that it is not enough to say Lord, Lord; but that we must also do His will, in order to enter the kingdom of heaven.

Catholic bishop of Vincennes, by the appointment of the successor of Peter, the vicar of Christ on earth, and visible head of His Church, in communion with all the other successors of the apostles in all the dioceses of the immense Catholic Church, I do, in life, or in death, humbly rejoice before my God; but it is the continual sorrow of my heart to see those who have assumed the ministry of so many self-created sects, engaged without mission, authority, promises, or graces, of God, in opposing the Church their true Mother, and all the institutions of Christ trusted to her. May God grant them to consider their arbitrary, and equally unauthorized, various manners of ministry. Let the fourth chapter of Ephesians show them how the true pastors must have their mission from Christ; I also suggest to them to keep in mind His frequent denunciations, and, after Him, that of the apostles, of Peter, Paul, John, and Jude, against the making oneself the leader of the blind and author of schisms that destroy the unity of the Church of God.

✠ Simon G. Bruté, Bishop of Vincennes.[10]

As the venerable prelate's strength diminished his devotion increased. In the midst of his sufferings for which he sought no alleviation he preserved perfect calmness of spirit and continued eager to labor and to do good. As a meteor, whose light becomes most brilliant the moment before it bursts, did the life of Bishop Bruté, lighted up by the flames of his all-embracing zeal and charity, glow more brilliantly as his dissolution approached nearer. When unable to walk or stand, he would at least sit up and write to any one whom he could hope to benefit by his correspondence, while to those around him he would speak on pious subjects, such as the love of God, conformity to His Holy Will, or devotion to the Blessed Virgin. The last precious days of his life were thus entirely occupied with works of charity, consoling those who were with him, and in intimate and affectionate communion with his God. He preferred often to be left

[10] *Researches* (ACHS), XIV (1897), pp. 101–102.

alone that he might the more freely indulge his pious feelings, consequently, he would allow no one to watch with him at night, until his mortal agony had begun. When his friends sought to relieve his sufferings, he designated a chapter of the *Following of Christ* which he desired to be read to him.

On Friday, June 21, Bishop Bruté received all the rites of the Church. On the same day he rallied and the physician promised him a temporary recovery. Those in attendance were also hopeful. "Yes, doctor," said the Bishop, "I shall be better these three days." He then gave orders for his tomb to be prepared and directed the mode of sepulchre and proper rites to be observed. This was discharged as calmly as any other ordinary duty. The dying prelate's prediction was verified; on Friday, Saturday, and Sunday he was able to walk about, but the night of Sunday to Monday was a restless night for the bishop, and in the morning he was so completely exhausted that he could scarcely move. On Tuesday, the eve of his death, he grew weaker, and at nine-thirty in the morning he addressed Father Vabret in the words: "Oh my dear child, I have the whole day yet to stay with you, tomorrow with God in heaven." To another friend he said: "I am going home." Then he requested this clergyman not to let him die without having recited for him the prayers for the dying. When Father Vabret asked the time he wished to have them said Bishop Bruté answered that there would be sufficient time after supper. The suffering bishop sat in his chair nearly all day dying; about three o'clock in the afternoon, with much pain and difficulty, he wrote a letter to some ladies who had unfortunately abandoned the practice of their faith. He told them that it was the eve of his death; that tomorrow he would be in eternity, and that he thought it his duty to entreat them at his dying hour to return to the true Church, to the practice of their religion.

The prayers for the dying were recited after supper as requested, but with Bishop Bruté prayer was the constant

THE LAST LETTER OF BISHOP BRUTÉ TO ARCHBISHOP ECCLESTON, JUNE 22, 1839

habit of his soul. It seemed perpetually to breathe forth from his heart like perfume from a flower. He answered all the prayers for his departing soul and with such angelic fervor that everyone present was edified at his devotion and affection for our Divine Saviour. At eleven o'clock the dying bishop sent Father Vabret to bed, saying it was too late for him to be up. Two hours and a half later, at one-thirty o'clock in the morning, the Father of the Diocese of Vincennes expired in the most edifying manner perfectly conscious to the last and speaking in the most affecting manner to the priests who attended him.[11]

On the following day when the announcement was made that Bishop Bruté was dead, sorrow pervaded all Vincennes. His death was deplored as a general calamity. He was especially lamented by the poor, the widow, and the orphan; while the city at large felt that they had lost a public bene-factor. His own flock, both clergy and laity, bewailed, as they well might, the death of such a shepherd. All with one accord mourned for the scholar, the philanthropist, and the saint. Crowds of people of every rank, and of all denomina-tions, visited his remains and such expressions as the fol-lowing were heard on all sides, and from all classes of peo-ple: "The best man in Vincennes has gone; if there was ever a saint on earth, it was Bishop Bruté; he will be sadly missed by everybody; the poor have lost their best friend, and his place can never be filled."[12]

From a tribute that appeared in the *Western Sun*, on June 29, 1839, we readily perceive that Bishop Bruté was the Prime Mover within the episcopal city and its environs as well as the Silent Power throughout the extensive diocese. This article written at the time of his death and coming from the pen of Elihu Stout, a Protestant, likewise, portrays

[11] *Indiana Catholic and Record*, VII (1916), No. 322, p. 14. Indianapolis; *The Catholic Record*, May 28, 1891, Indianapolis; Col. Blanchard, *History of the Catholic Church in Indiana*, pp. 59–60.

[12] *The Catholic Record*, May 28, 1891. Indianapolis; H. S. Cau-thorn, *St. Francis Xavier Cathedral*, p. 53; M. Meline—E. McSweeny, *The Story of The Mountain*, II, p. 379.

to us how universally the good bishop was loved and venerated.

It is with feelings of the deepest sorrow and grief, that we discharge the sad duty of announcing the death of Bishop Bruté, which took place on Wednesday morning at half past one o'clock. He died of consumption, with which he was affected for several years past, and which ran its course undisturbed, until within the last few weeks, when he yielded to the entreaties of his friends to avail himself of the relief medicine might afford him during the rest of his days.

The news of his death produced a general and almost unanimous expression of grief amongst our citizens: and well have we cause to lament this event, for to many, very many he was dear: to the one as a friend, to the other as a comforter; to the third as a teacher, or as a literary companion, and to all as a pattern of goodness, morality and pure piety. His character was truly amiable, and his manners so conciliating, that wherever he could not make friends, he was sure not to make enemies, and we can safely affirm, that he died without the latter. Much as we have lost in him as a friend, the literary world has lost more in him. With a finished scholarship, he combined talents of the first order, indefatigable industry, and an unquenchable thirst for literary research. His correspondence was very extensive, and his literary productions numerous. His extreme modesty prevented him from publishing much, but he left about 200 large volumes of his own manuscripts, which will, to some literary reaper yield a rich harvest.

During the short time that he was the head of the Catholic Church in this diocese much has been done for the Christian religion; many churches have been built through his instrumentality, and many poor souls, from the obscurity of their residence, would never have had the consolations of religion, had not our pious deceased Bishop under the severest privations, hunted up their cabins. Even the savages of the forest he visited in their wigwams, and preached to them the gospel.

His charity to the poor was almost unbounded, and he readily denied himself the comforts of life for the purpose of assisting the poor. Besides the individual charities which he bestowed, he

established in this place, at his own expense, a free school for indigent male children, and through his influence and with his pecuniary aid, a similar one for female children.

May heaven grant peace to his soul, and may he reap that reward
which the religion in which he has so faithfully lived, promises
him.[13]

The obsequies of the beloved bishop took place at six
o'clock on Friday morning, June 28, 1839. A requiem High
Mass was celebrated by Reverend Simon Lalumière who
also delivered a touching and scholarly eulogy. The cortege
passed through the principal streets of the city followed by
deposition of the remains beneath the high altar in St. Francis Xavier's Cathedral. Everything was done to render the
ceremony as solemn as possible. All business was suspended, public offices were draped in mourning, and more than
twelve hundred people accompanied by the mayor, the civil
authorities, and the Vincennes Historical Society, attended.[14]

Although the entire diocese and all who knew the venerable apostle lamented his untimely departure, and the clergy
were crushed at the thought of their sad loss, nevertheless,
relative to the event we find in the Old Cathedral register
nothing more than the following brief and simple entry enclosed in black lines.

Simon Gabriel Bruté, the first Bishop of Vincennes, Indiana, born
at Rennes in France, died on the 26th of June, 1839, at half past
one in the morning. He was buried on the 28th, with as much pomp
as we could. Most all the population of the town attended. Much
regretted by every one, even Protestants. High Mass and sermon
by S. Petit Lalumière, Vicar General. Consecrated Bishop on 28th,
October, 1834.[15]

[13] *The Western Sun and General Advertizer*, XXX (1839), p. 3.
Vincennes.
[14] M. Meline,—E. McSweeny, *op. cit.*, pp. 399–400;   *The Catholic
Record*, May 28, 1891;   H. S. Cauthorn, *op. cit.*, p. 54.
[15] Register, Old Cathedral Archives. Vincennes.

In responding to a letter addressed to Bishop Bruté, Father Lalumière conveyed the news of Vincennes' great loss to Bishop Blanc, of New Orleans, on July 17.

> Your letter addressed to our good bishop came yesterday, but Bishop Bruté could not be found, he is here no more, he died on June 26 at half past one in the morning—he is dead, but his name and his memory are not dead—they shall ever live in our minds and hearts. Our Bishop's death is lamented by every one, even the Protestants shed tears on the day of his burial. We had the most beautiful burial that was ever in Vincennes, probably in the West.[16]

It is not our intention here to be indulgent or to invite undue praise for the venerable prelate whose deeds have been recorded with exactness and, as far as possible, free from all conscious bias, but to acquaint our readers with the fact that Bishop Bruté did possess a singular sanctity— a sanctity that could not be concealed. Moreover, these sentiments were not merely the opinion of the minority of his acquaintances but they were universally maintained by hosts of his friends including many of our separated brethren. In testimony of this we here insert what others wrote and said of him. While attending the Medical College at Paris, Mr. Teysseyre, a fellow-student, spoke of Simon Bruté as "an angelic young man."[17] Likewise, after Simon entered the Seminary of St. Sulpice, Father Emery, Superior, tried to defer his ordination and thereby to detain him longer in their midst "because of his piety and great edification which he gave the seminarists and the faculty."[18] That Father Bruté was held in high regard at the Seminary of Rennes is revealed in Father Champion's letter of recommendation to Archbishop Carroll, wherein he stated: "This

[16] S. Lalumière to A. Blanc, 7–17, 1839. CA of A.

[17] Abbé C. Bruté de Rémur, *Vie de Monseigneur Bruté de Rémur*, p. 77.

[18] M. Emery to Madame Bruté, 8–26, 1807. Canon Bruté Collection, Rennes.

gentleman (Father Bruté) is a treasure which heaven confides to you.   Let us respect its decrees, and not speak of our regret at our loss which will be a rich gain to your country."[19]   Mt. St. Mary's revered the Mountain professor to a marked degree and conferred on him the appellation, "The Guardian Angel of the Mount."

From the writings of his colleagues in the apostolate we learn that everyone loved and venerated the good bishop. Turning to August 7, 1836, in the *Diary and Visitation* Record of Bishop Kenrick we read: "The Right Reverend Simon Gabriel Bruté, Bishop of Vincennes, celebrated Pontifical solemn Mass in the Cathedral Church of St. Mary. . . . He is a man to be admired by reason of his holy life and his learning."   Fifteen years later the same prelate, then Archbishop of Baltimore, sent two notes, of Bishop Bruté, to Reverend G. B. Allen, and added: "He was truly a just man, living by faith.   I am sure you will be edified by their perusal.   You may retain them as memorials of the holy Bishop of Vincennes."[20]

Bishop Quarter, the first Bishop of Chicago, when speaking of the departed prelate, said: "I never saw but one, and that one was Bishop Bruté, who exhibited so tender a piety as my mother."[21]   And the venerable Bishop Flaget of Bardstown when writing of Bishop Bruté, to Bishop Rosati, said:

> During these five days that I have been in the company of the successor of the Apostles, I have nothing to do but listen, admire, and bless Providence. . . . when he celebrates the Holy Mysteries, when he speaks of Jesus Christ, of His love for men, of his continual spirit of sacrifice, my heart dilates, is inflamed like that of the disciples of Emmaus.   I then hope against all hope, and I an-

[19] BCA.   Case 2–B[12].   p. 3.

[20] *Diary & Visitation Record of Rt. Rev. Francis P. Kenrick*, p. 127. Lancaster, 1916;   *Records* (ACHS), XXXI (1920), p. 185.

[21] J. E. McGirr, *Life of the Rt. Rev. W. Quarter, D. D.*, p. 15, N. Y.   1850.

ticipate miracle upon miracle to be wrought by this venerable Apostle.[22]

The pioneer missionary of Evansville, Father Deydier, in a sermon delivered during the first synod held at Vincennes, said: "Bishop Bruté set the example of the most brotherly affection. When he was with us we did not feel our weariness; nothing was hard to us, and we scarcely knew we were poor although deprived of almost every necessary of life."[23] And in a contribution, to the Alma Mater, written by Father Edmund Schmitt, we read:

> Bishop Bruté! Good Bishop Bruté, humble, learned, saintly, first Bishop of Vincennes! How happy to be one of his spiritual sons, to labor in the field consecrated by his heroic self-sacrifice. And who are they who may call him Father? Today the diocese of Vincennes—Indianapolis, Fort Wayne, the great archdiocese of Chicago, and the dioceses of Alton, Peoria, and Belleville.[24]

Father Kundek, writing from Jasper, Indiana, to the Leopoldine Society, on July 17, 1839, related:

> It is with deep sorrow that I send you the news of the death of Our Right Reverend Bishop, the first Apostle of Indiana.... The deceased could truly say 'I have fought a good fight, I have finished my course, I have kept the faith; now I await the incorruptible crown of justice, which the Lord will grant to all who love Him.' (2 Tim. 4:7–8). Maryland and Indiana will never forget him. A good tree, he had borne much fruit, and he left vigorous sprouts that give further promise to strong and fruitful growth. To the deceased these words of Scripture, I believe, may be aptly applied: 'How beautiful are the feet of them that preach the gospel of peace, of them that bring glad tidings of good things!' (Rom. 10:15). Yet we feel keenly that he left us orphans. His loss is irreparable.[25]

[22] *Alma Mater,* IV (1895), p. 479. St. Meinrad, Ind.

[23] H. J. Alerding, *History of the Diocese of Vincennes,* p. 184; Aubrey de Vere, *The Heroines of Charity,* p. 41, N. Y. 1916.

[24] *Alma Mater,* p. 475.

[25] *Berichte der Leopoldinen-Stiftung im Kaiserthume Oesterreich,* XIII (1840), pp. 10–19.

Father Felix de Andreis described Father Bruté as "the most holy, learned, humble, and affable man" that he ever knew. And John Quincy Adams of Massachusetts, the sixth president of the United States, 1825-1829, stated that Father Simon Bruté was "the most learned man of his day in America."[26] Sister Benedicta in a letter from Vincennes announcing the saintly prelate's death to Mother Rose, at Emmitsburg, wrote: "I shall try to get some of his hair to send you in this letter; I am sure many in the house will prize it as the relic of a saint, for if he is not one, I know not where we will find one."[27] In the volume entitled *Meine Reise nach Nord-Amerika im Jahre 1842*, Canon Joseph Salzbacher of St. Stephen's Cathedral, Vienna, related of Bishop Bruté that he won all hearts through the fear of God, zeal, meekness, prudence, and the unfeigned Christian humility which he possessed.[28]

Father Ernest Audran in a letter to Father Edmund Schmitt, dated January 26, 1892, also leaves us a beautiful account of the admiration manifested by the natives of Rennes for Bishop Bruté. This tribute is the more precious since it was written late in this venerable clergyman's life, and fifty-three years after the saintly Bishop's death and Father Audran's arrival in America.

[26] G. E. Greene, *History of Old Vincennes and Knox County, Indiana*, pp. 412–414. Chicago, 1911; *Sketches of the Life of F. de Andreis*, pp. 80–90.

[27] *Bruté—Seton Correspondence*, p. 586, 1886.

[28] Dr. Simon G. Bruté, starb leider im Jahre 1839, allzu früh für die junge und ausgedehnte Diöcese, die seines frommen Lebens und seiner rastlosen Thätigkeit noch länger bedurft hätte. Er hatte durch seine Gottesfurcht, durch seinen Eifer, gepaart mit Sanftmuth, Klugheit und wahrhaft christlicher Demuth, alle Herzen gewonnen, und die unzweideutigsten Beweise der Verehrung und Achtung nicht nur von Seite der Katholiken, sondern auch von Protestanten empfangen. Sein Tod ward aber auch gleich einem gemeinsamen Unglück betrauert; Alle stimmten in der Klage überein, es sei ein Gelehrter, ein Menschenfreund, ein Heiliger geschieden. Seine hohen Tugenden erwarben ihm auch während seiner Anwesenheit in Wien im Jahre 1835 allgemeine Achtung und Wertschätzung, und befreundeten ihn, den gelehrten, eifervollen und unermüdlichen Bischof, insbesonders dem Hochw. Hrn. Fürzerzbischofe Vincenz Eduard Milde, Präsidenten des Leopoldinen-Vereins. Dr. J. Salzbacher, *Meine Reise nach Nord-Amerika im Jahre 1842.* pp. 231–2. Wien, 1845.

Jeffersonville, Ind., Jan. 26, 1892.

Reverend dear Father;

....I saw Bishop Bruté in the city of Rennes the capital of the old province of Brittany. I was then a lad of about twelve or thirteen years old attending Catechism in the Church of St. Germain which stood in the most aristocratic part. L'Abbé Celestin G. de la Hailandière a cousin of mine and according to the Breton way of reckoning relationship my uncle, was one of the assistant priests. When the Catechism class was prepared for Communion Bishop Bruté who had come from America and had already been in the city for some time was invited to celebrate Pontifical High Mass—and I received Communion from his hands. It was looked upon by the city at large, by the parents, and by the children themselves, as a grand event to have him retained to distribute Holy Communion to the children of the Parish. The reason of it was that apart from other considerations he was looked upon as a saint wherever he went and that deep respect which only Saints can force from unwilling worldly people surrounded him wherever he happened to be.... The city and the country were moved by his presence. It occupied the thoughts of all. His whole manner served to increase the feeling of veneration with which he was approached. A man of middle stature, he was thin poorly dressed—age was telling upon him; his bright clear eyes beamed with gentleness. Simple in all his ways; whenever he spoke, whatever the subject, his words led all, young and old to the thoughts of God, as it were unconsciously. The learned spoke of his learning and consulted him. He was always amiable to all and, indeed, mirthful, also he had a keen mind—and the unpretentious holy Prelate when in conversation could now and then in an inimitable way draw a carricature in words, as telling and instructive and amusing as his skillful pen could with a few bold strokes draw it on the first piece of paper at hand.

Such appeared Bishop Bruté to me when I saw him as a child. He left France and on his return was followed to Vincennes by eminent men; his departure was also an event, both on account of those who followed him to the unknown wilderness—and of his very departure: For all knew they could see no more one of those holy and remarkable men, whom it is a rare blessing to meet even once in life.

When four years later, a youth, having finished my collegiate studies, I found myself in Vincennes, also attracted there in great part by the wonderful figure the memory of which has never left me, he had been dead three months. Waiting for his successor, his room had not been touched. The aroma of sanctity and learning of its late occupant still pervaded it. There stood in a corner the humble bed on which he had died—the crucifix, the sacred pictures—the piles of books filling up—encumbering the large room, in shelves from top to bottom, around, in the middle, everywhere, leaving only a narrow passage to the door.

The Priests who had been with him in his last moments Father Lalumière, Father Corbe, Father Parret, Father Vabret—fresh under the impression of the holy life—of which they had been—for a few years the close witnesses—and above all of his admirable death, never tired of recounting details of all.—Outside, in the city, it was the same among the people. Yet admirable and wonderful as were the testimonies of both priests and people—so deep was the impression which he had left on those who had seen him or heard him in Europe—that none of us—the newly arrived—were surprised—nay that every one of us could have instinctively, as it were, given full details of all that was recounted to us as if we also had been there and seen all.[29]

The Catholic Telegraph, likewise, rendered a beautiful tribute to the deceased prelate shortly after his death. This eulogy, copied by practically all the Catholic newspapers of the day, elicited a universal expression of sorrow throughout the Church in America. The following excerpt taken from the above weekly confirms the foregoing statements made by individuals.

The memory of the deceased will be ever cherished by the Catholics of the Union. His character was enriched with every trait to make him loved by his fellowmen. His knowledge was immense, but at the same time it was so void of pride and permeated with

[29] E. Audran to E. Schmitt, 1–26, 1892. Transcript in CA of A.

God that his conversation was loved by the ignorant as well as by
the enlightened. In his death the Church has lost a friend upon
earth, but gained one in heaven. May we imitate his virtues, and
be ever ready to sacrifice as he did every temporal comfort to advance the glory of God by the extension of his Church upon earth.[30]

In addition to the numerous tributes incorporated in our
story we are happy to record one rendered by the much
loved and highly esteemed late luminary in the hierarchy of
the American Church, His Eminence, James Cardinal Gib-
bons. This worthy dignitary attended the golden episcopal
jubilee of Archbishop Kenrick on November 30, 1891. Enroute to Baltimore, on December 4, 1891, His Eminence
escorted by three dignitaries, Archbishop Gross of Oregon,
Bishop Kain of Wheeling, Va., and Bishop Keane of Washington, D. C., stopped at the Union Station in Vincennes
where he was tendered a reception by a concourse of people
under the guidance of Father McCabe and Mr. E. Breivogel.
In the course of a brief address His Eminence expressed
regrets that the time would not allow him a visit to the
tomb of Bishop Bruté. He then added: "Worthy citizens
of Vincennes, you need not go on pilgrimages to visit the
tombs of saints. There is one reposing here in your midst,
namely, the saintly Founder of this diocese, Right Reverend
Simon Bruté."

Said the Very Reverend John McCaffery, seventh presi-
of Mt. St. Mary's and an ardent admirer of Bishop Bruté:

> The merits of such a man cannot be summed up in a few words.
> It is only by borrowing the language of sacred inspiration, that we
> can represent his character in worthy colors. I would therefore
> liken him to "Simon, the high priest," "who took care of his nation,"
> and "obtained glory in his conversation with the people," and apply
> to him the splendid eulogy which we read of that great man in the
> fiftieth chapter of Ecclesiasticus:
>
> "He shone in his days, as the morning star in the midst of a
> cloud; and as the moon at the full, and as the sun when it shineth,

[30] *The Catholic Telegraph*, VIII (1839), p. 238.

so did he shine in the temple of God. And as the rainbow giving light in the bright clouds, and as the flower of roses in the days of the spring; and as the lilies that are in the brink of the water; and as the sweet-smelling frankincense in the time of summer; and as a bright fire and frankincense burning in the fire; as a massy vessel of gold adorned with every precious stone; as an olive tree budding forth, and a cypress tree rearing itself on high; when he put on the robe of glory and was clothed with the perfection of power. When he went up to the holy altar he honored the vesture of holiness; and when he took the portions out of the hands of the priests, he himself stood by the altar. And about him was the ring of his brethren; and as the cedar planted on Mount Libanus, and as branches of palm trees, they stood round about him, and all the sons of Aaron in their glory.... And finishing his service on the altar to honor the offering of the most High King, he stretched forth his hand to make a libation, and offered of the blood of the grape.... Then all the people together made haste, and fell down to the earth upon their faces to adore the Lord their God, and to pray to the Almighty God the most High.... Then coming down, he lifted up his hands over all the congregation of the children of Israel, to give glory to God with his lips, and to glory in his name."[31]

Countless tributes to the deceased prelate could be quoted here but we shall close with the following one which, although last, is far from being the least noteworthy. It has been left to us by Bishop Bruté's worthy successor, Bishop de la Hailandière, another native of Brittany, who occupied the See of Vincennes from 1839 to 1847:

Almighty God in his admirable designs upon this immense diocese, had bestowed upon it for its first Pastor and founder, a man who was simple and upright, one of those whom Providence reserves in the treasury of his mercies for the happiness and salvation of mankind. The Right Reverend Doctor Bruté was that man, possessing an unshaken faith, a burning charity, an unrelenting zeal for the House of God. To these virtues were added the qualifications

[31] M. Meline—E. McSweeny, op. cit., pp. 376–7.

which distinguish men of the highest order: the most extensive knowledge, a delightful imagination, an extraordinary understanding. But these qualities had taken in him a particular form which rendered him one of the most amiable of men, they being united with great humility, simplicity of manners, love of the poor, devotedness to the flock which had been entrusted to his care, and the most loving heart. The love of the poor! they were in his eyes the living members of Jesus Christ. How many times did he not take off his own garments to clothe them! What miserable cottage did he not enter, to relieve and console its suffering inmates! Such was his love of poverty, that in the judgment of unreflecting men, he was not blameless; but they neither knew the secret of his own poverty, nor did they comprehend the excellence of that virtue. But who was ever possesed of a better heart? Who was acquainted with Bishop Bruté and did not love him, and find in him an affectionate friend? With regard to the salvation of men, "who was weak, and he was not weak? Who was scandalized, and he was not on fire?" (2 Cor. 11:29). How many times did I not see him prostrated before the Holy altar, with his face bathed in tears, his heart burning within him—or offering up the Divine sacrifice to the Father of mercies for the conversion of sinners, for those who were wandering from the true ways of salvation! for he would have all to be just and holy. He appeared indeed to have had only one grand object in view, and that was perceptible in all his actions, viz: the greater glory of God! and salvation of souls: all his words and actions, and even his appearance, were calculated to inspire those around him with heavenly thoughts. Vessel of election! Fundamental stone built upon the foundation of the Apostles and Prophets (Eph. 2:20), for the permanent establishment of the Church of Vincennes! Was it not written of him too, beloved of God and men, whose memory is in benediction (Ecclus. 45:1). But this sainted Pontiff, this wonderful man Providence had scarcely shown to you when he was taken away from you; he departed this life, he went to his home, to the realms of eternal bliss, to enjoy the rich reward which his immense labours had merited; at least we have every reason to hope so. This hope is our only comfort in the privation we have to sustain in seeing him no longer among us.[32]

An indefinite number of pages could be filled with eulogies but tributes and eulogies contain merely the judgments of men that for the most part are unstable, impressionable, and vary with the seconds of time. The only permanent eulogies are written by the fruits of men's deeds. "By their fruits you shall know them" (Mt. 7:16). Since they alone are beyond deception we shall now view the imperishable fruits of Bishop Bruté's labors and read their tribute to him. But might we not ask where should we seek the fruit that developed from the venerable prelate's restless activity? Evidently it is not to be sought amidst accumulated personal wealth for so universal had been the bishop's charity that at the time of his death his personal estate, excluding his manuscripts and library, was a mere trifle. Practically his entire supply of clothing had been given away, while that which remained was well worn and almost thread-bare. He left but one suit of clothes, a brown cloak that has been used for years, and two worn shirts of coarse material. Thus the saintly prelate's remains had to be robed for burial by the charity of surviving friends.[33]

The fruits of this learned pioneer prelate's labors are found increasing continuously and abundantly in the bosom of Holy Mother Church throughout the entire United States and their perpetual tribute is universal. Notwithstanding this fact, we are, for the present, concerned only with this dignitary's last field of labor—his apostolate, the See of Vincennes. When Bishop Bruté took possession of his Episcopal See on November 5, 1834, he found himself in the most trying circumstances. The diocese was without priests, churches, and means to provide them. The venerable prelate was a stranger, poor, and alone. He saw around him little more than the wrecks of the Catholic faith. There

[32] *Pastoral Letter of the Right Reverend Bishop of Vincennes,* *January, 1840.* Vincennes. 1840.
[33] H. S. Cauthorn, *op. cit.,* p. 51; *Catholic Record,* May 28, 1891.

was indeed an immense field for labor, but everything was to be commenced and all was to be accomplished by himself. *The Metropolitan Catholic Almanac* portrays the status in which Bishop Bruté found the diocese upon his arrival at Vincennes, as follows:

Vincennes, St. Francis Xavier, Rt. Rev. Simon G. Bruté, D. D.

Black Oak Ridge, Daviess Co., Rev. Simon Lalumière.

Duckee River........

Logansport, visited occasionaly by the Rev. S. T. Badin.

Fort Wayne, visited occasionally by the Rev. S. T. Badin.

Racoon Creek, Vacant.

Independence, Vacant.

Mississinaway, Vacant.

Mt. Pleasant, visited occasionally.[34]

Despite this sad condition the good bishop applied himself courageously to the allotted task and prayed fervently and confidently to the "Lord of the harvest that He would send laborers into His harvest" (Mt. 9:38). In less than nine months the zealous prelate had visited a large portion of the diocese and had departed for Europe to procure the assistance that he needed to further his labors. The bishop's previous residence at Vincennes had made such a favorable impression on the inhabitants that upon his return with the band of missionaries from Europe he was welcomed by the citizens of all denominations.

At this date commenced a new series of labors. In a short time the indefatigable apostle had founded a seminary, a college, free schools for both boys and girls, and aided in the erection of many new churches. Even after his precarious health caused the weight of the episcopacy to be felt more keenly he still continued to urge the erection of new churches wherever possible. In order to carry on these

---

[34] *The Metropolitan Catholic Almanac and Laity's Directory*, p. 64. Baltimore, 1835.

The above list, as the reader will remember from Chapter XI, is incomplete. At this date Father Ferneding was ministering to the Catholics at New Alsace and vicinity; Father St. Cyr, a priest of the St. Louis Diocese, was stationed at Chicago.

numerous praiseworthy labors the self-sacrificing bishop submitted to many privations; nevertheless by his apostolic zeal he encouraged the faithful, sowed the good seed throughout the extensive territory under his administration, and had the consolation before he died to see the wilderness blossom with hopeful prospects for an abundant harvest.

In less than five years the diocese advanced from the foregoing humble beginning to the following status, an advance which would scarcely seem credible to those who were not acquainted with Bishop Bruté's wonderful activity of mind and his powers of endurance.

INDIANA

Vincennes, Cathedral of St. Francis Xavier,
Rt. Rev. Celestin de la Hailandière, D. D.,
Rev. J. A. Vabret, Rev. Peter Berel, Rev. A. Parret.

Duchee River, Queret Prairie, Carlisle, Shaker's Prairie and Lawrenceville, are attended from Vincennes.

Daviess county, Washington, Rev. Simon Lalumière.
St. Peter's and St. Mary's, Rev. Maurice St. Palais.

Mount Pleasant, Paoli, etc. are occasionally visited by the same clergymen.

Jasper, Rev. Joseph Kundek.

New Albany and Assumption at the Knobs, Rev. Louis T. Neyron, who also visits occasionally Jefferson, Charleston, Corydon, etc.

St. Mary's, near Rome, Perry Co., Rev. Julian Benoit, who also attends Cassidy and Troy stations.

Evansville and Newark, Rev. Anthony Deydier, who attends Mt. Vernon, New Harmony, Princeton, etc.

Madison, Rev. Michael Shawe, who also visits Vernon, Lancaster, Salem, Vevay, etc.

New Alsace, St. John's, St. Paul's, Blue Creek's, Salt Creek's, Rev. Joseph Ferneding and Rev. N. Schneiderjans.

Lawrenceburg, Napoleon, Harrison, Brookville, Richmond, Abington, etc. are attended by the same.

Shelby, Rev. Vincent Bacquelin, who also visits Columbus, Indian-apolis, Greenburg, etc.

Logansport, Rev. Claude François, who attends also Lafayette, Independence, Williamsport, Delphi, Peru, Wabashtown, Nobleville, etc.

Fort Wayne, Rev. Lewis Mueller, who visits Legros, Huntington, Goshen, etc.

South Bend, Rev. M. Bernier, who attends St. Mary's of the Lake, Laporte, Elkhart, Indian station of Pokagon, Michigan City, etc.

Terre Haute and St. Mary's, at Thrall's Settlement, Rev. Stanislaus Buteux, who also attends Montezuma, Clinton, Merom, etc.

ILLINOIS

Chicago, Rev. James O'Meara, who visits also Grand Calumet and Small Fork.

Joliet, Rev. John Plunkett, who attends also the Illinois canal.

Paris Prairie, at Bodin's, Rev. S. Buteux, who attends also Darwin, York, etc.

Shawneetown, Carnia, etc., visited by Rev. M. Ward, of Kentucky.

St. Francisville, Rev. John Corbe, who attends also Mt. Carmel, Albion, and Coffee.

Piquet Colony, Rev. F. Czakert, who visits also Tutopolis, a German settlement.

Recapitulation

Churches, ... 27
Churches building, ... 4
Other stations, ... 30
Clergymen in the ministry, ... 22
Clergymen otherwise employed, ... 3
Theological Seminary, ... 1
Ecclesiastical Students, ... 20
Religious Communities, ... 2
College for young men, ... 1
College attendance, ... 79

After comparing the status for these two given dates our readers will agree that the tireless prelate was never a barren fig tree in the Master's garden, and, likewise, that his imperishable fruits record a very truthful eulogy in the trinity of brief but expressive words—The Silent Power.

CHAPTER XV

BISHOP BRUTE—THE SILENT POWER

The seal of eternal peace has rested upon the span of Bruté's fruitful career for almost a century. But the surpassing splendor of his life-record has never ceased to manifest itself and to continue the influence that he so powerfully wielded in spreading God's kingdom in the United States. Unfortunately Bruté has not received his due from the forgetful hearts of men. While hosts of worthy prelates have found their biographers, one of the most learned and influential apostles has evidently been forgotten. The great and noble deeds of his colleagues have not only been recorded but in numerous cases have found more than one biographer. Obviously these worthy apostles were not self-sufficient; their fruitful labors were not accomplished solely by individual efforts.

Beyond this simple truth lingers another, namely, that often the prime mover of heroic deeds either passes unknown from the midst of society or he is forgotten and his accomplishments ascribed perhaps to another. Time also persists in consigning these Silent Powers to oblivion. Thus have time and wonted neglect of mankind dealt with the silent, prayerful, though active and energizing, Simon Bruté de Rémur.

We have followed this beautiful character from his birth to the close of his mortal career. We have studied him at every milestone in life—infancy, childhood, youth, manhood, and old age. We have beheld him a feigned orphan on the arm of a beggar lady, a child in the schools of Rennes, a Tarsicius of the Revolution, a medical student, a doctor, a seminarian, a priest, a professor, a foreign missionary, and a member of the hierarchy.

Who could behold him otherwise than a Silent Power during the Revolution? Then but a boy of tender years with a full knowledge of the danger risked Simon Bruté carried his Eucharistic Lord to the prisons of Rennes, charmed the guards, and strengthened the captives with the Bread of Angels.

No one with a knowledge of the progress of the Church will question the statement that practically every phase of development witnessed by the American Church within the three decades from 1810 to 1840 bears the indelible touch of this worthy priest's personal efficiency.

Our readers may ask how was this effected when the greater portion of this luminary's career in America was spent in seclusion as professor at the Mountain Seminary. The answer is found in the simple fact that Father Bruté's time was divided between labor and prayer. Frequently he spent whole hours, even nights before the Blessed Sacrament and when morning dawned and he returned to his ordinary duties the marks of converse with his God were so perceptible that they could not be concealed. Consequently, he was at all times a living example of all he taught.

To form a true picture of Father Bruté's interior life we need but to read a letter penned to a young seminarian, later His Eminence, John Cardinal McCloskey, who was to be ordained to the priesthood and to be made professor in Nyack Seminary. The spiritual monitions in this letter opened with the pertinent query: "What is a Catholic priest?" to which he wrote the immediate response, "*Sacerdos alter Christus*. A pontiff that offers a divine sacrifice to God and imparts its graces to men—*Dispensator mysteriorum Dei*."

This [said Father Bruté] is the priest, for this he preaches, for this he confesses, that the sacrifice of the Holocaust of propitiation may be known and offered, and improved upon earth to the greatest glory of God and the salvation of souls, according to its divine institution and first consummation by Jesus Christ, Whom he now represents, with Whom he makes himself one person, as it were, at the heavenly altar.

Following this we find a succinct relation of the consequences of this belief as they should appear in the daily life
of the priest, as realized in the life of Father Bruté.

A perfect and perpetual sense of unworthiness; an eternal horror of sin, of the smallest deliberate venial sins; prayerfulness
through life, watchfulness, a delicacy and purity of conscience with
the early meditation of every day can alone keep up; a scrupulous
care in celebrating the Holy Sacrifice as perfectly as possible; a
great zeal to have the faithful instructed in the nature of the
divine sacrifice; a vivid sense of sorrow for the profanations of
unworthy communicants, heretics, and bad priests.

Father Bruté, the model professor then closed this letter
with the following seven practical points concerning the
office of teaching:

Often cherish in meditation the most exalted and heavenly motives of our commission. *Pro Christo ergo legatione fungimur
tanquam Deo exhortante per nos.*

Think of pleasing God above all—*Est qui judicet;* of pleasing
men only for God's sake. *Mihi autem pro minimo est ut a vobis
judicer.*

Yet for God's sake pleasing all as much as we can.

Most attentive to cultivate sound doctrine: study best principles
both for dogma and morals. Never lose sight of our most approved
authors. Doctrine is a trust of the most sacred kind for Catholics.
Depositum custodi.

Attention to composition, order, style, manner of delivery,
particularly during first years, that proper habits may be acquired
for life.

Make best use of all the time that can be had with this intention.
Woe to a too yielding temper to every call of worldlings or good
people who are ignorant of the true priestly engagements. Be
resolute to save time with more jealousy than the statesman or
judge in session. *Nescitis quia in his quae Patris mei sunt oportet
me esse.*

Study best models, either living or recorded in print. Be not seduced from the holy, solid, and most profitable views of preaching and instructing—not seeking applause.

This is only one of many examples of the zealous professor's untiring solicitude for the spiritual welfare of each individual seminarian committed to his charge, all of which shows that Father Bruté possessed an incomparable appreciation for the priceless gift of a priestly vocation and consequently he availed himself of every opportunity to counsel and to guide those whom God had chosen to serve the Church. This appreciation he imperceptibly, by his example, inculcated into the hearts of future priests, bishops, archbishops, and our first American Cardinal. A few days prior to the ordination of Father John McCloskey, the inspired professor of the Mountain Seminary penned another letter of timely advice for the benefit of his student.

Adore and embrace the Will of God, with your whole soul.

Put all your confidence in your Lord, all love!

Think only of doing faithfully your best as duty, no self, no desire of personal consolation.

Place entirely yourself in the hands of God under His man for you on earth, your Bishop.

To return to the primary principles with piety your main purpose —*pietas ad omnia utilis est*—true prayer *petite et accipite*.

Once the priest, let your altar be all in all.

Piety alone can obtain and form a pious clergy. Nay solid piety alone can form a truly learned clergy as clergy—Else want of self-denial.

Be a disciplinarian of principle, affection, and example—love discipline—even if not observed enough, and you still keep to it, save what you can; it will reclaim and maintain.

Have most regular hours—Early morning. But rather not too early—Early rest at night, indispensable.

As you have your family in New York, I would as a faithful friend summon all your courage to keep yourself as independent as possible of them, not accepting family care and interest, nor calling them to attend on the college or seminary.

As for own circumspection and humble observance of the best rules, also of every good book concerning the care of your domestic life, take from the beginning strict habits, although silently and without affectation—be certain that it adds considerably to the safety and good odour in Christ of your sacerdotal life—and that example you owe at the seminary to the young clergy destined to go from it to Calvary as both the light and the salt of this earth.

If to be soon ordained, retire, do retire from the world—either in this house or at Nyack—be sure that in the result all will approve you for refusing the rounds of invitations at so sacred and decisive a time—you need to be entirely by yourself.

Let prayers, my friend, be prayers indeed, so that you may all your life remember before God how you did offer yourself and call for His grace—make at such a time your communion with the Saints as if in their presence in heaven in sight of the seat reserved there for you, and pray now fervently to secure it particularly I say: 1. Blessed Virgin. 2. Holy Angels. 3. The Apostles and Holy Doctors.

Read some select part of these last, e. g. of St. Jerome's *Epistles*, St. Augustine's select chapters of the *Confessions*, but particularly of St. Chrysostom *de Sacerdotio*....

Study and practice perfectly the ceremonies of Mass, in order to begin well—then be most exact in observing them—all interior and exterior application to the Sacrifice.

Mind in all your conduct the utmost simplicity and purity of intention, the soul of your life and your eternity.

After weighing this counsel in the scales of spirituality our readers will quickly perceive how Father Bruté became The Silent Power in the lives of those around him. His humility, piety, and learning made him a model professor and it was he who stamped Mount St. Mary's with a true ecclesiastical spirit and made it a nursery of an educated and zealous priesthood. While his cheerful piety, amiable manners, and lively interest in the welfare of his students won their hearts, his eminent holiness of life secured their respect and veneration and made him one of the most influential leaders of souls that America has ever known.

Owing to the scarcity of clergymen in the United States at that epoch the Church in America was comparatively weak and in many parts unorganized. For twenty years the saintly Mountain professor taught the American Church to entertain the brightest hopes; and he lived to see them realized. A succession of worthy priests went forth from the Mountain Seminary to every section of the country. It was Father Bruté, the solitary, who educated many of the bishops and priests that evangelized the United States, hence in all justice he deserves to be called Father of the American clergy.

He not only taught the true philosophy of ecclesiastical life but he lived it. All who read the following page from his memoranda entitled, "One day of a Priest" must acknowledge that a life filled with such admirable examples must necessarily work marvelous good.

4½ o'C. *Benedicamus Domino*—Praise be to God, on awakening; Vocal Prayer; Meditation before the Tabernacle. Rev. Mr. Hickey's Mass; Jesus Christ my Lord present.

6 o'C. Celebrated Mass; Jesus Christ present; Breakfast; bodily care. Returned to the Church (on the Mountain), opened the Tabernacle, and took out the Blessed Sacrament. Went with Guy Elder through the woods, our Blessed Lord on my breast. Said our Beads with acts of devotion to the Blessed Sacrament at the end of each Decade.

8 o'C. At Mrs. McCormick's; her lively marks of Faith and joy; heard her Confession; arranged the table; called the people; the young convert and her little one; her husband preparing for his first Communion; administered the Blessed Sacrament to Mrs. McC; spoke of Martha and Mary and Lazarus and Zaccheus, old friends of our Lord on earth; He still upon earth and we his present living friends. On our way to Emmitsburg recited the Miserere, our Father, Hail Mary; Hymn, 'Jesus, lover of my Soul.'

9½ o'C. At the Church in Emmitsburg; opened the Tabernacle and Ciborium. Went to see Mr.—, 10 years without making his Easter communion; good *moral* character, as they say; heard his confession: strong Faith, gave lively evidences of it; had a talk with him.

10¾ o'C. Coming back, baptized the child of Peters' wife; her abundant tears; her great difficulties; did not hear her confession at that time.

11 o'C. Returned to Church in Emmitsburg; restored B. S. to the Ciborium; stopped at St. Joseph's with Guy; paid a visit to the B. Sacrament; saw Mrs. Brawner.

12 o'C. Found at the College an old German woman waiting for me; no duty for ten years; sick and lame; looked very poorly; came to know if I would hear her; Sister Angela gave her a dinner; to come again on Sunday.

1½ o'C. Was called to see Glacken above Emmitsburg; went to the Church at Emmittsburg to get the Blessed Sacrament; this is the fifth time today that I have touched my Sovereign Lord, 'The King of Glory', as Mr. Duhamel has it embroidered on the inside door of the Tabernacle; carried it to the sick; administered the Sacrament of Extreme Unction; made a little address to those present—several Protestants.

4 o'C. Went to Mrs. Brawner's; heard her confession; recited my office; Oh! the wonders of that office of the Blessed Sacrament; and am now writing down these notes; but a thousand details, thoughts, and acts not told; how wonderful the day of a Priest. In the evening instructions for Confirmation.

On the same paper is written:

What have I done today for the house? Reviewed the 2nd Latin Class; had a conversation before God with one of the young men; Latin Lesson; Reviewed the 3rd French Class; Latin Lesson to Guy Elder; had a conversation with another young man who came to consult me; one with Mr. Hickey; one with the two Gardiners; wrote a Letter; the Dialogue for Baltimore, six pages; Spiritual Reading, the usual Prayers. If all done well, what a blessing it would bring; but oh! my Lord, so poorly, by halves—alas!

M. LE CHANOINE BRUTÉ DE RÉMUR

L'auteur de la

Vie de Monseigneur Bruté de Rémur

M. LE GÉNÉRAL BRUTÉ DE RÉMUR

MADAME LA GÉNÉRALE BRUTÉ DE RÉMUR

GRANDNEPHEWS OF BISHOP BRUTÉ DE RÉMUR

While on this occasion long before the morning dawned he arose to converse with God and to offer Him the first fruits of the day, more often he remained during the entire night in loving converse with his God. It was this love for his Eucharistic Love that made Father Bruté pen the words: "This is the fifth time today that I have touched my Sovereign Lord, the King of Glory." It was there at the tabernacle that he obtained the secret power and strength by which he silently accomplished such untold good. Truly Christ's love burned bright in Father Bruté's heart. Well did he merit the precious appellation of the "Angel of the Mountain" for like those ministering spirits who seek but to assist man in every way as he is tending towards that final union with his Creator, so, too, the saintly Bruté was spending himself that he might draw others to a more perfect love of their Creator, to seek but the things that are God's and to find their final reward in the glorious vision of the City of God.

The salvation of souls was the ruling desire of his heart and to accomplish this no labor was too strenuous, no weather too inclement, no distance too great for him to travel. We find a testimony of this in 1832 when the cholera visited Baltimore. Likewise, he would remain up far into the night to write letters to some one whom he desired to instruct, or to bring back some lost sheep who had strayed from the fold of Christ.

There is a spirit of tender piety, simple faith, burning zeal, and consuming charity permeating every page, yes, every line of Father Bruté's letters. While the saintly priest and prelate really tells his own life-story in his ever restless activity it is especially in his letters and notes that we have a picture of The Silent Power more vivid and affecting than any portrait could place before our eyes. It is there we live in his presence, feel his personality, and are awed by his saintly simplicity. Again it is there he taught his correspondents by tender and unaffecting example to have recourse in all things to the Sweet Mother of God to confide all to her protection. The words *Auspice Maria* "Under the protection of Mary" are to be found in every letter that came from his pen. Resignation and abandonment to the Holy Will of God and a constant mindfulness of Eternity were other timely lessons taught through his correspondence. His letters frequently bear the words, "God is All;" "His adorable Will be accomplished, all the rest is nothing;" "God will provide;" "Abandon your whole self to God;" while he never penned a message that did not either commence or end with the word "Eternity." He styled it his *old* word yet ever *new*. On numerous occasions he inserted references to eternity such as the following:

> A stillness of expectation of that grand, grand Eternity I hear, me-seems, drawing near, with its only praise, only love, only peace, and no more of offence; a silence and forgetfulness of our puny troubles in sight of that grand, beautiful, magnificent Eternity, filled with God alone, His majesty, sweetness, and goodness. O Eternity! O my God alone!

Casual readers find his notes and letters to be mere rambles, but a minute study of these writings proves them to contain solid spirituality. Father Bruté's ideas flowed so rapidly that on numerous occasions he would not stop to give them full expression in language, but he poured forth his subjects as it were in flashes of words and sentiment, leaving much to be supplied and felt by those to whom he addressed himself. Consequently, as a writer, not as a published author, he wielded perhaps a wider and more powerful influence than any man of letters of his day. This influence was not so much seen as it was felt. From his little corner room in the Mountain Seminary flowed much of the intellectual life that coursed in the veins of the American Church of that day.

There was still another sphere in which Father Bruté labored and over which he exercised an unequaled silent influence. This was the Sisterhood in St. Joseph's Valley. For many years he served in the capacity of confessor and spiritual director of the Sisters of Charity at St. Joseph's. Under his spiritual regime the small Community arose from the humblest beginnings to a state of prosperous maturity. However, he had no part in the material administration of the house. His arduous and responsible task was to strengthen vocations, foster piety, confirm virtue, instill unfeigned charity into the hearts of novices and professed Sisters, and to watch with angelic care the advancement of St. Joseph's School. That the grace of God was with him and God's blessings granted to his labors is evident, for we behold the fruits of his zeal in the numerous charitable institutions that have branched from the parent foundation and now adorn the country.

In the midst of all these quiet, unpretentious labors Father Bruté's life was eminently a life hidden with Christ in God, yet the flame of divine love that glowed in his breast was too strong and bright to be concealed; and much more than he desired did his light shine before men, so that seeing his good works they glorified their Father who is in Heaven. At this moment the eye of the distant Father of all the Faithful pierced the obscurity of the Mountain solitude and selected Father Bruté as the first bishop of the new See at Vincennes. Truly in this humble prelate's election God manifested His Providence, which infinitely surpasses all human prudence and wisdom. Indiana at that period was a sylvan wilderness and its homes were log cabins. Our readers know the story of the sufferings and hardships of the impoverished bishop, hence suffice it to say that he bore all in that calm resignation to God that is characteristic only of a holy soul schooled in virtue and devotion to God.

The greatness of Bishop Bruté showed itself in the building up of this vast diocese. From the beginning he wielded the same supereminent influence here as elsewhere and became The Silent Power in the forests of Indiana and Illinois. His lustre shone about him and spontaneously drew all hearts to God. All who met him were set on fire for religion, and ardently craved the Faith. The attractiveness of his personal sanctity was beyond description. In unfeigned truth and simplicity he could have exclaimed with St. Paul: "I became all things to all men that I might save all" (1 Cor. 9:22).

It must be borne in mind that Bishop Bruté spent but a brief period of his fruitful life in Vincennes; nevertheless, his work, for the kingdom of Christ, was indefatigable and in that short period of time he erected Christ's standard in all sections of his diocese. Whenever he heard of a Catholic family, the zealous bishop spared no pains or fatigue to find their cabin and visit them in their lowly surroundings. Sometimes it was a poor negro family from Maryland or Kentucky living in a remote corner of the woods that received his visit and apostolic ministrations. His solicitude for the salvation of the faithful within his diocese was universal and it may be said of Bishop Bruté that he awakened to a new religious life the whole western section of the country and became a victim to the hardships of the apostolate. He realized that we can do good to men only by loving them and it was this Christ-like love for the poor, neglected souls who were threatened and whom God had committed to his charge that urged him on daily to more sacrifices.

During his brief episcopal apostolate he was at all times a living model, an ideal worthy of imitation, a truly Silent Power to his priests in his exact fulfillment of his spiritual exercises and zeal for the spread of Christ's kingdom. It is especially related of him that when he celebrated Holy Mass his countenance was radiant with supernatural light and he seemed to be entirely carried out of himself at the moment of consecration. Likewise, his priests beheld him to be at all times simplicity personified. No charge or duty in behalf of religion was too mean or lowly for him to perform. Often he swept the church, stood on a chair to ring the bell and even cut the wood and prepared the fire to heat the church. What admirable unselfishness there was in all his work! "The charity of Christ presseth us" (2 Cor. 5:14).

If Bishop Bruté occasioned untold good to the Church directly he was no less influential in the educational field. He realized that religion and education are inseparable and that the foundations of our Christian civilization were laid by the Catholic Church through its system of Christian education; likewise, that the moral and social uplifting of our future depends upon the proper training of the youth. Consequently, he used every energy to establish schools to save the children of the diocese for the Church. He was also an artist in inspiring hearts to devote themselves to this work of the Master. Bishop Bruté was a prelate who labored, lived, and died not only for the children of his age, but also for the unborn millions. He noted the advantages of St. Mary's of the Lake as a location for a future institution. His agent and successor, Bishop de la Hailandière, induced Father Sorin of the Congregation of the Holy Cross, who had been deeply impressed by what he had seen of Bishop Bruté and who had then formed the intention of making a foundation in America, to carry out his project. Thus did Bruté's silent influence reach out and form one of the great living stones in the quarry that produced Notre Dame University and the labors of the Holy Cross Fathers and Brothers throughout the country.

After a few short years the venerable prelate's health and strength began to fail him under the excessive toils and colossal burdens of the episcopate. But still he remained The Silent Power of all, especially his priests. He visited again and again the growing settlements in his diocese and everywhere engaged in all the duties of an ordinary pastor. In this manner he spent himself to the last moment of his mortal career accomplishing good by deed and example. His last moments, likewise, were those of a holy man; his resignation to the Will of God was perfect, his calmness, patience, and cheerfulness in the midst of the most severe sufferings was astonishing. Thus he expired as he had lived and in his departure left the memory of his undying influence stamped upon his entire diocese.

That under God the entire nation is indebted to the ardent zeal of Bishop Bruté—The Silent Power—is unquestionable. Scarcely any life of the men who received their education at Mount St. Mary's is considered complete without giving us a vivid portrait of the "Angel of the Mountain." It was he who guided Bishop Kenrick through the critical period of the Church in Philadelphia; counselled Father Hughes in all his perplexities, aided him in debates with Protestant ministers, solved the trustee difficulties, and directed Bishop Hughes' early labors in New York. He, likewise, claims no small share in the colossal labors of His Eminence, John Cardinal McCloskey of New York; while no one can gainsay that the spirit of Bruté is not present in a notable degree in the accomplishments of Bishops Purcell of Cincinnati, Portier of Mobile, Quarter of Chicago, Gartland of Savannah, Blanc of New Orleans, Carrell of Covington, Whelan of Wheeling, Bacon of Portland, Young of Erie, Elder of Cincinnati, and McFarland of Hartford. In all their labors we catch a glimpse of the Christ-like man who sought and found the solution of every difficulty in the Heart of the God of peace dwelling within the tabernacle.

All that is mortal of the saintly bishop reposes within the limits of the see that he founded while his apostolic spirit furthers Christ's apostolate in a land where Bishop Bruté's name is and shall ever remain engraven among the shining lights in the hierarchal firmament. Not even death could silence the living counsels of The Silent Power. In the Old Cathedral crypt his venerated remains rest at the foot of a plain but beautiful statue of our Blessed Mother, one that the devoted bishop himself procured in France. There, between the statue of the Virgin of Virgins and the altar whereon the Virgin's Son is offered, his body sleeps while THE SILENT POWER wakes, preaching from his sepulchre and warning all his spiritual sons especially, by the expressive language of its presence in that consecrated spot, that the sure way to learn, and to acquire holiness, and to enjoy one day the respect due to saints is that which Jesus Christ himself pointed out to His beloved disciples from the Cross of Redemption; to behold in Her their Mother and to be to Her a son according to His own virgin Heart.

ETERNITY

Vivar semper - legi 6-22-31

INDEX